Trends, Experiences, and Perspectives in Immersive Multimedia and Augmented Reality

Emília Simão
Escola Superior Gallaecia University (ESG), Portugal

Celia Soares
University Institute of Maia (ISMAI), Portugal & Polytechnic Institute of Maia (IPMAIA), Portugal

A volume in the Advances in Multimedia and Interactive Technologies (AMIT) Book Series

Published in the United States of America by
    IGI Global
    Information Science Reference (an imprint of IGI Global)
    701 E. Chocolate Avenue
    Hershey PA, USA 17033
    Tel: 717-533-8845
    Fax: 717-533-8661
    E-mail: cust@igi-global.com
    Web site: http://www.igi-global.com

Library of Congress Cataloging-in-Publication Data

Names: Simao, Emilia, 1976- editor. | Soares, Celia, 1974- editor.
Title: Trends, experiences, and perspectives in immersive multimedia and
  augmented reality / Emilia Simao and Celia Soares, editors.
Description: Hershey, PA : Information Science Reference, 2018.
Identifiers: LCCN 2017051897| ISBN 9781522556961 (hardcover) | ISBN
  9781522556978 (ebook)
Subjects: LCSH: Mass media--Technological innovations. | Digital
  media--Technological innovations. | Social media.
Classification: LCC P96.T42 T74 2018 | DDC 302.23--dc23 LC record available at https://lccn.loc.
gov/2017051897

This book is published in the IGI Global book series Advances in Multimedia and Interactive Technologies (AMIT) (ISSN: 2327-929X; eISSN: 2327-9303)

British Cataloguing in Publication Data
A Cataloguing in Publication record for this book is available from the British Library.

For electronic access to this publication, please contact: eresources@igi-global.com.

Advances in Multimedia and Interactive Technologies (AMIT) Book Series

ISSN:2327-929X
EISSN:2327-9303

Editor-in-Chief: Joel J.P.C. Rodrigues, National Institute of Telecommunications (Inatel), Brazil & Instituto de Telecomunicações, University of Beira Interior, Portugal

MISSION

Traditional forms of media communications are continuously being challenged. The emergence of user-friendly web-based applications such as social media and Web 2.0 has expanded into everyday society, providing an interactive structure to media content such as images, audio, video, and text.

The **Advances in Multimedia and Interactive Technologies (AMIT) Book Series** investigates the relationship between multimedia technology and the usability of web applications. This series aims to highlight evolving research on interactive communication systems, tools, applications, and techniques to provide researchers, practitioners, and students of information technology, communication science, media studies, and many more with a comprehensive examination of these multimedia technology trends.

COVERAGE

- Audio Signals
- Multimedia Technology
- Internet Technologies
- Social Networking
- Web Technologies
- Multimedia Services
- Digital Games
- Gaming Media
- Digital Images
- Mobile Learning

IGI Global is currently accepting manuscripts for publication within this series. To submit a proposal for a volume in this series, please contact our Acquisition Editors at Acquisitions@igi-global.com or visit: http://www.igi-global.com/publish/.

Titles in this Series

For a list of additional titles in this series, please visit:
https://www.igi-global.com/book-series/advances-multimedia-interactive-technologies/73683

Cross-Media Authentication and Verification Emerging Research and Opportunities
Anastasia Katsaounidou (Aristotle University of Thessaloniki, Greece) Charalampos Dimoulas (Aristotle University of Thessaloniki, Greece) and Andreas Veglis (Aristotle University of Thessaloniki, reece)
Information Science Reference ● ©2019 ● 213pp ● H/C (ISBN: 9781522555926) ● US $145.00

Feature Dimension Reduction for Content-Based Image Identification
Rik Das (Xavier Institute of Social Service, India) Sourav De (Cooch Behar Government Engineering College, India) and Siddhartha Bhattacharyya (RCC Institute of Information Technology, India)
Information Science Reference ● ©2018 ● 284pp ● H/C (ISBN: 9781522557753) ● US $215.00

Intelligent Multidimensional Data and Image Processing
Sourav De (Cooch Behar Government Engineering College, India) Siddhartha Bhattacharyya (RCC Institute of Information Technology, India) and Paramartha Dutta (Visva Bharati University, India)
Information Science Reference ● ©2018 ● 429pp ● H/C (ISBN: 9781522552468) ● US $235.00

Real-Time Face Detection, Recognition, and Tracking System in LabVIEW™...
Manimehala Nadarajan (Universiti Malaysia Sabah, Malaysia) Muralindran Mariappan (Universiti Malaysia Sabah, Malaysia) and Rosalyn R. Porle (Universiti Malaysia Sabah, Malaysia)
Information Science Reference ● ©2018 ● 140pp ● H/C (ISBN: 9781522535034) ● US $155.00

Empirical Research on Semiotics and Visual Rhetoric
Marcel Danesi (University of Toronto, Canada)
Information Science Reference ● ©2018 ● 312pp ● H/C (ISBN: 9781522556220) ● US $195.00

For an entire list of titles in this series, please visit:
https://www.igi-global.com/book-series/advances-multimedia-interactive-technologies/73683

701 East Chocolate Avenue, Hershey, PA 17033, USA
Tel: 717-533-8845 x100 ● Fax: 717-533-8661
E-Mail: cust@igi-global.com ● www.igi-global.com

Editorial Advisory Board

Table of Contents

Detailed Table of Contents

This chapter uses an arts- and design-based research methodology to explore emergent possibilities in contemporary transmedia arts and design practices. Focusing in narrative and fiction creation for the development of participatory and performative events with emphasis in audience or community engagement and conveying inspiration from modernist and postmodernist movements, it reveals the role of participation design in connected and smart experiences for urban cooperative gaming and play. Mobile gaming and play technologies taking advantage of sensors and data tracking devices immerse us in a persistent and pervasive game of life which blur the boundaries between the real and the fictional world.

Chapter 2

The reengineering of life through the sense of presence in virtual and augmented reality raised in art and technoscience is the focus of the aesthetical, scientific, and technological potential for the changes to the ecological, social, environmental, and biological condition. Virtual reality immersion uses proprioceptive trackers for navigation and stereoscopy in kinesthesia generating compelling experience inside data landscapes. Nowadays, disruptive technologies melting biological, synthetic worlds (data-cyber) and physic spaces (biocybrid systems) allow synaesthetic embodied experience to the Spinozian body. In enactive affective systems, the sentient and pervasive technologies by the invasion of mobile technologies, physiological sensors, computer vision, locative, and geodesic dialogues of organisms/data and environment are in reciprocal and mutual exchanges. The ontology of life conciliates paradoxes and conflicts of emergent realities and self-organizing dialogues between artificial and natural modifying the concept of reality, which is always a philosophical concept.

Chapter 3
Paulo Cesar Teles, University of Campinas, Brazil

This chapter aims to highlight and discuss contemporary aspects of interactive art as the audience influence, the aesthetic technological impact, its targeting to art-education, and the cross-cultural aspects involved as well evidenced by an art and technology literacy event at two schools in the city of Osogbo, Nigeria for primary and secondary school teachers and students in mid-2016 and five months later the re-exhibition of its final artwork in museums and cultural centers in Brazil. For this propose, the author sought to highlight the density of the aesthetic experiences and the cultural addition that affected all the involved people in terms of interactivity and multi-technological connections. He also intended to point out and compare both the different interactive attitudes and the processes of comprehension and reframing that occurred during the stages of production and exhibitions under the prism of some contemporary theoretical perspectives and cases.

Chapter 4
Manuela Piscitelli, Università degli Studi della Campania Luigi Vanvitelli, Italy

The chapter analyzes, with particular regard to the Italian context, the aspects related to the fruition of cultural heritage and to the expectations of the potential public. There is often a lack of adequate media for communication, which should create interest in a non-specialist public. Multimedia and interactive technologies can be a valuable support to enhance internal and external communication for museums and cultural sites, reaching a wide audience in a differentiated and customized manner depending on their interests. The aim is to understand the link between the work of art and the geographical, physical, historical, and cultural context in which it was born, to open the horizon to a synoptic and organic understanding of heritage, contributing to its protection and educating citizens. Finally, a case study concerning the museum and territory of Mondragone (Italy) is presented.

Chapter 5

Henrique Silva, Escola Superior Gallaecia University (ESG), Portugal
Emília Simão, Escola Superior Gallaecia University (ESG), Portugal

In this chapter, the authors discuss the use of digital media in the creation of digital art, questioning the evolution of the relationship between technology and concept in communication through art. The intersection of new media and digital art have been opening interesting and seductive new horizons and in parallel, the concept, the understanding, the legitimacy of artistic creation, the role of the artist and the role of the spectator are also redefined. Based on two experimental works of the artist Henrique Silva, the authors analyze and reflect on the relationship of technology, art and virtuality, focusing on concepts like experience, sensory, immersion, communication and interaction in artworks created through digital media.

Chapter 6

Paula Guerra, University of Porto, Portugal

The importance of music concerts is all too revealing of a complex and malleable framework which operates at aesthetic, artistic, and emotional levels. We are faced here with a new type of relationship with music, in a way that we find not only the classic takes on music as an artwork to be admired, or as a collective identity-building activity, but also as a way in which festival "stages" serves as observatories of youth, cultural and artistic practices, and values in contemporary Portugal. This chapter addresses these questions via the analysis of the mobile photo-sharing application Instagram deposited by the managers of the page of Paredes de Coura's Festival—Portuguese music festival—between 2015 and 2017, and it is from here that the author will try to understand and analyze the dynamics underlying the festival as an immersive experience.

Chapter 7

Şükrü Oktay Kılıç, Kadir Has University, Turkey
Zeynep Genel, Okan University, Turkey

A handful of social media companies, with their shifting strategies to become hosts of all information available online, have significantly changed the news media landscape in recent years. Many news media companies across the world have gone through reorganizations in a bid to keep up with new storytelling techniques, technologies, and tools introduced by social media companies. With their non-transparent algorithms favoring particular content formats and lack of interest in developing solid business models for publishers, social media platforms, on the other hand, have attracted widespread criticism by many academics and media practitioners. This chapter aims at discussing the impact of social media on journalism with the help of digital research that provides an insight on what storytelling types with which three most-followed news outlets in Turkey gain the most engagement on Facebook.

Chapter 8

Johan Cavalcanti van Haandel, FIAM FAAM Centro Universitário, Brazil

This study sees the technology and communication interface in the radio universe. In the last 20 years, radio became multimedia with the use of digital codes, which uses transmedia storytelling to spread the contents in different media and platforms. The objective of this chapter is to observe the changes in relation to the production of content in the multimedia radio, the reception and interaction processes of the receivers in this new context, and the language changes that occurred during the process. As a methodology, it presents a review of the current radio theory and an observation of the phenomena resulting from the production of multiplatform content in radio stations operating in AM and FM.

Chapter 9

Celia Soares, University Institute of Maia (ISMAI), Portugal & Polytechnic Institute of Maia (IPMAIA), Portugal
Emília Simão, Escola Superior Gallaecia University (ESG), Portugal

This chapter describes the immersive multimedia's role in our lives, educational activities, and business, and social media benefits from the growth of this emerging reality. Consequently, this chapter analyses the impact and the use for immersive multimedia in different contexts. In the modern world, technological advancement led to the discovery of the powerful application of multimedia. Education and learning systems have significant contribution to improve this field of research. This chapter is going to help expanded the knowledge and information about multimedia in general and immersive multimedia in particular, and its strong influences on education. How technological innovation can be used by external stakeholders to direct and promote innovation in education, how teaching can benefit from the proximity to technology, and how social networks can seize the advantages of an immersive system are some of the answers the authors try to find in this chapter.

Foreword

Humanity is still living an era that corresponds to the most intensive technological development period of its existence. The second world war and the cold war that followed it, with the competitive star wars period, with the man on the moon, highly established a new technological development cycle for mankind. The transistor, the microprocessor and the personal computer with Internet's public telecommunications protocol associated to the World Wide Web in the wakening of the 20s was a gigantic leap for each one of us as individuals. Postmodernist philosophers like Gilles Lipovetsky understood this trend, and announced in the 90s much of what we consider today's properties of human-centric new media, obsessively worried in delivering personalization and usage to individuals. With the advent of computational power in a volume no bigger than a shoebox and now in the palm of our hand, new human-computer interaction paradigms emerged that augment our real context of use and in some instances by evoking virtual interaction scenarios, moments synthesized entirely in computers but lived as new immersive experiences. Some of these situations transport human beings into immersive sensorial and cognitive experiences; others keep the user at an immersive multimedia level.

This manuscript integrates a set of chapters that report very well on the diversity of new media as we know them today, namely augmented reality, virtual reality and immersive multimedia. Don't expect a pure technological manuscript, it isn't. Editors called on work that reported on trends, experiences and perspectives related with these new media and they were successful. All the chapters are centred in profound human-centric real contexts of use, with predominance for cultural and arts technology mediated scenarios. Education was not left out, nor was the radio as traditional media, considered in new trends correlated with the use of transmedia platforms to enhance traditional media. Online digital journalism is also included and discussed within the scope of the very trendy social media platform state-of-the-art impacts.

This is clearly a must have and must read book for scholars, a top grade student or business man that really wants to understand new media trends in the arts and cultural lead including the postmodern human-centric approach. The set of reported experiences, cases and studies situated in technological mediated real contexts of use around the world and correlated with multicultural backgrounds are enriching for anyone who wants to understand and build on a new media driven "global world construct" perspectives.

Óscar Mealha
University of Aveiro, Portugal

Óscar Mealha *is Associate Professor at the Department of Communication and Art, University of Aveiro, Portugal. He develops his research in the area of "Information and Communication in Digital Platforms" in the context of "Knowledge Media and Connected Communities" with several projects, masters and doctoral supervisions and publications on interaction design and analysis techniques and methods, namely for usability evaluation, UX and visualization of interaction/infocommunication activity. He is involved in infocommunication mediation projects such as "Visualization of Open Data Dashboards for Citizen Engagement and Learning" in intelligent territories, and "Knowledge Interface School-Society (KISS)" within the scientific network ASLERD - aslerd.com.*

Preface

INTRODUCTION

Terms like multimedia, immersion, virtual and digital are some of the key themes of the new society of 21st century. Technology is everywhere with everyone and everything is changing. Immersive digital environments, *avatarism*, organic interfaces, the first cyborg recognized by a European government, interactive museums, new media, Web 4.0, immersive art, e-learning, intelligent houses, artificial intelligence and a multiplicity of other concepts are extremely interesting but also quite controversial. At the same time that machine learning and artificial intelligence become more refined, immersive experiences will group up. The devices that deliver those experiences will inevitably get smaller, with a higher resolution, faster data handling, and inbuilt artificial intelligence. They won't just display information in ways we can interact with, they'll also gather information from the environment in real time and pass it back to an artificial intelligence for analysis that drives an equally rapid response. As that happens, digital experiences will become progressively multi-sensory, making them even more believably and incredible real. Virtual reality and augmented reality hardware has advanced so quickly that the limits of what's possible to do seem to be expanding every day. The speed at which these technologies are evolving are the best reasons to develop research in this area. There are countless ways they could be used, from design and maintenance to customer service, not forgetting the entertainment, education and health. It's not just that we'll use new tools to perform existing tasks like consuming content, viewing instructions, augmenting employee performance, or delivering more engaging customer experiences. It's that we could create completely new ways of doing things.

Immersive multimedia experience is the last form of engagement. They are custom designed to meet certain conditions and that means the engagement factor is increased even more. The engagement factor comes when technology and art come together to give the appearance that the user is part of the experience - and in several cases, user really is a part if the experience - in scenery or characters that respond to touch, movements and even facial expressions. Immersive media experiences can include things like: Floor-to-ceiling wall displays that react to your touch and movement when you moves in a certain space; Interactive table tops, that react when you touch or even when you put anything on the top; Lighting and staging experiences that give another dimensions to shows and events; Larger than life exhibits that completely surround your body and senses with interactive, immersive features; Games that are driven by body movement and gestures, pulling you into the story so you're not sure which world is real; Military serious games that allow to test war scenarios; Health simulations that allows surgeons to practice and training.

Entertainment, engineering, health, music, arts or in a more general approach, a large part of the economic, cultural, social, and personal spheres that surround us will probably all benefits from multimedia development. Suddenly, the magic has become real and humans enters other dimensions they only found before in their dreams, movies or imagination. We plunged into a sea of endless possibilities and experiences, where before the difficult was to enter but where now the difficult thing is to leave.

This capacity of crossing dimensions once-called imagination, that made us fight with pre-historical animals, go back to ancient times, or land on Mars, is known as virtual reality.

As the name suggests, this technology offer to the users simulated circumstances through the use of certain devices and programs, increasingly sophisticated. It allows users to replicate their physical world generated by the computer and create an interactive new presence.

This is both technology and narrative in its best and in its most evolved forms but in addition to enhancing its facets, it is also important to realize the impact on people's daily lives. Are we human beings prepared for such radical changes in social representations, relationships, life styles and other dynamics we integrate, whether individually or globally? Virtual reality is not so virtual anymore, virtual is real.

In an attempt to contribute to this very broad subject, *Trends, Experiences, and Perspectives in Immersive Multimedia and Augmented Reality* is not another technical book but a compilation of multidisciplinary reflections and approaches on topics usually associated with engineering, now focused on the user and how it can be influenced by multimedia devices, artifacts or experiences. Think virtual reality, immersive experiences and multimedia centered in human participation beyond its technical aspects are thus the main objective of this publication.

ORGANIZATION OF THE BOOK

This multidisciplinary book contains nine chapters that reflects an extensive and detailed approach of different perspectives on this matter. Subjects like transmedia, immersive spaces, interactive art, cultural heritage, digital media creation, immersivity in summer festivals, the technology impact on digital journalism, multimedia radio emergence and the information revolution influence on immersive multimedia are explored and discussed through the vision of experts - artists, university professors and reference academics - in these various areas, bringing some approaches unquestionably trends in this new digital age.

The first chapter, "Transmedia Experiences That Blur the Boundaries Between the Real and the Fictional World," is based in arts and design research methodologies used to explore the emergent possibilities in contemporary transmedia. The main focus of this chapter addresses the issue of narrative and fiction creation for the development of participatory and performative events. The author brings up to discussion the advantage of sensors and data tracking devices on gaming that immerse us in a persistent and pervasive game of life. The entertainment industry benefits from production of multimedia contents that have synergistic effects on one another and form an ultimately more desirable and marketable whole media product.

The ontology of life explored as concept that conciliates paradoxes and conflicts of emergent realities and self-organizing dialogues between artificial and natural modifying the perception of reality in a philosophical way, is also explored in this book. The second chapter, "Affective Presence in Enactive Immersive Space: Sensorial and Mobile Technologies Reengineering Life," focuses on the impact from reengineering of life through the sense of presence in virtual and augmented reality raised in art and technoscience, focused on aesthetical, scientific and technological aspects and gives the reader a perspective how virtual reality can be applied to art and science.

The third chapter, "Hi-Tech + Low-Tech: Aesthetic Reframing Processes Through Brazilian-Nigerian Art Literacy," discusses the contemporary aspects of interactive art and the impact brought to art-education when technological artifacts are used. The cross-cultural perspective is evidenced by art and technology literacy when comparing results of experiences in Nigeria and Brazil. For this propose the author sought to highlight the density of the aesthetic experiences and the cultural addition which affected all the involved people in terms of interactivity and multi-technological connections. Besides, he also intended to point out and compare both the different interactive attitudes and the processes of comprehension and reframing which occurred during the stages of production and exhibitions under the prism of some contemporary theoretical perspectives and cases.

"Multimedia Experiences for Cultural Heritage," Chapter 4, analyzes the Italian context related to fruition of cultural heritage. The focus is to make understand the link between the work of art and the geographical, physical, historical and cultural context in which it was born, to open the horizon to a synoptic and organic understanding of heritage, contributing to its protection and educating citizens.

Multimedia and interactive technologies are analyzed has a support to enhance internal and external communication for museums and cultural sites through a case study concerning the museum in Italy.

Returning to arts, Chapter 5, "Thinking Art in Technological World: An Approach to Digital Media Creation," focuses the digital media and how we can benefit from the evolution and introduction of digital technology in art creation. Taking as example two experimental works of the Portuguese artist Henrique Silva, one of the authors, there are addressed themes such as digital communication, creation vs artistic objects and digital/computational aesthetics, focusing on immersion and illusion created through digital media and the interaction between the public and artworks.

In Chapter 6, multimedia is understood as a key factor to guarantee the complete commitment of those who attend a concert and the performative artist is analyzed on the mobile photo–sharing application Instagram deposited by the managers of the page of the Festival Paredes de Coura – a Portuguese music festival – between 2015 and 2017, and it is from here that the author will try to understand and analyze the dynamics underlying the festival as an immersive experience. "Ceremonies of Pleasure: An Approach to Immersive Experiences at Summer Festivals" reveals the music concerts importance too revealing a framework which operates at aesthetic, emotional level and technological level.

Turning to a more communicational approach, the seventh chapter, "Impact of Social Media and Technology Companies on Digital Journalism," focuses on how the social media companies have changed the news media landscape in recent years and what can we expect in the future. The journalism are changing with the help of a digital research that provides new interacting ways. The readers are no longer exclusive readers, they are clients for a new business models for publishers and social media platforms. This new model of journalism attracted widespread criticism by many academics and media practitioners and this chapter aims the discussing the impact of social media with help of digital technologies.

Still in the scope of the media, Chapter 8 observes the changes related to multimedia productions the radio must control the contents creation process and must be capable to increase online participation. "The AM and FM Radio Changes in the Multimedia Radio Emergence" explores the technology and communication interface in radio universe. From the current radio theory emerges a new phenomenon resulting from production of multiplatform content in radio stations operating in AM and FM.

In the last chapter, "Immersive Multimedia in Information Revolution," the information revolution is explored as a mean to achieve the knowledge that allows the creation and use of technologies related to virtual reality. In the future it is assumed that technology will allow a revolution in the development of interfaces more capable to grant users immersion on more realistic scenarios. In modern world, technological advancement leads to discover the powerful application of Multimedia.

Education and learning systems have significant contribution to improve this field of research and here you can find an analysis impact for immersive multimedia in different contexts.

CONCLUSION

This book explores the idea that immersive multimedia and augmented reality are transversal to several areas: art, communication, journalism, music, culture, gaming and education can take advantage from these technologies, tools and contents. Therefore, is important refer that virtual reality immerses users in a completely virtual environment that is generated by a computer, and there are several aspects that needs to be improved. Many questions arise that can be related to the virtual reality and immersive environments growth. Disciplines such as neuroscience, ergonomics, life science or even formal sciences such as systems or decision theories, as well as theoretical aspects of computer science, among others can play a crucial role in this field. We believe that research on issues such as "immersion" and "reality" will intensify and will continue to be the subject of many discussions – technical, philosophical, anthropological, among others. If we think in the early 1990s, the racing simulator arcade games with their screens, working pedals, and haptic feedback in the steering wheel seemed completely realistic at the time, and now they are completely obsolete. Some studies say we're still five to ten years away from an actually convincing immersive digital world, capable to engage multiple senses and allows us to move through it in 360-degree space. When that possibility arrives, it will change our entire sense of what's real, what's relevant, and what we can tangibly affect. For now we have to use too many technologic artifacts and the engagement is often compromised.

The work found in this set of chapters attempts to help understand the trends in this area and shows perspectives that only technological approaches are not enough to respond. We believe that "Trends, Experiences, and Perspectives in Immersive Multimedia and Augmented Reality" is a useful book where researchers and students can find different facts, reflections and perspectives about these themes.

Chapter 1

Transmedia Experiences That Blur the Boundaries Between the Real and the Fictional World

Patrícia Gouveia
Universidade de Lisboa, Portugal

ABSTRACT

This chapter uses an arts- and design-based research methodology to explore emergent possibilities in contemporary transmedia arts and design practices. Focusing in narrative and fiction creation for the development of participatory and performative events with emphasis in audience or community engagement and conveying inspiration from modernist and postmodernist movements, it reveals the role of participation design in connected and smart experiences for urban cooperative gaming and play. Mobile gaming and play technologies taking advantage of sensors and data tracking devices immerse us in a persistent and pervasive game of life which blur the boundaries between the real and the fictional world.

INTRODUCTION TO THE TRANSMEDIA *GAMEFUL* WORLD

In essence transmedia is a term used to describe the process of creating a story world across multiple platforms using multimedia and cross media content. *In A Creator's Guide to Transmedia Storytelling: How to Captivate and Engage Audiences Across Multiple Platforms*, Andrea Phillips, considers that multimedia is nowadays connected with a very specific and narrow interpretation, "in the 1990s, the term took on a

DOI: 10.4018/978-1-5225-5696-1.ch001

very specific connotation: text, video, audio, and images delivered together through computer. Multimedia CD-ROMs of atlases and encyclopedias were common and profitable for a few years. They vanished when the new king of the multimedia experience arose: the World Wide Web." (Phillips, 2012, p. 18). The author of this chapter uses multimedia and cross media content as an equivalent to transmedia considering both in a broader sense, more than just a content platform jumper. According to Phillips, cross media refers to the release of the same content across a multitude of platforms. In that case the same product can be seen in different media, a TV show episode could be available on TV, mobile phones or else (2012, p. 19). Although in this text we use these terms as connected entities in a broader sense we think it is useful to define and classify possible differences to contextualise the reader in a clear path and to avoid cultural misunderstandings. It is our conviction that different countries have different approaches to the words transmedia, multimedia and cross media narratives and that each concrete project should be analysed as a complex emergent artefact which ask for connected interpretations and discourses. Words, in this particular context, are just guidelines and "it might take decades for the dust to settle. But there's no sense in waiting for consensus on a complete definition before you start making something amazing yourself. There's a lot of territory to explore, and it's going to be just as much fun no matter what words we use to label our work" (Phillips, 2012, p. 20).

BACKGROUND

In Lev's Manovich article "Post-Media Aesthetics", from 2001, the author considers that "along with the arrival of mass media throughout the twentieth century, and the proliferation of new art forms beginning in the 1960s, another development that threatened the traditional idea of a medium was digital revolution of the 1980s- 1990s. The shift of most means of production, storage and distribution of mass media to digital technology (or various combinations of electronic and digital technologies), and adoption of the same tools by individual artists disturbed both the traditional distinctions based on materials and conditions of perception and the new, more recent distinctions based on distribution model, method of reception/exhibition and payment scheme." (Manovich, 2001) The merge of various methods of distribution and the changes in reception, where people experience stories spread throughout several media but also create their own fictional path, is crucial to thing about narrative paradoxes where stories are simultaneously open for interpretation and action (Gouveia, 2009). In a recent conference at the Museum of Art, Architecture and Technology (MAAT, May 2017) in Lisbon, named "Post-Internet Cities", Giselle Beiguelman spoke about hybrid urban relations in city spaces like São Paulo. Beiguelman gave the example of *Connected Drains* (Sepiridião, 2014), a digital mobile application project that connects the town drains with citizens, creating a mobilization and decision taking environment around preventive and corrective actions for the social well-being. The aim of the project is to fight against accidents caused by lack of maintenance but also mobilizing people for a social cause in a cooperative and collaborative manner. If we want to solve the problems we've created for ourselves and our ecosystems we will have to get involved and transmedia experiences can help create participatory environments for people to connect.

Liquid and fluid interfaces mediate our experience with the world and they can contribute to engage people in a playful manner. The project *Saving Face* (Lancel & Maat, 2015) is a deconstruction of control technologies of surveillance and sensory perception to facilitate intimate meeting experiences. The project takes advantage of a fluid bio-feedback system for "a poetic 'meeting-through-touching ritual' where participants caress their own faces, to connect online with family, friends and strangers worldwide. They become tangible and visible for each other in a relational process, a 'social sculpture' in which we invite them to endlessly meet, caress, mirror and merge." (Lancel & Maat, 2015). This interactive city sculpture of networked identities shows how various interface states can merge in a collective action, an emergent portrait performance, a transmedia story.

MAIN FOCUS OF THE CHAPTER

Integral to the transmedia experience process is the engagement and active participation of the target audience in different countries and communities using various technologies from analog to digital media. New forms of performance and interactive art emerge from mixed audiences across the internet. The renowned internationally artist group, Blast Theory, uses interactive media art "that mixes audiences across the internet, live performance and digital broadcasting. (…) the group's work explores the social and political aspects of technology. Drawing on popular culture and games, the work often blurs the boundaries between the real and the fictional." (Blast Theory, 2018) Contemporary mobile gaming and play immerse us in a persistent and pervasive *game of life* (Conway, 1970) which blur the boundaries between the real and the fictional in a connected world. From smart cities to the internet of things we see ourselves in a *Black Mirror* (Brooker, 2011) of ludic screen interfaces where we can no longer distinguish fact from fiction. In the second volume of *My Struggle* (*Min Kamp*), (Kanusgård, 2015 [2009], p. 529) the Norwegian author considers the blur between fact and fiction taking into account that we access our world through fiction. In that sense, for Kanusgård, the diary and the essay formats, in contrast of fictions and documentaries, are the only interesting literary formats. In their diaries and essays people can translate their actual experience into a story world, merging fact and fiction in a holistic narrative. In this fashion people can present different points of view and help solve some of our contemporary challenges in a collaborative way.

Participatory and slow design merge real and imagined spaces that brings artists, designers and participants together in defense of six principles: to reveal spaces and experiences that may be forgotten including materials and processes; expand, taking into account the potential of artificially produced artefacts and environments, leading to more balanced consumption; engaging in open and collaborative processes based on information sharing, cooperation and transparency; encourage people to become active participants in design processes, strengthening a sense of community and social value; evolve, from experiences, artefacts and reflected environments (Correia, 2016). Participatory design is crucial to understand the role of technological mediated participation supported by digital media.

Looking beyond the immediate needs of everyday life participatory design is nothing new. It evolved from the seventies Nordic cooperative design systemic processes and the firsts attempts, in 1971, from the Design Research Society, United Kingdom, of defining this particular field in a conference named *Design Participation* (Correia, 2016, p. 57). In this context, arts and design merge the creation and solving of problems in a holistic manner incorporating systemic ideas and emergent behaviour. A critical analysis of participatory artworks, "do-it-yourself" practices and the aesthetics and culture of participation can be find in the doctoral thesis of Margarida Carvalho named *The Do-It-Yourself" Work: Aesthetics of Participation in Digital Arts* (2015). Grounded in a tradition of critical and interdisciplinary studies in humanities, Carvalho presents a concrete body of work to support her inquiry about the role of participation in digital arts. How cooperative gaming is built in this arts and design tradition was previously develop by the author of this chapter (Gouveia, 2015) and others (Manovich, 2001; Bogost, 2007; Flanagan, 2009; Deterding, 2014). Gaming processes interconnect various communities, countries, city spaces and people in a hybrid fashion creating a *gameful* world.

According to Steffen P. Walz and Sebastian Deterding in their text "An Introduction to the Gameful World" nowadays, when we consider the *gamification* i. e., the art of applying game design techniques in different contexts in a meaningful way (Gouveia, 2015) or, in alternative, the *ludification* of cultures and societies, we find optimistic and utopian versions of a "total" game design which will solve real world problems and enhance human beings capabilities (McGonigal, 2011) or we find a dystopian critical vision from academia and game design proponents who consider that *gamification* trends are just like the "latest form of ideology masking political disenfranchisement and exploitation of digital labor as playful self-realization." (Walz & Deterding, 2014, p. 5) The advantages and the dangerous powers of *gamification* and serious gaming were state elsewhere (Gouveia, 2015) and we consider crucial to analyse and question these fields and practices as part of our cultural discourse in arts and design transmedia experiences.

Walz & Deterding considered that "instead of using the value-laden term *gamification* or the narrower concept of *ludification*" they prefer to use instead "the gameful world." Following the authors "in this, we (…) suggested mapping the current use of games and play beyond leisurely entertainment along two dimensions: wholes versus elements or qualities, and *paidia* versus *ludus*" (Walz & Deterding, 2014, p. 7). Gaming and play rhetoric's are being used in a, sometimes, superficial and alien way for those who studied game studies for more than a decade but they can be also instrumental to generate critical thinking about our present-day life's.

Echoing Walz and Deterding, "What if all of our everyday life is turned into a game? What would be the consequences of life governed by a pervasive web of sensors tracking our every action, algorithms evaluating them against rules and goals set by ourselves and others, and effectuators constantly feeding back information on our performance, status, and progress? How would we work, commune, and act politically under such circumstances? How would it alter (and disturb) the ordering of our everyday interaction? And what happens to games and play themselves? What are the ethical ramifications of a societal panludicum — for policy makers, for designers, but also for individuals alternatively extending or replacing our will with technically mediated systems of goals?" (Walz & Deterding, 2014, p. 9) It seems that in today's fun culture people are not "escaping into the virtual world of games, but games escaping into everyday life." And we have to meet the "Frankensteinian daemons and Skinnerian dictatorships: as algorithms increasingly rule the world" (Walz & Deterding, 2014, p. 9) and dismantle them with our disruptive power of rebellion and resilience.

Transmedia content creation can include pervasive games and urban play in a broad perspective but also location-based games (LBGs) and hybrid reality games (HRGs). Sensor installations, augmented and virtual reality (AR and VR) interfaces (Gouveia & Martel, 2017, Gouveia, 2016) can be used to created embodied and performative first-person perspectives in short term sessions included in bigger storylines. These categories define different aspects of the relationship between game spaces, interfaces and time. (Silva & Sutko, 2009, p. 3) Connected play spaces aim to explore the social aspects of technology drawing on popular culture and games for the creation of mixed realities that blur the boundaries between real and fictional worlds. According to Silva & Sutko, "the idea of combining the physical and the digital is not new. In the 1990s, Mark Wieser (1991, 1994) envisioned a world in which objects in our daily lives would become "sentient" that is, they would be constantly connected to the Internet and able to communicate to each other and to us. (Silva & Sutko, 2009, p. 4) Nevertheless the authors remind "contrary to

VR [Virtual Reality], which attempts to bring us inside the computer, ubiquitous computing actually brings the computer outside, into our daily, lived experience. (Silva & Sutko, 2009, p. 5) Gaming and play are escaping into everyday life, they are everywhere we turn.

Andrea Phillips, suggested, in the previously quoted book, that there is a divide between two different types of transmedia, namely West Coast, Hollywood or based in a franchising like inspiration, and East Coast, which tends "to be more interactive and much more web-centric. It overlaps heavily with the traditions of independente film, theater, and interactive art. These projects make heavy use of social media, and are often run once over a set period of time rather than persisting forever. The plot is so tightly woven between media that you might not fully understand what's going on if you don't actively seek out multiple pieces of the story." These projects contrast with West Coast which "consists of multiple big pieces of media: feature films, video games, that kind of thing. It's grounded in big-business commercial storytelling. The stories in these projects are interwoven, but lightly; each piece can be consumed on its own, and you'll still come away with the idea that you were given a complete story." (Phillips, 2012: 13-14) As we will further develop in this chapter our approach to transmedia research is connected with the East Coast trends and strategies.

Issues, Controversies, Problems

Transmedia content creators and producer's challenges in a *gameful* world can be a tricky issue. These content creators and producers need to examine the marketability of a project from day one by determining whether or not there is a community already built around their story. If they work for a corporate world they need to ask which kind of entertainment experiences this particular audience is looking for (Bernardo, 2014, online). Beactive Entertainment is "an award-winning Film, TV and Digital studio with a decade of experience in story and format development, international co-production, licensing, production and distribution of entertainment contents across multiple platforms." (Beactive Entertainment, n.d.) Nuno Bernardo, founder and CEO of Beactive, states "A fully fleshed storyworld *'bible'* should include *detailed character profiles* and *backstories* and *extended story arcs*. Also, the bible needs to list historical and real world events that help define and authenticate your setting. Lastly, it's important to define *the rules of your storyworld* (if they differ from the rules of the real world) and the visual elements that distinguish or define your world." (Bernardo, 2014, emphasis from the author). The goal of a transmedia universe is to engage participants in a story world where they are simultaneously the authors of the plot, the narrators of the story they created and actors in a real-world theatre performance. In *The Producer's Guide to Transmedia* (2011) Nuno

Bernardo offers advice on how to fund, develop, produce and distribute content across multiple platforms for global audiences. The playful story world is designed with a participatory user-friendly experience which is "key to promoting and engaging with audiences around a traditional TV show, feature film, game or consumer brand" (Bernardo, 2011).

The idea of turning consumers into producers (*prosumers*) in transmedia experiences is not new. In gaming mainstream environments *crunch time* and work with no payment are diseases that we cannot subscribe. Game fans participate in the creative process suggesting ideas for brand loyalty and immerse themselves in the production stage with no monetary rewards besides their own satisfaction of playing the game and to belong to a community. Game designers sometimes turn themselves into puppet masters who generate orders instead of rulers and they can be manipulative inserting players into a suicide plot which reminds us the horror of *The Blue Whale* Game/Challenge (Budeikin, F57, 2013). The internet game was running in various countries and asks participants to accomplish a series of tasks during 50 days with the final challenge requiring players to commit suicide. In a critical perspective we have to avoid certain unethical behaviour and to keep in mind that the *gameful* world should be a meaningful and inclusive experience which builds on empathy and respect for the "other". Convergence culture demands well informed citizens.

According to Sebastian Deterding, "If there is one catchword for the current moment in the history of media, it is convergence: digital media, computing, and networking are decoupling the entities formerly known as "the media" into their requisite components — content genres and storage media, distribution networks and end devices, producers and audiences — to recombine them into unexpected, fleeting new formations (...). Thus, games can now be played on almost any digital device, anytime, anywhere. Game distribution is migrating from off-the-shelf physical copies to online streaming and a myriad of app stores across a myriad of platforms, and games are shifting from being finished products to interconnected, constantly evolving online services where "produsers" (Bruns, 2008) pay in the form of micro-transactions, personal data, content creation, and marketing work." (Deterding, 2014, p. 23) The cultivation of *ludus* and *paidia* in a mix strategy of chance, competition, simulation and vertigo, using Roger Caillois terminology and Huizinga's ideas, and the ludic and playful languages we speak are persistente entities in our contemporary pop culture and art which reaffirm, states the above quoted author, "the modernist notion that society can and ought to have spaces of noninstrumental, nonreligious aesthetics, and that games and play can and ought to be one of them." (Deterding, 2014, p. 26) There is also a postmodern shift that we have to take into account "that deemphasizes authority and economic achievement and foregrounds the maximization of personal wellbeing and self-expression." (Deterding, 2014,

p. 33) Gamers develop their creativity, knowledge, skills and aptitudes in systems thinking design, complex problem solving, collaboration and communication and these competences seem to be relevant to the twenty-first century workforce. In this sense games are sites of expression, meaning making and aesthetic experiences and they should be understand broadly as an aesthetic form "parallel to painting, music, film, or literature (…). Cultural participation today requires the acquisition of "new media literacies" (Jenkins et al., 2009), including the ability to appreciate and express oneself critically through the medium of games. Unsurprisingly, this rhetoric is particularly dear to the indie and art games communities." (Deterding, 2014, pp. 46-7)

For the purpose of this chapter the indie and art games rhetoric will be further develop as we belong to that thinking tradition but we also consider that different rhetoric's coexist in a *gameful* world where there is lots of diversity in terms of communities, discourses and practices, and our reality is "much more messy, random, unfair, and *beyond our control* than games. To think otherwise is to fall for "the ludic fallacy." (Deterding, 2014, p. 50) Our methodology considers a communication sciences approach which mixes arts and design-based research with game studies in a broad perspective emphasizing the idea that games are an aesthetic form.

Akira Thompson's game named *And Maybe They Won't Kill You* deal with "a performative empathy experience about being poor and black in America. Participants must journey to the local corner store in their own neighborhood while deflecting various micro-aggressions as well as harassment by law enforcement. Choose to speak out or remain silent and deal with the consequences of your choices." (RAINB, n.d.) According to Leigh Alexander this "striking work challenges one of the biggest misconceptions about police violence against black people in America, and offers privileged players the chance to experience the truth. As designed systems, games can create spaces for people to grasp how infrastructures work, to test theories—and often to internalize how the systems of our world may not work, may promote inequality. They can be tools to create empathy and reveal injustice; they can illustrate the often-complicated answers to the "why can't you just" and "but it's probably not really" that pervade rhetorical discourse." (Alexander, 2015)

Transmedia content creators and producers can engage in a forensic approach to societies complex opacity and instigate open source citizens. Echoing Daren's O'Donnell words in *Social Acupuncture, a guide to suicide, performance and utopia* (2008), "(…) there is the need for an understanding of art that goes not only beyond pleasant aesthetics, but beyond even typical ideas of creativity and imagination, directly engaging with the civic sphere. An aesthetic that can work directly with the institutions of civil society – an aesthetic of civic engagement. (…)" (O'Donnell, 2008, p. 24) And the Canadian author continues "(…) could we develop an aesthetic that favours work in which relational situations employ moments of antagonism toward a unification of oppositions in the civic sphere? Could civic engagement – the use of civil institutions as material – create the basis for an artistic practice?" (O'Donnell, 2008, p. 33). In the Mammalian Diving Reflex website (n.d.), Darren O'Donnell's project, we read "ideal entertainment for the end of the world" and we understand that "innovative artistic interventions" can be "a way to trigger generosity and equity across the universe." In this sense, founded in 1993, "Mammalian is a research-art atelier dedicated to investigating the social sphere, always on the lookout for contradictions to whip into aesthetically scintillating experiences." (Mammalian Diving Reflex, n.d.) In tune with O'Donnell's project the aim is to use arts-based research, in the production and dissemination of knowledge (O'Donnell, 2015, online), to create an aesthetic of participation that connects communities, several media and different cultures.

Inspired by [Kateřina] Šedá's creative work with communities O'Donnell considers that she "(…) is interested in changing real life and making people's lives better particularly those living in her own Czech village and surrounding villages. (…) She is able to obtain many of the objectives of the art-based researchers, revolutionizing social circumstances in small, temporary ways, introducing new dynamics, relations and connections between people. Here is a science-based artistic practice, focused on examining and affecting real life, managing to attend to the major concerns that have energized the turn toward a post-epistemological, relativist social science." (O'Donnell, 2015) If we want to solve our current problems we will need to involve cooperation and institutions for collective action. Transmedia creative experiences can be instrumental for that purpose in future.

According to the Urban Democracy Lab: "Through a fusion of art, pedagogy, and public policy" the once mayor of Bogotá, Antanas Mockus, "inspired citizens to work together in devising and applying solutions to the city's most pressing problems." (Urban Democracy Lab, 2015) The application of artistical and creative practices to reality can be seem in Andreas Møl Dalsgaard film *Bogotá Change* (2009) and it can inspire us for the design of future inclusive gaming interfaces.

If transmedia content creators and producers work for a more artistical oriented environment they can create a brand new atmosphere from scratch where they engage people in an alternative narrative or experience. Digital creators can use virtual and/ or augmented reality technologies to immerse participants or players in different contexts taking advantage of multiple realities and various technologies. QR codes connected to mobile phones can help solve mysteries in urban environments adding digital information to real settings. Virtual reality can enhance the feeling of presence and can be used in short term indie installations in the creation of narrative content and enhancing the sensorial experience using multiple platforms (cf. Gouveia, 2016). Even though VR attempts to bring us inside the digital space, which is not the purpose of transmedia experiences, as Silva and Sutko (2009) stated, it can also be used in short term creative sessions to make participants engage in deeper visceral and embodied experiences as part of the overall created performance.

SOLUTIONS AND RECOMMENDATIONS

Fictional content creation research and old school remediation techniques can be instrumental to engage contemporary audiences. Looking at the evolving ways in which stories are experienced to more accurately reflect the habits of contemporary audiences is part of the goal of cross media projects. By delivering independent, yet interconnected stories across multiple media platforms these projects help us research fictional content creation. In doing so, they unlock fresh creative possibilities, enable access to new revenue streams and promote deeper levels of audience engagement and brand loyalty. A transmedia project or franchise consists of various narrative storylines existing within the same fictional universe. We can think of transmedia projects involving different fields and platforms: internet, cinema, television, short film, broadband, publishing, comics, animation, mobile, special venues, narrative commercial and marketing rollouts, and other technologies connected to augmented or virtual reality (AR or VR). These narrative extensions are not the same as repurposing material from one platform to be cut or repurposed to different platforms, they need to be created in a transdisciplinary manner, converging knowledge from different areas. Interconnecting different pieces of narrative in a consistent plot and in a coherent manner is part of the creative process.

As stated elsewhere (Gouveia, 2013) we can witness a rebirth of creative old school techniques through the use of old visual imagery in new directions. Since the indie turn of the last decade gaming is prolific in using old school arts and design strategies to newer projects. From pixel art to film noir aesthetics everything became possible in a vintage turn to old cultural aesthetics which mix analog and digital media visuals. Visual aesthetics become a type of media archaeology where zombie arts from the past resurrected to new uses, contexts and adaptations. (Hertz & Parikka, 2013, p. 429) These transmedia procedural representations become "not only a method for excavation of repressed and forgotten media discourses, but extends itself into an artistic method close to Do-It-Yourself (DIY) culture, circuit bending, hardware hacking and other hacktivist exercises that are closely related to the political economy of information technology. The concept of dead media is discussed as "zombie media"—dead media revitalized, brought back to use, reworked." (Hertz & Parikka, 2013, p. 425) Using Hertz ans Parikka's ideas we can consider that besides games we can testify a return to old visual techniques in a broader sense.

In Moby & The Void Pacific Choir vídeo, "Are You Lost in the World Like Me?" from 2016, is curious to see how "zombie arts" from the past resurrected to new uses, contexts and adaptations. One simple and clear example of these artistical aesthetics is how "Director Steve Cutts took inspiration from Max Fleischer's animations from the 1930s to create an old-timey-looking but thoroughly modern world in which everyone is distracted by their devices. "For me the video is about our increasing dependence on technology and about human interaction today, or a certain lack of it. It focuses on the way tech is changing us – how we have become desensitized," Cutts said in a statement." (Rettig, 2016) We can with no doubt consider David Bolter claim about remediation in his *Writing Space* book, "(…) Remediation is a characteristic process not only for contemporary media, but for all visual media at least since Renaissance with its invention of linear-perspective painting." (Bolter, 2000, p. 25) An animation style from the thirties is remediated in a contemporary vídeo about how mobile technology is immersing us all in a screen device good enough to become our best window to the world.

According to Marsha Kinder "while those committed to the historical specificity of predigital media might question this strategy of rethinking old cultural forms through the metaphors of new media (perhaps fearing some kind of reductionism, say, in describing Giotto and Eisenstein as "important information designers" who deserve to be compared "alongside" contemporary giants like Allan Kay and Tim Berners-Lee), Manovich claims he is also motivated by an ethical obligation—to see old and new cultures as one continuum, and to enrich new culture through the use of the aesthetic techniques of old cultures. (Kinder, 2014, p. 8) Kinder in a critical reflection about medium specificity and transmedia challenges, quoting Edward Branigan, adverts "an art medium, whether old or new, elicits responses from us as it intermixes with memory systems." (Kinder, 2014, p. 10) The remix of different times and spaces in contemporary arts challenge our perceptual world in new ways.

The postmodernist erasure of the distinction between high and low culture is considered in Kinder's words, following British new media theorist Andrew Darley, as part of an assemblage between the "marginal practices" of avant-garde computer art and the "low" forms of popular entertainment under the scrutiny of cultural studies. (Kinder, 2014, p. 4) This approach of mixing arts and design practices from galleries, libraries and museums with popular artefacts from gaming and play is implicit in our own research in ludic studies applied to transmedia mediated experiences using various pieces of narrative and fiction. (cf. Gouveia, 2010a; 2010b) According to Andrew Darley, "art, like everything else, is a social phenomenon – one, moreover, that cannot properly be grasped outsider of historical development and the specificity of social context (see Wolf 1981)." (Darley, 2000, p. 5) Computer emergence and its ability to make tools to create other tools allows us entirely new ways to create and generate images "together with distinctive ways of assisting and augmenting traditional methods and techniques of moving image production have become commonplace within contemporary forms of visual cultural production." (Darley, 2000, p. 22) Transmedia experiences use and remix commercial visual materials with indie aesthetics. A good example of the use of these strategies is the company 42 Entertainment which considers that "audiences expect to go deeper" and the "internet has fostered an expectation that people will be able to delve into a story at different levels of involvement. They assume they'll be able to immerse themselves in a narrative at will. The more committed your fans, the greater need to reward them – because nothing brings in new fans like an enthusiastic evangelist." (42 Entertainment, 2016)

To integrate and reward fans a transmedia artist and designer is responsible for the long-term planning, development, production, and/or maintenance of narrative continuity across multiple platforms, and the creation of original storylines for new environments. The use of digital technologies, databases and search engines for the creation and production of new models of storytelling and generative narratives was inspired in modernist movements such as Dadaism, Surrealism and Post Structuralism, to mention just a few. This exploration was previously used as concepts in arts and literature environments and opened a path for "narrative experimentation that always leaves room for the unknown and that exposes the ideological implications of all databases and their search engines." (Kinder, 2014, p. 13) Recombinant strategies and "open-ended storytelling is not an oxymoron, as some theorists have argued, but a grammar that lies at the heart of narrative networks and predates Barthes's *S/Z.*" (Kinder, 2014, p.16) Marsha Kinder quoting Peter Brooks considers that, "the greatest narratives are usually so long (think of the work of Proust, Melville, Joyce, Scheherazade, and—one could add—Rushdie), and why, as we move through their expansive middles, we experience them as "force fields of desire." Instead of using the story of Oedipus as his master narrative, Brooks props his theory on Freud's *Beyond the Pleasure Principle* (which offers him Eros and Thanatos as primary engines of narrative drive) and on the *The Wolf Man* (an open-ended network of interwoven stories that uses transference and dialogue as models of interactive exchange)." The goal of Brooks strategy "is to design a new narrative grammar capable of delivering pleasure and sustaining desire." (Kinder, 2014, p. 17) Tv series nowadays exploit this model in various ways to immerse audiences around the globe.

FUTURE RESEARCH DIRECTIONS

Transmedia aesthetics and the interactive experience of participation in mixed, augmented and virtual reality can improve with a media art histories approach.

Conveying inspiration from several movements of the history of modern and contemporary arts, which promoted the transition from a passive spectator to the participant of the artistic systems, namely, Dadaism, Surrealism, Fluxus, Situationist International, Digital Activism, Net and Generative Art, among others, transmedia aesthetics merges arts and games territories in their historical specificities to create projects that take into account the transition from a visual arts aesthetics associated with the image to an aesthetic of the interactive experience present in media arts. Transmedia aesthetics, as the above quoted arts movements, also tend to merge arts and life, high and low cultures, different communities and countries, various technologies and platforms, in a pervasive mediated plot for a global audience.

The new media aspect of the "cross-media experience" typically involves, suggests Drew Davidson in the preface of the book *Cross-Media Communications: an Introduction to the Art of Creating Integrated Media Experiences*, some level of audience interactivity. In other words, it's an experience (often a story of sorts) that we "read" by watching movies, dipping into a novel, playing a game, riding a ride, etc." (Davidson, 2010, p. ix) The possibility of creating experiences across multiple media, transmedia, came "in the mid to late 90's the internet boom promised the incorporation of cross-media interactivity into transmedia experiences, but with the dot.com bust those promises have only now come into fruition. Currently, the technology is ubiquitous enough and the culture is more connected than ever. This has enabled more and more interactive cross-media experiences to begin being designed, developed and experienced. We are entering an era where our media experiences will be integrated together and we will be able to interactively participate in these experiences." (Davidson, 2010, p. ix)

Today's digital experiences are influenced and inspired by old forms of social interaction, considers Carolyn Miller, from religious rituals to analogue games. These experiences help us "define some of the critical components required to create satisfying interactivity. Namely, they are participatory; something important is at stake; rules and a structure guide our path through the interactivity; and the experience involves overcoming obstacles and achieving a goal of some sort. Furthermore, the act of participating in an interactive experience arouses some sort of feeling within us. It either involves us emotionally (as in religious rituals) or is enjoyable as a form of play (as in games). The experiments in narrative that were first tried in novels, theatre, and film have also helped point the way to creators of interactive media, particularly in new techniques of storytelling. These older works introduced the concept of hyperlinking; of unpredictability; of multiple pathways and multiple events occurring simultaneously within a fictional world; and of new ways to peer into the lives and perspectives of characters. Other narrative works have pioneered the breaking of the fourth wall that divides fiction from reality" (Miller,

2008, p. 14). The boundaries between the real and the fictional world are just getting blurred and Miller aims to articulate ideas of character design, structure, and other development techniques to forward a new way of telling stories.

The "total" mediated convergence experience can be created these days and analog and digital universes are explored in order to produce artefacts that promote the convergence of spaces (online and offline) and media (film and television, web and mobile devices, visual arts and design printing press, sound scales and radio, among other possibilities). Peter Weibel once describe the shift from the passive spectator to the active participant, "If there are any social aspects at all in modern art, then they must involve the spectator. We want to arouse the spectator's interest, to liberate him, to relax him. We want him to participate. We want him to seek interaction with other spectators. We want to develop together with him enhanced perception and action. A spectator who is aware of his power and tired of so many falsities and mystifications will be enabled to make his revolution in art and to follow these signs: act and cooperate." (Weibel, 2007, p. 48) To act and cooperate is leaving the spectator's role and becoming a participant in the transmedia created plot. It means to be aware that the action produced will change the overall story world. To act and participate in the creative story is exchanging pieces and bits of written and visual material in an open-ended fiction.

The spectator, the viewer, belongs to an ideological mechanism, states Erkki Huhtamo, which puts the work of art in a distance from those who experience it. According to the author, "touching with one's eyes only was a manifestation of an ideological mechanism, where the formation of the aesthetic experience was associated with "stepping back" – maintaining physical distance from the work: Touching a sculpture or a painting was not only deemed vulgar, but forbidden." (Huhtamo, 2007, p. 76) The rigid structure of game controllers and how we forget about our bodies (Sicart, 2017) in play experiences is something that new research in gaming devices will consider in future. Let's remember, as an inspiration, Isamu Noguchi's work on playgrounds and public spaces where visitors could physically and actively engage with art.

Following Roberto Simanowski's book *Digital Art and Meaning*, it is important not to forget that interactive arts must be analysed according to phenomenological and semiotic perspectives. In this context, it should be taking into account that interactive systems are both spaces with performative emotional and sensorial dimensions but also open to interpretations, thus combining phenomenological and hermeneutic analyses (Simanowski, 2011). In our game studies research (Gouveia, 2010a) we combined phenomenological sensorial dimensions in first-person perspectives with hermeneutic theories in an attempt to better understand the complexity of gaming and play spaces.

According to Whitney Quesenbery and Kevin Brooks, "stories have always been part of user experience design scenarios". We use tools such as storyboards, flow charts, paper designs, personas or identity card style character presentations "and every other technique that we use to communicate how (and why) a new design will work. As a part of user experience design, stories serve to ground the work in a real context by connecting design ideas to the people who will use the product." (Quesenbery & Brooks, 2012, p. xviii) Stories can be made of written, visual or audio materials and are a powerful tool in user experience design because they can help us understand participants roles and better communicate our design goals and strategies. (Quesenbery & Brooks, 2012). Narrative construction and processes are an essential part in the transmedia content creation and production design (Quesenbery & Brooks, 2012, p. 21) and they can be used to shape the interactive action in a meaningful way.

The narrative paradox and how we can design interactive fictions where actions and narrations can contribute for a more meaningful experience within an interactive setting was developed in a previous paper (Gouveia, 2009) and book (Gouveia, 2010a). Our previous research showed how pervasive gaming, where participants can cooperate and compete in the real application of tactics and strategies as they play the game online and offline, can contribute to create a more engaging environment where players are able to build their own stories. Player made content and hyperfiction are useful tools to better understand interactive fiction. For us interactive fiction is much more than just something which means "a very specific kind of computer game: the text adventure, as in games like *Zork* or *Moonmist.* (Phillips, 2012, p. 18) Our arts and design based research methodology aims to be holistic in connecting hypertext and interactive fiction with transmedia projects such as those which use playable media, serious gaming, alternate reality games (ARGs), VR documentaries, AR urban play and what else we can evoque to immerse players in a plot which blurs the boundaries between the real and the fictional in a postmodern way.

Gaming history is prolific in creating rooms or devices to enhance game experience and to create a perceptual feeling of presence and/or immersion. In a previous publish peer reviewed paper "Gaming and VR Technologies, Powers and Discontents" (Gouveia, 2016) we develop our research for the design of play environments taking into account augmented and virtual reality with concrete examples in terms of projects such as documentaries and games. Virtual Reality remains a vertigo (*ilinx*) territory, where users are so immersed in the digital environment that they can play with their own sensorial apparatus, but the all experience is so intense that it can ruin other game design attributes such as plot or story consistency, meaningful interaction and game play, game mechanics, among others. VR can be a truly meaningful experience but its effects are still not well tested.

In another previously peer reviewed paper named "Serious Gaming: How Gamers are Solving Real World Problems" (Gouveia, 2015) we developed gaming connections with serious gaming and gamification stating that these strategies can be used to help solve real world problems in education and health care. Serious gaming, which aims to merge digital and real world social environments, can be also instrumental to enhance connectivity among communities. Inspired in concrete projects and actions in the field of serious games, game based learning, *transmedia* experience and alternate reality games at that time we reviewed some literature and projects in serious gaming as future inspirations for the creation and production of a serious game design applied to education and/or health.

Playable fiction and gaming can contribute to recombine action and narration in connected ecologies and we think that implosive stories, in which everything happens simultaneously, present in transmedia spaces, allow us to better understand the difficulties of creating and developing consistent narrative in interactive environments that use mixed technologies. Inclusive spaces where gamers can learn how to deal with different media, various communities and cultures can enhance players ability to shape better narratives in order to design their own fictions and stories in real time.

In this context, we can consider, following Quesenbery & Brooks that "stories are more than just a way of broadcasting information. They are interactive, and come to life in the imaginations of the audience members. Stories are as much a part of the audience as of the storyteller. The Story Triangle describes the relationships between storyteller, story, and audience. Stories have many roles in user experience design: They explain research and ideas. They engage the imagination and spark new ideas. They create a shared understanding. They can persuade." (Quesenbery & Brooks, 2012, p. 52) The power of persuasive procedural rhetoric, a technique for making and unpacking arguments with computational systems and games, was explored by Ian Bogost (2007) and can be a resource for independent and activist artistical projects which aim to show and dismantle manipulative power rhetoric's. They can be used to disrupt and introduce noise in a renewed manner showing new ways of thinking about old problems. They can be used to help explain various points of view to achieve a certain level of transparency because only opacity is the darkness but "there is always a lot of light in the Heart of Darkness." (Oguibe, 2004, p. 9)

Artists and designers of transmedia content should be aware of the potential for continued accelerated growth and development of processes and techniques in the creative digital industries and should be professionally capable of anticipating such developments both as consumers and as providers of services to those industries with a wide range of capacities. Since software knowledge and engines are more available nowadays, we can also notice a boom in participatory practices where people find themselves through the web, work together without even meeting in real life, and find financial support for their projects also through social and crowd funding platforms such as *Kickstarter* (cf. Antrophy, 2012). In a convergence culture, where old and new media collide (Jenkins, 2006), do-it-yourself practices (DIY), a tool to engage people and generate creative content (Dezeuze, 2010), converge in a renewed community of artists, designers and programmers, which create transmedia experiences using fun theory to create a *gameful* world.

Artists and designers explore new strategies in serious gaming and game based learning (Blashki, 2013) in Transmedia environments. Nowadays, many urban game play settings and experiences, involving multiple strategies and locations, are created to generate greater participation among people after the dark diagnosis, from the MIT sociologist Sherry Turkle, in her *Alone Together* book, from 2011. Accordingly, to Turkle, it seems consequential, that research in participation, using Transmedia content production we would add, could be the key to solve the lack of care in multitasking digital natives. Some social dilemmas, among youth generations, could be tested and explored to generate greater creativity, engagement and participation.

CONCLUSION

Transmedia professionals need to be aware of the multidimensional territory they are creating for and they need to know there is a certain lack of narrative control in their works. In a diluted authorship profession, they also create and implement interactive content/activities to unite the audience of the property with the canonical narrative. They may originate with a project or be brought in at any time during the long-term rollout of the creative process in order to analyse, create or facilitate the life of that project and they maybe be responsible for all or only part of the content of the artwork. A transmedia artist and designer may also be hired by or partner with companies or entities, which develop software or apps and who wish to showcase these inventions with compelling, immersive, multi-platform content.

Transmedia content could be applied in creative industries in a broad perspective, from media arts and design, to film, music and television, journalism and advertising, among other possibilities of convergence. Transmedia projects are designed to encompass the key issues relating to the design, creation and production of content and creators need to develop a high level of competency in specific tools and techniques. Transmedia content creators tend to be in close connection with a wide variety of communities. Social and cultural factors in creating participative communities of practice are relevant issues to take into account and consistent research is needed from the beginning of each project. A detailed understanding of cross platform applications for community engagement is fundamental to engage audiences and generate a high degree of problem solving and conflict resolution skills. Transmedia experiences can be designed as rich and meaningful environments where participants connect and communicate with various perspectives and points of view. Transmedia interactive spaces can generate care and empathy among human beings and can be instrumental to enhance transparency because, as stated before, only opacity is the darkness but "there is always a lot of light in the Heart of Darkness" (Oguibe, 2004, p. 9).

REFERENCES

42 Entertainment. (2016). Retrieved July, 30, 2017, from http://www.42entertainment.com/

AA.VV. (2015). *The Right to Have Rights: Citizenship Culture and the Future of Cities, with Antanas Mockus*. Retrieved July 26, 2017, from http://urbandemos.nyu.edu/event/the-right-to-have-rights-citizenship-culture-and-the-future-of-cities-distinguished-faculty-lecture-with-antanas-mockus/

AA.VV. (2017). *Noguchi's Playscapes*. Retrieved July 30, 2017, from https://www.sfmoma.org/exhibition/noguchis-playscapes/

AA.VV. (n.d.). *The Blue Whale Game*. Retrieved July 30, 2017, from https://en.wikipedia.org/wiki/Blue_Whale_(game)

Alexander, L. (2015). *Carry the frustration of injustice in this game about racist police violence*. Retrieved July 30, 2017, from http://boingboing.net/2015/08/05/carry-the-frustration-of-injus.html

Anthropy, A. (2011). *Rise of the Videogame Zinesters: How Freaks, Normals, Amateurs, Dreamers, Drop-outs, Queers, Housewifes and People Like You Are Taking Back an Art Form*. Seven Stories Press.

Beactive Entertainment. (2017). Retrieved from http://beactivemedia.com/

Bernardo, N. (2011). *The Producer's Guide to Transmedia: How to Develop, Fund, Produce and Distribute compelling Stories across multiple platforms*. Lisbon: beActive Books.

Bernardo, N. (2014). *How to build an exciting and convincing transmedia storyworld*. Retrieved July 26, 2017, from https://www.mynewsdesk.com/ie/beactive/blog_posts/nuno-bernardo-how-to-build-an-exciting-and-convincing-transmedia-storyworld-27070

Blashki, K., Lim, L., & Kristensen, M. (2013). The Social Translator: A Game Based learning Simulator to foster cross cultural understanding and adaptation. *IADIS International Journal, 11*(1).

Bogost, I. (2007). *Persuasive Games, The Expressive Power of Videogames.* Cambridge, MA: MIT Press.

Bolter, J. D. (2001), Writing Space, Computers, Hypertext, and the Remediaton of Print (2nd ed.). London: Lawrence Erlbaum Associates.

Caillois, R. (2001). *Man, Play and Games.* Urbana, Chicago: University of Illinois Press. (Original work published 1958)

Carvalho, M. (2015). *A obra "Faça-Você-Mesmo": Estética da Participação nas Artes Digitais* [The Do-It-Yourself" Work: Aesthetics of Participation in Digital Arts] (Unpublished doctoral dissertation). Faculdade de Ciências Sociais e Humanas, Universidade Nova de Lisboa.

Correia, V. (2017). *O Design e a Cultura da Participação na Era dos Média Digitais* [Design and the Culture of Participation in the Era of Digital Media] (Unpublished doctoral dissertation). Faculdade de Ciências Sociais e Humanas, Universidade Nova de Lisboa.

Darley, A. (2000). *Visual Digital Culture, Surface Play and Spectacle in New Media Genres.* London: Routledge.

Davidson, D. (2010). *Cross-media Communications: an Introduction to the Art of Creating Integrated Media Experiences.* Carnegie Mellon University ETC Press.

Deterding, S. (2014). The Ambiguity of Games: Histories and Discourses of a Gameful World. In S. P. Walz & S. Deterding (Eds.), *The Gameful World: Approaches, Issues, Applications* (pp. 23–64). Cambridge, MA: MIT Press.

Dezeuze, A. (2010). *The Do-it-yourself, Artwork, Participation from Fluxus to New Media.* Manchester, NY: Manchester University Press.

Flanagan, M. (2009). *Critical Play, Radical Game Design.* Cambridge, MA: MIT Press.

Gouveia, P. (2009). Narrative Paradox and the Design of Alternate Reality Games (ARGs) and Blogs. In Proceedings of IEEE Consumer Electronics Society's Games Innovation Conference 2009 *(ICE-GIC 09)* (pp. 231-38.). London Imperial College.

Gouveia, P. (2010a). *Artes e Jogos Digitais, Estética e Design da Experiência Lúdica* (11th ed.). Lisbon: Edições Universitárias Lusófonas.

Gouveia, P. (2010b). Playing With Poetry a Portuguese Transmedia Experience and a Serious ARG. In *GIC 2010 Proceedings of 2nd International IEEE Consumer Electronic Society Games Innovation Conference* (pp. 150-56). Hong Kong, China: Academic Press. 10.1109/ICEGIC.2010.5716904

Gouveia, P. (2013). Transmedia experience and the independent game industry: the renascence of old school visual and artistic techniques [Esperiência transmedia e a indústria de jogos independente (indie): o "renascimento" de expressões artísticas e visuais do tipo "old school"]. In Comunicação e Antropologia Social, Seminário Internacional de Rede ICCI Imagens da Cultura Cultura das Imagens (pp. 78-89). ECA, USP.

Gouveia, P. (2015). *Serious gaming: how gamers are solving real world problems.* Academic Press.

Gouveia, P. (2016). Gaming and VR Technologies, Powers and Discontents. In Proceedings of Videojogos'16. Covilhã, Portugal: Academic Press.

Gouveia, P., & Martel, P. (2017). Player Experience, Gaming and VR Technologies (extended version). Journal of Computer Sciences.

Hertz, G., & Parikka, J. (2012). Zombie Media: Circuit Bending Media Archaeology into an Art Method (pp. 424–430). *Leonardo, 45*(5), 424–430. doi:10.1162/LEON_a_00438

Huhtamo, E. (2007). Twin-Touch-Test-Redux: Media Archaeological Approach to Art, Interactivity, and Tactility. In O. Grau (Ed.), *MediaArtHistories* (pp. 71–101). Cambridge, MA: MIT Press.

Huizinga, J. (1955). *Homo Ludens.* Boston: The Beacon Press.

Jenkins, H. (2006). *Convergence Culture: Where Old and New Media Collide.* New York University Press.

Kinder, M. (2014). Medium Specificity and productive precursors, an Introduction. In M. Kinder & T. McPherson (Eds.), *Transmedia Frictions, The Digital, the Arts, and the Humanities* (pp. 3–19). University of California Press.

Knausgard, K. O. (2015). *A Minha Luta 2: Um Homem Apaixonado.* Lisboa: Relógio D'Água Editores.

Kutner, M. (2017). *What is the Blue Whale Game, The Russian 'Challenge' Blamed for Suicides?* Retrieved July 30, 2017, from http://www.newsweek.com/what-blue-whale-game-russia-suicides-637798

Manovich, L. (2001). *Post-media Aesthetics*. Retrieved November 30, 2017, from http://manovich.net/content/04-projects/032-post-media-aesthetics/29_article_2001.pdf

McGonigal, J. (2011). *Reality is Broken, why games make us better and how they can change the world*. New York: The Penguin Press.

Miller, C. H. (2008). *Digital Storytelling: A Creator's Guide to interactive entertainment* (2nd ed.). Focal Press.

Montola, M., Stenros, J., & Waern, A. (2009). *Pervasive Games, Experiences on the Boundary Between Life and Play (Theory and Design)*. Burlington, MA: Morgan Kaufmann.

Museum of Art, Architecture and Technology. (2017). *Post-internet Cities*. Retrieved November, 30, 2017, from https://postinternetcities.weebly.com/

O'Donnell, D. (2008). *Social Acupuncture, a guide to suicide, performance and utopia*. Coach House Books.

O'Donnell, D. (2015). *So You Want to be an Artist: when social scientists don the beret*. Retrieved July 30, 2017, from https://medium.com/@darrenodonnell/so-you-want-to-be-an-artist-when-social-scientists-don-the-beret-a9d32f272fb5

Oguibe, O. (2004). *The Culture Game*. Minneapolis, MN: University of Minnesota Press.

Phillips, A. (2012). *A Creator's Guide to Transmedia Storytelling: How to Captivate and Engage Audiences Across Multiple Platforms*. McGraw Hill.

Quesenbery, W., & Brooks, K. (2012). *Storytelling for User Experience: Crafting Stories for Better Design*. New York: Rosenfeld Media.

Rainb. (n.d.). Retrieved November, 30, 2017, from http://rainb.ro/

ReflexM. D. (2017). Retrieved from http://mammalian.ca/

Rettig, J. (2016). *Moby & The Void Pacific Choir – "Are You Lost in the World Like Me?"* [Video]. Retrieved July 27, 2017, from http://www.stereogum.com/1905565/moby-the-void-pacific-choir-are-you-lost-in-the-world-like-me-video/video/

Saving the Face. (2015). Retrieved November, 30, 2017, from http://connectingcities.net/project/saving-face-0

Sicart, M. (2017). *Queering the Controller*. Retrieved August 30, 2017, from http://analoggamestudies.org/2017/07/queering-the-controller/

Silva, S. A., & Sutko, D. M. (Eds.). (2009). Digital Cityscapes, merging digital and urban playspaces. New York: Peter Lang.

Simanowski, R. (2011). *Digital Art and Meaning: Reading Kinetic Poetry, Text Machines, Mapping Art, and Interactive Installations*. University of Minnesota Press. doi:10.5749/minnesota/9780816667376.001.0001

Speridiao, A. (2014). *Connected Drains*. Retrieved November, 30, 2017, from http://www.bueirosconectados.net/

Theory, B. (2018). Retrieved July, 30, 2017, from http://www.blasttheory.co.uk/

Turkle, S. (2011). *Alone Together, why we expect more from technology and less from each other*. New York: Basic Books.

Walz, S. P., & Deterding, S. (Eds.). (2014). The Gameful World: Approaches, Issues, Applications. Cambridge, MA: MIT Press.

Weibel, P. (2007). It is Forbidden Not to Touch: Some Remarks on the (Forgotten Parts of the) History of Interactivity and Virtuality. In O. Grau (Ed.), *MediaArtHistories* (pp. 21–41). Cambridge, MA: MIT Press.

Wikipedia. (2018). *Blue Whale Game*. Retrieved July, 30, 2017, from https://en.wikipedia.org/wiki/Blue_Whale_(game)

Chapter 2
Affective Presence in Enactive Immersive Space:
Sensorial and Mobile Technologies Reengineering Life

Diana Maria G. Domingues
University of Brasilia, Brazil & University of Campinas (UNICAMP), Brazil

Mateus Rodrigues Miranda
University of Brasilia, Brazil

ABSTRACT

The reengineering of life through the sense of presence in virtual and augmented reality raised in art and technoscience is the focus of the aesthetical, scientific, and technological potential for the changes to the ecological, social, environmental, and biological condition. Virtual reality immersion uses proprioceptive trackers for navigation and stereoscopy in kinesthesia generating compelling experience inside data landscapes. Nowadays, disruptive technologies melting biological, synthetic worlds (data-cyber) and physic spaces (biocybrid systems) allow synaesthetic embodied experience to the Spinozian body. In enactive affective systems, the sentient and pervasive technologies by the invasion of mobile technologies, physiological sensors, computer vision, locative, and geodesic dialogues of organisms/data and environment are in reciprocal and mutual exchanges. The ontology of life conciliates paradoxes and conflicts of emergent realities and self-organizing dialogues between artificial and natural modifying the concept of reality, which is always a philosophical concept.

DOI: 10.4018/978-1-5225-5696-1.ch002

INTRODUCTION

This essay focuses on discussions on virtual reality immersive spaces in various issues coming from the artworks raised in the field of Art TechnoScience and their aesthetical, scientific and technological appeal There are topics related to the humanization and naturalization of technologies, the transcendent and consciousness states claimed for immersion in VR (Virtual Reality) and urban mixed life in AR (Augmented Reality). It is emphasized the qualities of immersion, navigation, proprioception amplified to synaesthesia that reshape the consciousness issues in data landscapes and mixed realities. In the beginning, synthetic data created Virtual Reality scenes that went into the frames that were expanded in order to make "a room with a view" (Sandin, De Fanti, & Cruz-Neira, 1993) or CAVEs (Cave Automatic Virtual Environment). After, the VR scenes and objects escaped to the physic space to be mixed and to live in physic and hybrid space of the AR Augmented Reality. By adding the mobile devices, the MAR (Mobile Augmented Reality), mixed data landscapes and data objects to human biocybrid (bio+cyber+hybrid) scenario.

All those aspects are considered because every technology promotes changes in the field of perception in its potential to expand and modify the sense of presence in the world. Perception and cognition resulting of human experience facing technologies expand the world and the body apparatus living in. This is the main secret topic must be analyzed when facing the creative technologies and innovation for the expanded sensorium and respective aesthetical responsive actions in the world. The reengineering of life expanded in the perceptual experiences by the sense of presence in Virtual Reality and Augmented Reality using mobile devices (MAR) Mobile Augmented Reality is the seminal theme of the present essay. The investigation lead in transdisciplinary collaborative practices and confirms that the artists´ creativity when connected to the inventiveness of scientists make available the mutual capacities for the reciprocity of the generation related to enactive immersive sensorial landscapes.

The ontology of life towards different levels of reality that attempt to conciliate paradoxes and conflicts related to changes and challenges of human condition are the recent scene which embraced the effects of technologies. Art and TechnoScience are in theirs roots and deal with emergent realities and self-organizing dialogues between artificial spaces and the natural signals, natural and artificial, human and non-human, life and synthetic life, modify the concept of reality, which one is always a philosophical concept. We propose immersive and mixed reality affective environments with embedded multisensory systems, responsible for the strong experiential nature in synthetic spaces of virtual reality and in the moistures with physic and hybrid spaces of mobile augmented reality. There are experiences of spaces constructed biologically, transduced by algorithmic codes. They are shaped by algorithmic laws and Cartesian and geodesic coordinates, transformed and transduced into process of natural and mainly physiological laws in signals processing and code. Through internal interfaces of the program, the system: hardware and software are able to perform the body and environmental laws functions. Mutant renderings make visible the dynamics and kinematics of synthetic territories; topographies and objects evolve in their mutant destiny; physical phenomena manifest natural laws, responding to the behaviors of the system updater. The body experiences inside the data landscapes all the qualities of VR manifested in navigation and immersion by proprioception and visual stimulus of stereoscopy which amplify the degree of having the body enveloped by images on a human scale. Body/system feedback establishes a perceptual continuum in a relationship in which the body feels in a space that "feels" the body. Displacements to the right, to go ahead, pushing, blowing or other gestures and actions create another reality to be lived in.

In the historical list of performance, the first discuss was using two immersive environments one for artistic and other training. Metaphorically, in those artworks VR immersion is suggested to be compared as performance and body/experience. In ritualistic practices, people can get powers of acting in the fantastic cosmos propitiated by the trackers inside artificial landscapes and by generating mutant scenes and natural phenomena. The magic of acting and updating a technological cosmos always has enchanted people by offering realities that replicate or transgress our human condition here provided by VR and immersion. Turmoil birds, sky rotation, lights, fire enveloped people in a shamanistic dream. At the same time, and in great application in recent years, the VR, from its origins, has returned to application for trainings of pilots, engineers, doctors, used for psychological treatments, educational, sightseeing and tourism, meetings in artificial worlds in online synthetic environments. This topic is presented with research in cross sensoriality and immersion to collaborate with immersion as a digital world for expanding the human factor of technologies.

On the other hand, the AR, with the mobile devices and the GPS (Global Positional System), biosensors, computer vision, satellites, modem, gyroscopes and other technological systems makes a Reengineering of Reality that push us to ask:

What is the sense of presence modified by technologies? What spaces are we living in now?

The collaborative practice at the Laboratory of Research in Art and TechnoScience (LART – University of Brasília - Gama) consider virtual reality and augmented reality as parts of the ecosystem, abandoning the original idea of synthetic separated worlds (Domingues, 2003). Enactive bodily interfaces in their sophisticated connecting manner bring a novel kind of art related to aesthetic, anthropological, philosophical changes and challenges in life experience and social relationships. Locative interface activates an interstitial zone between physical space and data space and configures a biocybrid existence (Domingues, 2008). The transdisciplinary research in the domain of Biomedical Engineering and Computer Science and Health, Science and Technologies for affective experiences and the expanded sensorium investigate problems regarding enactive systems. These systems enhance the sensorial apparatus by adding technologies for experiences that amplify kinesthesia (displacement, movement, gestures). The sensations are configured in response to the enactions to the physical world, by embedding and making the transit in all sensorial system, transferring sensations, which aesthetically constitutes the principle of synesthesia. The entire body sends signals and the expanded perception is not only a retinal vision, but a complete sensorial body exchanging with the environment as "living maps" (Massumi, 2002; Domingues et al., 2016).

In the beginning, virtual reality systems for immersive experience used different types of proprioceptive devices and movement trackers to map a participant's displacements or gestures and provide a feedback for navigation and positioning. This principle constitutes the basic idea of kinesthesia in the domain of aesthetics, which was largely explored in applications in virtual reality. This historical approach related to the Kinetic Art of the 80s and the recent experiences in virtual reality and mobile augmented reality. Those disruptive technologies for perception and sensorial measurement offer a compelling experience in data landscapes for visualizing and inhabit data landscapes with the all the senses. Simulators add to the displacements the effects of collisions, vibrations, trepidations etc., when inhabiting the synthetic spaces. Also, the historical intuitive interfaces, such as shutter glasses, data gloves, trackers, emitters, force biofeedback devices, joysticks, among others, are empowered by biosensors that capture physiological signals in order to enhance the immersion experience and make it more intense.

The embodied experience then corresponds to a Spinozian body with the affective ability to communicate with the environment through the several measured signals. This body sends and receives data, as it exchanges energies and signals with the environment, in an enactive condition, described by Varela (Domingues et al., 2014). We present enactive systems inside the Caves by configuring compelling experiences in data landscapes and human affective narratives. The interaction occurs through the acquisition, data visualization and analysis of several synchronized physiological signals, to which the landscapes respond and provide immediate feedback, according to the detected participants' actions and the intertwined responses of the environment. The signals rates for analyses are the results of the human states include the electrocardiography (ECG) signal, the respiratory flow, the galvanic skin response (GSR) signals, plantar pressures, pulse signals and others. Each signal is collected by using a specifically designed dedicated electronic board, with reduced dimensions, so it does not interfere with normal movements, according to the principles of transparent technologies. Also, the electronic boards are implemented in a modular approach, so they are independent, and can be used in many different desired combinations, and at the same time provide synchronization between the collected data. To collect the signals while the participants live the immersive experience, the authors developed special support biomaterials, such as an insole made out of Brazilian latex. This is a biocompatible material that helps fixing the electrodes in the participants' skin, without displacements during the experience and without risks of allergic or other undesired reactions. This is especially important for easily positioning the plantar pressure sensors, through an easy-to-put insole with the electrodes already.

The enactive human context to affective narratives in the scenario/body/technologies mutual exchanges generate living maps, by body narratives through body in action. (in action, Noé, 2010). The enactions propitiate enactive landscapes, experienced in locative bodily mobile and ubiquitous computing (Weiser, 1991) which generate ecological affordances. In the similar James Gibson way, Diana Domingues discuss the Oroboric perception and the ancient mythic desire by the intertwined relationships of body/environment/nets, and co-location in physical and data world (Domingues, 2016).

Another research of this group describes an experimental platform used to evaluate the performance of individuals at training immersive physiological games. The platform proposed is embedded in an immersive environment in a CAVE of Virtual Reality and consists on a base frame with actuators with three degrees of freedom, sensor array interface and physiological sensors. Physiological data of breathing, galvanic skin resistance (GSR) and pressure on the hand of the user and a subjective questionnaire were collected during the experiments for training conductors of cars, planes. The theoretical background on Biomedical Engineering and Ergonomics and Creative Technologies present an evaluation of a vehicular simulator located inside the CAVE. Images captured through time at the embedded experience and data collected through physiological data visualization (average frequency and RMS - Root Mean Square - graphics) empowered the subjective questionnaire which register the strong lived experience provided by the technological apparatus (Miranda, 2015). The affective enactive biocybrid condition is expanded beyond art and entertainment to automotive issues. In fact, the kinesthetic sensations amplified by synesthesia replicates the sensation of displacement in the interior of an automobile, as well as the sensations of vibration and vertical movements typical of a vehicle, different speeds, collisions, etc.

The authors expand kinaesthesia, or motion sensors activity, that recognizes the environment for kinesthetic proprioception (Berthoz, 2000), body movement schemes, by adding physiological data from all directions by signal processing, skin temperature, heart rate, cardiac flow, breathing, muscles rhythm. Human actions in enactive processing systems and the processes of knowing, learning and teaching about their affections generate living maps in synesthesia and affective geographic narratives of ecological perception. (Gibson, 1979). One important innovation is the application of that system for diagnosing and treating diabetes, as well as other applications in m-health. As seen at PhD thesis by Tiago Lucena and the Post Doc work by Prof. Suélia Rodrigues, integrating the two laboratories (LART/FGA and Camera Culture/MIT – Massachusetts Institute of Technology) in a series of activities in the last years. Using physiological sensors attached to the insole, it acquires physiological data (galvanic skin response, foot pressure, temperature) combined with locative tools (GPS), allowing the creation of a kind of affective living map of the city. Following the user along his/her daily life, the proposed system is as a kind of tool to tell stories about user's habits and urban activity. While this insole does not supplement human ability, it provides an intuitive tool to see where and when the body responds less than optimally.

Finally, the authors insist in the proposal of the enactive systems to empower the emergence of affective condition of human narratives coming from physiological signals in the mutual and reciprocal influence of data spaces, and bodies' performance as the experience inside the hybrid landscapes. The complex enactive effects in a constructed perceptual experience of living maps, towards the naturalization of technologies are traces of the enactive aesthetics in that world increasingly technologically dependent.

VIRTUAL REALITY: PHILOSOPHICAL ISSUES

The virtual reality seems to constitute the contemporary technological version of the fantastic artistic desire to make us feel that we inhabit and act in another places, in another times, in another realities. The experiential nature of events living inside synthetic immersive environments that involve the entire body offer sensations that cause the boundaries of the corporeal and the dream to become diffuse, getting close to a perceptive and cognitive magic space responded by the fantasy of living in artificial spaces. These post-biological immersive forms of existing in virtual reality homologue high levels of sensorial responses to human actions. Immersive places for the enveloped body, totally involved in a diving sensation and *dissolution of its corporeal boundaries* melt up the organism with the environment.

Consequently, when Joël de Rosnay (2000) casts his glance to the third millennium and proposes the classification of a "symbiotic man", can be considered for analysis the virtual reality immersive environments as an expressive example on the aesthetic approach. The symbiotic man coupled to computer generated environments and tracked into the data world responds to the author understanding of symbionomy in the different aspects of the human connectivity with engines in connections between the computer and the ecosystem, living states of emergency of artificial complex systems and their qualities of self-organization, self-selection, co-evolution (De Rosnay, 2000, p. 68). Another author fascinated by virtual reality, Howard Rheingold (1991, p. 138) describes these symbiotic experiences in virtual spaces corresponding to manipulations of molecules with the hands. Because the haptic devices we used to act in the virtual world can be compared to actions with a microscope to the mind and not only to the eyes. By tracking the body's actions and provoking changes in the synthetic territory we control data units and the body is part of a complex system with the brain, cells, muscles, neurons in symbiosis with a numeric artificial system.

The fact that interactive technologies are cerebral prostheses provide us cognitive and mental stages, allowing propagations of consciousness lived in a symbiosis with technologies. The philosopher Daniel Dennet (1991, p. 159) proposes consciousness states related to the science of complexity and different levels of emergency. The validation is based on millions of instructions per second manifested trough behaviors that evolve in simulated environments following computational paradigm that works as the human body/brain laws and replicates coming-into-being states for processing information. Following this philosophical perspective, bodies gain "introscopic functions" (De Rosnay, 2000) because they provide us the condition to act in microstructures of the numeric code of infraworlds in real time. (apud Domingues, 2003).

VIRTUAL REALITY AND SENSORY APPEAL

Immersive environments offer greater sensory simulated spaces and their relationships with the real stating that it is not a matter of imitating the real but of replacing it through a logic-mathematical model which does not intend to be a simulacrum or a deceiving image of the real, but rather an interpretation of reality formalized by scientific rationality laws. The term "artificial real" is used by Myron Krueger (1991), i.e. worlds produced by machines or a "virtual real", which deals with simulated spaces by numerical models or even an "augmented real" to avoid the "virtual reality" paradox. The constitution of these environments as "responsive environments" (Krueger 1997, p. 104) can be checked in the very sense of our behaviors in tridimensional space corresponding to our actions and providing intensive psychic states which intensify these levels to be immersed in dreams. Inhabiting virtual worlds as "a "metaphysical laboratory", a "tool to check its sense of reality" (Heim, 1999, p. 287), by using interfaces, we exceed the human condition, acting in the field of phenomena, experimenting calculation of numeric code and invisible forces within simulated environments immersed inside infraworlds in correspondence with some acts we have in real worlds. The fact that interactive technologies are cerebral prostheses provide us cognitive and mental stages, allowing propagations of consciousness lived in a symbiosis with technologies.

Scientific researches in the important book Multimedia From Wagner to Virtual Reality, edited by Randall Packer and Ken Jordan (2001), the authors put together seminal and original texts related of the pioneers in this field of investigations. In the overture they comment some important issues concerning these themes and they highlight the desire to be transported to another world by the realm of imagination is now being fulfilled by VR immersive worlds.

The old historical ritual practices considered in Lascaux's pre-historical caves from 15,000 B.C., places for performances and rituals takes the perspective to be inside a room with painted walls. Those places were visited to gain the power of mystery and to trigger altered perceptive states as immersive space propitiated in the interior of the cave with its aisles and large chambers for the body. Other historical examples for immersion are Greek Theater, Europe's cathedrals, Richard Wagner's opera Gesamtkunstwerk, which mixed the truthfulness of the drama, visual effects in the amphitheater, surround-sound acoustic effects, the darkness of the room among other effects which created immersion for the public.

The representation and the illusionism of the observer condition changed of the contemplator condition in sensoramas, panoramas never placed the spectator inside the scene. Only the virtual reality tridimensional environments place the spectator located inside the virtual environment. The spectator in no more in front of the image. Olivier Grau (2003) reports the tradition of illusory visual spaces: "the gigantic paintings of the roofs of the Baroque churches, the panoramas of the 19th century, the cineramas, sensoramas, movies of third dimension, movies of 180th and IMAX, the multimedia installations are part of these attempts". Grau highlights those examples that sum the technician-illusory ability, based on the physiology of the perception and of time "are the goal of visionary artist-scientists like Alberti, Piero, Leonardo, Barker, Daguerre, Prampolini, Eisenstein, Youngblood or, recently, artists of art computational as Krueger, Davies or Sommerer, have been trying to also unite their artistic visions the innovative visual techniques that themselves developed.

RESPONSES IN A FEELING SPACE: SENSORIAL AND IMMERSIVE WORLD

The interfaces send the signals to the data environments built upon Renaissance principles of geometry and linear perspective based on the Cartesian coordinates which became haptic and responsive. Lunenfeld (2001. P. 87) distinguishes the virtual reality worlds, understanding that both allow dialogues and interactions, but what distinguish them is the interaction possibility in the immersive aspects, as something penetrable only possible in synthetic 3D worlds that offer sensations of being visited and allowing to inhabit and to act within the virtual world. Three main qualities of VR worlds are: immersion, proprioception and stereoscopy are the main sensitive qualities of these artificial spaces where sensory stimuli allow the body to take different positions physically in the environment and to change images and sounds in correlation with the body movements surrounded by low or high relief images called stereoscopic images.

The immersive stereoscopic visual only occurs in digital environments when wearing devices such as head–mounted displays, and/or eyeglasses, emitters, trackers and googles for stereoscopic vision. Inside caves, or immersive cubes, the notion of reality by sensory experiences propitiate forms of existing in computer-generated artificial environments that can be inhabited in the physical scale for senses, entering into the space with the entire body and having a total immersion. Those spaces built in numeric language are worlds of a conceptual realism, based on calculations, done by algorithms and functions that generate scenes and mutations for syntactic associations of the programming language. Algorithm's functions generated narratives propitiating events and behaviors in simulated degrees to virtual world. The situation places the interactor in a mixed condition: to live a dream drive by our amplified consciousness and resulting of decisions guided by the rationality of dialogues with computer decision and the classes and functions of the software.

The conceptual realism of synthetic environments allows some behaviors close to communication processes of life, in degrees of realism and dream beyond the appearance of former artistic projects. The body is responded in a feeling space sensorial and immersive world where the actions, updating elements of simulated worlds trigger up poetic and aesthetic situations to the actuator-subject who actives elements enabling to check levels of fiction inside artificial reality and its experiential nature, no longer using contemplation of scenes, but putting the viewer inside the scene. Behaviors provoke an immersive simulation granting abstract and figurative levels of "reality" within virtual worlds reaching rates of surprising actions, generating at times effects of dynamics and kinetics where people's feedback gives "veracity" of the real in degrees not reached before. The immersive interactive technologies allow a tactile relationship, i.e. with some kind of contact in the virtual environment. So immersive virtual environments offer a "being there" (Barthes, 1984) in another degree of presence. They are artificial landscapes with proprioceptive (Quéau, 1993, p. 184). qualities, which answer or reply to spatial situations experienced by body displacements in the real world. The body goes out and about and experiences daydreaming states in the mutating environment. Responded behaviors and not just only in the appearance and morphology of the forms, configure another level of presence.

BEHAVIORAL INTERACTIVE SIMULATION

Digital realism offers fictional worlds that respond exactly to respective actions and provide experiences lived in worlds of fiction related to behavioral interactive simulation. Even abstract themes in digital environments can take rates of surprising realism and behave as figurative scenes. The simulation in virtual reality generates times effects and dynamics, where the feedback is totally realistic. For example, the action with a tracking allow to play a virtual sphere as is it were a ball because of the return received trough that interface that captures the gesture. The control of the sphere in a dynamic way, makes the sphere behave as an object-actor in real time. See Figure 1.

Virtual reality 3D images result of fantastic advances in graphic libraries, interfaces with special effects, visualization displays making possible manipulations of the simulated world in real time. What matters are not only the animations, but also the special condition to experiment the virtual territory and the objects in all their

Figure 1. Environment behavior inside a CAVE

dynamics. The viewer is no more an observer contemplating scenes but can check levels of fiction inside the world living and acting its experiential nature. The origin of virtual reality is to create living systems possibility physic phenomena based on a numeric model and behaving as a new kind of reality. Quéau affirms that they are "intermediary" worlds in the sense Aristotle classifies as rationality entities and symbolic representation that simulate levels of reality using a mathematical model.

In immersive universes there is a correlate body-environment awareness, in a relativity space, space-time-body, through the interactions exchanged in real time, whereas the self-organization capacity in the participant's mind also takes place inside the system which respond on mutating states corresponding to those actions. Following Couchot's (2001) second interactivity theories, the system answers the external actions and internally the software regulates the dialogue of the synthetic objects as actors-objects changing form, color, position, displacement, speed in a complex relationship among them. The synthetic objects became "actors" capable to behave no longer as "things" with unalterable properties, but in a more sensitive, more alive, more autonomous, even more intelligent ways. Algorithms with specific functions generate complex events. The scenes do not come from the real but result from the manipulation of mathematical units or numerical entities which translate numeric concepts into virtual worlds.

The events lived inside the virtual can be totally imagined and the objects and scenes can behave having artificial and autonomous qualities when compared with the physical world. Inside virtual reality unexpected behaviors occur that confirm the system complexity, and its emergency. These are possibilities that enhance the artistic qualities of the virtual because there are some functions and classes managing the system and giving them creative actions. Experienced with special devices, these synthetic worlds offer other experiential perceptions in Euclidean space with numeric spatial logic. Optical is linked to haptic allowing perceptive experiences increasingly more performatic. Coming from the Greek *haptikos* "grasp", VR consists of touching with devices according to physics and dynamics laws, in scenes governed by mathematical models for the generation of force, vibration, which increase the immersion capacity and allow to the participant to feel the consequences what is being done. The tridimensionality of sounds generate sensations with depth illusion of spatiality.

COGNITIVE SPACES FOR EXPANDED AESTHETICAL EXPERIENCES: THE "POINT D'ÊTRE"

Derrick de Kerckhove (1997, p. 39) affirms that proprioception is a tactile perception of the event experienced and extended to the environment that feels and changes in reciprocity with the actions. Orders of the inner world expressed by the actions of the body and the answers of the system in feedback witness that artificial systems are cognitive spaces for expanded esthetic experiences. The author says: "By proprioception, I mean the sense of one's own body "being there"; Proprioception creates the own internal sensation and of events and sensations in one's immediate or electronically extended surroundings". It would be an affirmation of the "I am here" and the awareness of the immersive space that changes in a direct relationship of correspondence of the body with the environment (Kerckhove, 1997). The viewer acts in the environment that takes on mutations according to the viewpoint of the participant. What the author calls the "point d'être". In VR these situations enhance the spatial experiences of the interactor physically located and living sensorial stimulus in proprioceptive correlation between the body actions and the space.

The esthetical visualization of immersive virtual environments offers 3D visual qualities to multisensory spaces trough stereoscopic vision, made possible by head–mounted displays and eyeglasses equipped with liquid crystal screens and emitters. The stereoscopic vision adds tridimensionality to the vision and augment the sense of real. On the other hand, in virtual reality immersive worlds stereoscopy even bestows a sensation of tridimensionality by images "relief" that fluctuate around the participant. They provide the visualization with devices that augment the sensory dimension and the sense of artificial reality. Technically, stereoscopy bestows visual qualities of depth thus generating a different image for each eye, presenting them separately according to the difference existing between the projections on the retina. Illusion degrees of relief increased by the stereoscopy explores the binocular vision, where both eyes see, each one in a different way, the same object, generating in the brain a sensation of a world in depth. It was around 1833 that Charles Wheatstone verified that it was possible to give relief and depth to images, starting from equipment he called stereoscopic.

The same scene, drawn lightly with two points of view in different times, creates a perspective illusion that takes to an immersion degree in the space for the depth and relief generated by the device. The illusion of being in an inhabited place with images in relief and in action creates the sensation to be dived in some degrees of immersion. If the helmets are uncomfortable when dressed, the glasses are better adapted allowing the users to go and to return in their displacements in the real world, visualizing the virtual world.

On the other hand, the shutter-glasses used for virtual reality with the two LCD (liquid crystal display) displays which alternately obstruct the vision of each eye cause this alternated obstruction to be synchronized with the projection system in such a way that each field updated in the system is alternated on the generated image. In immersive universes there is a correlate body-environment awareness, with stereoscopy in a relativity space, space-time-body, by the answers that are being exchanged in real time, whereas the self-organization capacity in the participant's mind also takes place inside the system which takes on mutating states corresponding to those actions.

"A ROOM WITH A VIEW": IMMERSIVE CAVE/CAVERN/CUBE

Daniel Sandin, Thomas DeFanti and Carolina Cruz-Neira conceived this system and in the article *"A Room with a View"* (Sandin, DeFanti, & Cruz-Neira, 1993: 266) they explain that the users do not need to wear helmets "which would limit their view and mobility in the real world to experience virtual reality". Inside the caves the viewer is surrounded by images as in a virtual movie theater. The authors add that immersion in the cave goes back to Plato's cave and evokes the metaphor of reality representation trough shades, suggesting how perception is always filtered through the veil of illusion. All sensations lie between the real and the virtual. So, perception field expansion takes place esthetically in the cave virtual environment offering possibilities to replicate and expand sensations experienced by the body in real space.

The caves are the more intensive experience in VR, when the body totally involved inside the data landscape has the sensation of presence and to be enveloped by liquid images living the multisensory stimulus. The immersive space is a place for the enveloped body, totally involved in a diving sensation and dissolution of its corporeal boundaries melt up with the environment. The experience is fascinating offering spectacular situations. Caves in Virtual Reality and the feedback devices really create collective places for sensory experience and until now the caves are the most efficient places for full immersion. Movements are tracked in a physical way giving the illusion we are living in a liquid virtual world, which create a multisensory atmosphere.

The stereo glasses for stereoscopic visualization of the scenes and of the objects are integrate to the trackers allowed for manipulation which control the scenes in real touching the images and using the transmitter attached to them. These trackers can be attached to the glasses and determine different view of the virtual scene when the participant walks, touches or moves.

The participant is inside the cubic space and surrounded by overhead projections all over, in a scale that involves the human body, feeling totally immersed in the environment that changes in relation to position and movements. The choices of body/environment spatial relationship cause us to have the sense of presence in the space that gains a state of emergency by means of changes occurring in response to the system in real time trough technologies as trackers which are capture systems for direction and movement. Technically, this happens by rendered in real time of the "virtual territory" and of the objects with which it may be experimented in all their tridimensionality. The environments are endowed with hardware and rendered plates in real time and sensory simulation. Spaces may also be provided with other interfaces to act trough breathing, heart beats, touch devices with many variables such as datagloves, cameras, systems with magnetism, sound waves, infrared sensors, brain waves scanners, eye-tracking or other haptic devices and technologies to acquire and communicate signals.

DAILY RITUALS AND MIXED REALITY: THE BIOCYBRID BODY AND THE NATURALIZATION OF TECHNOLOGIES

The human factor always has been considered in the Diana Domingues's research when investigating interactive technologies in their potential to transform ways of living. She argues how we can understand types, levels and intensities of changes in post biological, posthuman, neobiological, transhuman life installed by technologies. At the end of the 20th century, when interactive technologies – and mainly the inclusion of the World Wide Web – started to invade and feed the creative minds of artists in the Media Art scenario, she had already anticipated:

"Without intending to be taken for a visionary I dare to forecast that in the next couple of years, people will normally use wireless interfaces, and matter-of-factly will be connected in all microtimes of their lives. Existence will become a cybrid existence during the twenty-four hours of life time. People will increasingly have interfaces and will be rather TV like, to use an analogy to the contemporary technological and the society of the spectacle. Symbiotic technologies will be facilitated as permanent prostheses and they will be attached on us and into our bodies and thus we will be reinventing our lives and the ultimate nature of our species." (Domingues, 1998)

Nowadays by the effects of mobile technologies as calm and transparent interfaces installed "in the periphery," as proposed by Mark Weiser's ubiquitous computing, (Weiser, 1991) in the post desktop era, the computer is almost invisible and has disappeared in the hybrid world. Notwithstanding, technologies have gained biological tasks and are increasingly installed in our habitat. The naturalization of technologies and how they are enhancing the humanization technologies scenario. HCI (Human-computer interaction) technologies, with their devices and systems take part in our organisms and work as part of our nature by expanding our sensorium as living systems in our landscapes and in the social engine. (Dyens, 2016).

During AfroBrazilian rituals, entities such as Ogum, Oxum and Iemanjá, who are called 'guides' or spirits are incorporated by the participants, who are in mediunic states. These guides provide their own identities and expand our potentials to act as human beings. In a similar way, we can experience human altered identities during social, cognitive and emotional behaviors shared with the responsive environments of social platforms, mixed reality, or other technologies. We are in enaction, reaffirming the ecological perception with the environment, and the mutual influences exchanged with the invisible data modify our perception and cognition. In the case of the recent mobile technology, the interfaced body feels and acts by sharing qualities that come from the connectivity of the synthetic vision of cameras, satellites, physiological sensors, Bluetooth, tags, codes, wireless devices, GPS, or other technological components that transmit and exchange data, and collocate us in virtual and physical worlds, thus transforming us into biocybrid humans. All those technologies provide us with altered limits of the human condition.

The enactive condition is referred in the theories of embodied cognition. It is about the interdependence between the organism and its environment, and their mutual, reciprocal exchanges, bringing the idea of autopoietic and emergent phenomena. In the relation with mestizaje, it gave me the inspirational figure of ouroborus to make visible the seamless condition lived by the interface of body and technologies. When compared to a ritual, it implies the logic of participation, tribal logic, collaborative actions, spirit of communion, of object taboos, like that logic implicit in the offerings of religions: offering and receiving, sharing and attempting to get to invisible forces. Technological apparatus and artificial systems empower artists' exploration of how technologies are changing our world perception.

OUROBORIC PERCEPTION AND POETICS

Mestizaje and ouroborus are inspirational seeds to discuss Diana's artworks through a poetic lens (Domingues, 2016b). These metaphors have guided her interactive art of Media Art since the beginning and are expanded in the recent domain of Art and TechnoScience in BioArt and innovation.

The ouroboric perception and poetics was discussed in Diana's interactive artworks since her first cyberinstallation in the 90s, Transe my body, my blood, (Domingues, 1997) which became an emblematic artwork and inserted the theme of interactivity and ritual into the artistic and scientific community. It is related to AfroBrazilian popular religions as in a shamanic trance. Northeast Brazil's Inga Stone's projections show metamorphoses sprouting from prehistoric inscriptions. People interacting become metaphorically shamans who consider the stone as a 'veil' between their world and the 'spirits' world. The software "shaman 32," based on artificial intelligence researches, has autonomy to self-regenerate the life of the cavern and the 'mutant visions' by surprising people with unexpected emergent 'realities'. In 2007, the piece reincarnated in a new, more complex version called The Cavern of Trance, a more complex version of the embedded system – it was expanded to immersive and crossmodal technologies, multisensorial interfaces and immersive multidisplay synchronized large screens in VR – and it was also adapted for mobile connections. (See Figure 2).

In a dark room, a large panoramic screen offers images and sounds as if on the walls of a cave: scenes, textures, lights, gleams, animals in stereoscopic vision allow a spatial navigation responding to bodies' motions and gestures by providing a ritual: sets of video images changed through three levels of a shamanic trance; infrared sensors captured the body heat and a bloodlike liquid kept moving in a bowl, like an offering to life. A special quality of this artwork was to provide physically impaired people with equal capability to act using infrared sensors zones and/ or by multisensorial interfaces of sound interfaces using AfroBrazilian musical instruments: flute, maracas, whistles, afuches, rain sticks, shakers and other ritualistic instruments. People were tracked to synthetic objects that moved according to sounds and noises. Non-mobile people could only interact with their mouth making sounds with whistles, flutes, or singing, making noises, and so interacting with the system

Figure 2. The Cavern of Trance, 2005, 2007, 2009. Ingá Stone projections. Memories of the Future, 10 Years Art and Technology, Instituto Itaú Cultural São Paulo, Brazil. © Diana Domingues/CNPq

in a kind of ritual. On the other hand, people's displacements and gestures generate several proprioceptive interactions. A wireless tracker and an accelerometer with a gyroscope provide responses and motions in proprioceptive interaction, and by focusing with a flashlight the walls of the cave, magically people manipulate the objects: thunders, butterflies, spiders, vases, crosses, worms, animals appear in the room in stereoscopic visions creating a sensation of enhanced trance.

In the field of VR and immersive poetics inside a Cave, Diana highlighted the magic of HEARTSCAPES. (Domingues, 2005) It allows responses from synthetic objects and navigation in the 3D ground, and offers the atmosphere of a ritual, metaphorically giving shamanic powers inside data landscapes of a heart, and the immersion in a synthetic landscape, mixing visual effects with noises of indigenous rituals, natural environments and phenomena of the ecocosmos. The result of this investigation is published in the chapter "Human biology" in Stephen Wilson's recent book Art + Science Now. (Wilson, 2010) Physiological devices and biofeedback of electrical waves in EOG electrical signals offer mutations of forms in real time and are also commanded by another biological interface that captures heartbeats, sending signals from the participant's heart to the system. The interactivity of physiological signals results from the heartbeat frequency (ranges 60/80, 80/100, 100/200, 120/140, 140/160). The action of the biofeedback sensors activates a VR particle system of HEARTSCAPES, move the position of the objects, and changes colors on the screens, confirming the dynamics and kinematics of the virtual, by communication by the electric waves of the eyes with the VR world. See Figure 3.

Figure 3. HEARTSCAPES, 20052009, NTAV CAVE, immersion in a data landscape of the heart controlled by trackers, stereoscopic glasses, biofeedback of heartbeats and electrooculogram (EOG). Brazil. © Diana Domingues/CNPq

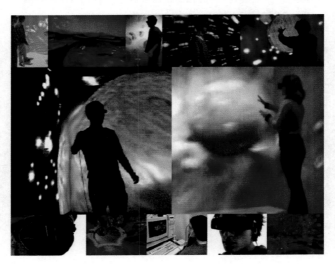

Another immersive environment that mixes virtual and augmented reality installed in a cave is VR AQUARIUM. (Domingues, 2005), see Figure 4. Telepresence images of fish living in an aquarium of the Natural Science Museum next to the cave on the same floor are transmitted and combined with synthetic 3D scenes. The body enters the cave populated by real and synthetic animated fish in relief seen through stereoscopic glasses that let the synthetic fish pass through the immersed body of the visitor. The interaction with the virtual fish uses a body movement tracker, enabling the participant to touch the creatures by simple gestures and activating an artificial life boids algorithm that gives them a collective behavior. The virtual fish move together, showing a behavior like the biological world. The interfaces blur the real and the virtual, confirming the magic of interactive technologies.

BIOCYBRID SYSTEMS AND THE REENGINEERING OF LIFE

An evolution of the prime research using physiological sensors is the researches in Biocybrid Systems.

"Electricity is life," says the futuristic premise. From now, the main subject of the researches is to include sensors in embedded systems that allow electrical signals' embodiments and enactive affective aesthetics, adding further data of all senses in the principle of synaesthesia, thus enhancing the kinesthetic laws of movement and proprioception.

Synaesthesia, meaning all the senses together, enhances aspects of motion, electricity, graphic design to the translation of signals of data from the other senses.

Figure 4. VR AQUARIUM, telepresence, immersion, and Alife in the CAVE. © Diana Domingues/CNPq, 2005-2009

In an analogy to smallest units such as phonemes, graphemes, morphemes etc., Diana had chosen to use 'kinemes' and 'synaesthemes' to express parts of a ritual motion and body language. Experts in human motion explain the nature and effects of movements and gestures in rituals (e.g. candomblé, samba, tai chi). Thus, by studying rituals we can see how everyday gestures such as grabbing a glass or extending a hand can help health research, rehabilitation and wellbeing investigations. Body movements, gestures, postures, fragmentation, reinstatements, dynamics, internal external connections and motor schemes deal with gestures, rhythms, not only at each stage of the movement, but also considering what affects the participant and the environment in a mutual exchange.

The artwork Biocybrid Ouroborus: Ecstasy's Geographisms (Domingues et al, 2012) at the Oncena Bienal de La Habana (2012), see Figure 5 explore during AfroAmerican rituals, simultaneously, information generated visualizations and sound patterns. The concept of trance that I proposed in the 1990s was modified by the discussions with the expert in Brazilian Maria Aparecida Donato, CNPq fellowship holder (PDJ). Discussion in her postdoctoral research, focusing on body and Bioart, at LART (UnB), under Diana Domingues' supervision. Rising from ecstasy in Brazilian rituals such as carnival and candomblé, research results affirm that shamanic trances differ from ecstasy states. In an ecstasy state, sensations, emotions and thoughts come from bodies that are conscious of their sense of presence, albeit the condition of transcendence ecstasy here is significantly different. Trance is an unconscious and mediunic state, while during ecstasy we are aware and live rhythms and structures of the body autopoiesis with the environment. Using data visualization and signal processing we create 'biograms' (data visualization) of corporeal living maps in kinesthesia and synaesthesia as a result of perceiving and processing data of human physiology for the understanding of body actions and their cosmic relationships in daily rituals. The workshop and exhibition related to

Figure 5. Biocybrid Ouroborus: Ecstasy's Geographisms, 2012. Workshop and exhibition. The Oncena Bienal de La Habana. © Diana Domingues/CNPq

the Habana Biennial developed specific software for the analysis of measured data of physiological rates and motion traces for the generation of graphics visualization that changed dynamically during the rituals offering data visualization landscapes of a new abstractionism. In the exhibition, two large screens presented impressive body rituals and data visualization landscapes.

The workshops demonstrated the importance for artists and scientists to engage in the processes, and methods for creating common viable systems from which artists as well as scientists can benefit and express a systems' capacity for processing data, and human cognitive capacities for dealing with logic and hermeneutic dialogues. The results confirm the possibilities or human/ systems sharing introspections and poetry, revealing complex behaviors and human identities taking the remote history of the rituals, which present actions and gestures of our daily life. The rehabilitation field in health and wellbeing is confirmed as a rich domain for this kind of artwork. Or for art to reinvent the ultimate nature of our species, close to ancient beliefs.

Toward the Urban Mixed Life

Intervention in urban life, using mobile augmented reality (MAR) and computer vision, GPS and net connections, allows the ecological geolocated art event celebrating Borges Fantastic Creatures in Buenos Aires' streets (Domingues et al, 2010). Synthetic creatures appear in the physic space of Buenos Aires city. Using mobile and locative interfaces in mixed reality we inserted 3D virtual reality models of biomorphic shapes, such as serpents, minotaur, pigs and others, from the fantastic imaginary of the Argentinean writer Jorge Luís Borges in 2010.

The artwork BIOCYBRID FABLES: BORGES' FANTASTIC CREATURES, in two modalities –urban intervention in MAR Mobile Augmented Reality and Installation in AR – translates imaginary creatures into synthetic objects. Modeled in 3D and distributed in tags, the synthetic creatures are scattered by geodesic coordinates, and through tags, are stored in a satellite. The intention is to create a mysterious vision near the Cultural Center San Martín (Buenos Aires, Argentina). The Augmented Reality Mobile Technologies (RAM) distributed transbiomorphic shapes as snakes, minotaurs, pigs, tigers, among others translated from the reading of Jorge Luis Borges' fables in "The Book of Imaginary Beings." The urban intervention used to use mobile technologies and computer vision, GPS, network connections, to insert Borges' synthetic creatures in real scale, providing a geotagged vision in the streets of Buenos Aires. Another biocybrid artwork was the response to the invitation for special guest artist at the Art exhibition "La cultura argentina en la edad digital" at the San Martin Cultural Center. The use of tags allowed the act of reading a book in computer vision and augmented reality. Reading the book, every page showed animals of the 'bestiarium' growing from the paper and thus reinventing daily life things in domotics and the act of reading a book. See Figure 6.

For the apparitions, we used the same procedure of tag code geolocation by GPS as in the 14-Bis plane, but this time using virtual models located in the ground and mixed to local people in the urban flow, instead of the sky. Computer vision of the mobile cellular phone was responsible for reading the code translated into data visualization of synthetic animals. Synthetic senses of technological apparatus allow the reengineering of life and offer a different scenario for human narratives. See Figure 7.

MOBILE WEARABLE CONDITION

Regarding vision, urban life, our habits, landscapes, survival and biodiversity, and societal challenges in terms of anthropological issues, the mobile condition amplifies the phenomenology of 'being here'.

Computers have disappeared, and technologies are transparent, cyberspace is everywhere, as Gibson states. Life is altered by cyberspace, and the use of cell

Figure 6. BIOCYBRID FABLES: BORGES' FANTASTIC CREATURES, 2011. Urban intervention in MAR (Mobile Augmented Reality) and Installation in AR, Buenos Aires. ©Diana Domingues/CNPq

Figure 7. Views of two cell phones showing the virtual 14 Bis, in the biocybrid system. Latin America Memorial, São Paulo, Brazil. September 2010

phone, mob cameras and locative and geographic interfaces radically change our landscapes. Data visualization and computer vision allow the post biological extrusion of human vision, and in terms of Bioart and biomedical investigations, peripheral perception provoke the post biological extrusion of human vision into an altered process of perception/cognition. The post biological extrusion of human vision in the act of seeing shared with the eye in the sky, and with the eye in the hand, i.e. the act of seeing shared with the eye of the satellite in the sky and the eye of the mobile device in the person's hand, configure an enactive act extending the sense of seeing or expanding human perception by the extrusion of our visual apparatus. AR tags placed on GPS, and the possibility of seeing in computer vision using geodesic coordinates create a collocated event for the human body.

Bioart and health are also included in the study of Brazilian rituals in a transdisciplinary approach in the fields of arts, humanities and sciences. This approach was dealt with in the project Reengineering Life: Creative Technologies for the Expanded Sensorium, developed at the Camera Culture Media Lab at the Massachusetts Institute of Technology (MIT).

The artworks of LART collection are now in the phase of expanding the sensorial apparatus in terms of physiological signals. The background of this investigation was published in the chapter `Human Biology,' in the recent book. Simulators technologically add to the displacements the effects of collisions, vibrations, trepidations etc., when inhabiting synthetic spaces.

Also, the historical intuitive interfaces, such as shutter glasses, data gloves, trackers, emitters, force biofeedback devices, joysticks, among others, are empowered by physiological sensors that capture physiological signals in order to enhance the immersion experience and make it more intense. The embodied experience then corresponds to a Spinozan body with the affective ability to communicate with the environment through the several measured signals. This body sends and receives data, as it exchanges energies and signals with the environment, in an enactive condition described by Varela et al. (Domingues et al., 2014)

In this context, the human actions and interactions generate living maps, body narratives through enactions in an ouroboric perception8 corresponding to Gibson's concept of ecological perception.9 In this work, the Laboratory of Art and TechnoScience (LART) at the University of Brasília at Gama, in Brazil, intends to collaborate with discussions on embodiments, data visualizations and immersions with enactive affective systems, which echo the enacionist theory of autopoiesis and to the naturalization of the technologies.

The Cave Automatic Virtual Environment (CAVE) has important applications in biomedical engineering, body arts, product design and others. The Cave is also a special place for aero spatial Engineering raining. In fact, the kinesthetic sensations replicate the sensation of displacement inside an automobile, as well as the sensations of vibration and vertical movements typical of a vehicle, different speeds, collisions, etc. These various conditions may be created by the system in terms of physical sensations and synthetic data provided by actuators, as well as by the biofeedback using breathing, heat, heart beats and other signals collected by our physiological sensors. For embodiments and aesthetic affective emotions inside the CAVEs, our systems configure compelling experiences in data landscapes, by providing human narratives in biocybrid spaces.

APPLICATIONS IN M-HEALTH

The act of walking and the use of embedded systems to analyze relations between people and space as well as the proxemics involving inhabitants, patients, doctors, places and things etc. are the object of innovation of a system to diagnose diseases – mainly diabetes – and for other applications in wellbeing similar to a personal assistant who gives information in mHealth and mobile applications. (Domingues et al., 2011) The innovation is the application of that system for diagnosing and treating diabetes, as well as other applications in mHealth. This is a project resulted in the PhD dissertation by Tiago F. R. Lucena and the postdoctoral research Suélia Rodrigues, integrating the two laboratories LART/FGA and Camera Culture/ MIT/CNPq in a series of activities of the Program MIT International Science and Technology Initiatives MITBrazil Seed Fund/CNPq – Project titled: "Reengineering Life: reative Technologies for the Expanded Sensorium." Directors Adson Ferreira da Rocha and Diana Domingues and American Research Leader: Ramesh Raskar/ MediaLabMIT.

The prototype called Cidadepathia consists of a sensorized insole built with Brazilian latex (Havea brasiliensis) as a mobile (wearable) device. Lucena defends that the insole is a sensorial device to capture the energy and the pathos of the city. The insole made with a biomaterial acquires physiological data combined with locative tools. (Lucena, 2013) I make a similar reference to the ouroboric perception when creating living maps of the city. Processing signals and data visualization reveal enactions and affective narratives of passersby. The tool tells stories about people and urban activity in a kind of bio(geo)graphies recording journeys. Although Lucena alludes to the mythological figure of Hermes and his winged sandals, I prefer to insist in sandals like the ouroboric serpent and the reinvigoration when giving and receiving energy in the autopoietic feedback with the ground. See Figure 8.

The cinematic floor was another prototype used to study the enactive affective systems. To enlarge the corporeal sensations offered inside the CAVE, a treadmill is used for the displacements in the floor which responses for the immersion in the

Figure 8. Cidadepathia, 2014. Brazil. a) sensorized insole. b & c) living maps in enactive affective systems and innovation for art and technoscience and health. © Diana Domingues/CNPq

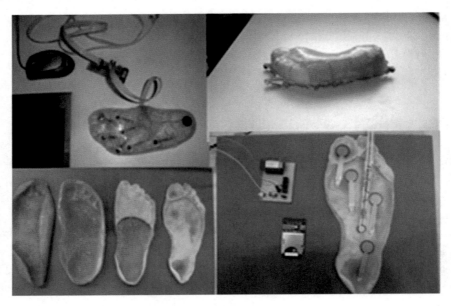

data landscapes. We have adapted: (i) A single-phase induction motor, a power of 0.5 hp, (ii) a sliding belt and (iii) a pair of pulleys, to establish its sliding velocity.

By default, the treadmill provides the user a sense of displacement by sliding action caused by the spindle motor. However, it is interesting to include a sense of unbalance to generate uncomforting to the user. In this sense, four springs of different sizes were fixed in the structure of the treadmill. Thus, the users try to adapt their movements to compensate the oscillations of the treadmill as well as to reestablish equilibrium. Then two sensations can be experienced in the treadmill, with sensations of: such as (i) movement or displacement, and (ii) unbalance or oscillation. Thus, some episodes are performed, and different scenarios emerges from the immersion with respective physiological rates. The physiological sensors measure the behavior of the user in the context and provides input to the simulation to adapt the image and situations according the synaesthetic responses. See Figure 9.

An example with the use of the enactive affective system in engineering research is the vehicle simulation. This research consists in an experimental platform used to evaluate the performance of individuals at training immersive physiological games. The platform proposed is embedded in an immersive environment in a CAVE of Virtual Reality and consists on a base frame with actuators with three degrees of

Figure 9. Unbalance Treadmill - LART 2014 - (A) User testing the oscillatory motion and (B), detail of springs of different sizes

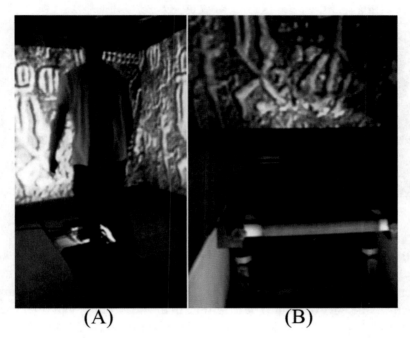

(A)   (B)

freedom, sensor array interface and physiological sensors. Physiological data of breathing, galvanic skin resistance (GSR) and pressure on the hand of the user and a subjective questionnaire were collected during the experiments.

The theoretical background used in a project focused on Software Engineering, Biomedical Engineering in the field of Ergonomics and Creative Technologies in order to presents this case study, related of an evaluation of a vehicular simulator located inside the CAVE. The analysis of the simulator uses physiological data of the drivers obtained in a period of rest and after the experience, with and without movements at the simulator.

The set of sensors placed in a volunteer sitting in the driving position simulator can be seen in Figures 10 (A and B).

The biocybrid condition regulated by biofeedback is very shamanic in the sense it gives the power to capture biological information from the body moving in the physical space, and they exchange energies. Body and environment send signals and the system is performed by inputs and outputs of wireless sensors embodied in a network area (Rocha, 2008). New states emerging from the body in the environment connected to cyberspace and governed by the experience of its presence status in reciprocal behavioral changes reaffirm the enactive interfaced by the very alive human

Figure 10. Affective Enactive Vehicle Simulator LART 2014 – A volunteer sitting on the simulator and the sensors attached to his body (A) and A volunteer with the sensors during the tests, sitting on the simulator within the CAVE (B)

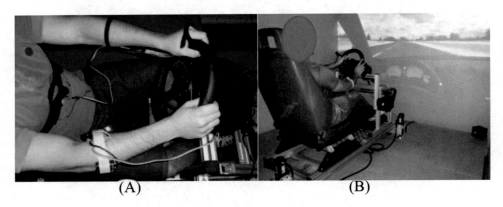

(A)   (B)

condition transduced by the sensorial physiology of the body and the qualities of urban life in which the enaction occurs. The structure of the sensory-motor interfaced subject contextualized by mobile devices determines how to act and be modulated by events in the environment. These results, in the near future, will offer biocybrid systems which allow to interact with everything, with everybody, with every space, and everywhere, with nobody, with humans and non-humans. By sharing internal and external signals, feelings, beliefs, values, emotions and desires, during rituals - the flâneur of the 1900s is alive and acting located in the mixed landscapes and expand the vital signals to biocybrid life.

Finally, following Diana Domingues´ humanization and naturalization of technologies principles, we accept the challenges of the world, increasingly faced by circuits of sensors and transparent technologies which are blurring the limits of the natural and the physical, and are reengineering our life. We are facing the transformation of our existence and the nature itself, signaling the emergence of the naturalization of technologies and the engineered and creative reality for a healthier future.

REFERENCES

Barthes, R. (2002). *A Câmara Clara*. Editora Nova Fronteira.

Berthoz, A. (2000). *The Brain's Sense of Movement* (G. Weiss, Trans.). Cambridge, MA: Harvard University Press.

Carvalho, H. (2005). Data fusion implementation in sensor networks applied to health monitoring. In *Departamento de Computação*. Universidade de Minas Gerais.

Couchot, E. (1998). *Between trance and algorithm. In Transe: My body, my blood. Exhibition catalogue*. Caxias do Sul: Lorigraf.

De Kerckhove, D. (1997). *Connected Intelligence – The Arrival of the web Society*. Toronto: Somerville House Books Limited.

De Rosnay, J. (2000). *L'Homme Symbiotique*. Paris: Éditions du Seuil.

Dennet, D. C. (2000). An Empirical Theory of The Mind: The Evolution of Consciousness-1991. In Cyber _Reader. Critical writings for the digital era. Phaidon.

Domingues, D. (Ed.). (1997). *A Arte no Século XXI: A Humanização das Tecnologias*. São Paulo: Ed. Unesp.

Domingues, D. (1998). The desert of passions and the technological soul. In *Digital Creativity* (Vol. 9). Lisse: Swets & Zeitlinger. doi:10.1080/14626269808567101

Domingues, D. (2003a). *Cyberinstallation exhibited firstly at ISEA 97, at the School of Art Institute in Chicago Isea Montreal, Modern Art Museum, Buenos Aires, 1999, II Bienal do Mercosul, VII Bienal de la Habana, when receiving the 2000 Unesco Prize, Lima 2000, Kibla Multimedia Center, Maribor, Slovenia, 2003 and Exhibition Valfisken Gallery*. Simrishamn.

Domingues, D. (2003b). *Heartscapes*, Diana Domingues and CNPq collection. The artwork was installed in a cave. *Art + Science Now*.

Domingues, D. (2005). VR AQUARIUM. In *Heartscapes, 2005-2009*.

Domingues, D. (2008). *Research Project: Art and TechnoScience: Expanded Interactions and Cybrid Condition in Software Art*. CNPq Minister of Science and Technology.

Domingues, D. (2012). *Biocybrid ouroborus: ecstasys' geographisms*. The 11th Havana Biennial.

Domingues, D. (2016). Ouroboric perception and the effects of enactive affective systems to the naturalization of technologies. *Media-N, Journal of the New Media Caucus, 12*(1).

Domingues, D., da Rocha, F. A., Hamdon, C., & Miosso, C. J. (2011). Biocybrid Systems and the Reengineering of Life. IS&T/SPIE Electronic Imaging.

Domingues, D., Hamdan, C., & Augosto, L. (2010). Biocybrid Body and Rituals in Urban Mixed Life. In Congreso Internacional Mujer. Arte y Tecnologia en la Nueva Esfera Pública-CIMUAT.

Domingues, D., Lucena, T., Rosa, S., Miosso, C., Torres, R., & Krueger, T. (2016). Walking and health: An enactive affective system. *Digital Creativity, 27*(4), 314–333. doi:10.1080/14626268.2016.1262430

Domingues, D., Miosso, C. J., Rodrigues, S. F., Rocha Aguiar, C. S., ... Raskar, R. (2014). *Embodiments, Visualizations and Immersion with Enactive Affective Systems*. IS&T/SPIE Electronic Imaging. doi:10.1117/12.2042590

Dyens, O. (1995). L'émotion du cyberspace. In *Esthétique des Arts Médiatiques. Presses de L'Université du Québec*.

Dyens, O. (2016, March 1). The Human/Machine Humanities: A Proposal. *Humanities (Washington), 5*(1). Retrieved from http://www.mdpi.com/20760787/5/1/17

Fischer, S. (2001). Virtual Interface Environments. In *From Wagner to Virtual Reality*. New York: W. W. Norton.

Gibson, J. J. (1974). *The perception of the visual world*. Westport, CT: Greenwood Press.

Heim, M. (1999). Virtual Realism. In Media and Social Perception. UNESCO/ISSC/EDUCAM.

Krueger, M. (1991). Artificial Reality Art. Addison-Wesley.

Lucena, T. (2013). *Sistemas enativos afetivos em arte e tecnociência: experiências vitais dos deslocamentos na cidade* [Enactive affective systems in art and technoscience: vital experiences of displacement in the city] (PhD diss.). UnB.

Massumi, B. (2002). Parables for the Virtual: Movement, Affect, Sensation. Durham, NC: Duke University Press.

Miranda, M. R. (2014). *Desenvolvimento de Bancada para Simulação Veicular Integrando Realidade Virtual e Medição de Dados Fisiológicos*. Tese de Doutorado em Ciências Mecânicas.

Miranda, M. R., Cota, H., Oliveira, L., Bernardes, T., Aguiar, C., & Domingues, D. M. (2015). *Development of simulation interfaces for evaluation task with the use of physiological data and virtual reality applied to a vehicle simulator*. SPIE/IS&T Electronic Imaging; doi:10.1117/12.2083889

Noë, A. (2006). *Action in perception*. Cambridge, MA: MIT Press.

Quéau, P. (1993). Le virtù e le vertigini del virtuale. Bologna: CAPUCCI, Pier Luigi Realtà Del Virtuale. Rappresentazioni Technologique, Communicazione, Arte. Editrice Bologna.

Rocha, A. F. (2008). As redes de sensores e o monitoramento da saúde humana. In L. Brasil (Ed.), *Informática em Saúde* (pp. 489–510). Brasília: Universa.

Weiser, M. (1991, September). The computer for the twenty first century. *Scientific American.*

Wilson, S. (2010). *Art + Science Now*. London: Thames & Hudson.

Chapter 3

"Hi-Tech + Low-Tech":
Aesthetic Reframing Processes Through Brazilian-Nigerian Art Literacy

Paulo Cesar Teles
University of Campinas, Brazil

ABSTRACT

This chapter aims to highlight and discuss contemporary aspects of interactive art as the audience influence, the aesthetic technological impact, its targeting to art-education, and the cross-cultural aspects involved as well evidenced by an art and technology literacy event at two schools in the city of Osogbo, Nigeria for primary and secondary school teachers and students in mid-2016 and five months later the re-exhibition of its final artwork in museums and cultural centers in Brazil. For this propose, the author sought to highlight the density of the aesthetic experiences and the cultural addition that affected all the involved people in terms of interactivity and multi-technological connections. He also intended to point out and compare both the different interactive attitudes and the processes of comprehension and reframing that occurred during the stages of production and exhibitions under the prism of some contemporary theoretical perspectives and cases.

INTRODUCTION

Cultural globalization and multi-media connection in this second decade of the XXI century has brought closer (since the end of the last century) people and entities from different backgrounds and cultural capital (Bourdieu, 1977); [1] in terms of individual and collective (Murray, 2001), multidirectional and decentralized modes (Deleuze,

DOI: 10.4018/978-1-5225-5696-1.ch003

1997), hitherto it was impossible in previous moments of our history. Hence, these technological mediated contacts have provided exponential growth in meetings and events that have disseminated cultural exchanges, among people, collectives and institutions from different cultures. and continents.

Technological headways that have taken place throughout human history, such as transportation and media, have led people to encounters, confrontations and dialogues, mutual appropriations and, also, a techno-socio-cultural syncretism between "high" and "low" technology.[2] Usually, the first is seen as electronic and digital devices emerging and / or commercially newly consolidated, while the second is treated as obsolete devices or ancestors manufactures. These concepts, however, can vary within each culture or society (the use of chopsticks to have a meal, in general – whether made of wood or metal - is known to be regarded as a "new technology" to many Western people).

What is nowadays considered as a "post-digital trend" does not necessarily need to be the abandonment of electronic and algorithmic technologies in search of a vintage nostalgia or even a radical return to a way of life based exclusively on "non-electronic" craftsmanship (Sennet, 2008).[3] One can also look at it as a way to integrate, in many ways, objects, equipment, as well as social and artistic behaviors from many cultural background. However, in spite of a number of historical happenings of these cultural miscegenation, the increasing access to digital media, in an increasingly distributed and individualized way (Trible & Jana, 2006), produced several other ways of artistic experience and understanding from the audience that are very active and immersed in the work itself (Couchot, 2002; Hansen, 2003; Gianetti, 2006; Lipovetsky, 2011).

Therefore, in order to promote new experiences pointed to those conceptual frameworks on art and technology through art-education, the author has developed and triggered a set of international workshops that built interactive and mixed-media art installations, targeted initially to art teachers, and their 09 – 14 years old students as well. Entitled *The Wishing Tree*, they aim to disseminate transdisciplinary art and media literacy within art-educational environments. Initialized in 2012, it already took place at several elementary and secondary schools in five different continents.

These art and technology workshop group was originally created to address interactive and participatory processes to the teachers and students involved by a fusion of digital technology, audiovisual media and fine arts. These happenings in schools of different countries broadened our conceptual spectrum in the inter- and cross-cultural fields as a way to reframe what occurred in each of these places, most of the time unlike and in varying degrees of intensity among the involved local cosmologies.

Once they occurred, the observed literacy's impacts led us to search for a set of other cases and researches that would meet our actions, attitudes and results, but also for the concerns that have arisen throughout them. In order to have a broad and well-founded understanding, so far these workshops have been studied and looked through in an "interactive" co-authorship audience scope (Giannetti, 2006) the procedural Gilles Deleuze's cartography (Deleuze, 1997)[4], or "participative" performances (Freire, 1982; Soares, 2011) which consider the pupils' protagonism on their self-knowledge besides the objects, materialized information and also the places and framework.

The Nigeria *Wishing Tree* workshop case is particularly highlighted and debated in this chapter due to the resulting mixed-media assemble from the interactive installation built on that workshop have expressed a singular cross-cultural aspect (Santos, 2013) which jointed in the same artwork the Nigerian ancestrally and contemporaneousness (Willet, 2002) with the audiovisual, digital and interactive Brazilian and Western creativeness. Moreover, after the exhibitions of that installation in Nigeria and also in Brazil, both countries in 2016, the author also realized about the very distinct reactions and understandings caused in both country audiences.

The first topic discusses the initial proposals, the methodology, the multi-disciplinarily developed by the international workshops *The Wishing Tree*. The second topic approaches the Nigerian and Brazilian experience features as the assembled shape design; the audience behavior; the exportation of its installation to Brazilian museums and events; and the Brazilian audience behavior as well. Both topics brings also other specific cases which carry, even partially, similar features with our experiences such as reused objects assemblage (Kee et al., 2013); digital literacy (Lee & Shieh, 2017) and *ancestrofuturism* (Santos, 2013; Borges, 2017; Garcia, 2017). At the end of this Chapter, the author brings a brief analysis of some impacts over the production and exhibitions occurred were listed about the same work in both countries.

THE WISHING TREE: ART AND TECHNOLOGY LITERACY FOR A POST-DIGITAL EDUCATION THROUGH ART

The Wishing Tree is a multimedia workshop project originally designed by the author in partnership with Mousumi De, US-based PhD candidate at the University of Indiana. In 2011, after five years searching and developing artistic work with sensorial touchless artistic interface, (Teles, 2009), The author was encouraged by her to use artistic work in an inclusive way through educational art literacies based on her previous experiences, among them an accomplishment of collage of papers workshops inspired in the legend of the wishing tree produced in partnership with the English art educator Roberta Altman in New York and New Deli in 2010. He realized that he could make a rereading of that legend and build the tree with recycled material. Moreover, it could be added ultrasonic motion sensors to trigger videos, sounds and animations with all wishes of the attending kids.

Trees have occupied the human semiotic imagination by endless mythologies, legends and folklore worldwide. Hindu mythology presents a divine tree, Kalpavriksha, mentioned in the Sanskrit literature (*Mänäsara*) as the *Tree of Life* responsible for the birth of Ashikasundari and Aranyani, daughters of the deities Siva and Parvati (Toole, 2015). On the other hand, in the Japanese Buddhist tradition a tree, *Tanabata*, is built or chosen to collect desires written on small pieces of paper, which are then burned or thrown in running water of some river so the wishes come true. (Flood, 1996; Garbick & Schafer, 2011).

In these legends' reframing, the author decided to handle with two types of "wishes" in these trees built during these workshops. The first consists of those who (still) live in the participants` imagination. They are expressed through the drawings, writings and interviews carried out by the students and "accessed" through touchless sensory interactions. The second, on the other hand, consists of a series of wishes that "came true", in many cases daily, that express themselves through discarded, recycled and reused materials to constitute the tree sculpture of the installation.

This way, this experience combines a set of mixed-media artistic ways that merges manufacturing with electronic, media and digital features all in the same artwork. Both in all different steps of the whole process and in the final presentation of the results, there were cross-cultural experiments of an interactive, participatory and collaborative nature in the behavioral and technological fields, whose nature contrasts according to the proximity and distances between our cultural framework and the participants' in each of the countries where it happened.

The first of those workshops took place at *SESI Santos Dumont* school, in Campinas City, Brazil, in 2012, with around 30 students. About 100 people had attempted in the exhibition of the resulting installation. Still in that year, another workshop held at 2/3 João Meira school in Guimaraes City, Portugal, with more than de 150 students and 10 teachers in the installation exhibition. In 2014 they occurred at *Tulla Realschülle*, in Kehl city, Germany, and at *Oreokastro* secondary school, in Thessaloniki, Greece as well, with 60 and 20 students each workshop, and 120 e 300 students each exhibition. In 2015, it took place at Somerville Intermediate School, in Auckland city, New Zealand. There, there were more than 600 pupils and 50 guests interacting with the installation. The following year, another workshop occurred in Nigeria, in Osobgo city, at two schools: Kingdom Kids School and Excellent School, having more than 600 people, among students, teachers and guests. In 2017, there was another one at Annapurna Secondary School in the village of Sikles, in Nepal, with nearly 50 attending pupils and some guests.

The workshops were originally designed to be addressed to the educators of those schools. The reach to their students varied according to their criteria. However, the author recommended them to recruit the students aged between 09 and 14 years old were interviewed, however it was not a restrictive measure. By choosing this age range the author have considered the cognitive development, emotional and also the social aspects all well observed, mostly, in the genetic epistemology by Jean Piaget (1981) that ponders this age range which become those kids able to reflects on "the formal and concrete operations" as the abstract thought (Consani, 2015), besides some "moral judgment" (Oliveira, et aluii, 1992: p. 48).[5]

Methods and Early Results

In the course of this workshop, teachers and students involved are encouraged to collect recyclable materials from their surroundings and, by an assemblage way, they build a three-dimensional sculpture tree that could make references to some local tree. All students with that age group are also invited to express their wishes through writing, drawing or gluing. Teachers select about twenty students to make their wishes through recorded statements on digital footage and then photographed. In the interviewing, the students, one by one, say their names, their ages and, then, they say their wish.

The lecturing author's role, however, did not rely on watching and coaching those activities. His action-research way became him effective part of the process by lectures about art and technology, since primitives to present and available tools and media. He also records all the interviews and work in all further digital steps. The shot material is saved along with some of the chosen drawings, which are scanned. Then they are animated with nearly one second of duration each.

Figure 1. Photographic assembly with The Wishing Tree interactive sculptures built in world tour between 2012 and 2015. (Author's personal file)

Ultrasonic motion sensors are connected in the sculpture's trunk and branches. They are able to detect any material proximity movement and, then, generate alphanumeric codes to be interpreted by software "Isadora Core" in order to project and interact the sounds and images simultaneously.[6] Two of them trigger a set of animated drawings and the sampler's the sound track. The third one, often placed in front of the screen views, triggers on the screen the face of all students and their interviews' speeches as well. Both the animations, the images and the soundtracks are swapped according to the movement and closeness of the people towards the sensors.

The sensory technology used was originally developed in partnership with the technological artist Aidan Boyle, whose research began in 2005 (Teles & Boyle, 2015: p.155). Later, Juliano Prado (developer) Eduardo Santana (programmer) and Igor Salinas (electronics technician) improved it from the use of a controller interface, "Arduino" brand. In some of these meetings it was also possible to produce and execute "interactive music". The "original" instruments were scanned separately,

Figure 2. Excerpts from different moments of the workshop:(from right to left) building the tree in Brazil (2012 in Portugal (2012, student draws his wish in Germany (2014), student records his wish in Greece (2014); exhibitions and interactions in New Zealand (2025) and Nepal (2017). (Author's Personal file)

resynchronized and algorithmically connected to the sensors in order to be triggered and remixed by the audience interacting by walking around the 3D sculpture and also shaking their arms and hands toward the sensors.

The installations were exhibited in the last day of the workshops as a *grand finale*. In some cases, it took one day more in order to all the schools' students could participate. Once the installation was done and working, the attendees were invited, in groups of three or four people, to interact with the work. So each group is guided to know where the sensors are and from this point, moving backwards and forwards. This way they start exploring available contents in the spaces provided by each sensor. Besides the sculptures, in 100% of these experiences, all the sounds and projected imageries, all peoples' movements and actions become effectively part of the artwork, by showing somehow, even involuntary, a kind of improvised choreography.

From Interactive Art to Participative Art: Brief Analysis of the Observed "Double Protagonism" Features

It is well known that actions and connections of this kind of activities have grown, becoming an increasingly interdisciplinary trend in the fields of Multimedia, Art and Technology, Art-education and Education through Art. The assemblage of recycling and reuse of discarded objects for the re-reading of these folklores, as well as the technology used, once materialized in the final works carried out, sent us directly to the "postmodernity" of Dadaist anti-poetics, manifested in the artworks of Marcel Duchamp (Alexandrian, 1976)[7] as well as the post-kinematic technological reuse exhibited in the Bill Viola's (Townsend, 2004)[8] and Peter Weibel's interactive artworks (Szope, 2003).[9]

There are several artistic workshop focuses as to the technological handling as to recycling process for education through art all over the world. Two of them are highlighted due to the closeness of their proposals with our experiences. *Art as Aché – Rhe Unpacking Student Identities project* is an extracurricular workshop that also promotes creative assemblage in a collaborative way. Occurred at Ashé Cultural Art Center in New Orleans, this project – developed by Jessica Kee, graduate instructor from Dillard University – is target do 6 – 14 years-old students (K-12) under supervision of the performer artist Kesha McKey, it "comprises a tree-dimensional sculptural form of collage combining found and altered objects with mixed-media processes." (Kee et al, 2016: pp. 14 - 19).

At the beginning of the project, 24 K-12 students participating of this extracurricular art class each received an antique hard-shell suitcase. We guided them to develop two- and three-dimensional art techniques to transform their suitcases into mixed-

media artworks representing their personal, family and community identities – reflecting the cultural "suitcases" of diverse influences, we all carry with us as we move through the world. What emerged was both a colorful installation art series and intergenerational learning community of working artists. (Kee et al., 2016: p. 14)

This project aimed to increase the cultural curriculum of that art school and its students as well, by (re)building some of the individual and collective social and cultural identities expressed in that cases. Occurred at the Kuumba Institute in New Orleans, USA, It's final results was exhibited in a gallery of the New Orleans Healing Center. The authors achieved to attest how that assemblage process can provide "a complex creative medium for constructing and expressing identity through art."(Kee et al., 2016: p. 16). According to them, "as assemblage artists, students not only express their identities; they also curate and construct them in real time by choosing diverse visual elements of their life to create complex three-dimensional self portraits." (Kee et al., 2016.)

An action Research Photography Education for Vocational School Students in the Post-Truth Era, by this way, was an action-research focused on digital photography literacy. It was conducted at "a vocational high school in Taichung City in 2016 school year (from September 2016 to June, 2017). There were 192 11th graders from four different classes, including majors of art and design and multi-media animation" (Lee, 2017)[10]. Leaded by Ching Fang Lee, PhD Associate Professor at the National Changhua University of Education, Taiwan, and Min-Ying Hsich, from Department of Multimedia Animation at Ta-Ming High School, this project was not limited to the instructional-technical methodology, but it aimed to open the student's mind about the "post-true era" framework by digital post-photography practice. (Lee, 2017).

By promoting the use of photo-editing software features and techniques, as well as digital assemblages and pieces of similar image textures to suppress specific elements of any digitalized image, they attempted to clarify the students about how procedures like that can produce fake images which take many people to believe in the "truth" of those ones. Then, "the image reading and writing abilities of students can be further enhanced and promoted, so that the design group students from vocational schools in Taiwan can grasp a whole new vision and visual thinking with a post-modern photographic perspective" (Lee, 2017).

Both examples above have the participatory processes embedded in their scopes. Moreover, the post-modernity evidenced as in New Orleans as in Taichung City, is expressed by each own way of reuse and assemblage of their objects and images. The artistic-technological activities of the *Wishing Tree* workshops, however are at the same time interactive and participatory. They permeate as the agent role of the individual (Murray, 2001: pp. 149 – 150; Ryan, 2001: pp. 216-217;) as well as the

"Educomunication" method (Soares, 2011)[11] empowerment even without having any instructional purpose.

The set of literacies developed in these workshops has not been limited to the production of knowledge based on bodily experiences of different interactions, immersive (Murray, 1999) and endo-aesthetic procedural reactions (Giannetti, 2006). From different levels and automation expertise integrated in affective connections and agency actions (Hansen, 2006), it was possible to detect some micro-social aspects in the treatment among people involved with both an available technology to the populations of the places visited, and with those newly introduced.

The interactional process with the addressed fusion of the sensorial technology with manufactured fine-art has been the most relevant cross-cultural *hi-tech + low tech* issue. In 100% of those exhibitions, when the audience realizes that they are able to change the installation's audiovisual aspects, they begin to accurate their bodily movements in order to explore the feeling of getting an extra touchless power. On the other hand, the wishes expressed by those kids have brought us some of their social and affective perspectives about their current and future life. Due to the personal or ideological messages, some of them have caused many emotional impacts in the participants no matter if they were colleagues, teachers or visitors. Likewise, the amount of "fulfilled wishes" embedded in the tree has achieved to make them and the public in general, to reflect on the daily consumerism. The artistic recycling of discarded objects had also huge appealing to many participants in the schools over there.

IGI AA MU EROGBA SE (THE "MADE IN NIGERIA" *WISHING TREE*): FROM ART-TECHNOLOGY LIGTERACY TO A TRANSCULTPRAL ARTWORK

By encompassing and interacting with cross-cultural meetings, this set of workshops achieves to integrate different cultural backgrounds in two distinctive ways. During the proceedings of the workshop until its final exhibition the author were focused on the step by step integration of the technoscience (Santos, 2013) of electronic and digital art with the traditional expressions of fine art education. On the other hand, when its final results were exhibited outside its original environment, there was a series of aesthetic, technological and documentary reframing grown by the new audiences.

Once being in Nigeria, the personal contact that the author had *in sito*, as well as bibliography checked later, kept us abreast of the artistic ancestry and all its cultural density. The Africanness carried by them through the same work, on the other hand, also brought to the Brazilian public an international and intercultural experience, even in terms of art and technology. Due to of these issues, our interactional experiences with Nigerian art and culture should be observed initially as a meeting of different artistic perspectives.

Nigeria is a country that, even its people are "connected" with multimedia smartphone technology[12], its culture still retains most of the African artistic tradition, in particular, the Yoruba nation. The city of Osogbo is an important reference in the national artistic context. The artistic and cultural trajectory of the "School of Osogbo" (Willet, 2002)[13] is an important reference for the historical and contemporary art of that country. Furthermore, *The Osogbo Sacred Grove* is a natural park containing a giant open-air art museum comprised of a magnificent collection of small and monumental sculptures in wood, metal and masonry (this one seen in large extent) produced by local artists of various generations. The abstraction and subjectivity contained therein stands out in the traits employed and in the folkloric symbology contained.

However, we cannot say the same about Brazil, since its original inhabitants were almost decimated, and the rest were confined to dwindling "reserves." Brazil currently lies in the dominant condition of a broadly globalized Western subculture,

Figure 3. Adobe sculpture in "Osogbo Sacred Groove" park. Osogbo, Nigeria, 2016. (Author's personal file)

with African (music, cooking and some religious syncretism) and Asian influences (especially cooking) and, with the exception of the daily full body shower, almost nothing from its local ancestral culture was left. Being an industrialized country, Brazil's technological infrastructure much resembles those of "first world" countries. Technical and university education, at times, also equates with European, North American and Asian internationally renown universities, which provides abundant specialized technical labor. Thus, the profusion of Brazilian technological artists (largely Euro-descendants and more affluent social classes) it is, in a way, the fruit of these conveniences.

From Brazil to Nigeria

The Nigerian experience, held in the last week of June, 2016 in the city of Osogbo, in partnership with the elementary schools International Kingdom Kids and Excellent School, and the Osogbo's fine artists Sunday Olaniyi and Babalola Mahmood. This event became possible due to previous contact with Olaniyi, who was art teacher at both schools in that time. In both schools the author had a warm welcome with celebrations, presentations and speeches by their directors Olaide Aboujan and Solomon Oladapo. The affection, appreciation and respect expressed by all of them leaded the author to adopt a more affectionate and respectful behavior towards all those involved. The author also should point that, according to both principals' testimonials, it was the first time which their schools had experienced a foreign workshop in.

The Nigerian experience was designed to take place although a week, from June 24th to July 1st of that year. The meetings were adjusted according to the daily schedule of the teachers and students. In both schools, the same procedure steps of the previews workshops took place there. Initially, the lecture was given to the teachers of each school. During the speech the author approached historical and contemporary aspects of and procedural nature in the artistic and technological in terms of material, electronic and digital arenas. Through explanation and dialogue, he aimed to demystify the commonly attributed reductionism that makes people understand technology only as something that is solely electronic and / or digital and point out the possibility of interdisciplinary integrations with it in the art-education field.

By choice of Nigerian art-teachers, the sculpture to be assembled by them and the students involved in both schools (some parts would be built in one school and elsewhere in the other) should represent an *Baobá* tree, a giant typical tree in Africa sub-Saharan Africa. The main materials reused by them were cans of beer and soda,

Figure 4. Reception at Kingdom Kids School (left) and Excellent Schools (right). Osogbo, 2016. (Author's Personal file)

which were cut into small squares and glued on hardboard; beverage caps (oil, water, etc.) painted with oil paint; tubes of cardboard coated with cut-out packs; used waxed papers and cut like tree leaves; and some "flowers" made of green beverage bottles placed at the ends of tree branch.

Ten students from each school were chosen by their teachers to express their wishes on video. Ten among the drawings produced by them and all their other classmates were selected to be scanned and then animated. The multimedia exercise of the children involved in making their wishes by spontaneously way in order to express both the particularities of their momentary local contexts (family, profession, city / community / environment issues) and those that are widely globalized (about sports, wealth, material goods). All this information would grant us and the audiences of all the exhibitions too, a small but important sample of the connections and affections of these young students from Osogbo with their surroundings in the personal, local and global aspects.

In the mean time the soundtrack was produced at *Harmonious Sound*, a small musical studio in Osogbo, by the musician and sound technician Adedeji Adebimpe. The music was sampled in digital keyboard with sound emulations of percussion, guitar, bass guitar and piano to be played continuously in looping mode. The instruments were recorded separately in different digital files. The synchronization

Figure 5. Tree assemblage steps at International Kingdom Kids School (left), At Excellent School (center) and at Blue and White Hotel (right). Osogbo, Nigeria, 2016. (Personal file)

between them was done by a digital metronome in order to keep them with the same speed and be able to be resynchronized during the presentation, so that they did not miss the timing.

In the full assembly of the installation, the posters with the original student's drawings were displayed near the walls around the environment. The ultrasonic sensors were connected to the controller board and attached to the tree's built. As well as the previously installations, the images and animations were diagrammed in the projection screen, besides being programmed and distributed in the algorithms of connection and responsiveness of each sensor to be exhibited and changed by anyone who approached them. Likewise, the interviews recorded were programmed to play continuously. Each musical instrument recorded, on the other hand, was programmed to have its volume increased and decreased according to people's proximity while it was playing synchronously.

The *grand finale* was as remarkable as the reception. Both schools suspended official classes and took all their teachers and students to the exhibition. It happened in the lobby of the "Blue and White Hotel" of Osogbo for more than 500 people, among teachers, students, crew, technical and administrative staff from both schools, family members and guests. The event lasted a full day (from 9 am to 4 pm) and was

Figure 6. Sound track production with the Nigerian music Adedeji Adebimpe (left) and final tests with the installation. Blue and White Hotel (right). Osobgo, Nigeria, 2016. (Personal file)

preceded by speeches from the directors of both schools, prayers and blessings of a Baptist minister, as well as dance performances by invited students and guests. The preliminary presentations concluded with the Olaniyi's speech about the importance of the artistic reuse of discarded packaging and objects in order to avoid unnecessary environmental pollution.

During the exhibition of the installation only the students (about 150 from each school) could interact with the tree. They were organized by a crew of monitors in groups of four people, one for each sensor and during five minutes, each student had to switch their positions among them around the sculpture. As they came closer to the sensors, they activated the sounds of the interviews and the tracks with their movements. When they came closer to the sensors, they also triggered and altered their movements, the sounds of the interviews, the tracks, the images and the animations were projected on the screen. The slower were the movements, the more accurate was the responsiveness of the motion sensors.

At the beginning of the interactions, the children did not seem to understand very well how to proceed with the sensitized sculpture. It was necessary the monitors to guide each group showing them how to interact with it. Their legs were barely moving, while their arms were limited to follow instructions, fearing to move their bodies

Figure 7. Students from International Kingdom Kids School (left) and Excellent School interact with the installation by exploring sensory affected space.Odogbo, Nigeria, 2016. (Personal file)

spontaneously. However, as the other pupils watched the previous performances of their classmates, their curiosity and anxiety for the experience increased, and when their turn came, they already stretched their arms toward the tree, without knowing properly for what, though.

The shyness of these children was, in fact, the aspect that particularly observed by us in this presentation. There was an obvious fear of "disobeying" the monitors' instructions. Their impression was that they were playing a similar role of an actor in an elementary school theater. The author could attest the body self-mitigation of these students when they were next to the sensorial spaces mapped. On the other hand, he could also highlight their clear consciousness that they played an effective protagonist role in the scope of this artwork, even in a "managed" state. For the audience who sat in the audience's chairs, composed of family, relatives, teachers and friends, it was almost an abroad spectacle that counted on the participation of the students, just like a "multimedia" recital. They could pay many attention and then become quite touched with the expressed children's wishes in the interview.

Something that also should be emphasized is a huge effort from the directors, teachers, and all the school's and hotel's staff, who did their best in order to make everything happen the best possible way, given the very poor electric infrastructure.

For both lectures, other activities planned at both schools and also the grand finale at the hotel, the arrangement of energy generators in addition the transport required a considerable physical and logistical effort from all the adults involved. On the exhibition's day, the brightness entered strongly in the lobby of the hotel. Canvas were used on both side walls to reduce the light. Even so, the sharpness of the projection of the images on the screen was partially compromised.

The Nigerian Wishing Tree experience lead us to search for additional post-digital perspectives that achieved to contemplate those interdisciplinary and cross-cultural aspects contained both in the technological-art hybridism such as the *transculturalism* (Santos, 2013), the *ancestrofuturism* (Borges, 2017; Garcia, 2017) and other diasporas in which some of its characteristics and affirmations were also evidenced in the set of our artwork. In this way, Brazilian *tecnoshamanism* and *afrofuturismo* cultural movements, as well as the transnational *Amazonia* opera (Santos, 2013), has revealed the multiple cultural cosmologies existing within the same country, and the peculiarities of their fusions *hi-tech + low-tech* as well.

The ancestrofuturism, manifested through tecnoshamanism meetings (Borges, 2015, 2017) establishes dialogical relationship between local references and global trends. They merge digital technological art with traditional local art and ancestral tribal rituals in order to promote the conservation, preservation, and other ways

Figure 8. Grand finale's event Banner (above). Students and others present at the event (below). Osogbo, Nigeria, 2016. (Personal file)

to rescue the indigenous and other ethnic minorities as well Barbara Garcia sees technoshamanism as a movement that "build bridges between technology and ancestral tribes to recover ideas for a better future lost in the past (Carcia, 2017)." Fabiane Borges adds:

... techno + shamanism has three quite evident meanings: 1. the technology of shamanism (shamanism seen as a technology for the production of knowledge); 2. the shamanism of technology (the pursuit of shamanic powers through the use of technology); 3. the combination of these two fields of knowledge historically obstructed by the Church and later by science, especially in the transition from the Middle Ages to the Renaissance (Borges, 2015)

Borges's concept about anscestrofuturism (2017) also proposes a fusion of ancestral perspectives based on "devoid of proof" knowledge, with a progressive vision of the future from "evolutionary development dominated by science and technology" (Borges, 2017). Garcia (2017) considers it as "the union of two kinds of thought traditionally separated by the church and later by science," which "problematizes hugely this idea of evolution preached by modernity".

African cultural and geographic diasporas, on the other hand, are the spreading of cultural expressions originating in the African continent that have come to express themselves and to influence the "Western" culture through the creation of imagery and musical artistic works of all kinds, as well as the design of objects, clothing and cuisine (Farrel, 2004). *Mocambos* is a Brazilian activist network that represents this type of action in seeking to preserve what there is still of African culture in Brazil[14] through a network that integrates 200 Brazilian *quilombola* communities in which digital archives are produced and stored in a collection named *Baobáxia* in order to protect the "ancestral wisdom".

Besides implanting a local node ... it also plants in each of them a Baobá tree, which means the future perseverance of the African culture in Brazil, connecting it with an ancestral practice. These trees can live thousands of years, meaning that process the creation of a millennial Afro-Brazilian future. (Garcia, 2017)

Laymert Garcia dos Santos' literary work *Transcultural Amazonian: Shamanism and Technoscience in the Opera* reports a collective international remake - coming from three distinct cultures: German, Brazilian, and Yanomani indigenous - from the Greek narrative *Orpheus*. According to the author this project had as objective:

... to create a common ground in which cultural differences over the creation of opera were proposed and counter proposed, not in the search for common denominator, a

synthesis, or a negotiated accord, but so that the sharing of knowledge and practices could stablish parameters to help us work with diverse visions of the forest in a productive manner. (Santos, 2013: p. 13)

The *Amazônia* opera was created and produced by means of a partnership between researchers and artists of the University of Campinas; of the *Göethe Institute* of São Paulo, both in Brazil, and the *Zentrum für Kunst und Medientechnologie* (ZKM) in the city of Karlsruhe, Germany, and members of the Brazilian Yanomani tribe. This artistic work refers to the promotion of a cross-cultural artistic production (Santos, idem) through an instrumental and mediatic multifacetism between electronic-digital technologies and ancestral ritual expressions. Santos calls for a liberation of the art of shackles of (techno) science and points out the role of Yanomani ritual reopens the possibility of the same dialogue with traditional knowledge.

Contemporary technoscientific knowledge, for example, as a matter of principle, gives no credit to traditional knowledge, because its discourse by its very nature serves to negate all forms of knowledge that preceded it. Art, however, which emerges from different premises, may be less limited than science in its ability to risk hearing what indigenous peoples are saying. Art relates readily to myth, and the aesthetic has nothing to lose in opening itself to this dimension. It's here that the Yanomani enter the opera. (Santos, 2013, p. 44)

The "Nigerian" *Wishing Tree* sound and visual assemble, by this way, ended up in an interactive technological installation that, at first, could be seen as an international and contemporary technological art expression. Despite this part was mixed, edited and mapped by a Brazilian multimedia artist, the sculptural design of the tree built by those Nigerian fine-artists and students for this installation, in addition sincere drawings and testimonies - which expressed the living and real thoughts of those children - brought to light the local artistic talent of a visible "African" artwork.

During the exhibition at Osogbo, the author has attested that, in one hand, the Brazilian technology art focuses on aesthetic-affective experiences through technological reframing, quite close with Western technological art trends. On the other hand, the set of chromatic and geometrical patterns expressed by the assemblage tree brought to light deep references to the Nigerian current fine-art trend. It has achieved quite similarity to the artistic traditions of the "Osogbo school" as described by Willet (2002). Likewise, the symmetric pointillist detail exposed has also catapulted this sculpture's shape to Nigerian ancient period which used ink points to ritualistic ceremonies and also reframed the continental art tradition that dates back to the Neolithic period (Hauser, 1995, pp. 9-18; Bourcier, 2001, p.7).

The sensorial technologic impact, by this way, was quite similar to the other previous workshops. Even shy, the students that interacted with the tree have a first touchless sensorial experience in their lifetime. On the other hand, the ecological consciousness has emerged specially in the Excellent School pedagogical practice. Oladapo, its principal, related to the author that "the school has created the awareness of the need to let the children always think about what they can make from the waste materials. During the Christmas period, the students decorated their classes which such waste material that they put together."[15]

From Nigeria to Brazil

Once this specific literacy achieved to joint a particular sort of Western "thecnoscientific contemporary knowledge" (Santos, 2013; Lee, 2017) with Nigerian contemporary and ancestral fine-art expressed by a assembled sculpturing (Kee, 2016; Borges, 2017; Garcia, 2017), the author, back to Brazil realized that the result of this experiment should be more widespread and the installation could be displayed again in different conditions for other audiences. It led the author to seek conditions to take this exhibition to Brazil, along with some oil paintings of Olaniyi and Babalola, two of the main mentors and directors of the entire Osogbo event; part of the photographic documentation produced in that workshop; and all the wishes spoken by those children were subtitled in Portuguese.

Thus, through a partnership among the Institute of Arts of Unicamp, the African Cultural Center of São Paulo, the Campinas museums Museum of Image and Sound and Museum of the City, the relatives of Babalola and also the voluntarily of Rosana Bernardo, Brazilian art-educator and Edilene Roppoli, PhD media-education researcher, Olaniyi and Babalola were able to travel to Brazil and then had their first artistic, cultural and human experiences out of their native country.

In November and December of that same year, the installation "made in Osogbo" was finally exhibited in Brazil. It premiered in the lobby of the Mário de Andrade Library, in the city of São Paulo, at the event *II Ilè-Isèse Prize for Combating Religious Intolerance* promoted by the African Cultural Center at Brazil. Then, it was also exhibited in the *Museu da Cidade* and the *Museu da Imagem e do Som*, both in Campinas. In the places where the exhibitions occurred the environments were semi-open (Museu da Cidade) or closed (Biblioteca Mário de Andrade and Museu da Imagem e do Som). Undoubtedly, this gave more prominence to the projected images and made possible a clear reading of the subtitles.

Figure 9. Pictures of Sunday Olaniyi (above and left), Mahmood Babalola (above and right), with the authors on the side, and printed photo documentation (below) exhibited at the City Museum. Campinas, Brazil, 2016. (Personal file)

Sao Paulo's event was allowed only for special invited people. Most of them were African immigrants and Brazilian African descendants. There is some Brazilian non-African people, who are engaged in African studies and/or trading. More than 500 people in the event and about 30 people interacted directly with the tree.[16] The Nigerian children's wishes projected and subtitled were watched by the audience stopped around the screen. The balance of the volume of the instruments on the track, set according the people's closeness to the sensors, made many of them feeling that they played a certain instrument while they "dancing" around the tree. Therefore, their dancing movements became them a special complement of that artwork, buy enjoying their own aesthetic experience and, at the same time, promoting a "bodily performing spectacle" for the other present ones.

The exhibitions that occurred at Campinas museums, however, the author and the Osogbo's artists achieved to bring the "complete" Nigerian production with the original tree's Nigerian sculpture. They also borrowed some points of led light that, when illuminating the sculpture, caused an interesting visual effect when reflected in its small metal squares of tin. The exhibitions length to nine days in the *Museu da Cidade* (Campinas City Museum) and three more days in the *Museu da Imagem e do Som* (Image and Sound Museum). There was about 30 people in each exhibition opening section and around 20 people each exhibition day. The audience behavior in a few moments looked like São Paulo's, due to the rhythm provoked by the sampled sound track when they came close to sensors. However, in many cases, the exploring desire about the audiovisual responsivity, as well as and the accuracy of those sensors, has provoked slower and softer movements from most of the audience.

The changing framework in every way produced some new meanings both the ontological and procedural character of that artwork. Different in several aspects of the Osogbo's participants and audience, in the exhibitions in Brazil, the interactive bodily movement was more spontaneous and noticeable. Furthermore, the Brazilian interator people did not have any previous relationship with the installation. For those people, it was an "interactive documentary" that brought some knowledge from another country and / or culture, linked with an interactive audiovisual experience through touchless body movements around a sculptural Nigerian tree. Thus, the endo-aesthetic awareness of their performances was also distinguished from the Osogbo's students, since their body movements made them act less as "actors", like the Nigerian students, and more as "musicians", once they realized how they can handle the sound track, while watched by the rest of the audience.

Figure 10. From left to right: The Wishng Tree (Igi Aa Mu Erogba Se) exhibitions at Biblioteca Mário de Andrade (Sao Paulo, Brazil, 2016), Museu da Cidade and Museu da Imagem e do Som (Both in Campinas, Brazil, 2016). (Personal file)

CONCLUSION

The propose to share these technological art experience aimed to show how these systemic aspects which were emerged from this set of those experiences allowed the author to get important exchanges and addition of vital knowledge for the understanding of the study, production and teaching of (and through) technological and multiplatform art in its particular way. Thereby, this artistic and technological partnership established between Brazilian and Nigerian artists, teachers and students achieved to produce a *hi-tech + low-tech* installation that effectively interacted with many of the current and rising concerns surrounding the contemporary artistic field in post-digital contexts, not only in Brazil or Nigeria, but also in a broader global context.

The aesthetic reframing pointed out during the workshop, through South American and African artistic reinterpretation about original Asian folk narratives, brands the production of this particular installation. On the other hand, the different interactive behaviors detected in each of these both countries discussed in this chapter pointed us multiple and differentiated glances that, in fact, "are not subordinate to the One, but they gain self-consistency" (Deleuze & Guattari, 1997).

Hence the author can state, based on these different experiences under technological, expressive and cultural perspectives, the multiplied characters of this interactive and immersive artwork and, also, how much the attitude and behavior of people – from diverse background and "fresh" incorporated culture as well – could transform one single artwork in many others, albeit under the same materiality and informational content. In this way, by the facts described and analyzed above, the different aesthetic attitudes from the distinct audiences on this same artwork piece have, in effect, generated a set of procedural and multidirectional experiences that made them unique, as in terms of a participatory multi-technological and multi-cultural art literacy as in terms of a contemporary transcultural interactive and immersive experience.

REFERENCES

Alexandrian, S. (1976). *The Surrealism* (Brazilian edition). Sao Paulo: Edusp.

Appardurai, A. (1996). *Modernity at large: cultural dimensions of globalization.* Minneapolis, MN: University of Minessota Press.

Borges, F. (2015). *Tecnoxamanisms, etc.* Avaliable at http://revistageni.org/10/tecnoxamanismos-etc/

Borges, F. (2017). *Ancestrofuturim: free cosmology – do it yourself (DIY) rituals.* Available at https://tecnoxamanismo.files.wordpress.com/2016/05/ancestrofuturismo-cosmogonialivre-rituaisfac3a7avocc3aamesmo.pdf

Bourcier, P. (2001). *Historie de la danse en occident.* Sao Paulo: Martins Fontes.

Bourdieu, P. (1977). Cultural reproduction and social reproduction. In *Power and ideology in education* (pp. 487–511). New York: Oxford University.

Consani, M. (2015). Moral narratives, Piaget and the flies. In Educommunication and human rights. Sao Paulo. ABPEducom.

Couchot, E. (2002). Real time on artistic devices. In L. Leao (Ed.), *Labyrinths of contemporary though.* São Paulo: Iluminuras.

Cunha, M. (2007). Cultural capital Pierre Bourdieu's concept and its ethnographic legacy (Brazilian Edition). Perspectiva, 25(2), 503-524.

Deleuze, G., & Guattary, F. (1997). Mille plateau (Brazilian edition). São Paulo: Academic Press.

Farrel, L. (Ed.). (2004). *Art of contemporary African diaspore.* New York: Museum for African Art.

Flood, G. (1996). *An Introduction to Hinduism.* Cambridge University Press.

Freire, P. (1982). *Cultural activism for freedom.* Rio de Janeiro: Paz e Terra.

Freire, P. (1987). *Pedagogy of the opressed* (17th ed.). Rio de Janeiro: Paz e Terra.

Garbick, J., & Schaefer, S. (2011). In L.A.'s Little Tokyo, a place for your wishes. *Los Angeles Times.* Available at http://articles.latimes.com/2011/aug/14/opinion/la-oe-wishing-tree-20110814

Garcia, B. (2017). *Technoxamanism: when indigenous and kackers get togethet to save the planet.* Barcelona: Laudano Magazine. Available at http://www.laudanomag.com/tecnochamanismo-indios-hackers/

Giannetti, C. (2006). *Digital Aesthetics.* Belo Horizonte: C/Arte.

Hansen, M. (2003). *New philosophy for new media.* London: MIT Press.

Hauser, A. (1995). *The story of the Art and the Literature.* M. Fontes.

Hegel, G. W. (n.d.). *Vorlesungen über die ästhetik* (Brazilian edition). Sao Paulo: EDUSP.

Kee, J., Bailey, C., Horton, S., & Kelly, K. (2016). Art at Aché. Collaboration as Creative Assemblage. AAEA Art Education, 69(5).

Lee, C., & Shieh, M. (2017) *An action research in photography education for vocational students in the post-true era. 2017 InSEA World Congress. Abstract and power-point presenteation given by the authors.*

Murray, J. (2001). *Hamlet on the Holodeck: the future of narrative in cyberspace* (Brazilian edition). Sao Paulo: Itau Cultural.

Neumaier, O. (2004). Space, time, vídeo, Viola. In C. Townsend (Ed.), *The art of Bill Viola*. New York: Times & Hudson.

Ryan, M. (2001). *Narrative as virtual reality: immersion and interactivity in literature and electronic media*. Baltimore, MD: Johns Hopkins University Press.

Santos, L. G. (2013). *Transcultural Amazonas: shamanism and technoscience in the opera*. Sao Paulo: N-1 Ed.

Sennet, R. (2008). *The Craftsman*. London: Penguin Books.

Shobat, E., & Stam, R. (2002). *Unthinking Eurocentrism, multiculturalism and media*. Barcelona: Paidos.

Soares, I. (2011). Educommunication: Proposals for a high school reform. São Paulo: Ed. Paulinas.

Szope, D. (2003). Peter Weibel. In J. Shaw & P. Weibel (Eds.), *Future cinema: the cinematic imaginary after film*. Cambridge, MA: MIT Press.

Teles, P. (2009). *Touchless sensor interfaces: systemic poetics and interactive music* (Unpublished doctoral dissertation). Pontifical University of Sao Paulo, São Paulo, Brazil.

Teles, P. (2015). *The Wishing Forest*. Available at https://www.youtube.com/watch?v=8EmZM_Ybvlw&t=6s recovered at 09/09/2017

Teles, P. (2017). Protagonism, recycling and new sensibilization in technological art international workshop. In Educomuinicação e suas áreas de intervenção: novos paradigmas para um diálogo intercultural. São Paulo: ABPEducom.

Teles, P., & Boyle, A. (2015). Psytrance influences on touchless Interactive experiences: new roles for performers and audience within the electronic music scenario. In E. Simão, A. Silva, & S. Magalhães (Eds.), *Exploring psychedelic trance and electronic dance music in modern culture*. Hershey, PA: IGI Global. doi:10.4018/978-1-4666-8665-6.ch007

Tinhorão, J. R. (1984). Short histoty of Brazilian popular music – from "Modinha" to the "Tropicalism". Sao Paulo: Arte Ed.

Toole, S. J. (2015). *Origin myth of me: reflections of our origins creations of the Lulu.* Lulu Press.

Willet, F. (2002). *African Arts.* London: Times & Hudson.

KEY TERMS AND DEFINITIONS

Ancestrofuturism: A concept given to ritual actions and artistic events, promoted by a collective composed of artists and scholars of the human sciences together with indigenous or other communities holding "ancestral knowledge" in the search for a hybrid cosmology that promotes a sensorial and cultural elevation to this set.

Controller Board: Electronic-digital boards that connects devices and objects of various natures (by cameras and/or a sort of different sensor features) to computers and gives them the role of peripheral controllers (mouse, pen tables and/or keyboards, for example) of actions and events in those systems.

Interactive Music: Every music that audience participates, collaborates, and interferes with its execution can somehow be considered "interactive." In the context of this chapter, the author refers to experiences in which digital interfaces of interaction give the spectator an opportunity for interference and rearrangements in the volume or course of different tracks of a specific song.

Led Spots: Light spot composed of small bulbs of high luminous intensity with low energy expenditure, whose colors and intensity can be controlled and constantly altered.

Responsiveness: Logical and temporal ability of a hardware or software to "return" to imputed commands.

Sampled Instruments: Sounds recorded or produced by electronic and/or digital instruments that imitate other "original" musical instruments or creation of new sonorities.

Ultrasonic Sensors: Small devices that detect how close/far objects are through ultrasonic waves that "echo" the objects found within range.

ENDNOTES

[1]   Pierre Bourdieu's approach on cultural capital (Bourdieu, 1977; Cunha, 2007) argue on the shock of distinct symbolic heritages within the struggle

against the hegemony of one single and "central" culture. He considers this term, in a critical mode, as the acquisition and consume of new knowledge and experiences from a kind of mainstream Western-culture diffuser.

[2]   Arjun Apparduray names this socio-cultural dynamic procedure as *technoscape* which, according to him, is "the global configuration, also ever fluid, of technology and the fact that technology, both high and low, both mechanical and informational, now moves at high speeds across various kinds of previously impervious boundaries." (Apparduray 1996: p. 34).

[3]   In consonance with Sennet's arguments, this is important to highlight the "non-electronic" craftsmanship feature in this case. According to him, "practical skills still sustained the ongoing life of the city but were not generally honored for doing so... People who participate in "open source" computer software, particularly in the Linux operating system, are [also considered] craftsmen..." (Sennet, 2008: p. 45)

[4]   Deleuze proposes for a systemic human relationship, "a social cartography that is linked to the fields of knowledge of social and human sciences rather than physical mapping, it deals with movements, relationships, power plays, subjectivity of aesthetic itself, practices of resistance and freedom. It does not refer to the method as a set of rules, procedures or research protocols, but rather as a strategy of critical analysis and political action, a critical look that accompanies and describes relations, paths, rhizome arrangements, the composition of devices, pointing out lines of escape, rupture and resistance." (Prado Filho and Teti, 2013: p. 47)

[5]   Piaget`s theory of development has been revised and discussed by many authors, educators and researchers even after his death. There are many factors, mainly resulting from the individual, coming from his socio economic situation (Freire, 1987) or combining media and technological access human being has (Vigotsky, 1989), which complement Piaget´s studies. Despite all this, it is still seen as a solid primary reference for many subsequent theories that agreed, disagreed, complemented and its general assumptions.

[6]   Since 2011 the author uses "Isadora Core" software from Troikatronix company in our sensory installations. It allows determining, among other factors, the distances of actions of the sensors (some have three meters in range, others reach up to six meters).

[7]   Marcel Duchamp, during the first decades of the XXth century, "studied the way of transforming a common object into a rare one by the intervention of a personal detail; it was called *ready made*. Featured in *The Bicycle Wheel* (1913), *The Trap* (1917), which was a floor-mounted hanger, *Recent Widow* (1920), and the controversial inverted urinal, entitled *Fountain* (1917) (Alexandrian 1976: p. 39).

8   "Like several other contemporary video artists. Viola increasingly renounces the use of the classical means of representation in the medium, namely the TV monitor, and instead creates spaces - even in those works where he still makes use of monitors. And even in these cases, they are often employed by Viola in unusual ways. In *The Sleepers* (1992), for instance, the sleeping people are shown on black-and-white monitors lying at the bottom of seven white tin barrels, filled to the brim with water" (Neumaier, 2004: p. 48).

9   "Weibel's consideration of the problems of the internal and the external viewer in connection with interface, is also in evidence in, amongst other things, a computer installation entitled *Die Wand, der Vorhang* (Grenze, die), *fachsprachlich auch Lascaux* (1994). In this interactive opus the image of a brick wall is stored on a computer and projected automatically onto a wall ... the viewer has become part of the image. He is at once a real, internal viewer and a simulated external viewer who appears to be pressing against the wall from the rear." (Szope, 2003: p. 190)

10   The authors have attended in their researcher's lecturing about this theme in the 2017 Insea (International Society of Education Through Art) International Congress. Later, they sent us the paper's resume as well as their screen presentation frames, used by then during their Congress's speech.

11   *Educommunication* is a pedagogical philosophy of socio-constructivism which is sedimented in the connection of the media with education. It promotes the protagonism of the Freirean construction of knowledge itself through the production of content and representation to be transmitted on media and communication devices, See Soares (2011) and Consani (2015).

12   While the author was in Nigeria it was noticeable that internet is accessed through smartphones. There are many TV channels, but one of them is spoken in Yoruba. Additionally, its film production is highlighted not only in Africa but also worldwide.

13   *The Osogbo School of Artists* consists not only of these and other untrained artists, who discovered their undeveloped talents in the summer school, but a number of others who were encouraged by the artists Ulli Beier and Susanne Wenger to develop themselves artistically long before the summer schools were started" (Willet, 2002: p. 241).

14   During the seventeenth and nineteenth centuries, Brazil was the largest recipient of slaves from the African continent. The current estimate indicates that 45% of the slaves going to America came to Brazil. That means 5.5 million black people brought by force to that country. According to calculations, 12% of them did not land here. See more at https://noticias.uol.com.br/cotidiano/ultimas-noticias/2015/04/13/perto-do-fim-da-escravidao-60-dos-negros-trazidos-ao-pais-eram-criancas.htm

15   Oladapo's testimonial extracted from particular Facebook chat between him and the author about the impacts on the school's students one year after the Osogbo's workshop.

16   For the exhibition at the Mário de Andrade Library in Sao Paulo, there was no time enough to bring the Nigerian tree and the artist's paintings either, due to Olaniyi landed in Brazil almost at the time of that event. The author then used the first "tree" of this series, produced by the art-educator Lúcia Camargo in the Brazilian workshop (in Campinas, in 2012). It was made on cardboard, wire, bitumen and yellow caps, which representing an *Ipê*, a traditional Brazilian tree.

Chapter 4

Multimedia Experiences for Cultural Heritage

Manuela Piscitelli
Università degli Studi della Campania Luigi Vanvitelli, Italy

ABSTRACT

The chapter analyzes, with particular regard to the Italian context, the aspects related to the fruition of cultural heritage and to the expectations of the potential public. There is often a lack of adequate media for communication, which should create interest in a non-specialist public. Multimedia and interactive technologies can be a valuable support to enhance internal and external communication for museums and cultural sites, reaching a wide audience in a differentiated and customized manner depending on their interests. The aim is to understand the link between the work of art and the geographical, physical, historical, and cultural context in which it was born, to open the horizon to a synoptic and organic understanding of heritage, contributing to its protection and educating citizens. Finally, a case study concerning the museum and territory of Mondragone (Italy) is presented.

INTRODUCTION

The total difference between the supports for communication and learning used especially by younger people and the didactic supports usually used in cultural sites makes it appear unattractive and difficult to understand archaeological sites, museums, exhibitions organized according to a traditional approach, without attention to a communication policy able to reach and interest a wide audience. This is the major challenge of the future, particularly in a context, such as the Italian one, where cultural sites are so widespread that they are largely unknown by the wide

DOI: 10.4018/978-1-5225-5696-1.ch004

public. Moreover, in Italy, compared to the great foreign museums, the attention to these aspects is arrived late and is not organically coordinated on the territory, often carried out on the initiative of a single museum or to the maximum of a single regional ambiance.

New technologies are the most suitable instrument to make the exhibits talk about their past with the typical methods of the multimedia and integrated communication to which the public has grown accustomed in every other context of the everyday life. Too often instead, the lack of didactic supports and an overly technical language makes it difficult to comprehend, and therefore to appreciate them by a non-specialist audience.

For some years, more attention has been devoted to these issues, and new professional figures are involved in the design of cultural products according to various meanings: the design of pathways from the point of view of the usability and aesthetics, the shared management, the graphic and visual design. The concept of fruition has also expanded to include not only the accessibility of a site, but also the possibility to understand the objects observed. It has also included the study of virtual access modes where the physical accessibility is precluded for different reasons.

This attitude is evident from the recommendations issued by the organizations dealing with the enhancement of the cultural heritage.

The ICOM's ethical code in the museum's definition also focuses on communication-related aspects. "A museum is a permanent, non-profit institution serving the society and its development. It is open to the public and conducts research on material and immaterial testimonies of humanity and its environment: acquires, preserves, communicates and, above all, exhibits them for study, education and pleasure." (ICOM, 2004).

ICOMOS documents also highlight the importance of communication with the public as an essential element of the process of conservation and management of cultural heritage, recognizing that each act of conservation is implicitly a communication act, since it presupposes a choice about what to preserve and above all how to present the preserved objects to the public. "Presentation specifically concerns a planned communication of an interpretative content by collecting information of the same nature through physical access to the cultural heritage site. It can be transmitted through various technical means, including elements ranging from information panels to a museum presentation, from recommended itineraries to conferences, guided tours and multimedia applications." (ICOMOS, 2008).

According to ICOMOS, the principles on which the interpretation and presentation should be based, are unrelatedly with the used medium, which may vary by choosing from time to time the most effective and appropriate one, in relation to the specific context. In all cases, it should facilitate understanding and appreciation of cultural heritage sites and promote public awareness and commitment for their protection and conservation, communicating the significance of cultural heritage sites to different interlocutors through a profound and well-documented recognition of this meaning through recognized methods of scientific analysis and research in addition to the living cultural traditions.

Multimedia communication represents an extraordinary opportunity to widen the enjoyment of cultural assets to a wider audience than just specialists or admirers, safeguarding the cultural and landscaping heritage (the first step for safeguarding is the knowledge and appreciation, in particular by residents), and creating new skills.

In support of these considerations, in addition to the proposition of numerous significant examples, it is described here a case study, conducted in the academic field. The application concerns the development of an interactive platform for the museum and the territory of Mondragone (Caserta, Italy). The demo, which is thought as a model exportable to other similar contexts, has two main objectives. The first is to reconnect the exhibits in the museum with the sites where they were found and the historical era of belonging. The second is the search for a captivating and immediate understanding language to communicate with the public, offering the possibility to customize the itineraries according to their own interests. In fact, the active involvement of the public in building their own cognitive process and the constructive dialogue between the museum institution and the community of its users are considered a priority.

COMMUNICATION FOR CULTURAL HERITAGE IN ITALY AND ABROAD

Demand for cultural heritage in Italy has shown a steady growth for at least 20 years until the beginning of the crisis in 2012, when the economic difficulties of many families led to a contraction in cultural consumption.

However, this demand has not been intercepted and appropriately addressed to the several proposals of the rich Italian offer, but oriented itself in an autonomous and often unexpected manner, with difficulties of managing unsustainable numbers for some sites, at the expense of others almost unknown to the public while they could meet the interest of many.

One of the first great events in the cultural field that attracted a huge audience, unexpected from the organizers and archaeologists, who were even irritated, was the exhibition of the Riace Bronzes at the beginning of the Eighties in Rome and in Florence. Salvatore Settis on that occasion stressed "the absolute, disarming inability to anticipate the public reactions: this gigantic cultural event happened, so it seems, not only beyond, but against the intentions of who would have to foresee and handle it. Archaeologists have been astonished and unbelieving, and so little they were prepared for what happened, that were busy looking for all-extrinsic reasons, ending to blame the mass media for such an annoying success." (Settis, 1981, p. 15-16).

Since then, many steps have been taken in the dialogue with the public, but in many cases, there is not still an exact will to find a language to communicate with them. There is still a slight incentive for an active participation of the citizens, depositors of history, traditions and shared memory, which should be the first aim of communication.

The problem of the communication and the transmission of information and "tales" that protected objects may allow, should be of an urgency and importance similar to that of the protection, because of it is a condition and a justification (perhaps not only in the eyes of the public opinion). (Ricci, 1996, p. 52).

Even with respect to the Italian brand abroad, in the absence of specific promotional campaigns, there has been a steady decline in attractiveness for the past few years. One of the reasons for this decline is the lack of communication of Italian cultural assets with respect to the great foreign museums. The diffusion of social networks and new digital communication technologies has profoundly changed the habits of travelers seeking to plan their cultural visit getting useful information and materials before leaving, to personalize their experience basing on their own interests. The Italian heritage in this sense is mostly behind. According to the estimates of Eurobarometer 278 - European cultural values - Italy is, in fact, the last in Europe to access and use digital resources. "In this context, cultural institutions show more than others an incredible delay, probably due to a way of thinking about the cultural heritage inherited from the past, mainly oriented to protect, preserve and maintain the *status quo*." (Federculture, 2014, p. 23).

In the present world, instead, it is essential to share information, so that an event such as the visit to the *Domus Romane* at Palazzo Valentini in Rome, accompanied by lights, video and digital installations, has attracted greater success and appeal to the collective imagination than the visit to archaeological sites of greatest interest, but lacking support for the visit. Enthusiastic comments on the web contributed to a virtuous circle promoting the event.

An active and constant communication policy with the audience through social networking has been applied for years by the most visited museums in the world, such as the Louvre in Paris, the Metropolitan Museum of Art in New York, and the British Museum in London. This did not happen in Italian museums, which often have no information in different languages, sometimes neither in English.

The role of museum communication with its public on the web is considered to be of great importance for the growth of the museum institution. "The future of the museum may be rooted in the buildings they occupy but it will address audiences across the world – a place where people across the world will have a conversation.

Those institutions which take up this notion fastest and furthest will be the ones which have the authority in the future". (Serota, 2009).

At the Tate Modern in London, for example, every visitor can leave a comment about his experience, ask questions about contemporary artists who exhibit their works, or just recommend the visit to others. In this way, the museum enhances its "web reputation", that is, its reputation on the web, fundamental from the time when the tour operator's figures directed to customers disappeared globally, and the visitors are now oriented by the opinions of other forum visitors in a kind of powerful word-of-mouth.

In communication strategies developed by Tate, is central the differentiation by public categories, from children to academics, as well as the dialogue between users and artists. (Stack, 2010).

The first category is made up of "Tate Kids", children involved through a playful approach. The site promotes creativity allowing children to create their own works, to show them next to those of artists, to comment the works of others. In addition, a series of interactive games bring children closer to the universe of contemporary art by encouraging them to explore collections. The second category is "Young Tate", teen and young people participating in a community where is possible to develop their creativity through artistic competitions and to virtually expose their works and discuss them with other members. "Schools and teachers" is a purely didactic area where you can participate in art projects and make use of resources for e learning. Even adults who want to get closer to learning art have a dedicated space in which "Adult learners" can access resources for learning, creating, sharing, and commenting works. The "Scholarship and research" category, on the other hand, has a more specialized, public and shared research area, allowing researchers and students to interact in a virtual community, exchanging comments and knowledge.

The report on "Tate Digital Strategy 2013-15" also highlights the new strategy for creating a link between the external and internal communication for the museum. This is possible through a web site specifically designed to be used in the museum galleries from phones and tablets, thanks to the availability of a Wi-Fi connection, to help people to understand the exhibited works and plan their own visit path through multimedia contents. (Stack, 2013).

The example of the Tate demonstrates how, besides what we can call communication outside of the museum with the aim of arousing curiosity in the potential visitor, the internal communication within the museum is essential too. It is the degree of visitor involvement in understanding the exhibition path. Obviously, the two communication instances are closely related, as it is also evident from the aforementioned example of the *Domus Romane* of Palazzo Valentini in Rome, and mutually reinforce each other.

The first communication error that persists within many Italian sites is to consider the audience as a homogeneous set, so a single, often standardized, display mode is offered to everyone, addressing to visitors indifferently. Instead, the public is strongly differentiated, first regarding the age: children, young people, adults; and then for their linguistic provenance; finally depending on the cultural level in general and the specific skills in the field in particular. A communication specifically addressed to each of these groups as in the example of the Tate is definitely winning.

Not differencing, however, translates into the attendance of cultural sites only by the public with a medium-high level of education, which considers their preparation sufficient to understand the exhibited collection or the site. In practice, cultural consumption is directly proportional to the cultural baggage of an individual, so those who have already visited cultural sites tend to visit others. (Pennella & Trimarchi, 1993).

While it is relatively easy to remedy the difficulties of physical access, it is more difficult to improve the accessibility of information, in the sense of making the paths suitable for those who are potentially interested but culturally inadequate to understand the content for how it is actually exposed and presented. Reaching this potential audience would bring enormous advantage in terms of benefits to the educational contribution offered from the museum to the community, which is one of the tasks that a museum needs to fulfill.

It seems that the information media of many Italian museums are designed and realized without taking into account the visitor's profile and its actual capacity for appropriation of the cultural message transmitted through them. This obviously leads to a disempowerment of the effectiveness of the whole museum's communication process and, therefore, to the enhancement of its collections, which ends to damage its own capacity to fulfill its institutional goals in terms of social development and support for the intellectual growth of the community.

Finally, it should be noted that the resulting intellectual and cognitive "loss" is sometimes further amplified by the visitor's spatial disorientation, which occurs in all cases where the internal signage (maps, directions of paths and services) is inadequate or absent. (Associazione Studi e Ricerche per il Mezzogiorno, 2010, p. 106).

A valid communication system should remove those "non-physical" but "informative" barriers to access, structuring the cultural path to amplify the attractiveness of the audience less interested in traditional proposals. (Prentice, 1994).

In a country like Italy, this public should first include the Italian citizens who must recognize, from the years of schooling, the distinct identities of their own cities as part of a common and diverse Italian national identity, a connective tissue that includes people and monuments, language, theater and cinema, and so on. The foreign costumers formed by non-Italians visiting Italy or living there should not be treated as a foreign body, but on the other hand should be involved in the same communication strategies, encouraged to feel at home in Italy, and to understand the many facets of Italian culture and tradition.

INTEGRATED COMMUNICATION FOR VALORISATION

An effective communication strategy for cultural assets in Italy must be able to make a system that means not focusing on the spectacular of a single event that could be realized everywhere and that would bring an ephemeral notoriety. Instead, it should be improved a constant communication (internal and external) of a widespread patrimony, in which each piece can be related to others through a mutual promotion action that would at the same time favor the understanding of the heritage as a whole. To understand the link between the work of art and the geographical, physical, historical and cultural context in which it was born means to open the horizon to a synoptic and organic understanding of Italian heritage, contributing both to the protection of heritage and to education of citizens. Museums, excavations and archives have to be increasingly conceived as sites of research and education, that elaborate knowledge and access strategies to their heritage both for specialists and for the public.

Communication can certainly benefit from the use of digital information systems, interactive and customizable, for a differentiated access depending on the interests of the individual user. In fact, virtual reality, augmented reality, and computer simulation allow overcoming the space barriers determined by the workspace container. (Medri & Canonici, 2010).

This is the case of virtual museums, a limit case where there is no need to preserve and exhibit the artworks, so the museum role is completely focused on communication. This type of museum is not discussed here in cases where it is disconnected from the physical context. It is interesting, instead, to discuss how these same digital technologies can be a tool for expanding knowledge during a real visit, and for integrating the visit through virtual spaces associated with the physical ones.

In the case of the Italian heritage, it is considered essential to involve the visitor in a real visit to the site or the museum. Creating connections on the site can contextualize the exhibits displayed expanding their ability to communicate and stimulate the curiosity and the interest of the visitor, who may choose to continue the visits in the future linking to other sites or environments to which the objects displayed are connected. Thus, a system for cultural heritage is created, where each element is understood as a part of a more complex system, and the interpretation of each object is clarified. (Scaltritti, 2012).

Heritage should therefore be able to activate knowledge processes creating a system of connections between its widespread elements. To achieve this goal, it is necessary to establish a system in which major sites, with a number of visitors too high for a sustainable management and enjoyment, can be the cognitive tool to promote less known sites, potentially able to attract visitors if appropriately understood through geographic, historical, and stylistic links.

Crucial in this regard is the role that local communities should take. They are no longer called to be only organizational sites for receptive activities, according to globally valid models, but should be active subjects in proposing cultural and behavioral models that provide interpretative keys to local resources, giving them a specific added value. It is the information that builds up a territory, representing the material and cultural resources that make up its specificity, as well as the user chooses among the various possibilities, building and expressing his identity (Urry, 1995).

In this context, the traditional figures of cultural mediators are also evolving. In the past, the most important mediators of cultural tourism experiences came from the field of art history: they were people who knew the value of art and heritage. Today we are observing the emergence of a new category of creative mediators that in many cases do not come from the cultural or tourist sector. Architects, designers, multimedia producers and many other people from the "cultural industries" in fact design creative tourism products and experiences.

Art often has to combine different elements of experience - teaching, aesthetics and entertainment - into one attraction. In this sense, while museums try to learn from thematic parks, architects and designers are playing an increasingly important role in the cultural tourism. The museum, to be still attractive, will have to transform from a conservation site into a meeting and learning place, able to satisfy interests and curiosities, and to live an interactive experience.

INTERACTIVE TOURS IN MUSEUMS AND CULTURAL SITES

Education for understanding works of art by the public is not a function of newly proposition for a museum. Already at the beginning of the nineteenth century, the archaeologist Quatrèmere de Quincy wrote: Fine works of art, those produced by the profound sentiment of their agreement with their destination, are those who lose most to be condemned to the inactive role that expect them in the museums. To prevent this, it would be, from the audience, one stretch of imagination, a feeling that no one is capable to have in that place where no accessory sentiment prepares the soul and has to work corresponding affections. (Quatrèmere de Quincy, 1815, p. 44).

The main problem of communicating within the museum is the discouragement of finding completely decontextualized objects far away in space and time from the context in which they originated and which is a key for their interpretation.

The exhibited objects are communicative artifacts: the task of museums is to make them speak, find a way through which a communicative channel can be activated between the work and the public, so that the exhibition has the sense of transmitting culture and each opera successfully reaches its addressees. (Antinucci, 2014).

New digital technologies can be of support in this research, activating the possibility of interaction between the visitor and the information content. Interactive museums are real museum containers where the potential of digital technologies is exploited for a more dynamic and engaging communication, which has the explicit objective of rethinking the museums communicative mechanism as a whole. (Ribaldi, 2005, p. 20).

The visitor is involved in the cognitive experience, has the opportunity to personalize his own path, to access the information he thinks more relevant for his own interests, to observe the works historically and geographically linked through virtual simulations, and to explore thematic itineraries.

An example of interactive museum is the Virtual Archaeological Museum of Herculaneum, a 5,000 square-meter physical structure on three levels located in the heart of the city, proposing a new mode for cultural enjoyment. The visitor can explore the streets of Herculaneum, the interior of the library, the spa and the forum, reproduced through three-dimensional reconstructions within the museum structure. Through multisensory effects, interactive interfaces, virtual books, holograms, synchronized multi-projections, visitors can relive a typical day in the old city. Scenario reconstructions, visual interfaces and holograms lead the visitor to a virtual dimension, where they can experiment in a playful and interactive way the new opportunities that multimedia technology makes available for the enjoyment of archaeological heritage.

In addition to the innovative communication within the museum, there is also good external communication activity, through the web, the coordinated image, the social networks, and the activities of scientific dissemination.

The interactivity within the museums, especially the scientific ones aimed at a young and very young audience, is becoming almost an obligation, with the risk of transforming the museum into a very ludic and in fact very little educational form. For this, it is necessary to clarify the meaning of interactivity and how it can be translated into a factual educational tool for improving the understanding of the exhibitions.

In this regard, Patrik Hughes, an expert in technological and interactive communication, observed that there is often no real interaction, but the simple operation of activating a display. While interaction should be "some form of reciprocity or exchange between two elements (for example, a person and a machine), in which the action or behavior of the one has an effect on the other. Switching on and off a light bulb does not create a reciprocity relationship between us and the bulb!" (Hughes, 2001, p. 178).

In fact, the only presence of videos that can be activated by the user is often unattractive, and the public after having driven them moves away looking for anything other stimulating their curiosity. The observation of a simple video, therefore, cannot be considered an interactive feature within a museum. On the contrary, interaction can already be mentioned when there are prototypes that can be touched by the user to understand their task by activating a tactile interaction with the object in question.

In this direction, technologies are rapidly evolving, replacing traditional audio guides with specific media applications that can be used by the own smartphone or tablet, or alternatively on touch supports (interactive tables, walls or totems) along the exhibition path. These tools can be used to create a connection between the museum and the territory. A simple insertion of a QR code into the caption accompanying the exhibited works allows the visitor to place it with his or her device to access additional content online. It is so possible to view the territory to which the finds belong, to plan visits outside the museum through the geolocation of the sites virtually linked to it, to interact with other users breaking the isolation mechanism of the decontextualized work that had been identified as one of the main limitations for its understanding.

Other interactive help tools are the augmented reality and the projection mapping. The term "augmented reality" means a set of techniques that allow smartphones and tablets to recognize objects framed with the camera, and to obtain digital information related to them. This is a more sophisticated evolution of the Qr code framing system described above, based on the optical image recognition and the GPS triangles of your device. The term "augmented reality" focuses on the fact that the user is in a real environment, but he may receive additional information, increasing his natural perception of the surrounding environment. (Rheingold, 2003, pp. 144-145).

Applications are of course endless, and cultural heritage can be one of the areas of major interest to the benefits of this kind of interactive and stimulating communication, differentiated by user typology, to learn in a playfulness mode, to stimulate their curiosity, or to receive scientific information.

An experimental application in the archaeological field was made in 2015 at Trajan's Markets at the Museum of Imperial Forum in Rome, where visitors, through eyeglasses with an augmented viewer, approaching the artworks could receive textual information, images, audio, and video.

In many other museums, similar experiments have been carried out not only with eyeglasses but also with tablets and smartphones, both to access to information contents or three-dimensional reconstructions, and for more playful aspects such as games and treasure hunts to discover works of art with the active participation of more visitors. (Ciotti & Roncaglia, 2000).

The projection mapping is instead a technology that is most relevant to the artistic performance than to the museum education. In fact, it is the projection of lights and videos on real surfaces, whose perception is altered by this virtual "second skin", creating surprising and spectacular effects, much appreciated by the public. In fact, projection can be two-dimensional or three-dimensional, enriched by music and audio comments, sometimes by smells and movements, to engage the viewer in a completely immersive experience.

The chosen real location, with its peculiarities, gives character to the work and profoundly influences the performance. In fact, works are specifically designed to be represented on a particular site, where they establish relationships with the space, giving it new meanings, reinforcing the cultural milieu, enabling them to be understood from the citizens who, as usual, live in the urban path system. In this way, these works deeply affect the memory of the users, telling the story of the place with innovative technologies.

Another term used to define this practice is "architectural dressing," referring to the practice of attributing new meanings to the architectural envelop. A public space or parts of a building transform itself into a narration and reflection moment.

An interesting example in this regard is the digital work *Magnificent,* created by Felice Limosani and narrated by Master Andrea Bocelli, projected on the partitions of the Armory Hall of the *Palazzo Vecchio* Museum in Florence from May to October 2015. The main pictorial works and sculptures from the Renaissance have been elaborated with digital techniques in an engaging and innovative sequence of actual episodes and anecdotes, symbolically represented in a plot that leaves space for reflection on man's magnificence. The walls of the Hall of Arms were transformed into monumental screens, increasing the visual and emotional impact that would have been projection on a normal anonymous screen.

The spectacular nature of these projections is due in fact to the context, and to the proposition of a way of alternative use of museums, archaeological sites, public spaces, which tell themselves in an entirely new and engaging way for the spectator.

A CASE STUDY:DESIGN OF AN INTERACTIVE PLATFORM FOR THE CULTURAL HERITAGE OF MONDRAGONE

Basing on the expressed considerations, the author developed an integrated and interactive communication project, exploiting the possibilities offered by digital technologies to enhance the knowledge and enjoyment of the cultural heritage of Mondragone (Italy). The location was chosen because the area has a vast and articulate heritage, but hard to understand due to the large temporal and geographical distribution. Housed since prehistoric times as evidenced by exhibits preserved in the local civic museum, in the Roman era was founded the city of Sineussa, which gained great importance as a commercial port and a resting place with spa treatments for the aristocracy. From the Middle Ages are the ruins of the castle Montis Dragonis, from which derives the name of the city of Mondragone, while of the later period there are several churches and palaces. (Greco, 1927).

Now, the Archaeological Museum of Biagio Greco, inaugurated in 2000, exhibits discoveries from prehistoric, Roman and medieval times. The surrounding area is characterized by several excavation areas, not all accessible to the public. They are the archaeological site of Rocca San Sebastiano on Mount Petrino, where prehistoric remains were found. The finds of ancient huts between the Bronze Age and the Iron Age known as the Cyclamen Village. The excavations carried out on Mount Petrino that brought to light the remains of the village of Ausoni-Aurunci digging along the Appia Street at the city cemetery. Several discoveries of remains of late-republican villas and other Roman material dating back to the ancient Sinuessa today submerged; and the excavations of the medieval fort Montis Dragonis.

From the point of view of the fruition, in addition to the limited accessibility and the lack of knowledge of many of the aforementioned sites, it is noteworthy the public's difficulty in bringing back the visible finds in the museum to the areas where they were found and at the time they belong. In the same way, in the face of the scarcely visible archaeological remains on the territory, there is a difficulty in understanding the original form and once again of the connection with the historical period and with the exhibits visible in the museum.

Hence, the idea of creating an interactive system able to recapture finds, sites, history, and to propose virtual cognitive paths, with information and reconstructions, but also physically accessible following the traces of finds to the areas where they were found. The goal is not only to expand the knowledge of the cultural heritage of the area making it virtually accessible from remote locations. It is also and above all to enhance understanding and therefore a participatory usability and to guide visitors to one of the sites of the Mondragone area, building a wide and stimulating personalized pathway, to persuade them to continue their visit including other sites related to the first.

The project exploits different technologies to achieve the aforementioned aims. Within the museum and some of the main sites, a touchscreen interactive table is provided, whereby can be obtained information, virtual reconstructions, a customized route based on their interests, complete with maps and travel times, to be followed outside the museum. Information should be integrated with a downloadable application on your smartphone to continue your chosen path outside the museum and reach the other sites. Among them, in the main ones you should find an interactive screen or totem to continue accessing the information content. In the smaller sites, instead, a poster should offer the first information, while for the in-depth information it would be necessary to frame a QR Code with the own tablet or smartphone, to connect with the interactive content related to that area, also visible in the museum, the main sites, and present on the Web. The same QR code could be included in the explanatory brochures of the routes, and on informative posters in churches and palaces of the city, within an integrated communication project, where the web, the museum, the cultural sites, and the whole territory participate in a unique integrated and interactive dialogue with users.

The project was partially developed as part of the thesis in Design and Communication from the student Francesca Spina entitled "Art meets technology" of which the writer was supervisor, who made a demo of the interactive platform.

The name given to the platform, imagined as exportable to other contexts and museum paths, is ArTour that is made of the union of the English terms Art and Tour.

Starting the application, an interactive map appears showing the sites of interest in the area. It is organized according to two thematic itineraries: religious and cultural. Each site is represented by a pictogram that summarizes the features for an immediate fruition, and allows the access to the informative contents. The goal is to reconnect the museum to the surrounding area, and encourage the visitors to extend their visit including other sites. Visitors can customize their cultural path including sites that match their interests by style, age, or in a thematic mode. The route thus built will include road signs and travel times.

The application can be realized through commercial software for multimedia management of interactive touch tables, which enable to create multimedia applications including interactive maps based on background images with sensitive areas, (in our case displayed through the sites pictograms), and allow to connect to Google Maps for help on the road to be followed and the travel times.

A specific forum section will allow people to submit comments and photos about their experience, and to share it with other users creating an information channel that can be the starting point for new visitors in a virtuous circle of promotion of the site.

Additionally, within the museum, the same platform enables the hologram technology to bring virtually back inside the museum rooms objects found in the area, but currently preserved elsewhere, such as the famous statue of Venus of Sineussa, exhibited in the Archaeological Museum of Naples. The technology to achieve the hologram is rather simple: it consists in projecting through a holographic projector an image taken from different angles, which thus reproduces the effect of three-dimensionality and can be observed from any point of view. It is not a technology innovative in itself, but thanks to modern techniques for modeling three-dimensional objects and the improving of the projections quality, provides spectacular effects highly appreciated by the public.

Figure 1. The graphic interface of the interactive application for the cultural heritage of Mondragone. Source: work of degree thesis by the student Francesca Spina, supervisor Manuela Piscitelli

Virtual reconstructions of Mondragone's ancient sites through augmented reality will also allow a better understanding of the context to which the finds belong and where they can be virtually recaptured.

A further tool to make the public aware of the rich history and cultural tradition of Mondragone is the projection mapping. Every year, during the summer, various visits and cultural activities are organized attracting tourists and citizens. The most suitable to be enriched with additional contents has been identified in the "lumina in castro" event, organized annually in the early September. It allows the visit of the ancient ruins of Rocca Montis Dragonis to a group of participants accompanied by a guide. A part of the path is done on foot climbing on the slopes of the mountain in the evening, with the suggestive light of torches and lanterns. At the top of the mountain, characters in costume recall important historical events concerning the fortress, which for the occasion is fully illuminated. The projection of lights and images with the projection mapping technology on the rock walls could enrich the narration in a highly suggestive way, increasing the participation, and becoming a driving moment to attract the public to engage also in the other paths that have been mentioned.

Figure 2. Monuments selected for the cultural itinerary, represented by pictograms. Source: work of degree thesis by the student Francesca Spina, supervisor Manuela Piscitelli

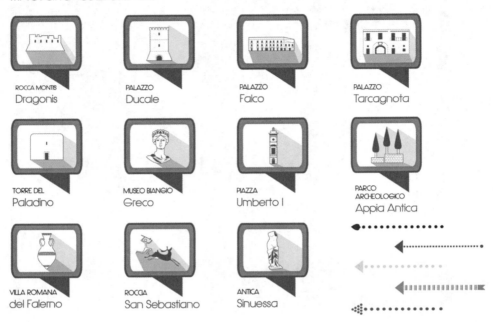

Itinerario CULTURALE

ROCCA MONTIS
Dragonis

PALAZZO
Ducale

PALAZZO
Falco

PALAZZO
Tarcagnota

TORRE DEL
Paladino

MUSEO BIANGIO
Greco

PIAZZA
Umberto I

PARCO
ARCHEOLOGICO
Appia Antica

VILLA ROMANA
del Falerno

ROCCA
San Sebastiano

ANTICA
Sinuessa

In addition, through the interactive platform, the video of the event may be accessible by other users, through the web or from the touch screens in the museum and the other sites. The sharing of images, comments, emotions in the specific forum section can be an opportunity to let others know the places visited, through the approach of the digital participatory storytelling.

FUTURE RESEARCH DIRECTIONS

The use of multimedia and interactive technologies for a better fruition of the cultural heritage is still little widespread in Italy. Most applications concern museums of a scientific nature, in some cases contemporary art museums, while rarely include the enjoyment of historical and archaeological museums and sites, which would benefit of it, in terms of communication and understanding from a wider audience.

Even with regard to exhibition spaces, new environments specially designed for participatory fruition by the public have been realized quite only for these types of

Figure 3. Monuments selected for the religious itinerary, represented by pictograms. Source: work of degree thesis by the student Francesca Spina, supervisor Manuela Piscitelli.=

Itinerario RELIGIOSO

museums. For example, the MAXXI, the National Museum of Arts of XXI Century in Rome, designed by Zaha Hadid, surpasses the idea of the traditional museum building through a highly articulated spatial and functional plan that visitors can cross through different and unexpected paths. The fruition is conceived since from the spatial design to be interactive, and to host not only exhibitions, but also live events, educational spaces, experimental productions. In the science field, the most innovative project of recent years in Italy is the Muse, Science Museum of Trento, designed by Renzo Piano as a new generation museum, featuring spaces that offer a flexible set-up and integration of events, temporary exhibitions, and educational workshops. These museums, conceived from the beginning in innovative terms, also have effective communication strategies both internal and external to the museum. The spaces that host historical and archaeological finds, instead, are usually historical buildings adapted or specially designed to the museum purpose in the past, when the exhibition criteria were very different from the present ones. Among the rare exceptions, there is the already mentioned MAV, the Virtual Archaeological Museum of Herculaneum, which is housed in an ex school building, that has been adapted thinking to the virtual and interactive contents that should have hosted. A future

Figure 4. Hologram of the statue of Venus of Sineussa in the Museum of Mondragone. Simulation. Source: work of degree thesis by the student Francesca Spina, supervisor Manuela Piscitelli

research direction of great interest can therefore address the changes needed to adapt the existing museum spaces for the new ways of interactive enjoyment. The same considerations can be applied to the cultural heritage. For example, should be useful to rethink the paths currently provided inside the archaeological sites, adapting them for an integrated use of the real space and the additional information provided by the augmented reality.

There is also a great fragmentation in the heritage communication. At present, there are no applications or systems that can reconnect the rich cultural heritage spread across the territory, allowing a global understanding. The development of applications to integrate the exhibits stored in the museums with the territory from which they come, as in the case study presented here, undoubtedly constitutes an innovative research direction and a useful support for knowledge. For this purpose, it is necessary to involve different professionals besides the museum staff, as research staff, communication experts, and cultural mediators.

Instead of aiming at the creation of great stereotyped events that are reproducible in other contexts, it would be useful promoting traditional festivals and events, that

Figure 5. Hologram of the castle of Montis Dragonis in the Museum of Mondragone. Simulation. Source: work of degree thesis by the student Francesca Spina, supervisor Manuela Piscitelli

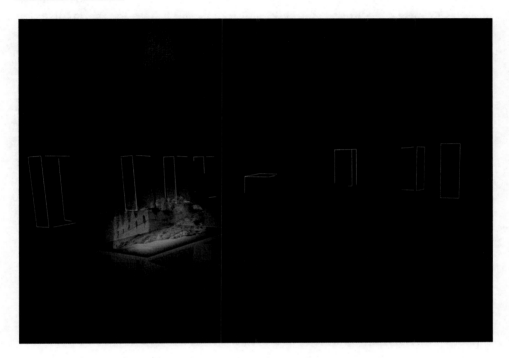

historically take place in many Italian little localities. These particular moments scheduled during the year should be integrated in the cultural offer. It should include the provision of supporting the traditional ways of the local festivals with the spectacular effects permitted by multimedia techniques to trace the history of the places (as the projection mapping or the augmented reality). Such events could represent a moment of great attraction, imposing the attention of the public on many small towns of great historical value but little known, in a perspective of sustainability of tourism, avoiding the concentration in a few key places with already too high numbers of visitors.

Future directions of research should also include a detailed analysis of the current and potential public, differentiated into homogeneous categories by age, interests, language, level of education and computerization, to meet their needs through a specific offer. Based on this kind of analysis, it would be possible to select, within the multiple and varied contents of which museums are rich, an appropriate use for each target identified, including the selection of the experiences to provide, and the language and communicative tool addressed to the different users. (De Biase & Valentino, 2016).

Besides the interactive products from the museum's contents, of which the author already discussed the utility, an additional tool of great help for the involvement of the public could be the realization of a digital open space. It would allow the creation, communication, and sharing of contents and information by the museum institution, and of real or virtual experiences, opinions and impressions by users. The advantages would be of various types. First, the user generated contents in text and multimedia format involving an active participation of the public, who at the same time stands as a user and a propagator of ideas and information. Second, the sharing of experiences, opinions and knowledge leads to the creation of a community of users with similar interests, creating a virtuous circle of promotion of cultural events. Finally, the dissemination of the museum image could be helpful in identifying the potential public, the most suitable communication channels, and the services to offer, expanding the number of users of cultural products. (Kolb, 2000).

CONCLUSION

Multimedia technologies, as well as distance learning supports, can be a valuable communication tool within the museum or sites to enhance the understanding of the exposed materials and to personalize the visit. A widespread use should stimulate the curiosity of visitors including younger generations, contributing to the knowledge and thus to the preservation of heritage. Globally there is an audience mainly composed of digital natives, but not only, which already makes a non-marginal use of digital media to get in touch with the world of art and culture. Analysis in the field has highlighted a preference of these users for cultural sites that offer a dynamic and interactive communication both external and internal to the museum.

On the other hand, however, the creation of a suitable language for the dissemination of collections is still not among the objectives of most of the Italian sites, where the professional figures employed in the museums have often been formed using traditional communication tools. It would therefore be useful to strengthen the research of new languages and cultural content. The final goal is to create a system with less "one way information" and greater "interactive storytelling".

The realization of the demo about the museum and the territory of Mondragone has shown how it is possible to make appear clear the link between the artwork and the geographical, physical, historical and cultural context where it was born. The adoption of similar applications in analogous contexts, and above all, the connection between the information about the different museums and cultural sites that today appears disorganized and fragmented in a unique interactive system, could open the horizon to a synoptic and organic understanding of cultural heritage.

The achievement of these objectives could have positive repercussions on many aspects: in the protection of heritage, the education of citizens, the sustainable development, and the creation of new professional fields in the cultural industry.

REFERENCES

Anceschi, G. (2005). Come si costruisce un'identità istituzionale. In M. Rossi (Ed.), *Oltre il logo. Nove progetti di comunicazione visiva per il Palazzo dei Pio a Carpi.* Carpi: APM edizioni.

Anholt, S. (2005). *Brand New Justice. How branding places and products can help the developing world* (revised edition). Elsevier.

Antinucci, F. (2014). *Comunicare nel museo*. Roma: Laterza.

Associazione Studi e Ricerche per il Mezzogiorno. (2010). *Mezzogiorno e beni culturali. Caratteristiche, potenzialità e policy per una loro efficace valorizzazione.* Napoli: Cuzzolin.

Augé, M. (2004). *Rovine e macerie. Il senso del tempo.* Torino: Bollati Boringhieri.

Ciotti, F., & Roncaglia, G. (2000). *Il Mondo digitale*. Roma, Bari: Laterza.

De Biase, L., & Valentino, P. A. (Eds.). (2016). *Socialmuseums. Social media e cultura, tra post e tweet.* Milano: SilvanaEditoriale.

Federculture, F. (2014). *Cultura & turismo. Locomotiva del paese.* Febbraio 2014.

Greco, B. (1927). *Storia di Mondragone*. Napoli: Giannini.

Henrion, F. H. K., & Parking, A. (1976). *Design coordination and corporate image.* London: Studio Vista.

Hughes, P. (2001). Making science 'Family fun': The fetish of the interactive exhibit. *Museum Management and Curatorship, 19*(2), 2001. doi:10.1080/09647770100501902

ICOM. (2004). *ICOM Code of Professional Ethics, adopted in Buenos Aires in 1986, renamed ICOM Code of Ethics for Museums in Barcelona in 2001, and then revised in Seoul in 2004.* Author.

ICOMOS. (2008). *ICOMOS Charter for the interpretation and presentation of cultural heritage sites called Ename Charter.* Prepared under the auspices of the Scientific Committee of ICOMOS on Interpretation and Presentation of Heritage Sites (April 10, 2007). Ratified by the 16th General Assembly of ICOMOS, Quebec (Canada), 4 October 2008.

Kolb, B. M. (2000). *Marketing cultural organizations: New strategies for attracting audiences to classical music, dance, museums, theatre and opera.* Dublin: Oak Tree Press.

Medri, M., & Canonici, T. (2010). L'immagine ricostruttiva nei media: una indagine nei musei archeologici italiani. *Virtual Arcaeology Review, 1*. doi:10.4995/var.2010.5134

Pastore, A., & Bonetti, E. (2006). Il brand management del territorio. *Sinergie, Rapporti di Ricerca, 23*.

Pennella, G., & Trimarchi, M. (Eds.). (1993). *Stato e mercato nel settore culturale.* Bologna: Il Mulino.

Prentice, R. (1994). Perceptual Deterrents to Visiting Museums and Other Heritage Attractions. *Museum Management and Curatorship*, *13*(3), 1994. doi:10.1080/09647779409515408

Quatrèmere de Quincy. (1815). *Considérations morales sur la destination des ouvrages de l'art, ou de l'influence de leur emploi sur le génie et le goût de ceux qui les produisent ou qui les jugent.* Author.

Rheingold, H. (2003). *Smart mobs.* Milano: Raffaello Cortina Editore.

Ribaldi, C. (2005). *Il nuovo museo. Origini e percorsi.* Milano: Il Saggiatore.

Ricci, A. (1996). *I mali dell'abbondanza. Considerazioni impolitiche sui beni culturali.* Roma: Lithos.

Scaltritti, M. (Ed.). (2012). *Comunicare i beni archeologici.* Milano: FrancoAngeli.

Serota, N. (2009). *The Museum of the 21st Century.* London School of Economics.

Settis, S. (1981). Introduzione. In N. Himmelmann (Ed.), *Utopia del passato. Archeologia e cultura moderna.* Bari: De Donato.

Stack, J. (2010). *Tate Online Strategy 2010–12.* Retrieved from http://www.tate.org.uk/research/publications/tate-papers/13/tate-online-strategy-2010-12

Stack, J. (2013). *Tate Digital Strategy 2013–15: Digital as a Dimension of Everything*. Retrieved from http://www.tate.org.uk/research/publications/tate-papers/19/tate-digital-strategy-2013-15-digital-as-a-dimension-of-everything

Urry, J. (1995). *Lo sguardo del turista*. Roma: Seam.

KEY TERMS AND DEFINITIONS

Augmented Reality: A view of a real environment augmented by computer generated information, such as graphic, texts, virtual reconstructions.

Digital Storytelling: A narration made with digital instruments (web apps, web ware). It consists in organizing selected contents in a coherent system based on a narrative structure, so that a story is composed of multiple elements of various formats (video, audio, images, texts, maps, etc.).

Hologram: A photographic recording used to display a three-dimensional image of an object.

Interactivity: With regard to the communication between a human and an artifact, interactivity refers to the capacity of the artifact to react at a human behavior.

Multimedia: A content composed by different media, such as texts, videos, images, audio, maps, usually organized in an interactive mode.

Projection Mapping: Also called video mapping. A technology used to turn object, buildings, and environments into a surface for video projections.

QR Code: A bi-dimensional graphic code used to create a link through a tablet or a smartphone to related information on the web.

Chapter 5

Thinking Art in the Technological World:
An Approach to Digital Media Art Creation

Henrique Silva
Escola Superior Gallaecia University (ESG), Portugal

Emília Simão
Escola Superior Gallaecia University (ESG), Portugal

ABSTRACT

In this chapter, the authors discuss the use of digital media in the creation of digital art, questioning the evolution of the relationship between technology and concept in communication through art. The intersection of new media and digital art have been opening interesting and seductive new horizons and in parallel, the concept, the understanding, the legitimacy of artistic creation, the role of the artist and the role of the spectator are also redefined. Based on two experimental works of the artist Henrique Silva, the authors analyze and reflect on the relationship of technology, art and virtuality, focusing on concepts like experience, sensory, immersion, communication and interaction in artworks created through digital media.

INTRODUCTION

The diversity of the latest contemporary artistic forms has been (almost) rendering outdated some arts like sculpture, painting, drawing, music or literature, essentially those which remain within the traditional canons of creativity, creation, tools, techniques, exposition, dissemination and relation with the public.

DOI: 10.4018/978-1-5225-5696-1.ch005

In the field of digital and computational we are expose to massive stimulations that transposes the most basic senses and feelings. In the digital society, the communication as process gained a new breadth as well the artistic manifestations, as powerful forms of communication. Art is contaminated (and simultaneously contaminates) and by digital tools, concepts and practices and in turn, end up contaminating the public that is no longer passive, instead he interacts, participate sometimes even integrates the process. Digital art promotes immediate and horizontal sensations - contrary to the verticality of the so-called traditional arts – and the changes are increasingly evident.

Nowadays, digital literacy influences the assimilation of the world around us - including art - in this information society where digital technologies have unprecedented developments. However, the ability to read and interpret these new artistic manifestations and its concepts is also dependent on each background, working as *self made* dictionary to interpret and classify the relations between subjects, objects and its legitimacy as creators and artworks, respectively.

Our memory functions can be metaphorical understood as a big computer that reacts based on data stored throughout life and experiences. This data and its respective decoded process activate the imagination and the creativity itself and can delineate the deductive capacities of each.

People also understand what surround them according to cultural values, creeds and traditions but interpretations are not only related to the influences received from the outside, they are also affected by inner experiences, feelings and experiences with specific techniques, aesthetics and technologies – maybe the *alpha tools* of digital media art creation.

In the communication process, the languages are determinant as well the participants and their interpretations (not excluding of course, the remaining elements of any communicative process). Focusing on the participant, the degree of culture or the knowledge about the subject can be determinant in understanding and decoding information. Regardless of whether information is transmitted through sounds, gestures or perceptible clues, the messages can be decodable in the first place based on background and other variables, as we already mentioned, but it doesn´t mean those messages will influence the public as receiver. These experiences are especially interesting when it comes to communicate through a work of art. Contrary to what one might think, a high cultural level person is not necessarily able to better read an object and its message, harmonize with the speech of the artist, understanding the technological implications or the work of art itself better than a lower cultural level person, especially when there is a physical interaction. Technical skills or higher sensory can be more important than academic level or education? Based on these more recent intersections between art and digital technologies what is communicating, the artist, the object, the environment or the media?

It seems that we have entered a new artistic paradigm, emerging from the technological society. Conceptions as interaction, immersion and illusion are no longer theories and practices of engineering or digital worlds instead they have already been absorbed by the social sciences and are frequent in digital art, especially when real and virtual intersects. We paradoxically live between the present and the future, where the future seems to be more close than the effectiveness of the presence and the difficulty to establish references and concepts tend to be diluted between the multiple analysis and reflections inter-influencing each other – each artist, each artwork, each public. Nevertheless, throughout this chapter, we will try to make some contribution based essentially in literature review articulated with *a/r/tography* (Irwin, 2009) direct observation and participant observation on the long artistic practice of Henrique Silva [1] (co-author), experimental artworks and artistic research: The first work *Hologram 360° 3D,* explores the reality sought between the introspection of the characters for a *collective blossoming.* This expression arises as synonym of the capacity of human connection beyond the individualism that characterizes our current society through the duality between the real performance in the tangible world and its virtualization in the illusory three-dimensionality of the hologram (See Figure 1 - *Hologram 360° 3D*). The second work "Interatividade Imersível" (in english *Immersive Interactivity*) put forward a sensorial experience

Figure 1. Hologram 360° 3D, Henrique Silva 2017

through the union of a tangible object – a bicycle - and its digital representation on a ride between the real, the ephemeral, the illusion and the immaterial. This second artwork is an interactive piece with visuals activated on a screen according to the movements of the pedals (See Figure 2 - *Interatividade Imersível*). In both cases the visuals themes for these interactive installations at *Escola Superior Gallaecia University,* Portugal.

THEORETICAL FRAMEWORK

Between Media and Society

Digital age can be frightful and simultaneously engaging and alienating. We can travel in physical and mental ways like it was never possible before and this technological is running us to other ways of living and experiencing the world. There are disagreements between the new realm of digital experiences and the physical experience of sitting at the computer. The rise of processes technological production such as 3D printing or generative design has been accelerating the discussions about the contamination between digital formats and tangible physical formats. However, if the real and the virtual have long been antagonistic realities, they are no longer, we live in communion with new medias and technology, we complete us with extensions

Figure 2. Interatividade Imersível, Henrique Silva 2017

to improve our experiences and our existence in physical and comfort aspects but also in personal and emotional levels (Simão et al., 2015).

Postmodern society needs to understand everything but are also living the era of subjective readings. An object can be perceived through various senses and physical and virtual boundaries are interweaved, as well as in art. With new technologies, objects and narratives gained the ability to generate new languages. From the cinema or the first optical image to the illusion of movement, from web 1.0 to web 3.0, from unilateral communication to new media and immersive environments, are digital the new god (or new evil)?

Following Lucia Santaella approaches on this field, from pottery and sculpture of the Greek world and the wonderful oil paintings of the Renaissance to photography in the 19th century, all the artists inherited the means and techniques of his ancestors, though they has also found new possibilities from the technological, scientific, artistic and cultural development of each time (Santaella, 2003). Although the media and its evolution are historical landmarks, they do not deplete themselves. It is the artist's role to reinvent and give a new body to the meanings and languages ransomed of the past, while exploring the *still brutal resistance of the materials and means of his own time* (Santaella, 2003: 152). Throughout the history, many transitions marked the implementation of new forms of producing languages and new means of communication. At an early stage the new media stood out among the older media then, these new media were taken by artists and becoming objects of research and experimentation, but at some point, the age of convergence begins to lighten this separation between means and communication techniques (Jenkins, 2006). On other hand, like Marshall McLuhan (1967) once said in his revolutionary essay *Understanding Media: the extensions of man*, the media really became the message itself. Taking for example the artist Andy Warhol[2] (1928-1987), the forerunner of the appropriation of the *media technologies*, he created parallel languages that overcame the mere entertainment and transfigure the reality that cinema intends to display in a subjective pictorial language, he communicated without narration, which lead to transcendental readings.

The study of new media and its languages has been generating attentiveness among academic research on communication, information science, technology, anthropology, philosophy, arts and other knowledge areas. From political, educational, commercial, ideological, cultural to all the actual personal and social spheres, the use of digital media is omnipresent. Media are even powerful opinion makers, mind makers e more and more inhibitors of personality, according with Noam Chomsky theories of media mind manipulation (Chomsky, 2002). Media are transversal, multidisciplinary and multitask insofar as they are simultaneously communication means and communications tools.

Between Art and Experience

In the artistic field, the initial enthusiasm on new digital instruments gave rise to some questions like what kind of knowledge is needed in digital art creations, what skills are eventually necessary and who have artistic legitimacy to create or produce digital art? The digital media art creators are artists, programmers, computer engineers or all in one? From the effective and material objects to its virtual representation entirely digitally conceived there is a legitimately quantitative leap, although, there are evident connections between both worlds. The creation, manipulation and production of objects and artworks cross the domain of virtual and computational languages and allow a deep connection between the digital and the physical, essentially through interactivity. Not only digital literacy but also digital skills beyond the user's optics are crucial to this new generation of media artists.

The concept of digital medium-art is the result of the evolution not only of aesthetic and artistic movements but also of technology and science. We can also perceive digital media art as forms of plastic expressions that use technological resources, or artistic objects created through digital or computational technologies. In digital media art, the point is not only the final piece but also the process of the digital intervention in the artwork in the content, support, aesthetic dimensions, concept, matter and diffusion.

In this context, technology is taken as a tool and also as a creative way to express and produce contemporary art, but is obviously not restricted to the artistic creation through medias like television or Internet. Digital media art includes the experiences of dialogue, sharing, collaboration and creation of artistic interventions in the media, thus becoming an art of its own while expressing sensibility and knowledge of the current man (Machado, 2010). Digital mediation is like having a new skin, we are undeniably a being of technical mediation and in order to interact with the world he creates artificial ways to invent new senses, interactions and environments, this is the new society (Domingues, 2010).

We must not forget that we do not live in an entirely digital, virtual, or merely material world. Most of what surrounds us (our bodies, our houses, the chair we sit, the car we drive) are and will remain material, at least in a near future. The computers, smartphones, tablets, televisions, projector, and a long list of different sorts of electronic devices involves software but also hardware, so the media we use to access to and create digital artifacts are still in part, material (Stallabrass, 1997). On other side, for several centuries, societies have been influenced by religion and the religion is far from being a material reality, it is more a set of immaterial ideas and beliefs. Considering that, we can assume that material and immaterial are combined and complement each other, both in the past and in the present (Miller, 2015).

Since the emerging artistic vanguards of the 60s (the conceptual art, the happenings, the *Fluxus Group*[3], the performance, the land art, the pop art, the video art, and other contemporary artistic tendencies), technological, audiovisual and more recently multimedia languages have been present and crucial within the diversity of artistic exploration. The artistic creation through digital means can be passionate and revolutionary, essentially when exploring virtual concepts and digital creation also came to rescue and redefine previous practices and visions about the artistic tooling.

After the 90s, with the advent of digital media we also faced a growing development in the research of new concepts that can meet the specificities of the artistic practices in the digital era. In the media art universe, we have been also faced with designations such as *digital art, interactive art, net art, glitch art, immersive art* and others, hereafter it will be necessary to understand where these concepts or designations differ, cross or complement. Being art a social practice, what kinds of relations are created between the artists, the artworks and the publics? Artists have been striving for complex applications of technology in media arts, creating and shaping worlds throw out the use of technology to appeal to *multisensory* experiences. With the creation of environments in virtual reality, the artist is delivering to the audience more than just interaction he is shifting their perception of time and space (Grau, 2003). By combining image, sound, time and space, digital artworks have enabled the artist to more efficiently bring the public into his own reality, delivering not just a sensory experience, but more effectively communicating his narrative (O´Sullivan, 2001).

Besides the mental interaction, there is a precondition for the reception and assimilation of art, in general. For example, some works in the digital and computational art are interactive and requires action form the public. The communication occurs in a more effective level and beyond the emitter and the receiver, there is a mutant message that depends on that interaction. Interact with an artwork can give the impression that we are a part of it and in some cases, that we belong in. This interaction can be more or less controlled and sometimes dialogue with the work is not so random, instead the public is following a set of rules, structures and codes, pre-established by the artist, translated into a programming language and embedded in hardware-software configurations.

Is the relation between the audience and the artwork dependent upon an audience's pre-concept? The effectiveness of the immersion it is as complex as human interactions, and it rests only on the audience's senses. By switching the sense of reality and the audience's perception, immersive art is transforming the audience itself (Douglas & Hargadon, 2000). The conscious decisions made by the user, physically or perceptually, cause the physical engagement for the embodied experience, allowing the user to explore and engage in the artwork (Kwastek, 2009).

Between Interaction and Immersion

Digital media world is a whole new universe where *organic senses* seems to give way to *mental senses* through illusion, surrounding vision and immersive experiences capable of modify concepts and sensations of what is real and what is unreal. Some immersive experiences allowed by the digital tools enable to create in the viewers or participants the illusion of being inside the work of art, being part of it. In interactive artworks, the public is even able to change the objects or environments through gestures, actions and decisions. When immersed, they are confronted with a set of sensations that allows experiencing the space and time inside the narrative of the artistic object, resulting in both illusory and sensorial states. Immersion is more effective when the illusion is intense and illusorily real as possible, and digital technologies have a key role creating these possibilities. Some authors compare the interaction with digital art to game playing, where interpretations are intimately connected to the user/viewer context that must have certain skills and a preconceptual disposition to engage in a proposed interaction (Ermi & Mäyrä, 2005).

Interactive art can be an individually created or selected configuration, presented to mediate an idea, motivate a reflection or stimulate an action. Many works of interactive media art are not represented for the contemplation, they are rather systems that allow individual exploration of pre-produced situations, enabling manipulation of processes that generate outcomes (Kwastek, 2009). The multidisciplinary emerging field human-computer interaction tells the interaction with digital objects happens in an increasingly fluid and integrated way. More than substitutions, interfaces are extensions of our bodies (Shneiderman, 1996), they integrate us, that´s why we can consider the public as being a part of the artwork. From the *instrument body* to the *mutilated body* to the *spectacle body* (Devillard, 2002), there have been several conceptual appropriations of the subject, today we can point the interface body. In interactive art, we can have the digital object as medium – for example in an artwork with digital sensors – but we can place the medium onus on public – when the body is the interface. Immersive art also proposes more than contemplation, it defies the user to be part of the artwork by immersing itself within the piece using their body as an interface (Mitchell, 2010). By being present in both physical space and cyberspace, the artist is asking to the audience to activate a combination of senses and to act and perceive in the virtual world as in the real world (Biocca, 1997). We can now easily assume that the audience must have an active role on the building of the artwork since its construction and effectiveness depends upon the audience's predisposition (Grau, 2002). Immersion is characterized by immateriality, deterritorialization, and disembodiment (Aretio, 2007). In what way does the immersion works as a narrative, and how is the narrative established? The identification of this type of narrative's construction is investigated, as well as the tools for the communication between the audience and artwork. And as the social integration for the human kind is becoming more and more cyber-immersive, a sensorimotor interface into everyday communication is also becoming mandatory. Online social networking is striving for immersion - why would the arts' communication be any different? Using the body as an interface, the user is receiving the information in an immersive way, having the artist communicating to the user's whole body. In what way did this affect our perception of the dialogue between audience and artwork shifted? The physical and emotional experience has always been a tool for the dialogue between the artist and his public - what has changed with immersive art? If we assume that the effectiveness and the aesthetics of immersive art lays on the experience itself, then we should analyse the results on the user's perception. Knowing that the artwork's effectiveness depends on its *polysensoriality*, its role in artistic paradigms is also analysed (O'Sullivan, 2001). By bringing the user to the construction of the narrative, the artist initiates a process of collaboration. Where did this need for a tighter relation arise? In order to better understand the established relation a study of existing written material on the subject is proposed. By analysing and comparing the latest immersive artworks, a connection between the construction and deconstruction of narratives in virtual ambient will be established. The use of virtual and augmented reality will also be analysed, constructing a comprehension of mediums in order to ascertain possibilities. The effectiveness of immersion does not rely on the proposed narrative, neither on the graphics: it solely relies on the user. The main tool for immersive art is neither virtual reality nor augmented reality: it is the human body acting like an interface. Sensory engagement and human perception are the keys to the understanding of immersive art, and the artwork lives on the audience experience itself. The audience is asked to make decisions, to react, revelling effects and consequences thus allowing a larger involvement. Immersion is not only dependent on the technological tools, it also depends on the mood of the audience to engage, their pre-conception of the artwork, the surroundings in which they experience it and finally, the audience's cognitive, physical and emotional traits.

Digital art artifacts like digital and computer art exploit interactivity, information and communicational expressiveness with great potential and are frequently inducers of artistic and cultural action-intervention. In their deepest essence, more than artifacts to be passively appreciated, they are naturally virtual, interactive or immersive objects, leading the public on a journey of polysemy and aesthetic contemplation (Marcos, 2012).

THE ARTIFACTS

Artists have always been researchers picking through different fields of science in order to build their creations. Technological tools and web open-source contents have brought an easy way to share knowledge, bringing artists into the fields that were so out of reach not so long ago. Artists became more aware of the potential of merging art and technology, building a new kind of new media artists with multidisciplinary backgrounds (Seo, 2015).

The *Hologram 360° 3D* and *Interactividade Imersível – Immersive Interactivity* are concrete examples of this connection between artistic traditional skills and more technical *artengineer* skills. As we could observe and now based on our own reflexions the general concept that prevails over the production in digital media art is based on the need to create interaction. The public is no longer a spectator but an actor with active participation in the artwork, and in some cases is even the responsible for the process: without the public interaction some artworks doesn´t work. The dialogue between a media art installation and the public becomes richer and more engaging in the cases where there is a close relationship between them. This relationship is created by the effectiveness of interactivity in order to produce a closeness that allows a complete interpretation and in some cases immersion by the spectator/actor.

In these art experiences, viewers and creator alternate frequently their roles considering that the public can be the decoder of the message of the work and simultaneously responsible for its performance. *Hologram 360° 3D* is media art installation is basically a hologram that pretends to create the illusion of a three-dimensional theater scene, placing the viewer in a theater room to move (physically) around actors, seeing their faces and replacing all the audience surrounding the scene, such as in a real theater. Here we must distinguish between the effect caused by the physical content and the content of the hologram itself, even though this content is only valid if containing a dialog with messages able to activate the deductive capacity of the viewer. New technologies should be channeled towards collective actions to motivate young people to be positive collectivist, instead of being negatively competitive. In this case, this work turns out to be a metaphor on young people's enthusiasm for new technologies, existential dilemmas and illusory relationships often taken to extremes. Illusion is the main concept - as the message - and the medium - as the technique for the hologram. Holograms are 3D images obtained from the projection of light on two-dimensional figures formed through the process of holography. In a generic definition, the holography consists in a three-dimensional image simulation technique that basically uses the reflection in lenses placed at a 45° angle of projected images through a screen. The holography technique was developed in theory in 1948, but it was only applied in practice in 1960, after the invention of laser technology. However, in the last decade the hologram has gained popularity in the arts by the illusory effect of creating *ghost images* in the air apparently with no support. With the holography technique, artists like Pierrik Sorin have been creating authentic illusory spaces of representation, combining the games of optical illusion with video art and animated dioramas (for example, interesting artifacts like the *Optical Theater*). The optical theater is based on the *Praxinoscope Theater* created by Émile Reynaud in 1879, and later used to animate characters of the first 2D animated films (Clee, 2005). This technique gives the illusion of movement of the characters and is basically created within a fixed scenario through the principle of optical compensation.

In some experiences with *Hologram 360°-3D* we observed diversity in the participants involved, principally on their origin (Portuguese, Brazilian and Spanish people) ages and social credentials. Derived from this punctual observations we could confirmed the relation with the artwork is conditioned or empowered due to the previous familiarization with technological and virtual experiences. We also verify that educational background influences as well since the majority of the intervening public were students and professors of Fine Arts and Multimedia from *Escola Superior Gallaecia* University, in Portugal. On other hand, it was supposed that most of them have some background on programs and concepts of media application in the artistic areas, contrary to the general public who had contact with the work while exposed and have different experiences.

The set designer Acácio de Carvalho[4] directed the content of the hologram - a narrative based on a welcoming dance to the flowering of spring. This deep dance occurred in a completely black scenario with actors also dressed in black wearing white masks and gloves. The white elements created the movements essentially hand movements belonged to the four faces. This artifact was built in a small booth with four led projectors directed to the center of the space completely black, and four 4 Wi-Fi-4K cameras on all sides. For the display of the hologram, it was made a black cube of 60 x 60 cm with a video screen inside. Inside this cube was a 2 mm glass pyramid where the four images of the screen were reflected creating the illusion of a 360° 3D image in suspension.

Also based in direct observations of several public experiences with *Interactividade Imersível – Immersive Interactivity,* we explored principally the physical and virtual locomotion as the basis of an interactive installation. In this installation there a clear interaction between *effective* reality and virtual reallity where the public has a fundamental role. In virtual reality experience there are induce cognitive effects associated with the feeling of being immersed in a computer-generated environment. This produces simultaneous sensorial stimuli directed to vision but also to hearing and touch, simulating in particular the sensation of movement (Ribeiro, 2012). In a more technological definition, virtual reality allows users to be convinced that they

Figure 3. Hologram pyramid, work in progress, 360° 3D, Henrique Silva, 2017

Figure 4. Hologram Box, Henrique Silva, 2017

are in an alternative space different from their own, replacing the sensory input with information produced by a computer (Heim, 1993). In this case, the responsibles for the input are the participant-spectators movements processed by sensors. The material artifact is an exercise bike with a television screen, triggered with by the action of the participant-spectator and processed with *Arduino* nano sensors[5] . When cycling, a virtual route is activated through the some spaces of *Escola Superior Gallaecia University* (where there is a bicycle fixed to the floor).The spectator is in the real place and without moving physically he can circulate around several spaces just by pedaling the bike. The experiences have different levels due the interaction of the participants-spectators and the images on the screen are also variable. The intensity of interaction, namely the strength of pedal movements will dictate the variety of images visible in the screen.The bicycle works as a medium between the man and the machine, the movement and the behavior of the artifact, the movement of the participant-spectator and what he is able to see. The experiences can sometimes be similar but in most cases observed, experiences were different since they vary according the movements. This artifact explores the human transfiguration processed through the consumption of its own energy, consisting in a virtual transposition to the screen. This transpositions place the participant-spectator in a virtual scenario shared with a representation, also virtual, of some places of the outer space. The intention and the movement are certainly the most determinant variables of the process.

We emphatyze the non-linear use of the equipments composing this work, that goes beyond the functions predicted by they manufacturers. A bicycle and a TV screen has not originally intended to be presented in art galleries nor to be principal components of artistic installations. The specific purpose of things can refer us to unexpected uses and realities, establishing unexpected contacts with subjective objectivities of the so-called real reality.

The Legible City of Jeffrey Shaw (1944)[6] is a revolutionary interactive art installation, also consisting in riding a bicycle through a simulated representation of a city. This artwork is composed by computer-generated with three-dimensional landscapes (Shaw, 2017) and explores the interaction between physical and virtual locomotion, having several similarities with Henrique Silva´s *Interactividade Imersível.*

CONCLUSION

Art pieces are symbolic objects that stimulates emotions and senses, they are displayed by physical materials combining patterns to produce aesthetic compositions. Digital art objects do not differ so much from conventional, except by the use of computers and computer-based artifacts that manipulate digitally coded information and opens

Figure 5. Work in progress, Interatividade Imersível, Henrique Silva

more possibilities in interaction, virtualization and manipulation of information (Marcos, 2009). The definition of media art digital creation is not consensual between artists, art experts and artistic researchers nor the definition of media art works (or projects, or installations, or pieces, or artifacts - an evidence not only of the plurality of styles within the scope of media art but also of the different forms artists fit in both technical and conceptual terms). Digital media art can still be considered an emerging artistic practice and the debates around definitions and positions remain very dynamic. The same happen with the question of conceptualization that suddenly became a liquid definition. Sometimes, the lack of concept is the concept itself. We believe only time will give place to concretes and consensual definitions about the status of objects as art creations, their underlying concepts, the artistic typologies and even the legitimacy of the artists.

In order to contribute to this quest, through teaching, artistic practice and research we continue to observe, analyze and search for new evidences, rules of composition and patterns of artistic creation. The artifacts mentioned on this chapter are a part of a complex path of artistic research on forms, contents, concepts and public interactions, but there are other works produced by the co-author Henrique Silva that fits on this mission: "A catedral do ego" - *The Cathedral of the Ego* - (2013) – is an exploration of (de)mystification of *the being* and its own ego; "O homem som" | *The sound man* (2012) – is an unobstructed speech of complexes of solitude and guilty, but there are more. The common point of all these works is the exploitation society´s anguishes, the social relationships and the human being trough different languages where digital technology is the pivotal element.

Everything has becoming more fast and vague in present technological age, information is more and more ubiquitous, media are converging and publics are increasingly demanding and participatory. Digital media art, as multidisciplinary and collaborative creation, has enable to explore, through the creation of open and collaborative works, the exchange of knowledge and sharing of experiences among students, teachers from different scientific areas, researchers and professionals. Artworks use to be the result from the relation between forms and contents, this relation will define the perception of the viewer and this perception is created by experience, background and/or predisposition. Assimilate, interpret or interact with digital media works also requires a combination of these variables where digital literacy - or lack thereof – is also determinant. With the development of digital technologies and by inheritance, the technical competences of artists, media art is also replying to new challenges. The roles of the artists and the publics are constantly changing and the artworks are creating news forms of creation, interpretation and participation/interaction. Thus, understand the role of digital and computational media in artistic creation is important, as well the role of the publics in the whole process. Creaton, conceptualization, research and artistic pratice may seem a paradoxal combination but it can lead to serious reflexions about the way we communicate. We´ve been living between dialogues, shapes, concepts, values and dogmas once acquired as being reality, but what is reality anyway? Following Gilles Deleuze, maybe reality is only a result of our perceptions, be it real and sustained in objects, or virtual and sustained in images (Deleuze & Parnet, 2004).

Where does the human being end beside rampant consumerism, slogans and corporations? Maybe we all are experiencing a false sense of well-being or a new one, as a consequence of the realization of technological society. If on one hand everything seems relativized, on the other everything appears overvalued: times are really changing, the reality is changing, man is changing.

The evolution of man, its techniques, technologies and communication rituals are avowedly inseparable and by inheritance, the arts do not outflow. The artworks/artifacts where we have based our reflexions have a *partial virtual* component, since they share physical/organic reality but there are many artists who already place their works entirely in virtual contexts. In this cases the notion of immersion and the immersive experience intensifies since when totally devoid of the physical world, its common to reach higher levels of abstraction. The virtual reality is no longer a slogan in the world of technology, it is (the next) great platform for all artists to show their innovations. And while VR platforms take some time to become a reality for everyone, there are those who are so ahead of everyone in creating art in virtual reality (Sharma et al., 2018).

Today´s society and all its components having a technological and a human side that complement, influence and prolong each other (Myeung-Sook, 2001). Digital media art prolongs the human experience and concepts like unconscious, irrational, illusory, immersive and virtual can act together on digital media art but more than explore empirical definitions form other authors, media art artists will always need to firm intellectual and methodological work, observing, comparing and reflecting. We believe that is the more profitable way for an *artcademic* journey.

Fine arts conceptualizes ideas, fantasies and phantasms of its authors
in a parallel reality expressing proposals that oblige the spectator
to penetrate in a language where there is neither dictionary
nor translation, just thoughts suggesting
other worlds and other experiences.
In my journey in the so-called media arts I try to transfigure daily realities
from images retained in memory and remake them, plastically,
in the utopia that is still possible in this context,
beyond the weight of an increasingly
materialistic and xenophobic world,
without philosophical values and without mercy.
Henrique Silva, August 2011

REFERENCES

Aretio, L. (2007). *De la educación a distancia a la educación virtual.* Barcelona: *Ariel.* (in Spanish)

Biocca, F. (1997). *The Cyborg's Dilemma: Progressive Embodiment in Virtual Environments.* International Cognitive Technology Conference. Retrieved February 20, 2017, from https://onlinelibrary.wiley.com/doi/full/10.1111/j.1083-6101.1997.tb00070.x

Chomsky, N. (2002). *Understanding Power.* New York: The New Press.

Clee, P. (2005). *Before Hollywood, from shadow play to the silver screen.* New York: Clarion Books.

Deleuze, G. (1987). Qu'est-ce que l'acte de création? Paris: Conference. (in French)

Douglas, Y., & Hargadon, A. (2000). *The Pleasure Principle: Immersion, Engagement, Flow.* Retrieved December 15, 2017, from ftp://ftp.cse.buffalo.edu/users/azhang/disc/disc01/cd1/out/papers/hypertext/p153-douglas.pdf

Ermi, L., & Mäyrä, F. (2005). *Fundamental Components of the Gameplay experience: Analysing immersion.* Retrieved May 2018, from http://citeseerx.ist.psu.edu/viewdoc/download?doi=10.1.1.103.6702&rep=rep1&type=pdf

Grau, O. (2003). *Virtual Art: from illusion to immersion.* MIT Press.

Heim, M. (1993). *The metaphysics of Virtual Reality.* New York: Oxford Press University.

Irwin, R. (2009). A/r/tography: A metonymic métissage. In R. L. Irwin & A. de Cosson (Eds.), *A/r/tography: Rendering self through arts-based living inquiry.* Vancouver, Canada: Pacific Educational Press.

Jenkins, H. (2006). *Convergence Culture: where old and new media collide.* NYU Press.

Kwastek, K. (2009). Embodiment and Instrumentality. *Proceedings of the Digital Arts and Culture Conference: After Media, embodiment and context.* Retrieved December 21, 2017 from https://escholarship.org/uc/item/0zg3t13v

Machado, A. (2002). Arte e mídias: aproximações e distinções. *Galáxias, 4*, 19-32. Retrieved October 11, 2017, from https://alldocs.net/philosophy-of-money.html?utm_source=ecoacoes-uma-instalacao-de-media-arte

Marcos, A. (2012), Instanciando mecanismos de a/r/tografia no processo de criação em arte digital/computacional. Invisivilidades. Revista ibero-americana de pesquisa em educação, cultura e artes, 3, 138-145.

Marcos, A., Branco, P., & Carvalho, J. (2009). The computer médium in digital art's creative process. In J. Braman & G. Vicenti (Eds.), *Handbook of Research on Computational Arts and Creative Informatics.* IGI Publishing. doi:10.4018/978-1-60566-352-4.ch001

Miller, D. (2015). *Technology and human attainment. Postdigital Artisans. Craftmanship with a new aesthetic in fashion, art, design and architecture.* Amsterdam: Frame Publishers.

Mitchell, B. (2019). *The Immersive Artistic Experience and the Exploitation of Space.* CAT London Conference. Retrieved February 10, 2018 from https://www.bcs.org/upload/pdf/ewic_ca10_s3paper2.pdf

O'Sullivan, S. (2001). The aesthetics of affect, thinking art beyond representation. *Angelaki, Journal of the theoretical humanities, 6*(3), 125-135. Retrieved May 13, 2018, from https://simonosullivan.net/articles/aesthetics-of-affect.pdf

Ribeiro, N. (2012). Multimédia e tecnologias interactivas (5th ed.). Lisboa: FCA Editora Informática.

Santaella, L. (2003). *Culturas e artes do pós-humano. Da cultura das mídias à cibercultura.* Paulus Editora.

Seo, J. (2015). Aesthetics of Immersion in Interactive Immersive Installation: Phenomenological Case Study. *Proceedings of the 21st International Symposium on Electronic Art.* Retrieved May, 13, 2018 from http://isea2015.org/proceeding/submissions/ISEA2015_submission_237.pdf

Sharma, A., Bajpai, P., Singh, S., & Khatter, K. (2018). Virtual Reality: Blessings and Risk Assessment. *Indian Journal of Science and Technology, 11*(May), 2–20. Retrieved from http://www.indjst.org/index.php/indjst/article/view/112577/87304

Shaw, J. (2017). *Jeffrey Shaw Compendium.* Retrieved January 11, 2017, from http://www.jeffreyshawcompendium.com/

Shneiderman, B. (1996). *The Eyes Have It: A Task by Data Type Taxonomy for Information Visualizations.* Retrieved December, 22, 2014, from ftp://ftp.cs.umd.edu/pub/hcil/Reports-Abstracts-Bibliography/96-13html/96-13.html

Silva, H. (2015). *O homem, a obra e o pensamento de Henrique Silva: a intemporalidade ou a temporalidade da obra de arte numa perspectiva polissémica (cosmológica, moral e técnica)* (PhD thesis). Retrieved February 21, 2018, from http://hdl.handle.net/10400.2/5336

Simão, E., Silva, A., & Magalhães, S. (2015). Psychedelic Trance on the Web: Exploring digital parties at Second Life. In *Exploring Psychedelic Trance and Electronic Dance Music in Modern Culture.* Hershey, PA: IGI Global. doi:10.4018/978-1-4666-8665-6.ch005

Stallabrass, J. (1997). Money, Disembodied Art and the Turing Test for Aesthetics. In J. Stallabrass, S. Buck-Morss, & L. Donskis (Eds.), *Ground Control. Technology and Utopia* (pp. 62–11). Black Dog Publishing.

KEY TERMS AND DEFINITIONS

A/r/tography: Methodology of educational research and artistic creation based on the hybridization of artist-researcher-teacher.

Artifact: An object produced by mechanical work, also an apparatus or device. In digital media artifacts are objects that can be tangible or immaterial, and also can be an expression of the individual or collective imagination and reflect a cultural and artistic phenomenon.

Digital Media Art: Artistic area in contemporary art can also be described as an artistic form that uses digital tools or is support based on computational or digital technologies. Digital media-art includes all aesthetics that exploits digital media and computational media, providing alternatives to the communicational / informational phenomenon through art and its various representations.

Hologram: Unlike the photograph that only allows registering different intensities of light coming from the scene photographed, the holograms also record the phase of the luminous radiation coming from the object. The construction of a hologram requires a laser light source to illuminate the object to be registered or other image projection techniques through screens of liquid crystals or matrices of micro-mirrors with very small dimensions.

Spectator Experience: With digital art, the participant has been abandoning the role of mere observer and seeking/demanding interaction with the work, becoming a participant, and sometimes even a co-author of the work.

ENDNOTES

[1]   Henrique Silva (HS) is born in 1933 in Paredes, Portugal. Since 2009, he is the director of Fine Arts and Multimedia at the *Escola Superior Gallaecia* University, Portugal; was a fellow of the *Gulbenkian Foundation* in Paris from 1961 to 1963, attending *École Superieur de Beaux-Arts de Paris* and in 1977, he graduated in the University of Paris VIII in Plastic Arts for Teaching; was the executive director of *Árvore*, an artistic school from 1978 to 1995; was the director of the Professional School of Social Economy in 1989/91 and 1998/2000; participated in several seminars and international conferences (e.g. in Warsaw - 1983, Brussels - 1986, Crete - 1987, among others), about territorial and cultural development policies; director and co-founder Cerveira International Art Biennale from 1995 to 2008; director of the Museum of Contemporary Art of the Biennale of Cerveira, since 2003; in 2015 concludes PhD in Digital Media Art; since 1958, Henrique Silve had more than 50 individual and 200 collective exhibitions in Portugal, Spain, France, Belgium, United States and other countries.

[2]   Andy Warhol was a famous American artist and one of the major figure in the 60´s pop art movement. Warhol had peculiar and revolutionary ways to explore art by combining it with celebrities and advertising.

[3]   The *Fluxus group* was an artistic libertarian movement in the decade of 1960 and 70 who rebelled against traditional art forms and the merchandise

of artistic objects. They proclaimed themselves anti-art (Joseph Beuys and Marcel Duchamp are inscribed in this line of artists).

4   Acácio de Carvalho is a multi-faceted Portuguese artist (in drawing, painting, installation, engraving, public art, ceramics, graphic design and theater) and university professor. Carvalho participated in more than 50 theater productions and numerous collective art exhibitions.

5   *Arduino* is an electronic prototyping platform intended for creating interactive objects or environments, highly used in media art works. *Arduinos* sense surrounding environments by receiving sensor signals and interact with by controlling audio, video, lights and movements. Projects developed with *Arduino* can be autonomous but also or can communicate with a computer or other digital devices.

6   Jeffrey Shaw is a new media artist and researcher also one pioneer of interactive art installations and the use of digital media in virtual reality, augmented reality and immersive visuals.

Chapter 6
Ceremonies of Pleasure:
An Approach to Immersive Experiences at Summer Festivals

Paula Guerra
University of Porto, Portugal

ABSTRACT

The importance of music concerts is all too revealing of a complex and malleable framework which operates at aesthetic, artistic, and emotional levels. We are faced here with a new type of relationship with music, in a way that we find not only the classic takes on music as an artwork to be admired, or as a collective identity-building activity, but also as a way in which festival "stages" serves as observatories of youth, cultural and artistic practices, and values in contemporary Portugal. This chapter addresses these questions via the analysis of the mobile photo-sharing application Instagram deposited by the managers of the page of Paredes de Coura's Festival— Portuguese music festival—between 2015 and 2017, and it is from here that the author will try to understand and analyze the dynamics underlying the festival as an immersive experience.

PRAISE YOU, WE'VE COME A LONG WAY TOGETHER[1]

Since 2005 music has been an intensively approached benchmark, namely concerning its enjoyment, consumption and experience at major events and summer festivals (Guerra, 2010, 2015, 2016)[2]. That incidence is largely due to the fact that festivals seem to be an entirety of cultural production, mediation and reception in different scales/spheres of action whose motivation is music, but which go beyond it – they are

DOI: 10.4018/978-1-5225-5696-1.ch006

pluri-programmatic/pluri-sectoral. We can say that nowadays the festival arrogates itself as a "totem point", making available to "carnal experience", music, dance, sports, therapy, food, clothing, drink, sun, beach, forest, land, mud... As referred by Purdue *et al.*, festivals are " globalization's somatic multisensory" (1997, p. 662). Then, in the last decade of the twentieth century, festivals have acquired particular prominence in cultural programs around the world, largely because they are an "immense accumulation of spectacles" (Harvey, 1989) in an illogicality of instantaneity/perennially. In this sense, the festival is a striking case of Debord's spectacle (1992) in its relationship with (post)capitalist order.

Historically, festivals have become established as important forms of social and cultural participation: space-times for celebration and sharing of values, of ideologies, of mythologies, of beliefs. In anthropology, the festival is interpreted as a public ritual; a "carnivalization" of reality in which community members participate by (re)affirming and celebrating social, religious, ethnic, national, linguistic and historical ties, in an articulation between past, present and future (Bennett et al. 2014). In contemporary society, the festival arrogates itself to this same function, unfolding into a plurality of proposals – particularly regarding the expression of cultural identities and lifestyles (Bennett & Woodward, 2014; McKay, 2000).

This is where we find a cornerstone of the approach to festivals as space-times of articulation of identities referring to liminality. As liminal spaces – removed from the routine sphere of everyday life – festivals offer opportunities for experimenting with extraordinary identities – and in some cases, socially circumscribed ones (Guerra et al., 2016; Simão & Guerra, 2016). They are a fairly current synecdoche of holidays, of freedom, of a better world. In addition to their importance as spaces for acquiring and articulating identities, festivals also increasingly emerge associated with the (re) constitution of different lifestyles. As societies have assumed a constant evolvement of diversified lifestyles (tastes, beliefs, attitudes, orientations and opinions) (Chaney, 2002), this has been accompanied by the scenario of the global festival (Bennett et al., 2014). Music festivals are fundamental examples of a festival genre where identity and lifestyle merge and find collective articulation.

HOW SOON IS NOW?[3] THE *DEFENCE* OF SOCIAL NETWORKS

In this chapter, we will give a special emphasis on the analysis of the social network Instagram[4] of Paredes de Coura Festival[5], focusing on the editions of the years 2015, 2016 and 2017, in order to understand not only the dynamics of promotion and dissemination of the festival, but fundamentally the festival experience as a *social practice* considering the flows of images and modify them by scrolling, liking, and commenting. During the three years of analysis, there have been published 157 images/photos on *Instagram* of Paredes de Coura Festival – which are not limited to the four days of the festival. We are positioning ourselves before the capture of a photographic lens, but also before the interaction of those who follow the publications on this social network – the followers – and that shows their opinions about the published photographs, either through comments or likes. And why? Because we live in a world where the virtual conquers more and more space in the lives of individuals, merging or even overlapping the reality. Therefore, it seems essential to analyse the meaning phenomena inherent in the attendance/experience of a music festival:

Mobile practices - where Instagram fits – can be characterized as intense and as an immersive experience because users are linked to contexts and emotional moments and this move them away from other activities (Kuru et al., 2016). In the same way, music festivals can also be considered as an immersive experience, because individuals distance themselves from what is beyond the festival. In those days, only the festival matters (Carah & Shaul, 2015).

The definitions of immersion that we find in the literature are not unanimous. On the other hand, most of them refer to the *gaming* phenomenon and/or virtual reality and not so much to the musical and social immersion experienced in music festivals Nechvatal (2011), however, postulates that immersion is a state of mind in which the *selves* of individuals are reduced to a mediated, intensive and immersive total environment/context. This applies especially to festivals. Following Schafer's (1977) thesis, we can consider festivals as an example of *soundscape*, that is, a sound space in which an immersive process occurs, in which the participants feel part of a different reality, diametrically opposed to the daily routine. In which they are able to experience new selves and experiences. It is an extremely immersive process, in which the *festival-goers* become actors, far from mere passive consumers, and also, part of the experience for all other *festival-goers* (Jordan, 2016, p. 50).

In fact, we can allude to the development of a self/hetero-mapping of the real and virtual space of the festival that models new forms of spatial appropriation (Liew & Pang, 2015). Currently, smartphone apps are cornerstones of this mapping: they act as expert benchmarks of personal space and symbolic guarantees of ontological security. The mobile phone is everything: 'Big Brother's' and a key element of self-affirmation and realization with regard to others. As a matter of fact, new media and digital technologies have very relevant impacts not only in terms of lifestyle but also in the placement and spatialization of allegiances and collective memories (Bennett et al., 2014; Regev, 2011; Chalcraft & Magaudda, 2011; Tomlinson, 2004). In (post-traditional) festivals, the intensity and speed of mapping and appropriation of one's cyberspace is staggering and, it should be stressed, it is a prime setting for interaction (Kitchin & Dodge, 2007; Roche, 2011; Cummings et al., 2011). *Instagram* shows us the growing of a visual culture which links design to photography, resulting in a combination of a *media form* and a *particular content,* which Manovich (2016) calls *Instagrammism.* This social network has come to be seen by its users as a tool that allows them to "narrate their ideas and experiences, and connect to each other" (Manovich, 2016, p. 4).

Social networks, particularly Instagram, enable an even more immersive experience in the soundscapes that are the festivals. Instagram, due to its characteristics (MacDowall & de Souza, 2018), has a possibility to capture experiences and a complete immersion in a more whole and instantaneous way. Likewise, it reflects a growing passage to a visual culture in which the text is secondary" (Chesher, 2012, p. 106) But not only: Instagram is also an example of a" disseminating media "(Jenkins et al., 2013), which is shared by the audiences. That lets these images, and their instant will, to allow the appearance of a sense of visual co-presence, of you could be here with me. As it was expected, this was appropriated in terms of marketing. The bet on the divulgation in the social networks, by several promoters of festivals, is thus linked with the emergence of the experiential consumer. That is, the objective turns to be selling the experience, as well as allow the consumers, and potential ones, to interact with of the object of consumption (in this case, a festival).

Proof of the growing importance attributed to virtual and the new technologies is the creation – at Paredes de Coura Festival – of an area with hundreds of outlets that allows the festivalgoers to put their mobile phones to charge, as well as the organization's own divulgation of this space, warning festivalgoers not to run out of battery power – as you can see in the description of the shared photo on *Instagram* social network, where we see a number of festivalgoers around the outlets waiting for their mobile phones to charge (Vodafoneparedesdecoura, 2017).

As we can see in the example of Paredes de Coura Festival, the bet is on two levels: first, with the institution of a page managed by the Festival managers to publish photos (and the experiences that accompany them) and, secondly, the concern about providing locations for recharging mobile phone batteries. This is partly because of a reason: it is a way of outsourcing marketing to consumers. These, through their sharing, the dissemination of feelings, states of spirits, etc., related to the festival, are most probably one of the most effective means (with the advantage of being understood as "authentic" and not starting from any company or the organizers of the festival) to publicize the festival.

METHODOLOGY

In exploring the potentialities of using photography, video and hypermedia in ethnographic research, Sarah Pink favours a critical understanding of visual cultures, a reflective understanding of how visual and ethnographic materials are produced and interpreted (Pink, 2001, p. 4). We focus essentially on the use of these visual and digital materials and from them we make our analysis, because we believe that not only allied to ethnography confer an enormous potential of analysis of social phenomena, since they are highly inserted in our daily life, exceeding the "notion of interaction" (Pink et al., 2017: 18). The shared contents from Instagram social network are voiced by "subtle differences, the power of empty space, visual intelligence, and visual pleasure", which contrasts with the initial objective of the application, which resides on the assumption of the immediate, on quickness paired with the ease to create and share a content (Manovich, 2016, p. 25). With the emergence of the Instagram, our daily lives have been exposed and organized according to images in flow, where spaces of our intimacy – or other spaces and events that we attend – and our body are associated, for example, with trademarks. In that way, it is possible to say that "Instagram enables market relations to form through everyday life and cultural space around the production and circulation of images" (Carah & Shaul, 2015: 71).

However, few investigations are based on social networks, let alone on Instagram. Lupton (2012) points out that it's surprising given the fact that sociologists have been very involved with the Internet since a very early age. Therefore, advocates a "digital sociology" to study the impact, use and development of these technologies. Taking into account that digital technologies are increasingly prevalent in our lives, then they must be at the centre of sociological research concerns. Even without a robust theoretical body on research in social networks, it's possible to analyse the challenges that social networks can bring to research in the social sciences. The Social Media Research Group (2016) postulates a set, such as: it can cause validity problems, since users of social networks are not representative of the population at large, thus entailing biases; second, we are dealing with data created for purposes other than scientific research, which can mean analysis difficulties and a high number of data without any value for analysis; third, there is always the difficulty of establishing generalizations solely from the offline behaviour of the actors. Old ethical and deontological concerns are more pressing here. For example, who owns the data? The individuals or the platforms? How to deal with this issue? Similarly, social networks emphasize the need for even more demanding ethical standards (Evans et al., 2015). Given the precocity of social networks and the scarce theoretical output on how to proceed in this new medium, perhaps the possible advice is given by the Social Media Research Group (2016, p. 16): "researchers may need to make methodological decisions based on theory rather than prior practical experience ".

LET IT HAPPEN, JUST LET IT HAPPEN[6]

We proceed, in this chapter, with the chorus of the song most often heard in the enclosure of the Paredes de Coura festival in 2015[7] in order to demonstrate it's (re) construction in a quintessential musical scene-place in the region of Alto Minho, in northern Portugal and the country itself. In the early 1990s, more specifically in 1993, the festival of Paredes de Coura came into existence. Since then and uninterruptedly until today it has been populating the banks of the Taboão River in Paredes de Coura and has been established as the "natural habitat of music". This festival is the result of an informal initiative by a group of young people who at the time were avid readers of *the Jornal Blitz*[8], which showed the new music trends, and were also influenced by the TV program *Pop Off* (RTP2)[9]. At a time when a certain frenzy about alternative music was emerging in Portugal (Guerra, 2010) with the appearance of several garage bands and of significant radio and television programs, a group of young people (calling themselves *Incentive to Courense Culture*[10]) who were passionate about music and especially about the independent rock music of the 1980s, found there was a supply gap in the area where they lived and, moved by a certain idealism, decided to create a "night" of concerts by rock bands in Paredes de Coura. To that end they soon got in touch with the Town Council of Paredes de Coura, who were from the beginning an important interlocutor, proving to be very receptive and becoming decisive in the start-up and sustained growth of a festival that would come to be considered unique as well as a pioneer in the national context[11].

In fact, in its first two years the festival lasted only one day; later it was extended to two days and subsequently to three and four days. Time in contemporary societies is characterized by polychromic, homogenized, calendarized time that arranges everyday life. However, as Pais (1998) points out, in contemporary societies not even work time is absolute anymore, particularly if we consider the expansion of leisure time in today's society. Thus, leisure time has become decreasingly isotopic, i.e. it does not have the same subjective properties, but even so the less time we have, the greater the need for leisure time to break with other times. Therefore, it is here that the time for festivals is included, thus justifying the festival's extension to additional days. The Paredes de Coura festival has been progressively growing in several aspects, consolidating a "successful career" and even bringing about other festivals nearby and becoming an international reference – at least as far as Spain. This means that, as advocated by Geus et al. (2016), in its essence the Paredes de Coura festival was born of a "fortunate" interaction between the individuals and the "environment" of the event – the program, the theme, the scenario, the service and the other users of that environment.

The photos published on the festival's Instagram that capture the scenery show us a place where nature prevails, as if it were a reconstruction of nature bases on an idyllic construction principle. The layout of the main stage looks like a natural amphitheatre, lying at the bottom of an inclined plane surrounded by nature, which allows a good visualization of the concerts to all the people, even when they are in the back region. There are even those who prefer to watch from this region, since it allows them to escape from the crowd and to watch the concerts more leisurely – sitting or lying down – if this have little affluence and calmer rhythms (see Vodafoneparedesdecoura, 2017). On the secondary stage, in turn, the floor has no slope and has a covered area, with the area of the bars in the background (Vodafoneparedesdecoura, 2017).

Taboão River and its banks are a central element and one of the festival's trademark images. More than a place where individuals can be in contact with nature, diving and sunbathing, it is a space of sociability, where individuals meet and amuse themselves, with props and artefacts ranging from clothes, like swimwear, fashion accessories - such as sunglasses, hats, caps and others - and rubber buoys and rubber boats that they share with friends on the Taboão river. Smoking, drinking and eating is another recurring practice during sunny afternoons in Taboão, with some festivalgoers carrying portable coolers. There is a disorganized arrangement in which youth groups merge, there is no interest in distancing themselves from those they do not know or in establishing spatial boundaries. We would like to reiterate here, with Bauman (2006), the distinction between mixophobia (fear of being in physical co-presence with anonymous people, causing estrangement) and mixophilia (satisfaction through the experience of socializing with strangers, which induces fusion). Apparently, this arena is governed by mixophilia (see Vodafoneparedesdecoura, 2017), i.e., the occupation of the different spaces in the enclosure obeys massive rationales between day and night, ruled by the abovementioned *mitsein*. This festival is even interpreted in the image of a "Gaulish village" materialized into an indie community, for it is "as if Paredes de Coura were the indomitable *Gaulish village* heroically resisting the diabolical concessions of true music to global capitalism" (Nadais, 2010).

We are therefore witnessing the transformation of a festival that emerges imbued with a do-it-yourself (DIY) rationale based on the effort of a group of young people committed to opposing the more or less fatalistic idea that the "hinterland" location of their town would be synonymous with cultural dependence vis-à-vis the big cities. As early as its second edition in 1994, and benefiting from the lack of other festivals and/or events of the kind, the festival began to appear in full-page features in the national press (for example, the *Público* newspaper[12]).

On its 25th anniversary in 2017, all the media continues to consider Paredes de Coura a "unique festival", not only due to the natural setting where it takes place but also its program. As a matter of fact, this festival eventually achieved the image of being an experimental venue for new artists/concepts, having presented the largest number of debuts in Portugal until the appearance of the *Milhões de Festa* festival. Thus, a "well-received" performance in Coura became synonymous with subsequent success, i.e., the festival became a springboard for names belonging to the so-called alternative sphere. This option corresponds to the representations that the organizers and festivalgoers themselves have about their own musical tastes. If we claim, like Pais, that "hegemonic culture is much more of a culture of exclusion than of inclusion" (2010, p. 166), underground music pulverizes other musical manifestations, reserving for itself the primordial space of action and establishing itself as the legitimate form of musical creation in Coura.

If we consider the logic of free artistic expression, ranking will be carried out depending on authenticity – let us remember that authenticity is one of the core values of the indie scene. Thornton (1996) has told us that authenticity is linked to the notion of subcultural capital. In fact, at the Paredes de Coura's festival, journalists, bloggers and opinion makers – as cultural gatekeepers – have always "defended" Coura as an alternative, unique and singular, and it is unavoidable – year after year – that through their music tastes and recommendations – isochronous with those of the organizers – they gradually defined and built the subcultural capital of Coura (Jetto, 2010).

These memorable moments decisively contribute to structuring the relations of sociability established in the festival, and here it is pertinent to join Pais (2010) when he tells us that popular music is a unique field in which to analyse social constructs. Thus, the fact that there is a temporary suspension of everyday identity based on the notion of proxemics, underscores the importance of assuming a common identity, the knowledge of how to behave that is learned at festivals and that improves the chances of starting new relationships insofar as the distance between strangers is narrowed by the symbolic, sensuous sharing of common space-time. From this we can identify the emergence of groups of affinities established on the basis of elective affinities that may amount to friendship as an omnipresent modality of sociability.

Reflecting the way the playbills and the organization evolved, from 2007 on the festival there were several different stages: the main stage, usually associated with the major sponsor (Optimus, Super-Bock, Heineken, Nokia, EDP, Vodafone...); the *Ibero Sounds* stage (currently also associated with the major sponsor), for bands that were still relatively unknown; *Jazz on the Grass*, responsible for the afternoon entertainment in the enclosure closest to the river, where there is concerts and other activities such as the *Writing Voices* – since 2015 – in which musicians and other artists are invited to take part in some reading sessions; and the *After-Hours* stage, for more electronic-type sounds. Although in terms of the stages there is a certain distinction and separation between national and international names, this does not prevent the best-known Portuguese names (Mão Morta, Linda Martini, X-Wife,

Manel Cruz) from featuring side by side with the international attractions on the main stage. This proliferation of stages complies with the necessary coexistence of multiple musical worlds at the same festival, proving theses of increasingly eclectic and omnivorous music consumption (Guerra, 2010; Crossley & Emms, 2016).

There are other concerts that the organization takes to various points in the village, such as Music Sessions - created in 2013 and in undisclosed parts of the village, such as a shoe factory (Vodafoneparedesdecoura, 2017) next to the church or a private farm – characterized by a greater proximity and intimacy between the artists and audience, who is quite limited. In addition to these secret and intimate music sessions, The Festival goes to the Village is another initiative in which the festival organizes this link with the village, since it happens on the main avenue of the village, Cónego Bernardo Chouzal Avenue[13], on the days before the start of the festival and the access is free.

Speaking of the current structure of the festival, let us start by mentioning its location and its fruitful intercrossing with the "town" (village). Thinking about festivals as communities not only evokes the interactions established between subjects but is also related to the fact that music and musical performances can act as a means of connecting festival participants to the places where they are held, promoting the creation of a sense of identity and identification with them (Duffy, 2000). Frequent trips to the places where festivals take place favour the formation of these communities – communities of identification associated with spaces of allegiance and intensification of relationships. Simultaneously, music and performances can be considered to incorporate and give voice to the relationship established with the space, on the one hand, and on the other hand to offer, through participation, ways for individuals to identify and situate themselves (Hudson et al., 2015).

These activities promote not only contact with local community, but also contact with relevant political, institutional and economic agents. Can these be considered actual coordinates of local development? We do not know yet, but surely festivals cannot be forgotten when planning the development of counties and regions such as Paredes de Coura. Established 25 years ago, the festival takes on the central dimensions of cosmopolitan openness advocated by Skrbiš and Woodward (2011): belonging and becoming, or simultaneously the involvement with the county and the connection to the world; the physical and virtual mobility and perenniality of people (Hebdige, 1990); the "semiotic capacity" for reading *the other* (Molz, 2011). Urry, in his "aesthetic cosmopolitanism" model, speaks to us of the *topos* of festivals as spheres for "opening up about the divergent experiences of the present in national cultures" and the "search by and for contrasts between societies" (1995, p. 167).

DESIRE LINES[14]: APPROPRIATIONS AND MUSIC

Our gaze looks on pop rock – or its drifts of indie rock or electro pop – as a *social system* and not as an opaque cluster of individual activities, which implies its (re) creation in a space transformed into a *place-scene* within the framework of this chapter. The festival's line-up has been quite well defined since its first edition – independent rock. It therefore assumes an orientation criterion that allows one to identify it and distinguish it from others, marking its difference. At this level we are probably close to Hennion (1999), who invites us to take on a new kind of relationship to music beyond the orthodox postures of music as a work of art to be admired but also as a collective activity that transmits identities: the assumption of music as a performance of personal tastes. In the Coura's line-up, one seeks novelty. This requires constant updating based on research work where the Internet is an essential tool, and which also involves reading industry publications and attending other international festivals – Reading[15], Roskilde[16] and Benicàssim[17]. This is very interesting because festival's line-up, - as we can see on Instagram – seems like a live and ephemeral flow of images (Carah & Shaul, 2015, p. 72).

In order to publicize and promote the festival, in 2016 the organization of the Paredes de Coura festival opted to make a publication with a photograph and name of each artists or bands that were being confirmed to act in the natural habitat of music in the same year's edition (Vodafoneparedesdecoura, 2017) which occurred between February 29th and August 6th. This is a way not only of approaching audiences and keeping the festival alive in their minds months before it happens, but also to perceive public opinions about the invited artists or bands. The comments in these publications are divided between thanks to the organization for bringing the artist or band announced, requests to bring other artists and bands who would like to see acting at that festival, and identifications of friends in those publications, many of them with requests to accompany them in that edition. In the last edition, held in 2017, they adopted another strategy of disseminating the confirmed artists, placing only one image where four confirmed names are registered, followed a month and a half later by a new publication with another international band confirmed for the edition of the festival's 25th anniversary. Note that in this edition the disclosure of confirmations focused only on major international bands and artists, which had not happened in the previous edition (Vodafoneparedesdecoura, 2017). Read among the comments to the publication: "You are great!"; "Bring the glowers please! The glowers are amazing" [sic]; "Let's go!" [Sic] "Julian Casablancas @vodafoneparedesdecoura was also the cherry on the cake" [sic].

If festival confirmations were once given from the press, today festival organizations see a need to adapt to the audience, who are increasingly disconnected from traditional media and give exacerbated attention to social media. See the example of the Portuguese version of "Primavera Sound", which is held in Porto, whose poster of the 2017 edition was first published on Instagram stories[18] of festival's organization with features to videos that narrate a story, interpreted by a character, focused on emblematic buildings of the city - since the brand of the city is associated with the festival. This was preceded by several warnings to the public that they would be attentive to Instagram stories that would be released on that day and at that time, a whole marketing strategy that proved effective and that aroused the curiosity not only of the public, but also of the press. So, this question makes sense to Tia DeNora's concept of music in action (2003), in which music assumes itself as a social practice, endowed with senses. To these new forms of promotion and dissemination lies a link that is created between the festival and the public intermediated by the artists that constitute the poster - there is an identification with what the event involves that leads to the desire to remain in contact with it, namely from social networks. In the days in which the festival takes place, the artists that make up the poster are prominent on Paredes de Coura Festival's Instagram. Throughout these three editions - 2015, 2016 and 2017 - the organization shared several photographs of the artists and bands - as a rule there appears exclusively one element of the band at the time of the musical performance - that passed through the natural habitat of music, either by the main stage or secondary stage. What is behind this option of highlighting the artists during the festival against the other dimensions that constitutes and defines it? Is there a logic behind strengthening the association of the poster to concepts such as quality, originality and diversity through the creation and/or intensification of hypes?

Not always the headlines are those that reach a greater number of likes and comments on Instagram, although there is often a direct relationship between these aspects. Take the example of the last day of the festival of the 2017 edition, in which Ty Segall and Foals are the highlights of the poster and whose photographs reached 433 and 821 likes, respectively, compared to the 1218 likes in Benjamin Clementine's photo (Vodafoneparedesdecoura, 2017) or 607 likes in the photograph of the Portuguese artist Manel Cruz (Vodafoneparedesdecoura, 2017) who also performed on the main stage, but were less prominent in the poster. In the comments to the photos of these two are thanks, congratulations and compliments: "The best of the festival!"; "It was so good!"; "Amazing!"; "idol". Initiatives such as Jazz in the grass, Writing Voices and the after-hours do not have as much visibility on this social network, and in the case of the after-hours, there is no publications on Instagram in the last three editions related to the same.

The main point to bear in mind here is to understand how the programming is experienced and appropriated according to the subjective dispositions and objective possibilities of the actors at play in Taboão. We can say that there is no "strong" code of regulation – which does not mean that there is no order at the festival. There is, and it is precisely the order of improvisation, of disorganization. In the interactive framework, this is where the difference resides between being in (being cool) or out (being an outlier). The "art" of infraction demands that it be done naturally, like a "gift" one has, an expression of something that one effortlessly is – something spontaneous and unconstructed, unrehearsed. Here lies the true *knowing how to be* of the festivalgoer, i.e., the ability to "naturally fit in" within the space – or Malbon's (1999) coolness criterion. We are in the sphere of musicking, which is the way we act before music, the value we place on it, etc. In other words, we are talking about social skills in relation to music (Crossley, 2015, p. 473). And musicking can only be completely apprehended if we seek to apprehend its collective nature through the concept of music worlds and of the way it functions in the festival scene-place. The consequences of musicking are varied, cutting cross the whole festival experience. Fonarow (1997) speaks of "regions inhabited" by the enjoyers during the live shows: in "front of the stage" are the youngest and most enthusiastic; "behind the pit" are the older ones experiencing music without distractions; In the "back regions" are industry staff and other professionals, peacefully enjoying the distance. In one of the videos published on the festival's Instagram we see a whole frenzied audience before a concert of the Portuguese Orelha Negra, a band that is in its essence instrumental and that locates its sonorities between diverse musical genres like Soul, Jazz, Rock, the Funk or Hip-Hop. Once again, the diversity that the Paredes de Coura festival offers its audiences stands out, not being restricted to a genre or subgenre.

Festival authenticity can involve ignoring the rules ("everyday garb", for example) ostensibly and systematically (as a habit, therefore). Think of "finite provinces of meaning", as Schutz would say (Wagner, 1979). Other people purposely prepare for this place. The party – the "carnival" in which the masks invade the hosts (Bakhtin, 1981) and value scales are subverted: a different place, a different time and, above all, chronotopes. Convergence, orchestration – the expectations of what will be shared, the backward assumptions (Garfinkel 1967) evidenced by the people who dress for, who "commit" to the bands. Regev's (2013) perspective on pop-rock as a possibility for cultural approchement is, in this regard, exemplary. The expressive elements that different cultures use to show the uniqueness of pop-rock are very close to each other. While those differences and singularities do exist, the processes and instruments for expressing these particularities are very similar.

DIY is an ethos and a praxis that defy and subvert the codes of mainstream culture (McKay, 1998). In this sense, this festival takes on the role of an heir that lubricates this ethos. It is an "autonomous temporary zone where the fragments of everyday symbolic life are suspended, or like a cultural laboratory where dominant codes are summoned to enable the formation of experimental identities and forms of neotribal sociability, or temporary *communitas*" (Purdue et al., 1997, p. 660). Thinking about the festival's game of sociabilities leads us to think of the notion of an "exception regime" – of planned and organized (regime) lack of control (exception), with no contradiction in terms.

The multiplicity of aesthetic styles provides an explanation of itself. The heterogeneity of clothes, props and artefacts takes on a common value. The aesthetic function becomes an axis of signification that crystallizes (originates) the main dynamics engendering subjective polyvalence. Aesthetic issues are visible not only in the way individuals present themselves and through the artifacts they carry, but also in their appropriation of space in the camping zone. Along with the tents are placed cards with handwritten expressions related to the festival, with its practices or with identity aspects. Read on these posters expressions like "Take me to the Couraíso [Coura (the festival's and village's name) + *paraíso* (which means paradise in portuguese)]", "Danger Zone", "Beware, drunk are camping", "Eat, Sleep, Rave, Repeat", "Kamacoura, Bragasutra" (Vodafoneparedesdecoura, 2017).

Along with music, the wish to interact with the (known or unknown) *other* is one of the main motivations behind attending festivals: "there are people who get together and do not know what they are going to find. That is why we came here. We are people of different cultures, different nations, different religions, that is cool "(Larsen & O'Reilly, 2005, p. 7). At the same time, sharing the reality of the festival and a preference for certain bands is a reason for establishing new relationships. In this sense, and perhaps more important than the music itself, are the non-musical aspects of festival attendance. We could even speak of the formation of transitory communities based on an awareness of similar tastes and sharing of experiences. These are geographically and temporally limited communities, slightly different from the communities that are formed when attending concerts. The camping area is one of the highlights in the festival where these communities manifest themselves. It is in this area that festivalgoers meet basic necessities like sleeping or eating, cooking their own meals with equipment, utensils – portable gas stove, plates, cutlery, among others – and food that they transport to the festival, favouring fast and easy food, always in a great atmosphere of relaxation and permanent contact with each other (Vodafoneparedesdecoura, 2017).

The festival is a catalyst of a number of networks. There emerges a spontaneous reformulation of the festival's structure, interweaving the previous structure with personal reformulations about the festival. Thus, "the festival organizers weave a fabric of relationships that can be approached in different ways by individuals." (Purdue et al., 1997: 661). The music festival community can be perceived as "a means of promoting the identity of a community, or at least, the way the community would like others to see it." (Duffy, 2000: 51). In this respect we cannot but draw attention to Cummings's[19] research (2007a, 2007b) when he points out that although indie music is defined by its independence from mass "commercial" music, it is itself also commercialized and its idea of authenticity is also a marketing strategy. We can therefore suggest that festivalgoers often end up forming communities of individuals linked together because they are consumers of a particular brand. For this reason we can emphasize the fact that the brands that sponsor music events are important as symbolic elements connecting individuals who belong to music neotribes: the "Primavera Sound" brand is prototypical. The appearance on the scene of a growing number of brands, even in Coura, has met with the acceptance of the participants, leading us to believe that they have accepted the role of sponsorship and of brands as essential for the festival's continuity. Since this is a time for neotribes to gather, it is necessary that the presence of a particular brand be linked to the values inherent to the community of festivalgoers and to its symbolic universe (t-shirts, backpacks, mattresses, scarves, key rings, etc.).

FROM THE NIGHT AND THE LIGHT, ALL PLANS ARE GOLDEN[20]: (IN)CONCLUSIVE CLUES

As Dowd et al. observe: "Gathered from geographically disperse locations far from the normalized expectations of everyday life, fans and performers can immerse themselves in a particular culture and experiment with different identities" (2004, p. 149). As we have seen, in a festival the actors therefore tend to occupy mixed positions between creation, intermediation and musical enjoyment – referring to music *in ac*t. The festivalgoing way of life is made up of layers recreated from festivalgoing cultural capital constructed by total participation – body and soul – in the Coura place-scene. McKay (2000) revealed an interesting duality in music festivals that is also present in Coura: if on the one hand the festival has an emphatically dreamlike brand associated to pilgrimage and to divinization, at the same time it is very much rooted in the real world, the market and consumption, which is also denoted by use of social networks. The virtual has brought new forms of self-presentation and new forms of interaction not only between individuals but also between consumer products and the individuals. According to Carah and Shaul (2015, p.71): "the portability and habitual use of the smartphone within everyday life enables Instagram to extend the role played by images in the stimulation, capture, and modulation of attention". It is here that the sphere of action of the organization of Paredes de Coura's festival is inserted, through the use of Instagram: to communicate and interact with its public, capturing their attention.

In fact, there has been an exponential increase in the number of festivals in the UK and throughout the world: the music festival is now an economic figure in the popular music industry. More than that, these are constituents of urban repertoires of regeneration, of seasonal cultural economies, of ritualized collective events, of tourism, of museumization-*nostalgia*, of endogenous local development. Thus, the Paredes de Coura's festival also lives between these two levels and the music *in act* experienced there also suffers from this dualism. The search for the alternative is an impactful motive for action but it is always carried out within the framework of a symbolic, economic and cultural struggle for authenticity. The Coura festival's way of life is presented as a complex *utterance under construction* of beliefs, symbols, modes of interaction, values and ideologies around what is alternative – not to mention underground.

This festival is underlain by the way that experiences, and the search for experiences, have marked their unique presence: experiences of communion with nature, of enjoying the most "beautiful" amphitheatre in Portugal; experiences of direct contact with pioneering bands and with big names of alternative rock; experiences with festivalgoing authenticity as opposed to the mainstream. In all these experiences, or rather in the festivalgoing "economy of experiences", Coura has gained a competitive advantage because it has offered the best symbolic, musical, affective and emotional experiences. A significant aspect is that the rain has "already become a tradition": what would *a priori* be a competitive disadvantage of the festival has been transformed, over time, into absolute experiential capital – because it brings the experience of this Minho festival closer to the legendary Glastonbury (Geus et al., 2016).

The immersive analysis about Paredes de Coura Festival's Instagram was central to understand that Coura is music, but it is much more than music. Put another way, *musicking* can only be fully apprehended if we seek to grasp its collective nature through the concept of music worlds and the way it operates in the festival scene-place (Crossley, 2015). As we have seen through the analysis of the festival's Instagram, music *in act* is present not only on stage's performances but in the experience that it dictates in the festivalgoer's "world of life": at the camping site, at the river and its banks, the food, drinks and in the use of technologies and social networks... This issue helps us realize the complexity and heterogeneity that currently characterize the universe of music intermediation, which do not arise only from the coexistence of multiple forms of diffusion. They are also associated with trends that dilute the boundaries that traditionally structured, on several planes, the worlds of music. And festivals are quintessential place-scenes of this mix. The development of cultural industries and the flexibilization of their forms of productive organization have blurred the boundaries between work and activities of creation, diffusion and enjoyment. Alongside this, diversity is evident in the varied content offered by festivals, which are increasingly showing their awareness of the importance of dimensions other than music, despite the fact that music continues to be the key element.

REFERENCES

Bakhtin, M. (1981). *The dialogic imagination: Four essays*. Austin, TX: University of Texas Press.

Bauman, Z. (2006). *Liquid fear*. Cambridge, UK: Polity Press.

Beck, U. (2011). Cosmopolitan sociology: outline of a paradigm shift. In M. Rovisco & M. Nowicka (Eds.), *The Ashgate research companion to cosmopolitanism*. Farnham, UK: Ashgate Publishing.

Bennett, A., Taylor, J., & Woodward, I. (Eds.). (2014). *The festivalization of culture*. Surrey, UK: Ashgate.

Bennett, A., & Woodward, I. (2014). Festival spaces, identity, experience and belonging. In A. Bennett, J. Taylor, & I. Woodward (Eds.), *The festivalization of culture* (pp. 11–25). Surrey, UK: Ashgate.

Carah, N., & Shaul, M. (2015). Brands and Instagram: Point, tap, swipe, glance. *Mobile Media & Communication, 4*(1), 69–84. doi:10.1177/2050157915598180

Chalcraft, J., & Magaudda, P. (2011). 'Space is the place': The global localities of the Sónar and WOMAD music festivals. In L. Giorgi, M. Sassatelli & G. Delanty (Eds.), Festivals and the cultural public sphere (pp. 173-189). Nova Iorque: Routledge.

Chaney, D. (2002). Cosmopolitan art and cultural citizenship. *Theory, Culture & Society, 19*(1–2), 157–174. doi:10.1177/026327640201900108

Chesher, C. (2012). Between image and information: The iPhone camera in the history of photography. In L. Hjorth & ... (Eds.), *Studying Mobile Media: Cultural Technologies, Mobile Communication, and the iPhone* (pp. 98–117). New York: Routledge.

Clarke, E., Denora, T., & Vuoskoski, J. (2015). *Music, empathy and cultural understanding*. Swindon: Arts and Humanities Research Council.

Crossley, N. (2015). Music worlds and body techniques: On the embodiment of musicking. *Cultural Sociology, 9*(4), 471–492. doi:10.1177/1749975515576585

Crossley, N., & Emms, R. (2016). Mapping the musical universe: A blockmodel of UK music festivals, 2011–2013. *Methodological Innovations, 9*, 1–14. doi:10.1177/2059799116630663

Cummings, J., Woodward, I., & Bennett, A. (2011). Festival spaces, green sensibilities and youth culture. In L. Giorgi, M. Sassatelli, & G. Delanty (Eds.), *Festivals and the cultural public sphere* (pp. 142–155). New York: Routledge.

Debord, G. (1992). *La société du spectacle*. Paris: Galimmard.

Deerhunter. (2010). *Desire Lines. On Halcyon Digest* [CD]. London, UK: 4AD.

Denora, T. (2003). Music sociology: Getting the music into the action. *British Journal of Music Education, 20*(2), 165–177. doi:10.1017/S0265051703005369

Dowd, T. J., Liddle, K., & Nelson, J. (2004). Music festivals as scenes: examples from serious music, womyn's music and skatepunk. In A. Bennett & R. A. Peterson (Eds.), *Music scenes: Local, translocal and virtual* (pp. 149–167). Nashville, TN: Vanderbilt University Press.

Duffy, M. (2000). Lines of drift: Festival participation and performing a sense of place. *Popular Music, 19*(1), 51–64. doi:10.1017/S0261143000000027

Evans, H., Ginnis, S., & Barlett, J. (2015). #SocialEthics a guide to embedding ethics in social media research. *Wisdom of the Crowd*. Retrieved from https://www.ipsosmori.com/researchpublications/publications/1771/Ipsos-MORI-and-DemosCASMcall-for-better-ethical-standards-in-social-media-research.aspx

Fatboy Slim. (1998). *You've Come a Long Way, Baby* [CD]. London: Skint Records.

Fatboy Slim. (1999). *Praise you*. Retrieved from https://www.youtube.com/watch?v=ruAi4VBoBSM

Fonarow, W. (1997). The spatial organization of the indie music gig. In K. Gelder & S. Thornton (Eds.), *The subcultures reader*. London: Routledge.

Friedman, S., Savage, M., Hanquinet, L., & Miles, A. (2015). Cultural sociology and new forms of distinction. *Poetics, 53*, 1–8. doi:10.1016/j.poetic.2015.10.002

Frith, S. (1996). *Performing rites. Evaluating popular music*. Oxford, UK: Oxford University Press.

Garfinkel, H. (1967). *Studies in ethnomethodology*. Prentice-Hall.

Geus, S., Richards, G., & Toepoel, V. (2016). Conceptualisation and operationalisation of event and festival experiences: Creation of an event experience scale. *Scandinavian Journal of Hospitality and Tourism, 16*(3), 274–296. doi:10.1080/15022250.2015.1101933

Guerra, P. (2010). *A instável leveza do rock: Génese, dinâmica e consolidação do rock alternativo em Portugal* (Doctoral dissertation). Repositório Aberto da Universidade do Porto.

Guerra, P. (2015). Keep it rocking: The social space of Portuguese alternative rock (1980–2010). *Journal of Sociology (Melbourne, Vic.)*, *52*(4), 615–630. doi:10.1177/1440783315569557

Guerra, P. (2016). Lembranças do último verão. Festivais de música, ritualizações e identidades na contemporaneidade portuguesa. *Portugal ao Espelho*. Retrieved from https://portugalaoespelho.files.wordpress.com/2016/05/ficha_-lembrancas-ultimo-verao.pdf

Guerra, P., Moreira, T., & Silva, A. S. (2016). Estigma, experimentação e risco: A questão do álcool e das drogas na cena punk. *Revista Critica de Ciencias Sociais*, *109*(109), 33–62. doi:10.4000/rccs.6206

Hannerz, U. (2006). *Two faces of cosmopolitanism: culture and politics*. Barcelona: Fundació CIDOB.

Harvey, D. (1989). *The urban experience*. Baltimore, MD: Johns Hopkins University Press.

Hebdige, D. (1990). Fax to the future. *Marxism Today*, *34*(January), 1118–1123.

Hennion, A. (1999). Music industry and music lovers, beyond Benjamin: The return of the amateur. *Soundscapes*, *2*, 1–7.

Hudson, S., Roth, M. S., Madden, T., & Hudson, R. (2015). The effects of social media on emotions, brand relationship quality, and word of mouth: An empirical study of music festival attendees. *Tourism Management*, *47*, 68–76. doi:10.1016/j.tourman.2014.09.001

Ilan, J. (2012). Street social capital in the liquid city. *Ethnography*, *14*(1), 3–24. doi:10.1177/1466138112440983

Jenkins, H., Ford, S., & Green, J. (2013). *Spreadable Media: Creating Value and Meaning in a Networked Culture*. New York: New York University Press.

Jetto, B. (2010). *Music blogs, music scenes and sub-cultural capital: emerging practices in music blogs*. Paper presented at Cybercultures, 5th Global Conference, Salzburg, Austria.

Jordan, J. (2016). Festivalisation of cultural production: Experimentation, spectacularisation and immersion. *ENCATC: Journal of Cultural Management and Policy*, *6*(1), 44–55.

Kitchin, R., & Dodge, M. (2007). Rethinking maps. *Progress in Human Geography*, *31*(3), 331–344. doi:10.1177/0309132507077082

Klaxons. (2007). *Myths of the Near Future* [CD]. London: Polydor Records Ltd.

Klaxonsvevo. (2009). *Golden Skans* [Official Video]. Retrieved from https://www. youtube.com/watch?v=q-SJjFcnsGs

Kuru, O., Bayer, J., Pasek, J., & Campbell, S. W. (2016). – Understanding and measuring mobile Facebook use: Who, why and how? *Mobile Media & Communication, 5*(1), 102–120. doi:10.1177/2050157916678269

Larsen, G., & O'Reilly, D. (2005). *Music festivals as sites of consumption: an exploratory study.* Working papers 2005. Braford, The Bradford MBA.

Liew, K. K., & Pang, N. (2015). Neoliberal visions, post-capitalist memories: Heritage politics and the counter-mapping of Singapore's cityscape. *Ethnography, 16*(3), 331–351. doi:10.1177/1466138114552939

Lupton, D. (2012). *Digital Sociology: An Introduction.* Retrieved from https://ses. library.usyd.edu.au/bitstream/2123/8621/2/Digital%20Sociology.pdf

Macdowall, L. J., & Souza, P. (2018). 'I'd Double Tap That!!' Street art, graffiti, and Instagram research. *Media Culture & Society, 40*(1), 3–22. doi:10.1177/0163443717703793

Malbon, B. (1999). *Clubbing: Dancing, ecstasy and vitality.* London: Routledge.

Manovich, L. (2016). *Instagram and Contemporary Image.* Retrieved from http:// manovich.net/content/04-projects/145-instagram-and-contemporary-image/ instagram_book_manovich.pdf

McKay. G. (2000). Glastonbury: A very English fair. London: Victor Gollancz.

McKay, G. (Ed.). (1998). *DIY Culture: Party & protest in nineties Britain.* London: Verso.

Molz, J. G. (2011). Cosmopolitanism and consumption. In M. Rovisco & M. Nowicka (Eds.), *The Ashgate research companion to cosmopolitanism.* Farnham, UK: Ashgate Publishing.

Morey, Y., Bengry-Howell, A., Griffin, C., Szmigin, I., & Riley, S. (2014). Festivals 2.0: Consuming, producing and participating in the extended festival experience. In A. Bennett, J. Taylor, & I. Woodward (Eds.), *The festivalization of culture* (pp. 251–269). Surrey, UK: Ashgate.

Nachvatal, J. (2011). *Immersion Into Noise.* University of Michigan Library.

Nadais, I. (2010, May 13). A aldeia gaulesa. *Ípsilon*. Retrieved from http://ipsilon. publico.pt/Musica/texto.aspx?id=256596

New Musical Express. (2010). The 50 best festival road-trip songs. *New Musical Express* Retrieved from http://www.nme.com/photos/the-50-best-festival-road-trip-songs/309307

New Musical Express. (2015). 15 Songs you're going to hear everywhere at festivals in summer 2015. *New Musical Express Gallery*. Retrieved from http://www.nme.com/photos/15-songs-you-re-going-to-hear-everywhere-at-festivals-in-summer-2015/377826#/photo/1

New Musical Express. (2016). 30 Years of Festival Anthems: the massive songs which defined every summer, *New Musical Express*. Retrieved from http://www.nme.com/photos/30-years-of-festival-anthems-the-massive-songs-which-defined-every-summer/344628#/photo/14

Pais, J. M. (1998). As 'cronotopias' das práticas culturais do quotidiano. *OBS*, *4*, 7–9.

Pais, J. M. (2010). *Lufa-lufa quotidiana. Ensaios sobre a cidade, cultura e vida urbana*. Lisboa: Imprensa de Ciências Sociais.

Pereira, B. (2015, June 25). João Carvalho: 'Paredes de Coura tem uma magia que outros festivais não têm'. *Wav Magazine*. Retrieved from http://www.wavmagazine.net/noticias/joao-carvalho-paredes-de-coura-tem-uma-magia-que-outros-festivais-nao-tem/

Pink, S. (2001). *Doing visual ethnography*. London: Sage Publications.

Pink, S., Fors, V., & Glöss, M. (2017). Automated futures and the mobile present: In-car video ethnographies. *Ethnography*, *0*(00), 1–20.

Portes, A. (1998). Social capital: Its origins and applications in modern sociology. *Annual Review of Sociology*, *24*(1), 1–24. doi:10.1146/annurev.soc.24.1.1

Purdue, D., Durrschmidt, J., Jowers, P., & O'Doherty, R. (1997). DIY culture and extended milieux: LETS, veggie boxes and festivals. *The Sociological Review*, *45*(4), 645–667. doi:10.1111/1467-954X.00081

Putnam, R. D. (1995). Bowling alone: America's declining social capital. *Journal of Democracy*, *6*(1), 65–78. doi:10.1353/jod.1995.0002

Regev, M. (2011). International festivals in a small country: rites of recognition and cosmopolitanism. In L. Giorgi, M. Sassatelli, & G. Delanty (Eds.), *Festivals and the cultural public sphere* (pp. 108–123). New York: Routledge.

Regev, M. (2013). *Pop-rock Music. Aesthetic cosmopolitanism in late modernity.* Cambridge, UK: Polity Press.

Reynolds, S. (2011). *Retromania: Pop culture's addiction to its own past.* London: Faber and Faber.

Roche, M. (2011). Festivalization, cosmopolitanism and European culture: On the sociocultural significance of mega-events. In L. Giorgi, M. Sassatelli, & G. Delanty (Eds.), *Festivals and the cultural public sphere* (pp. 124–141). New York: Routledge.

Sandberg, S. (2008). Street capital: Ethnicity and violence on the streets of Oslo. *Theoretical Criminology, 12*(2), 153–171. doi:10.1177/1362480608089238

Schafer, R. (1977). *The Soundscape: Our Sonic Environment and the Tuning of the World.* Rochester, VT: Destiny Book.

Silva, A. S. (2014). A democracia portuguesa face ao património cultural. *Revista da Faculdade de Letras. Ciências e Técnicas do Património, 13,* 11–32.

Simão, E., & Guerra, P. (2016). Territórios e mobilidades da (transe) virtualidade. A segunda vida dos freaks. *IS – Working Papers, 3*(11), 1-19.

Skrbiš, Z., & Woodward, I. (2011). Cosmopolitan openness. In M. Rovisco & M. Nowicka (Eds.), *The Ashgate research companion to cosmopolitanism.* Farnham, UK: Ashgate Publishing.

Social Media Research Group. (2016). *Using social media for social research: An introduction. Government Social Research.* Retrieved from https://www.gov.uk/government/uploads/system/uploads/attachment_data/file/524750/GSR_Social_Media_Research_Guidance_-_Using_social_media_for_social_research.pdf

Tame Impala. (2015). *Let it happen* [Official Video]. Retrieved from https://www.youtube.com/watch?v=-ed6UeDp1ek

Tame Impala. (2015). *Currents* [CD]. Sidney: Modular/Universal Fiction Interscope.

The Smiths. (1985). *How Soon Is Now?* [7" single]. London, UK: Rough Trade.

Thornton, S. (1996). *Club cultures: Music, media and subcultural capital.* Hannover: Wesleyan University Press.

Tomlinson, J. (2004). Global culture, deterritorialization and the cosmopolitanism of youth culture. In G. Titley (Ed.), *Resituating culture.* Strasbourg: Council of Europe.

Urry, J. (1995). *Consuming places.* London: Routledge.

Vodafoneparedesdecoura. (2017). [Instagram]. Retrieved from https://www. instagram.com/vodafoneparedesdecoura/

Wagner, H. R. (Ed.). (1979). *Fenomenologia e relações sociais. Textos Escolhidos de Alfred Schutz*. Rio de Janeiro: Zahar Editores.

ENDNOTES

[1] This is a song by the musician and DJ Fatboy Slim. The song was released in 1999 as the third single from the album "You've Come a Long Way, Baby". Kasabian presented a cover of this song for their encore at the 2014 Glastonbury Festival because it is a simple, joyous song, fun and endorphin-inducing – all key attributes of summer festivals. This song appears on the list of the most easily identifiable and listened to songs at summer festivals (New Musical Express, 2016).

[2] We are referring to three research projects: the first one, developed between 2005 and 2009 and entitled "Urban cultures and youth lifestyles: scenarios, sonorities and aesthetics in Portuguese contemporaneity (SFRH/BD/24614/2005)" within the scope of the Institute of Sociology of the University of Porto (IS-UP), coordinated by the author of this chapter and financed by the Science and Technology Foundation (FCT).This project gave rise to the doctoral thesis "The unstable lightness of rock. Genesis, dynamics and consolidation of alternative rock in Portugal (1980 – 2010)", which will be referenced herein as Guerra 2010. Its acronym is musiCULT_2005 I 2009. The second project, entitled "Urban polycentrism, knowledge and dynamics of innovation (PTDC/ CS-GEO/105476/2008)", based at the Centre for Geography and Spatial Planning Studies (CEGOT), was developed between 2010 and 2013 and funded by the Science and Technology Foundation (FCT). The third project, still underway, is entitled "Portugal in the Mirror: identity and transformation in literature, cinema and popular music", and is led by the Institute of Sociology of the University of Porto (IS-UP) and financed by the Calouste Gulbenkian Foundation (FCG) under the Gulbenkian Program for Portuguese Language and Culture (PGLCP) (For further developments, see Guerra 2016).

[3] Since the spring of 1985 The Smiths' song "How Soon Is Now" has been touring the world, having become a forerunner of post-punk. Written by the vocalist Morrissey and guitarist Johnny Marr, it has forever remained the epitome of alternative rock (New Musical Express, 2016).

[4] Social network whose shared content is exclusively in image or video format, and the latter can not exceed 60 seconds in duration. This social network differs

from other photo sharing services because it provides tools for editing the images in the application itself and "this democratized making good-looking images" (Manovich, 2016: 4).

5   In this chapter, we will drop the usual naming of festivals that associates them with their sponsors – e.g. EDP Paredes de Coura, Vodafone Paredes de Coura, Sudoeste TMN, Meo Sudoeste – because given the volatility of the brands involved in each festival in the last 15 years, it seems to us an exercise that rather fragments the narrative coherence that is required here.

6   This is a song by Tame Impala – an Australian psychedelic rock band – released on March 11 2015 as part of the band's third album, Currents, https://www. youtube.com/watch?v=-ed6UeDp1ek. Tame Impala had top billing at the Paredes de Coura festival that same year and "Let It Happen" was the song most often heard at the venue during the festival. The song focuses on the inevitability of accepting the innumerable transitions of the self in a transglobal context, under an eight-minute base of melodic hypnotism. An important piece of information associated with this song is that it was one of 15 songs "that would be heard at all festivals during the summer of 2015", according to a list by New Musical Express (2015).

7   We cannot but cite an excerpt of the song "Let It Happen": "It's always around me, all this noise/ But not nearly as loud as the voice saying/ Let it happen, let it happen/ (It's gonna feel so good)/ Just let it happen, let it happen". Cfr. Tame Impala (2015).

8   Blitz was the first Portuguese newspaper specialized in music and pop culture, for a long time it was the one and only, later being made into a magazine that has been editing until today.

9   RTP2 is the second channel of the Portuguese public service of Radio and Television, its highlighted by its programming dedicated to culture, music, arts, science, sports others than football, rich in documentaries, series and infantile/juvenile shows.

10   "That group was formed by Vítor Paulo Pereira, José Barreiro, Filipe Lopes and João Carvalho. (...) they saw an "astounding place". Someone has an epiphany: "What if we made here a music festival for youth?" (...) in the night of fados de Coimbra (a Portuguese type of music), there were present the Town Council and a councilman. On an "urge", João Carvalho takes the initiative and presents the idea to them. On the next they have a meeting on Paços do Concelho, where they are given "180 contos" (900 euros) from the municipal budget to arrange the event. And so is born festival Paredes de Coura (PdC) which celebrates this year 25 editions that put the village, that now is confused with the festival itself, on the map."

11   João Carvalho, one of the founders of the festival, recalls that moment in 2015: "In Paredes de Coura we always had a group of friends who enjoyed and knew a lot about music, but who also enjoy and know a lot about independent cinema, architecture and painting. We were always interested people. The festival was born precisely at a time when everyone went off to study elsewhere, some to Porto, others to Lisbon, Évora, and I was the only one in Paredes de Coura. So it began as a kids' game where the goal was to have a good time, and the rest is history" (*in* Pereira, 2015).

12   The Público newspaper is a daily Portuguese journal founded in 1990. It was pioneer publishing collectible goods, as CDS, books, etcetera. It's also well known for its chroniclers among various fields of social sciences.

13   Cónego Bernardo Chouzal Avenue is the main avenue of the village, and due to its central location in Paredes de Coura that the events related to the festival take place in this avenue.

14   Desire Lines is a song by Deerhunter – an American indie band associated with 4AD, a major a British independent record label – blending a variety of musical genres and subgenres (noise rock, art rock, shoegaze and post-punk...), which also features in a New Musical Express list, this time intended as a ranking of the "best festival road trip songs" of 2010. See http://www.nme.com/photos/the-50-best-festival-road-trip-songs/309307 "Desire Lines" is acknowledged to be magnetic and an indie hymn to freedom and self-realization.

15   Reading and Leeds are a pair of festivals that take place annually in two cities in England, Reading and Leeds. They are both a music festival, renowned for being the number one in UK. More information can be found on their website: https://www.readingfestival.com/ ; https://www.leedsfestival.com/

16   The Roskilde is an annual festival held in the city of Roskilde, Denmark. Is considered one of the 3 biggest and most well-known festivals in Europe, being the largest in North Europe. Initially created for hippies, but nowadays is more eclectic and covers a more mainstream part of the youth. More information can be found on their website: http://www.roskilde-festival.dk/

17   The Benicàssim festival is an art and music festival that takes place annually on the city of Benicasim, Spain. It offers a place for art displays, short movies, theater, dance, fashion and various workshops and courses on these themes. More information can be found on their website: http://fiberfib.com/index.php

18   Instagram stories are a feature of this social network which allows its users to share content (images or short videos) with others only for 24 hours. The publications expire and are impossible to see again after this time limit.

19   In her reflection, Cummings (2007a, 2007b) mentions the American Vans Warped tour, associated with the punk music that connects many skaters. This event has the name of a brand of trainers that is strongly associated with that

community. She does so in order to compare this tour to the Australian Big Day Out festival which, by refusing to sell its name to a sponsor, has itself become a brand.

[20]   This is an excerpt from the song Golden Skans by Klaxons and marks the moment when the band moved from nu-rave/new rave to art-pop. With all its vocal falsettos, mystical lyrics and indie-disco drums, this song from the "Myths of the Near Future" album – winner of the Mercury Prize – dominated the 2007/2008 festival season and became part of the clothing and aesthetics of many festivalgoers (New Musical Express 2016; Reynolds 2011).

Chapter 7
Impact of Social Media and Technology Companies on Digital Journalism

Şükrü Oktay Kılıç
Kadir Has University, Turkey

Zeynep Genel
Okan University, Turkey

ABSTRACT

A handful of social media companies, with their shifting strategies to become hosts of all information available online, have significantly changed the news media landscape in recent years. Many news media companies across the world have gone through reorganizations in a bid to keep up with new storytelling techniques, technologies, and tools introduced by social media companies. With their non-transparent algorithms favoring particular content formats and lack of interest in developing solid business models for publishers, social media platforms, on the other hand, have attracted widespread criticism by many academics and media practitioners. This chapter aims at discussing the impact of social media on journalism with the help of digital research that provides an insight on what storytelling types with which three most-followed news outlets in Turkey gain the most engagement on Facebook.

DOI: 10.4018/978-1-5225-5696-1.ch007

INTRODUCTION

Globalization and advancing technological infrastructures have made it easier for people to reach the information. Rapidly increasing popularity of Internet encouraged many companies to launch their own websites and grow into new audiences and costumers by keeping them updated on their initiatives. Realizing the importance of digital world, they made significant effort to adapt to the strategies in order to be visible on Internet. Companies, industries and institutions, which were reluctant to shift their strategies to digital, faced with unpleasant financial consequences.-By the raise of digital spaces, "the business has started to transform their stories into the digital zones such as Google that accumulates and blogs good stories about the users utilizing its search services"(Alexander & Levine,2008:12). Additionally, social networks have gained rapidly momentum and become the most consuming platform of both traditional and new media.

Media companies also had to rethink their strategies in order to maintain their businesses in the digital world. Being able to create content formats that attract the online-news consumer became an important metric for the news media organizations for measuring their success. Therefore, many news-media companies around the world formed new departments in their online newsrooms to be able to be attractive to the users in newly emerging platforms.

Large technology companies such as Facebook and Google played important role in shaping the principles of changing communication ecosystem. It is suggested that, as the shift to digital continues to accelerate, the impact of big online companies on the journalism industry will make its presence more visible. As suggested by McLuhan, the medium has increasingly begun to shape the message (2013). The increasing use of mobile for accessing the information makes it inevitable for content creators to think about how to deliver their work to the audiences in faster and attractive ways. According to We Are Social's Global Digital Trends research released in 2017, video has become the dominant digital format in the Internet, because use of mobile devices for consuming content has increased by 30 percent since 2015 (We Are Social Report, 2017).It is considered that the social media and technology companies' shifting towards native content strategies will continue to have game changing impact on how the digital content is produced, distributed and consumed. Especially, the structure of social media companies has become a determiner of the news reporting formats regarding desired consumer interactions. Due to emerging popularity of social media digital formats consumption, news platforms have started to form their content by this new formats. From this point of view, the study aims to evaluate whether digital storytelling formats shape the journalism in terms of interaction. Interaction is determined as a key point to understand its effect on the news reporting. Because the digital communication platforms are considered has a dominant role in gaining audiences' attention. Attention is becoming the primary focus of companies and corporations to survive on cyber space. As a leading question, it should be evaluated that these digital storytelling formats will be dominant on journalism trends in next future. The study is inspired from Marshall McLuhan's theory, which explains the importance of media device's habitat on media issues. The main idea is evolved from the power of the new media devices on media content consumption and its results on journalism trends and influences. In the first part of the chapter, the revolution of social media that includes its interaction is explained to understand the importance of social media and its habitat in terms of audience attention and interaction. In the second part of the chapter, the raising popularity of social media is explained with its effects on journalism.

Within the scope of this chapter, the impact of shifting native content strategies of social media platforms and the rise of digital-born news media outlets on storytelling formats is revealed by analyzing the Facebook posts of top three most used Turkish-language media companies. For this purpose, the interactions that different content formats gain on Facebook pages of three news outlets were measured and compared. The main criteria is to understand what the particular content formats in news reporting generate most interactions and expose the reasons why video content perform better than any other content type in Facebook. Therefore, the interaction differences between formats and news in Turkish-language media have been analyzed by a qualitative methodology in order to reveal the halo effects of global trends in a local market. In addition to analyze, interviews are made by digital Turkish journalists to understand the importance of digital formats in terms of the future of journalism in Turkey.

It is considered that the present study will provide a new perspective of reframing digital context in newsrooms and be a sample study of the impact of social media companies on storytelling formats in news reporting. Additionally, the chapter is a source for journalism studies for both academic and professional practices.

SOCIAL MEDIA AND TRANSFORMATION OF COMMUNICATION

The term social network dates back 50's, but the meteoric rise of social-networking web sites like MySpace, Facebook and LinkedIn has turned a dusty sociological phrase into the hottest buzzword of the Internet age. For Kaplan and Haenlein (2009), the era of social media as it is understood today probably started about 20 years ago, when Susan and Bruce Abelson founded open diary, an early social networking site that brought online diary writers together into one community (60). Boyd and Ellison (2007) defined the social media as web-based services that allow individuals to construct a public or semi-public profile within a bounded system, articulate a list of other users with whom they share a connection, and view and traverse their list of connections and those made by others within the system (211). So, a characteristic of social media is to connect individuals on one network for interaction and provides them with technological systems so that they can share their thought, images, visual arguments or comments with each other.

According to the data of the Organization for Economic Cooperation and Development the social media concept that reached the supra-territorial popularity at 2005, is defined as "applications which media content in various forms being formed by last user and is generally open to public" (OESD,2009:61). Especially, the social networks such as Facebook has rapidly gain momentum and reach 60 million users by late 2008 who spend 6-8 percent of all their daily time online and 500 million global users by early 2009 (Skeels & Grudin,2009; Parrish et al., 2010). Increasing number of Web 2.0 tools and social media networks attract individuals to engage with these networks in their social and private lives due to the reason of being interacted. Twitter, Instagram, and YouTube started to monitor the interaction of many communities (Newman,2009). One of the most important features of this new space is being free from time and space that, as McLuhan and Powers(2015) describe, establishes a new type of world that is globalized. The globalized platforms created its unique communication environment that rule out every member to become an active and creative participant of the communication environment.

The second important characteristic of social media is that it allow users to participate the effect of the content. The opportunity of creating own and unique content was the one of the most attractive feature of the social media networks. This new electric media changed the communication influences of the individuals and bring its new information forms and patterns (McLuhan, 2013). Especially the increasing mobile usage leads to content and the format production gain significant importance. Its simplicity makes people prefer spending most of their online time on the mobile when compared to the stabile connections.

Pace has gained importance and responsive content have become the favorite of users. The structure of content transformed into more visual and easy-to-look forms such as info graphs, images, videos, and live-stream forms. Therefore, the social media networks have gained power on the issues that people pay attention all around the world. Especially, the content formats became a determiner for attention and daily agenda of the cyber communities. In an ecosystem that the content formats determine the interaction volume, the quality or characteristics of the contents remain to the background. This new tendency has affected all policies of the corporations. Most companies have started to improve their strategies in order to be in this new and sophisticated market.

To be able to be visible on the Internet has become very much dependent on creating content by paying attention to a set of rules determined by big online companies such as Facebook and Google since their algorithms decide what type of content is being shown to their users (Goodwin et al., 2016). As the online traffic is mainly shared by websites through these platforms, being in line with their rules in content creation and distribution processes defined the success of websites in terms of having a wider reach and a greater impact.

This new phenomena affected the news consuming habits as well as other areas. People start to follow news accounts via the social networks except news websites. The visiting traffic has started to decrease while the followers increases on social network accounts (Doğan, 2013). Social media accounts become the first-hand news sources for the users. For, the message cluster makes users improve a filter to select the attractive or interesting content by formats criteria. Especially the old fashion contents that are based on website traffic lost their potential, while the formats such as quizzes and videos gain the power to catch and sustain attention. In a similar way, many news corporation affected by this new trend in terms of creating their content and conveying the messages by digital communications platforms (Bell,2014). While they have advertisement income concerns, users visit to the news website become a unique achievement for news desk to gain attention.

As identifier factor content formats has changed the habitat of online journalism. Therefore, news corporations start to use digital formats in order to gain attention and traffic for sustaining their life-cycle in Web2.0. period, which makes them shape the content characteristic by the necessities of online attention. In this regard, the message is created by the rules of digital storytelling formats that make the message attractive in point of users and gain interaction to have a power on daily social agenda. To understand the importance of digital storytelling formats in online journalism, reviewing the changes in journalism is an important practice. In that reason in the following parts, the alteration of journalism are explained and the digital news formats are examined in terms of attention.

GAME CHANGERS OF JOURNALISM

In the 20th century, newspapers saw the arrival of new mediums that altered the way readers related to print news. The Internet "was one of the most significant game-changers of all" (Mesquita, 2017:54). Newspapers providing readers with news that take place the day before publication begun to have a difficult time with competing with digital publishers operating in these new mediums introduced by the Internet (Shapiro, 2014). Although the Internet gave digital publishers the ability to publish and update news stories anytime, the early news websites were created in order to deliver the online information to the users mostly via produced content commissioned for printed media, television or radio in the first Internet era. The number of traffic to websites generated through third-party platforms was the most important metric, with which the success of social media desks was measured (Franklin, 2014). Online departments of news organizations and digital-born start-up were not capable of producing a significant amount of original content produced exclusively for the digital platforms in Internet-specific formats since the technology was not advanced enough for them to create and publish multimedia material combined with videos, audios, graphics, and other interactive elements (Gwertzman,2001).

With the launch of Web 2.0., the role of the Internet plays in the audiences has changed for all parties that used to shape the knowledge.Web 2.0. allowed the new communication environment that enable creating and airing the content within micro-blogging sites, social networks, and online encyclopedias. The most important characteristic of Web 2.0 is that its tools gave people opportunity to get involved in information creation processes and engage with online content. Therefore, the authorities, which have used to have the control over the information, were affected from Web 2.0. As foreseen by McLuhan, this new communication tool had a big impact on societies in terms of various aspects from their social structures to communal living habits (2013). As people increasingly started to engage with each other, the impact of this new ecosystem on societies became more visible by transforming itself into a global universe, where people's sentiments and opinions continuously change (McLuhan & Powers, 2015). The medium that is used to deliver messages became more important than the messages' themselves in this new global village.

The early social media strategies of news media organizations considering these platforms as traffic sources to their websites were challenged by digital-born format web-sites such as Huffington Post and BuzzFeed. They embraced native content strategies of big online and social media companies such as Google, Facebook and Twitter by treating the platforms as not only traffic sources to their websites but also as tools, in which they provide their followers with content that they can consume without leaving the platforms they are on (The New York Times Company, 2014). In the second Internet era, social network sites like MySpace, Facebook, and Bebo began to attract millions of users by offering them the ability to connect with each other through public or semi-public profiles (Boyd & Ellison, 2007), thus bringing about "the extreme changes promised by" Web 1.0 (Küng,Picard&Towse, 2008). With the power of being able to control the attention of one-third of the world's population (Reuters,2017), the large online platforms have urged news media outlets to produce original content in some specific formats, which are unique to their platforms, and embrace their tools and technologies, which are designed to get their users spend more time on their sites. Additionally, the increasing consumption of online content via mobile devices made it inevitable for the publishers to think about more creative ways to present their reports because the users started to receive information in fully digital formats (PwC,2014:6). Many news media companies across the world have had to go through reorganizations in order to adapt to the methods introduced by social media and technology companies, which have gained a huge distribution power that major media companies had once desired in order to reach new and mostly young audience (Bell & Owen,2017). Therefore, the impact of a few social media and technology companies based in Silicon Valley on digital storytelling has begun to show itself since 2010 with the content strategies basically aiming to become the only hosts of all online content available (Nielsen & Ganter,2017).

Once the traffic sources to websites for news organizations, social media platforms, with their technologies, algorithms and tools now are able to determine what content their users see in their feeds, what specific formats content creators produce information with, and what kind of content types reach wider audience. Native social media storytelling formats such as live and social videos, stories, moments, 360° photographs and videos, newly emerging products and tools such as Google Accelerated Mobile Pages, Facebook Instant Articles, Snapchat Discover, Twitter Moments, and Instagram Stories have been adapted reluctantly or eagerly by a significant number of news media outlets around the world since it has become almost impossible for them to compete with the large online platforms in terms of the number of active users, who use the platforms on a daily basis (Bell & Owen,2017).

Along with developing new products and tools to host information natively, the social media platforms also signed deals with a limited number of major news media outlets and content companies in order to popularize specific storytelling formats, especially video, in their platforms. For instance, in 2016, Facebook paid 140 media companies and celebrities $50 million to use its live video tool (Perlberg & Seetharaman, 2016). Twitter, in the same year, also announced more than six live streaming deals including ones with Bloomberg, NBA, and CBS (Wagner, 2016). The video, with social media platforms' shifting towards native content strategies, has become the dominant storytelling format.

A very few U.S.-based news media outlets have been offered to have privileged access to new features, tools, and platforms before they are rolled out to all publishers. Those outlets have also gotten favoured by the networks' algorithms in exchange of helping them popularize new content formats and tools. Facebook, for instance, has been prioritizing video content in its users' timelines. In a similar way, Google has been helping publishers, which use its Accelerated Mobile Pages to be listed on the top in searches(Wagner, 2016). Many news media companies across the world have had to go through reorganizations to be able to adapt to the ways introduced by social media and technology companies in hope to reach bigger audiences and create greater impact even though they are offered very little by those companies (Kılıç, 2016). However, there are many of indications that legacy news media outlets, even the ones offered privileged deals, have started to realize that they should not rely on a few platforms in distributing their content but invest more in their internal platforms and technologies. Social media and technology companies haven't been able to put decent business models for news outlets in place for past seven years while they force news outlets to produce exclusive content for their platforms. Continuously changing algorithms determining what format of information flourishes have been unable to help users distinguish between quality and trash (Kılıç, 2016). Therefore, the social media platforms, especially Facebook, have been struggling with the amplitude of worthless content. The platform is now trying lots of things that have little to do with social networking because it's assumed that they know that its news feed will be outdated in the very near future.

Not only the U.S. media affected by the dominance of social media on news but also these trends expanded through the global cyber platforms quickly. Nielsen and Ganter argue that the relationships that news outlets are forming with platforms are shaped by "news media's fear of missing out, the difficulties of evaluating the risk and reward ratios, and a sense of asymmetry" (2017:12). Findings from 70 interviews with media professionals, and from content analysis in another study of US-based news companies support the argument that news media outlets are confused about how to deal with social media and search companies (Bell et al., 2017).

Even the other developing countries' media corporations are affected by the popularity of the social media platforms such as Facebook and Twitter. The digital storytelling formats that able to catch population's attention became the determiner of the news content. In order for having the role of daily speech, news corporations have started to pay attention digital storytelling formats more than contents or other news formats. Within this scope, it is considered that The Turkish media is affected by the new influences of social media platforms in terms of creating the news formats. By that reason in the following part of the chapter aims to reveal the Turkish media news trends in social media and the factors that determine this trends in terms of journalism. In order for examining this aim, a research is conducted to show, whether Turkish news corporations use digital formats in order to gain attention and which digital storytelling formats affect the interaction of Turkish news consumers.

The Challenges Turkish-Language News Media Outlets Faces

Digital-born news outlets started to gain popularity by implementing native content strategies and engaging with users in creative ways on social media platforms, urging legacy news outlets to rethink traditional approaches that they had been taking towards these platforms. Media organizations shifted their focus towards the strategies that basically aim to keep the users' attention alive and making them to want to interact with information (Pavlik, 2010).

With the realization of relationship between attention and interaction, digital formats have become a necessity for the productivity of news outlets. Bock (2010) explains video journalism as the process, "by which one person shoots, writes, and edits video stories, represents both a socially and materially constructed form of news and adds a new dimension to daily work practices" (706). The increasing popularity of video formats quickly spread all over the world through the diffusing effect of social networks sites and established its own hegemony on journalism (Foust,2011). According to a research conducted by Turkish Statistics Institute in 2016, 84 percent of all Turkish Internet user population use social media actively and 74.5 percent of which prefer to consume online content in video format.

The increasing demand for videos by both users and platforms left digital newsrooms in Turkey with a dilemma. On the one hand, publishers realized that video became a dominant content type on social media landscape, and producing content in this particular format is necessary to achieve new audiences. However, on the other hand, news outlets still have to convince as many social media users as possible to consume content they produce in their websites and mobile applications as they heavily rely on online advertisement as a source of income. In order to examine how digital newsrooms in Turkey are dealing with this dilemma, social media posts of the most-followed news organizations are analysed in following parts of the chapter. The main aim of this analysis is to reveal the reluctance of Turkish-language news outlets in adapting to newly emerging native storytelling techniques and to understand the reasons behind this reluctance.

Before going into the details of findings of the research, it is important to have an understanding of the state of digital journalism in Turkey and the challenges that news outlets are facing while trying to keep up with the changes taking place across mobile technologies, storytelling techniques, social networks. Interviews with 10 media executives and news editors conducted for a 2016 study aiming at examining the challenges that prevent digital news outlets in Turkey from adapting to new media lays out major issues that media professionals face, which are the dependency on digital advertising as the main source of revenue, journalist with traditional mind-set dominating the management roles in digital news organizations, the reluctance of media owners in allocating more resources into digital innovation, and the current political environment in the country (Kilic, 2016).

The most pressing issue of all is the media organizations' inability to develop a business model for their digital operations that can pay for quality online journalism, according to interviewed media experts. Historically, digital news outlets that are profit-oriented have two main sources of income. They can put a pay-wall around their websites and applications to build a business model relying on their readers' willingness in paying for original content. They can sell advertising spaces in their websites and applications to commercial companies. And finally, they can sell other products to their readers (Gallaugher et al., 2001; Ihlström & Palmer, 2002). Sales of advertising is the only online revenue source used by digital news media outlets in

Turkey since even the most-visited news websites have no dedicated reporters who can bring original news content from the field that readers would pay for. Therefore, all news websites in Turkey offer readers content for free, meaning that news outlets need to drive as much traffic as possible to their platforms to be able to generate income to keep their operations moving. According to Statista, a statistics portal, the revenue in the digital advertising industry in Turkey amounts to US$1,172m in 2017. The same amount for the US market, where whether or not the digital subscription model can pay for quality journalism has long been widely discussed, is US$90,472m in 2017, more than 80 times more than the Turkish market. Therefore, the high dependency on digital advertising as the only source of revenue is widely considered as the main challenge stopping news media outlets from developing native social media content strategies by media professionals in the country. Media professionals also state that they have a difficult time convincing the owners of their organizations to invest more in digital operations since there is no clear path for them to make money out of digital content in social media platforms (Kılıç,2016).

With the rise of new platforms and storytelling formats, more tasks such as editing videos, designing and tailoring banners and images, writing conversational and engaged social media copies have been added to journalists' daily routines, requiring them to learn new skills to keep their jobs. However, news editors interviewed for the study, argue that they are already working under very unhealthy conditions as they need to write as many as news stories during their shifts to maintain high web traffics and have very little time, if any, to learn new skills (Kılıç,2016). Additionally, almost all news websites in the country are being run by traditional journalists who shifted to digital in recent years and have no good grasp of digital news media landscape that would allow them to set training programs for their staff so that they can acquired essential skills, the interviewed media executives admit. While facing existential difficulties, media executives stress, topics related to digital transformation are not being discussed in newsroom meetings as the most important issue that needs to be addressed.

In these directions, it is aimed to show the importance of interaction for Turkish digital journalists and the digital-storytelling trends of the Turkish news, which are affected on user interaction, are being examined. Within this scope, to understand the Turkish digital journalists' expectation of the social media and to evaluate the most popular digital storytelling formats in terms of news in Turkish media. Two different researches are merged to reveal the influences about the digital journalism in Turkey.

The main argument of the chapter is to show the importance of digital storytelling formats in terms of gaining interaction or traffic. Therefore, to understand the journalists' approaches about the digital storytelling formats and interaction, five interviews are made with Turkish digital journalists of different media corporations such as TRThaber, Anadolu Agency, Doğan Media Group in Turkey. In the second part of the research, the digital storytelling formats, which are used to deliver news in Turkish media are analyzed to understand the influences of audiences in terms of news in order to show how the medium characteristic shape the consumption of news and journalism.

Methodology and Sample of the Research

Interaction as the new trend of journalism has been discussed among the digital media experts in last years. Having digital attention is the most important factor that shows the success of a media corporation in this new era. To understand the factors behind the importance of interaction five Turkish digital journalists have been interviewed from different news platforms. Interview has been used as one of the qualitative research methodology to understand whether digital storytelling formats provide interaction and interaction shapes digital journalism in Turkey.

In the analyze part of the research is based on benchmarking methodology to understand which formats of digital storytelling are more appealing than others to audiences. It is believed that the comparison is one of the most efficient ways of examining the role social media platforms playing in people's influences in their everyday routines. As Durkheim's methodology used in his book "Suicide", the benchmarking gives a wide perspective to understand reasons and roots of a social influences. The research sample consists of the posts of top three most-used Turkish-language digital news brands that publish content on their Facebook pages. The important criterion at this point is to reveal how the attention of news audience's changes depending on the different digital storytelling formats.

CNN Türk online, Mynet, and Hürriyet online, whose Facebook posts analyzed for this study, are the top three most-used digital sources for news in Turkey according to the University of Oxford's Reuters Institute for the Study of Journalism's Digital News Report conducted in 2017. CNN Türk and Hürriyet are traditional news media outlets that mainly repurpose the news content that first published in print (Hürriyet) or aired on TV (CNNTürk), whereas Mynet is a digital-born content startup that aggregates news from various sources including newspapers, news agencies, and television packages (Yanatma,2017). They are all privately owned media companies.

CNN Türk is a thematic news channel established by CNN International and Doğan Media Group in 1999. The channel has adopted online journalism since early 2000's, first through its official website and later by adding its social media accounts to the picture. CNN Türk online is among the top sources for people from many different segments of the society, especially for those who want to keep up with the newsfeed. According to 2017 data, it is the ninth news source based on web statistics and the fifth place among mobile news sources (Medyatava, 2017).

Founded in 1948, Hürriyet is not only one of Turkey's most established and credible news sources, but also has long been a decisive element in setting the country's agenda. Based on 2017 data, it is the most followed news source in Turkey. Hürriyet has stepped into the realm of digitalization with its online news website launched in 1997 and according to 2017 data, it is the most followed news website in Turkey both on computers and mobile devices. (Medyatava, 2017).

Launched in 1999 as a Turkish-language internet platform, Mynet has become an online platform followed by 49 percent of internet users in Turkey as of 2014. Based on 2016 data, it is the top second news source with over 4.5 million visitors. There are two significant reasons as to why Mynet news has been chosen for the research sample: it is a widely preferred website as it reflects the popular contents which young internet users look for in news and it represents the tendencies of this user group.

McLuhan's and Fiore study focus on interactions when analyzing formats of media products. Their research reveals that content formats affect tendencies of societies. From this point of view, it is considered that the format a story is presented with can determine the extent of its reach and shape news consumption habits on social media platforms. McLuhan and Fiore also state that different media invite different degrees of participation on the part of a person who chooses to consume a medium(2012). In this respect, this study aims to examine the impact of newly emerging storytelling formats and mediums on news consumption habits and on the content itself.

From this point of view, it is aimed to analyze the performances of digital content types that three Turkish-language news outlets implement in their reporting. Facebook, with its 2 billion active users is the most used social media platform as a source of news among users in Turkey (Doğan,2013). Facebook posts of CNNTürk online, Mynet, and Hürriyet online are analyzed and the performances of news content shared in different formats are compared with one another.

In this respect, 300 Facebook posts published by these three news outlets in a row in Facebook between 09/11/2017 and 09/14/2017 were analyzed in order to reveal which content types gain the highest level of interactions, including reactions, shares, and comments. Data analysis methodology is used in order to determine the volume of the interaction of each digital storytelling format published by selected news outlets' accounts.

Research Findings

The interaction is an important asset of digital journalism for the most participants. According to results of interviews, most of the participant interpret their effect on daily agenda by gaining interaction. Interaction means awareness and awareness brings trust in journalism for some of the participants. The digital storytelling formats is important to gain genuine interaction for shared news outlets, while it is not important in giving immediate notifications. Most of the participants giving their unique content by using video formats due to having new followers and generating diffusion to effecting daily trends.

Some participants believe that interaction is the most important indicator for news channels' success on social media while it is also a factor in sustaining the popularity of those channels' social media accounts. On the other hand, some web editors argue that boosting traffic through social media is a priority target. The most significant motive behind this opinion is reported as achieving a certain hit rate for the official website of the news channel and generating an advertising revenue accordingly. Another group of participants think that although newsfeeds, which are linked to headlines, that are attention-grabbing but do not comply with journalism ethics, in order to get more hits, help increase hits in the short term, they cause the website to lose a significant number of followers in the long run and put the news channel's presence on social media.

Some of the participants use video story formats as part of their efforts to become a unique news channel which catches the attention of followers while journalists, who aim to generate traffic to the official news website, also use links to such video stories to increase appeal. The reasons behind the popularity of video stories are reported as the interest in television content consumption in Turkey, the high ratio of mobile consumption among users and their avoidance of reading long contents, and the fact that such video contents generate interaction in users' posts.

Most of the digital journalists interviewed believe that soon social media's attention factor will affect and transform news formats and consequently, news content. According to them, the most important reason for this is that being an active and attention-grabbing news channel on social media also means maintaining one's existence in the digital world. Almost all journalists interviewed express that being at the forefront and finding a place among agenda-setting Twitter trends which drive interaction are the most important work targets. Another conclusion derived from the interviews is that videos and similar motion videos are increasingly used in journalism in an effort to grab attention and drive interaction. Especially, video stories, which are preferred in content production except instant notifications, increase viewers' loyalty to and interest in the news channel.

During the interviews most participants said social media companies have an impact on digital journalism trends and expressed concern about restrictions against formats,which are incompatible with certain social media platforms. There is widespread concern among participants over the fact that social media companies may consider newsfeeds as message noise due to lack of striking and platform-compatible formats and limit their visibility.

In this respect the second part of the research focuses on the digital storytelling formats that are used in Turkish media. All digital storytelling formats that are used by Turkish-language news media outlets are chosen to analyze in an attempt to improve the understanding of popularity of different formats such as link, text, image, live video and video which are used to attract the attention of their followers on Facebook. For this purpose, the following part of the research aims to reveal the interaction of digital storytelling formats and understand the next future of digital journalism in Turkey.

The Interaction of Digital Storytelling Formats in Turkish News Media

The most popular Turkish digital news platform have the most interaction on determining the agenda-setting of social media in national level. The overall interaction for each news platform has shown in first figure to understand the sampled Turkish news media platforms' situation in social media. The numbers shown in figure1 is about the follower numbers of each news platforms between 01-11 September of 2017.

Among these media outlets that were analyzed, Hürriyet has the most liked Facebook page with 2,811,852 likes as of research dates, followed by CNN Türk with 1,783,549 likes. Mynet's page is considerably smaller than Hürriyet and CNN Türk

Figure 1. The popularity of news media outlets

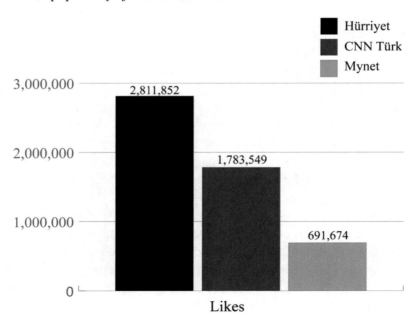

with 691,674 likes. The main reason for the gap in followers between two legacy news outlets and Mynet is that Hürriyet and CNN Türk are legacy news outlets within Turkey's biggest media cooperation with significant amount of resources that have been used to grow on the platform.

It is considered that producing content in different kind of formats is important for news outlets to increase the number of followers they have on their social media pages. Castells (2008) argues that those who manage to attract attention consistently in a network society are in a position where they can play an important role in determining what formats flourish. Hurriyet as a leading news source has important web traffic im comparision with its limited social media interaction. The main reason for that its shown as the adverstising revenue concern by the participants. Nevertheless, the interaction is the most precious result of a news outlet for the digital journalists. From this point of view, it's shown that what content formats Hürriyet Online uses to deliver its journalism to its users on Facebook. (Figure2).

Out of 100 Facebook posts shared by Hürriyet Online, 66 were image posts. (Figure2). It is considered that the main purpose of image posts is to drive traffic to its website. Bock (2010) argues that formats and strategies that are used to direct users from social media platforms to websites are not sustanaible and do not attract people's attention. According to results of journalists interviews, most of the participants think that traffic based formats cause loosing followers due to not meeting the users' expectations while only few of the participants pay attention to

Figure 2. The exhibition of Hürriyet Online news formats

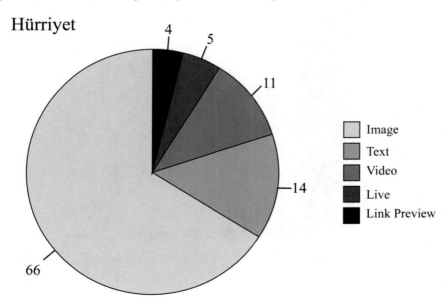

having traffic by social media news feeds. In terms of reach and interactions, it can be said that image posts of Hürriyet Online underperform on its page(Figure 3).

It was notable that 11 video posts gained more interactions (27,460) than 66 image posts had (21,599) on Hürriyet's Facebook page. The average number of interactions per video post was 2,496. In other words, the average number of interactions that a video post gained more than seven times bigger than an image post had. It shows that video posts performed way better than image posts, even though the number of videos posts were significantly less than image posts. The average numbers of interactions per link preview (4), live video(5), and text post (14) were, in order, 110, 79.4, and 31.7.

As Hürriyet uses image posts to generate traffic to its website through the platforms, CNN Türk prefers link previews that are shown with image, headline, and summary on the platforms's timeline for the same purpose (Figure 4). As shown on Figure 4, out of 100 analyzed posts in CNN Türk's page, 63 posts were published with link previews, 29 with videos, and 8 with live videos. These results shown that posts with link previews aiming at providing traffic to its website dominated CNN Türk's main

Figure 3. The interaction of Hurriyet Online news formats

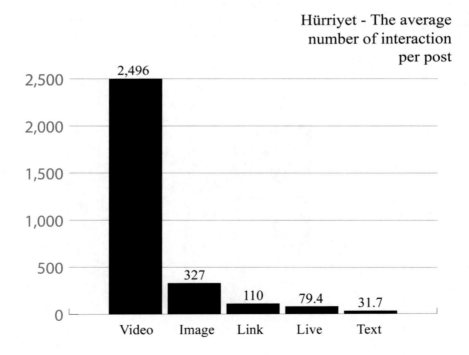

Figure 4. The exhibition of CNN Türk news formats

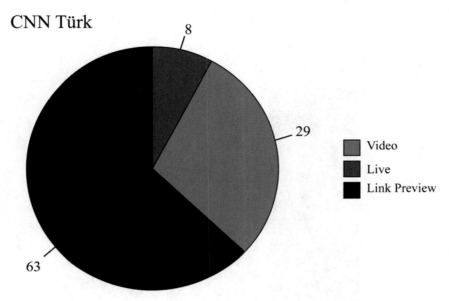

CNN Türk

Video
Live
Link Preview

Facebook Page although this format drives less interactions than other formats as shown in Figure 5. On the other hand, when CNNTürk's news formats are compared to Hürriyet Online news formats, it is noticed that with the advantage of being able to use its television content on multiple platforms, CNNTürk publishes more video content on its Facebook page than Hürriyet and Mynet do as shown in Figure 4.

As it's the case with Hurriyet, out of 100 posts shared by CNN Turk, the number of link posts were higher than video posts. However, the video posts gained more interactions than link posts did. As shown in Figure 5, the average number of interactions that a video post had was 487.3. The same number for a live video was 246.1, and for a preview link it was only 228.4. It's considered that with the newly introduction of 4,5G technology, video consumption among the Internet users will continue to increase in Turkey. Although Turkish-language news media outlets hesitate to pivot to video in their news reporting due to the fear of losing traffic to their internal platforms, video, as a storytelling format, is expected to dominate social media platofmrs. It can be seen that digital-born content website Mynet, either, was not able to fully adapt to video content (Figure 6, Figure 7).

Mynet is the only digital-born news website among Turkey's top three most-used online news sources. In spite of that, the number of video posts that Mynet published was only 15 out of 100. However, similarly with Hürriyet ve CNNTürk, it is observed that video posts shared by Mynet also attracted more user interactions (Figure7).

Figure 5. The interaction of CNN Türk news formats

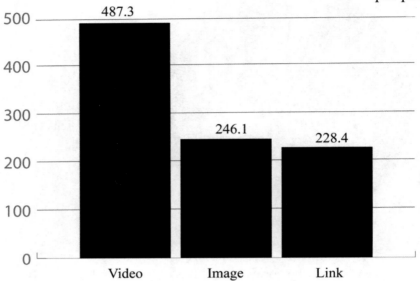

Figure 6. The exhibition of Mynet news formats

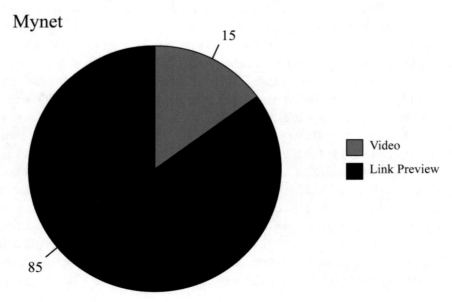

The average number of interactions that a video post gained (461.7) as shown in the figure 7 is five times more than a link preview had (84) in 100 analyzed Facebook posts. Although the number of video posts that the news outlets use on their Facebook posts is less than link and image posts, this study reveals that the number of interactions that they gain is significantly higher than any other content format.

FURTHER RESEARCH DIRECTIONS

The chapter provides an depth look at the state of digital news media in Turkey and reveals the reluctancy among news outlets in adapting to native social media strategies and content types. The study shows that user preferences in Turkey regarding in what news formats on social media they are most likely to interact with is very much in line with the global trends. Despite being aware of the fact that video content performs better than any other content type on social media, the chapter

Figure 7. The interaction of Mynet news formats

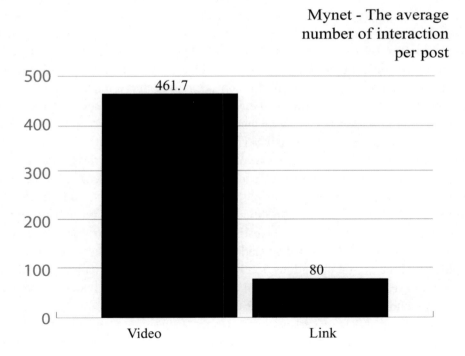

examines why digital news media outlets in Turkey are hesitating to embrace this content type. It is recommended for further studies to examine how news outlets in different countries are reacting to changes happening in mobile technologies, social networks, and digital storytelling methods.

CONCLUSION

The chapter reveals that video content of analyzed top three most-used digital news sources in Turkey performs better than any other content format on their Facebook pages. Social media users interact more with video format since it does not require them to leave the platforms they are on to consume the content. Facebook, just as Twitter, Instagram, and Snapchat, has been investing more resources into video content because it helps them get their users spend more time on their platforms. It has become almost impossible for news media outlets to grow organically on these platforms without providing its users with video content. However, the percentage of link preview and image posts (72.6%) shows that social media strategies of digital news outlets in Turkey still aim at directing as many readers as possible to websites even though video content they produce gain significantly more interactions than any other content type. Both legacy and digital-born news outlets in Turkey have been reluctant to use social media platforms as reporting tools rather than traffic sources to their websites despite being penalised by the algorithms that increasingly favour native content types on feeds and timelines. The main reason why Turkish-language digital news organisations does not seem to be interested in going through restructures to be able to provide their readers with content produced in newly emerging storytelling types on social media platforms is that their main, if not only, source of revenue is online advertising. The number of page views that their websites generate on a daily basis remains as one of the most important metrics for measuring the success of online newsrooms and social media departments because of the high dependency on online advertising displayed in their own platforms. Additionaly, the current state of highly polarized political environment with 73 journalists behind bars, media owner's reluctancy in investing more in digital operations as there is no solid business models developed by media companies or offered by social networks in place, and the digital operations dominated by traditional journalists are viewed as the main reasons that prevent digital news organizations from adapting to ever evolving technologies and methods in their news reporting.

Digital news outlets in Turkey, therefore, are struggling to find a balanced way between creating content in engaging formats, especially in video, on social media platforms and keeping their website traffic at the highest possible level. It can be concluded that although news outlets in Turkey are aware of the fact that video content performs well on their pages in social media platforms and help them increase the number of followers and likes, they do not take necessary steps to embrace this content type because of the fear of losing revenue.

New media transformation in the Turkish-language news media industry seems to depend very much on monetization opportunities of content on social media platforms. In conclusion, as long as social media platforms do not offer news media outlets solid business models in exchange of original content, the hesitation of Turkish-language news outlets in adapting to video content will continue.

REFERENCES

Alexander, B., & Levine, A. (2008). Web 2.0 storytelling emergence of a new genre. *Educause Review, 43*(6).

Bell, E., & Owen, T. (2017). The platform press:How silicon valley reengineered journalism. *Columbia Journalism School Tow Center for Digital Journalism.* Retrieved from http://towcenter.org/wpcontent/uploads/2017/04/The_Platform_Press_Tow_Report_2017.pdf

Bock, A. M. (2011). You really, truly, have to be there: Video journalism as a social and material construction. Journalism and Mass Media Quarterly, 88(4), 705-718.

Boyd D. & Ellison N. (2007). Social network sites: Definition, history, and scholarship. *Journal of Computer-Mediated Communication, 13*(1).

Castells, M. (2010). The rise of the network society. Wiley & Blackwell Publishing.

Doğan, B.A. (2013). Social sharing sites and participation: a study on academics in İstanbul. *The Journal of İstanbul University Communication Faculty,* (44), 67-84.

Foust, J. C. (2011). *Online journalism: Principles and practices of news for the web* (3rd ed.). Routledge Taylor & Francis Group.

Franklin B. (2014). The future of journalism. *Journalism Studies, 15*(5), 481-499. Doi:10.1080/1461670X.2014.930254

Gallaugher, J.M., Auger, P., & BarNir, A. (2001). Revenue streams and digital content providers: an empirical investigation. *Information & Management, 38*(7), 473-485.

Goodwin, I., Griffin, C., Lyons, A., McCreanor, T., & Barners, M.H. (2016). Precious poplularity: Facebook, drinking photos, attention economy, and the regime of the branded itself. *Journal of Social Media & Society, 1*(13). Doi:10.1177/2056305116628889

Gwertzman, B. (2001). *Interviewed by Bill Goldstein on The New York Times.* Retrieved from http://partners.nytimes.com/library/tech/reference/roundtable.html

Ihlström, C., & Palmer, J. (2002). Revenues for online newspapers: owner and user perceptions. Electronic Markets, 12(4), 228-236.

Kaplan, A.M., & Haenlein, M. (2009). Users of the world,unite the challenges and opportunities of social media. *Business Horizons, 53*, 59-68. doi. doi:10.1016/j. bushor.2009.09.002

Kilic, S. O. (2017). *The significant challenges preventing digital newsrooms in Turkey from adapting to new media* (Master thesis). Kadir Has University.

Küng, L., Picard, G. P., & Towse, R. (2008). *The internet and the mass media* (1st ed.). Sage Publications.

McLuhan, M. (2013). Understanding the media the extensions of man (3rd ed.). Gingko Press.

McLuhan, M., & Powers, B. (2015). *Global village [global köy]* (2nd ed.; B. Ö. Düzgören, Trans.). Scala Publishings.

McLuhan, M., & Fiore, Q. (2012). *The Medium is the message an inventory of effects* (J. Agel, Ed.; Haydaroğluİ., Trans.). MediaCat Publishings.

Medyatava. (2017). *Türkiye'nin en çok ziyaret edilen haber siteleri açıklandı!* Retrieved from http://www.medyatava.com/haber/turkiyenin-en-cok-ziyaret-edilen-haber-siteleri-aciklandi_150072

Mesquita, R. (2017). The transition of a traditional newspaper to the internet age: An historical account of Le Monde's case. *The Observatory Journal, 11*, 54–60.

Newman, N. (2009). *The rise of social media and its impact on mainstream journalism.* University of Oxford.

Nielsen, R. K., & Ganter, S. A. (2017). *Dealing with digital intermediaries: a case study of the relations between publishers and platforms.* Retrieved from http://journals.sagepub.com/doi/pdf/10.1177/1461444817701318

Nightingale, V., & Dwyer, T. (2007). *New media worlds: Challenges for convergence. front cover*. Oxford University Press.

OECD. (2009). *Education at a glance*. Retrieved from http://www.oecd.org/education/skills-beyond-school/43636332.pdf

Parrish, M., Elliot, N., Riley, N., & Wise, J. (2010). How to create an effective brand presence on Facebook. Forrester Research Online, 2(6).

Pavlik, J. (2010). The impact of technology on Journalism. *Journalism Studies, 1,* 229–237.

Perlberg, S., & Seetharaman, D. (2016). Facebook signs deals with media companies, celebrities for Facebook live. *The Wall Street Journal*. Retrieved from https://www.wsj.com/articles/facebook-signs-deals-with-media-%20companies-celebrities-for-facebook-live-1466533472

PwC. (2014). *The digital future of creative Europe*. Retrieved from https://www.strategyand.pwc.com/media/file/The-digital-future-of-creative-Europe-2015.pdf

PwC. (2016). *Leading in changing times making a difference*. Retrieved from https://www.pwc.co.uk/who-we-are/annual-report.html

Reuters Institute for the Study of Journalism. (2016). *Digital news report*. Retrieved from http://reutersinstitute.politics.ox.ac.uk/sites/default/files/Digital-News-Report-2016.pdf?utm_source=digitalnewsreport.org&utm_medium=referral

Reuters Institute for the Study of Journalism. (2017). *Digital news report*. Retrieved from https://reutersinstitute.politics.ox.ac.uk/sites/default/files/Digital%20News%20Report%202017%20web_0.pdf

Skeels, M. M., & Grudin, J. (2009). When social networks cross boundaries: a case study of workplace use of facebook and linkedin. *Proceedings of the Group 2009,* 95-104 10.1145/1531674.1531689

The New York Times Company. (2014). *Innovation*. Retrieved from http://www.niemanlab.org/2014/05/the-leaked-new-york-times-innovation-report-is- one-of-the-key-documents-of-this-media-age/

Turkish Statistics Institute. (2016). Retrieved from http://www.internethaber.com/iste-turkiyede-internet-kullanim-istatistikleri-foto-galerisi-1708499.htm?page=7

Wagner, K. (2016). *Twitter will livestream some Major League Baseball and National Hockey League games starting this fall.* Retrieved from https://www.recode.net/2016/7/25/12260820/twitter-livestream-mlb-nhl-games-mlbam

We Are Social. (2017). *Global digital trends report.* Retrieved from https://wearesocial.com/special-reports/digital-in-2017-global-overview

Yanatma, S. (2017). Overview of key developments (in Turkey). *Digital News Report 2017.* Retrieved from http://www.digitalnewsreport.org/survey/2017/turkey-2017/

Chapter 8

The AM and FM Radio Changes in the Multimedia Radio Emergence

Johan Cavalcanti van Haandel
FIAM FAAM Centro Universitário, Brazil

ABSTRACT

This study sees the technology and communication interface in the radio universe. In the last 20 years, radio became multimedia with the use of digital codes, which uses transmedia storytelling to spread the contents in different media and platforms. The objective of this chapter is to observe the changes in relation to the production of content in the multimedia radio, the reception and interaction processes of the receivers in this new context, and the language changes that occurred during the process. As a methodology, it presents a review of the current radio theory and an observation of the phenomena resulting from the production of multiplatform content in radio stations operating in AM and FM.

INTRODUCTION

Radio broadcasts have undergone several transformations since the beginning of their commercial use in 1920. Among these transformations is a scenario of hegemony of broadcasters in AM, which between the 1920s and 1950s were the main source of real-time information for society; the change of content by the emergence of television and the beginning of consumption in mobility, made possible by the development of transistor receivers; and the emergence of FM radio, which came to be used for music broadcasts, while the AM radio was dedicated to the spoken word. The current

DOI: 10.4018/978-1-5225-5696-1.ch008

period of the radio is marked by digital and multiplatform transmissions. The radio stopped transmitting only in analog broadcasting in AM or FM to broadcast also in digital broadcasting, using different standards such as the European Digital Audio Broadcasting (DAB) and Digital Radio Mondiale (DRM), the North American In-Band On Channel (IBOC) and the Japanese Broadbanding Services (ISDB-TN); in cable broadcasts (accessible through the television, which serves as an interface for receiving content, generally in subscription services, which displays not only transmitted sound, but visual content such as studio images, video clips of the displayed songs and news and interactions in the form of text) and the Internet (through streaming technology in a process called webcasting, which allows continuous downloading that produces real-time streaming of content, which can display both audio-only content and any type of language such as video, video with text, sound with texts, sound with photos, among others, since what is transmitted are binary codes that can be transformed into any type of language). Chris Priestman (2006, p.34) says that "the live streaming is truly the web equivalent of an analogue radio broadcast: it carries the output from the broadcast studio or an outside broadcast unit in real time". Therefore, we can say that the webcasting sound made by webradio is the equivalent to sound broadcasting on the Internet.

The webcasting process is based on packet switching technology. Wazlawick (2016, p.230) states that until the invention of packet switching in 1965 to transmit information between two points on a network, it was necessary to establish a connection between two points and to transmit all the information until the disconnection of the connection, which made the communication band dedicated from beginning to end, blocking the other messages, in which it was estimated that the bandwidth time was 90% wasted. With packet switching the information would be divided into small blocks and transmitted one at a time within the network in different paths, by other lines that were activated, in which when arriving at the receiver the data were regrouped. This action can be considered the genesis of streaming technology, where data is sent shortly after processing (for example, the first two seconds after sound production) and in small blocks are transmitted in separate paths and grouped on arrival to the receiver, which rebuilds on the machine the content transmitted by the station.

Based on Santaella (2007), we can affirm that radio was part of two generations of technologies: the second generation, called diffusion technology, in which products are developed through electro-electronic technologies, making possible the great irradiation of the radio signal and a great penetration of the content in several places, and the fourth generation, called access technology, in which are developed products for consumption in a virtual space, which have access through the graphical interface, which allows us access to the virtual content.

Twenty years ago, with the emergence of new media and the possibility of digital content transmission (through broadcasting, cable broadcasts and the Internet), radio broadcasts began to explore the visual matrix, which was not possible in previous years. The paradigm of a blind radio was broken. On the Internet, for example, web radio brings texts (which can explain advertising promotions or inform curiousities about programs and communicators) and videos (which can be viewed on demand, recorded before by radio broadcasters and downloaded by user's receiver, allowing it to be able to randomly access content, or live, in real time, following the idea that radio is a type of transmission that works with a synchronous transmission with running time). The web radio can also include new ways of distributing audio, such as the podcast, what brings content that is derived from the process of podcasting, which consists of the distribution of content by streaming on demand or download using RSS feeds to warn those who follow these new content is available. In the case of web radio, a podcast can display, for example, a recording of a musical program, an advertising piece or a radiojournal edition.

The personalization comes from the consumption of multimedia products in aligned paths, asynchrony comes from the consumption of products after the transmissions by the access of audio files or video on demand and the interactivity comes from the various platforms of interaction with the user, from the chatrooms to the recent lives on Facebook in which live streaming video is transmitted along with the broadcast on the dial and while the songs on the dial are displayed the conversation between radio and users continues on Facebook, making the narrative of the program into a transmedia narrative.

On the other hand there are new possibilities for producers, who in addition to exploring new languages, can use radio multimedia platforms as a promotional tool. This kind of use is not new, in early 2000's Pitts and Harms (2003) could saw webradio as a promotional tool. "The website can now be included in [the] list of media that can grab new audiences and recapture old audience members" (Pitts & Harms, 2003, p.274). Today this could be possible not only using its website, but all its ecology system.

Piñeiro-Otero and Ramos (2013, p.41) state that webradio focuses on a platform that covers the conventional radio with others in its multimedia essence, which allowed changes in concepts such as programming, radiophonic language, content listening community, among others. The authors (2013, p.42-44) cite two important changes: new product consumption trends (such as asynchronous access possible by hosted content for later listening and listening in a multitasking environment) and the user-listener's impact in the product prodution. But García González (2013, p.256) warns that the speech is imprecissible, as well as people who have the ability to explain things, to relate a song to a story, to tell an anecdote in the transmission or to recover a forgotten theme.

The emergence of digital media support allowed a change in the production of radio content, which became multiplatform, with a production that covers not only sound, but texts, videos, photos and others that are available in different types of media, such as social networks on the Internet (like Facebook, Twitter or Instagram), websites and instant messaging applications (like Telegram and WhatssApp), transforming radio production into a transmission of multimedia content that is accessed by users in a spread and propagated content context that, from the language point of view, has also changed, from being essentially sonorous-verbal to use a language of hypermedia, based on the three matrices of language and thought. This change, which began in the 1990s, was a global one and had repercussions on the radio stations that broadcasted AM or FM waves. Observing the consequences of these transformations for these types of broadcasters is important to understand what happened to their language, their reception and the production of content that emerged in this scenario. From the understanding of what transformations occurred we can understand the paradigm of the radio itself in the last fifteen years, which is no longer understood as a communication based on sound-verbal transmission to be understood as a narrative (Meditsch, 2010) that is based on sound, but which includes other types of language, which must have the presence of the four basic elements of sound (speech, music, effect or noise and silence) and have the possibility of transmitting each of them in real time (Medeiros, 2007; Prata, 2008).

Lev Manovich (2015, p. 73) states that, as digital humanists, we are interested in the investigation of historical artifacts, in the current visual digital culture, in professional culture, and in artifacts produced by occasional creators such as those who post content on social networking sites. All these phenomena are related to the universe of radio, an object of professional culture that marks its presence in history with content production, uses the contemporary digital visual culture and that suffers the influence of users who behave like occasional creators when interacting with the broadcaster in your posts.

The objective of this work is to observe the changes in relation to the production of content with the emergence of a multimedia production for the radio, that started to work with the three diferente kinds of language and thought and to develop products with audiovisual language in a transmedia narrative; the reception and interaction processes of the receivers in this new context and the language changes that occurred during the process. As a methodology we present a review of the current radio theory and an observation of the phenomena resulting from the production of multiplatform content in radio stations operating in AM and FM.

Some concepts covered are the technology and communcation interface (based on Neil Postman, Pierre Levy and Rogério da Costa), the transmedia narrative for the radio (based on Henry Jenkins, Sam Ford, Joshua Green, Frederico Belcavello, Marcela Castro Lewer Moreira, Carlos Scolari and Vicente Gosciola to understand the transmedia narrative and Fernando Ramos *et al* to understand the application of this narrative to the radio); the scenario of the media convergence, with the emergence of a multiplicity of content provision scenario (which can be observed in the works of Lúcia Santaella, 2004, 2005, 2007; Henry Jenkins, Sam Ford, and Josha Green, 2013, Cesar Ricardo Siqueira Bolaño and Valério Brittos, 2007, Lars Nyre and Marko Ala-Fossi, 2008); the production of digital content in the three types of language and thought (based on Lúcia Santaella, 2004, 2005, 2007); the concept and application of current media that can be spreadable in the media universe (based on Henry Jenkins, Sam Ford and Joshua Green, 2013); and the current radio scenario (based on Nair Prata, 2008; Marcelo Kischinhevsky, 2016; Andrew Dubber, 2013; João Paulo Meneses, 2012; Jorge Vieira *et al*, 2010; Chris Priestman, 2006; Paulo Portela, 2011; Sarah Helen Chiumbu and Dina Ligaga, 2003; Mariano Cebrian Herreros, 2008; and Wendy Willems, 2013), including an observation about the use of audio in this new scenario (based on Marcelo Kischinhevsky, 2016; Isabel Reis, 2012; Luís Bonixe, 2012; Aurora García González, [as cited in Ramos et al., 2012]; Debora Cristina Lopez, 2010; and Dominique Norbier, 2012). As expected results are the observation of changes in the production and reception of content, and the transformation caused by the use of new types of language, and a discussion of the consequences of these changes in the scenario of radio production and consumption.

BROADCAST ONLY RADIO

Before describing the current scenario of the radio it is important to understand what is the radio that operated only in broadcasting. This type of radio was present in our society between the 1920s and 1990s and was based on electromagnetic transmissions in amplitude modulated (AM) or frequency modulated (FM), which offered the reception of sound in real time by thousands of people who had receivers. As only sound was heard, it was not necessary to know how to read to consume radio, which made the radio accessible to all social classes. This, for example, is one of the reasons for the struggle for the possibility of communities transmit content to their surroundings, because everyone in this community can listen and understand what is said.

The AM transmission is characterized by long distances, but with a low quality signal: there is a lack of treble and bass and the signal suffers from interferences that cause noise in the transmission. The long reach of the signal, in continental countries like Brazil, facilitated the national integration, with a centralized diffusion that served like a national discourse. People who were far from cities could also access information through this transmission.

The FM broadcast is local as it has an average range of about 100 kilometers. This is because its signal is not radiated as high as the AM signal and this is what causes the FM radio to have less transmission noise. In addition, its signal is bigger and contemplates fully treble, medium and bass. As a consequence of its introduction, its general use was for musical transmission, whereas the AM radio was destined to the spoken word, because FM radio brings better quality of audio its musical transmissions bring similar quality to the recorded media as LPs or cassettes.

McLeish (2005) presents some characteristics of broadcast radio as the creation of mental images (because we only hear, which makes us imagine what is said), speak to millions and to each individual, be instantaneous, ephemeral, simple and without barriers. Broadcast radio presents some communication rules that remain valid for multimedia communication, because in any type of radio orality is the main point. Among some rules are clear language, use of small phrases, imagery in the listener's mind and repetition of key information needed by instantaneous and ephemeral nature of the radio.

Radio broadcasts began to work as a network, in which several broadcasters unified their broadcasts by delivering unique content, lowering costs and transmitting a unique speech. It was a practice initiated by AM radio in the 1930s and, later, FM radio started using the satellites to distribute the signal. In the 1990s broadcasters began expanding their productions to digital broadcasting, Internet and cable TV, which spawned a new type of radio, the multimedia radio, operating in the current context of media convergence.

MULTIPLATFORM RADIO

Aspects such as the interaction mediated by the computer and the access to digital contents in a hypermedia environment are marked by the digital culture, understood by Rogério da Costa (2003, p.13) as the capacity of relation that the users have with the information environments, called interface, which are positioned between users and what they want to get. This reality changed the way radio content was produced and distributed, forcing professionals working only with sound to work with multimedia content, with sounds, videos, texts, photos, etc., in a practice that emerges with the interaction mediated by the computer, the production of multimedia sites, maintenance of social networks and, finally, interaction through cell phones.

Some concepts of digital media come to be present in the radio universe: Use of interfaces, which mediates listeners and devices; interactivity, which manifests itself often as a stimulus of the transmitter, in the form of questions or call to participation, and response, in the form of commentary of the listener (this interactivity can be textual, sound or audiovisual); virtualization, because the contents of the stations are made exclusively for online transmissions; and convergence of media.

Neil Postman (1992, p.23-25) states that technological change is ecological, without adding or subtracting, but altering everything, like the things in which we think; the things with which we think and the nature of the community, which is where the thoughts develop. However, Pedro Portela (2011, p.58) says that technology has no power to produce social change, it is instrumental and only when its use has consequences in the social, political and economic dynamics of societies can it be considered as intervention agent changes. But Andrew Dubber (2013, p.26) argues that the change of the radio was a context, since what happened was a recontextualization, with a total change of its potential, meaning and 'flavor'.

We can say that effective technological use in the radio environment depends on the proposals of each broadcaster and even the personal proposals of each radio broadcaster, because if the radio does not have a common project for all, some may exploit more technological resources and others less, depending on your familiarity, curiosity or desires.

The beginning of the multiplatform radio was when radio stations started the transmissions in satellite broadcasting, that allowed the access of the radio through the TV, through parabolic antennas. Shortly thereafter pay-TV channels (satellite broadcasting or cable transmission) were tuned to radio stations. But the point of great transformation in the radio was the beginning of the transmissions by Internet.

From the technological point of view, Internet radio was only possible with the development of streaming technology, applied to radio in the second half of 1995. Rayburn (2007, p.3) says that term streaming in the English language is generally used for any audio or video content that is distributed over the Internet, being one of the existing technologies for delivering audio or video over the Internet. The streaming technology allowed the transmission of sound in real time in a process called webcasting. One of the needs for this type of transmission in the Internet scenario of the 1990s was data compression, since most users accessed content through low-speed modems. Ribeiro and Torres (2009, p.2-3) state that one of the reasons for the compression was to allow the transfer of multimedia content in a network, using the transfer rates that we have today (such as those with 128 kbps), which increase the speed of access to multimedia content.

Webradio works with a technology that allows a 'packet exchange' (Priestman, 2006, p.54), in which a packet is loaded while reading the packet that was previously loaded and so on. This technology enables the transfer of continuous and real-time radio audio between computers and also exploits visual-verbal elements, with which contents (such as texts, photos, videos and others) are transmitted, since everything that is transmitted is binary data that can be converted to any language.

The processes of radio transmission have different natures. For Priestman (2006, p.136-137) broadcasting is a process that 'pushes' content, with producers developing content that fills the spaces offered to the listener and webcasting is a process that offers content to 'pull', in which content is developed and made available for access by consumers. Priestman (2006, p. 13) asserts that the streaming broadcast infrastructure is one-to-one and is inherently a horizontal technology and is difficult to make it vertical, so those who want to have success in online radio need to adapt their transmissions to a horizontal way of thinking.

One of the advantages of this horizontal scenario is the possibility of the receiver to become an emitter, for example producing its own webradio and being able to be heard by commercial broadcasters, which previously were the only ones to transmit.

In addition to offering live content in real time, streaming technology also offers the on demand mode, in which all content is downloaded at once and allows random access by the user, which breaks the paradigm of instantaneous consumption of the radio.

Radio, understood as narrative (Meditsch, 2010), starts to explore different digital platforms. Then radio can be defined by actions such as its traditional broadcast, which is sound-based and continuous over time, and by its website, its applications on the mobile networks and its social networks (Bonixe, 2012, p. 183).

Lopez (2010, p.49-50) states that in the 1990s, when radio started to use the Internet as a medium of transmission, the web was seen as a threat to radio, so the adhesion of broadcasters operating in Internet broadcasting was low, but years later broadcasters began to explore not only the transmission of sound but to produce virtual spaces with texts about their memory or news presentation, which was also possible with the popularization of Internet broadband, that brought fast connections which allowed to read contents without the failures or delay of load of the data that occurred in the transmissions of 1990s.

RADIO CHANGES AND ITS NEW LANGUAGES

The radio currently shows characteristics such as free access, ability to be a secondary medium (enabling a strong multitasking context), ability to offer virtual company by voice, ability to offer breaking news in real time and ability to be available in various portable devices, which allows it to be ubiquitous (Vieira *et al.*, 2013, p.305-306).

With the adoption of digital support in radio broadcasts, we have the emergence of a new scenario for the radio. One of those responsibles for this change is the use of computers, which, according to Moreira and Belcavello (2012, p. 344), reshape society's way of thinking and modify the aspect of narrative expression by providing a new type of storyteller and enabling more peculiar and individualized circuits.

What happened on the radio was a radiomorphosis (Prata, 2008; Vieira *et al.*, 2013), a transformation of the way of being of the radio, process that is not new and has happened several times in radio history. This concept is based on the concept of midamorphosis (Fidler, 1997) that states that media do not develop spontaneously or independently, but emerge gradually from the metamorphosis of old media, in which the old forms evolve and adapt.

There are social contexts that have to be observed in this multimedia scenario of radio. The first is the access to technology, which is still expensive and therefore not accessible to poorer people. Without access to technology there is no access to content. The second is the need to know how to read interfaces, which breaks the radio's characteristic of being accessible to all: in each platform the information is written and presented in the logics of its interfaces, which forces the users to read this content. The third is the need to understand the logic of the transmedia narrative for the consumption of a story that unfolds on multiple platforms. The fourth is the context of access to interactive content, which can be at home or in situations where the listener is focused on the interaction device or can be in contexts where the user is in transit or performing some physical work, which may restrict the possibility for interaction.

Bonixe (2012, p.185) affirms that in online radio the listeners started to maintain a new relationship, different from what existed with the AM or FM radio, because with the Internet the listeners can select what they want to hear and the moment in which listen, in addition online radio provides continuous interaction with the user.

Pierre Levy (1997) argues that the network promotes the creation of a collective intelligence, distributed and based on the sharing of information, promoting and valuing the rapid circulation and instantaneous sharing of information rather than the aesthetic possession of information. In the virtual spaces that radio stations begin to maintain, such as their social networks, the posting of the listener is put into circulation and acts, when in conjunction with others, as a collective contribution, allowing what Norbier (2012, p.50) calls collective intelligence project.

Another element of change in the radio universe is its language. While acting as AM or FM broadcast it was only sonorous-verbal, as it only uses sound and text. At the moment when it begins to use new technologies for the transmission of content it starts to present new languages. In digital or cable broadcasts, digital contents are also accessed by a screen, which can be controlled by buttons. In this case you can either turn the images on or off by the buttons, making the image an optional element, which makes the radio have a sonorous-visual-verbal language. In online radio transmissions the language is different. Isabel Reis (2012, p.43) recalls that the web environment is hypertextual, multimedia and interactive. From the point of view of language, because it is hypertextual access to its contents is given by the graphic interface and therefore the image is necessary for access to the contents, which makes the radio have a hypermedia language.

The hypermedia language is based on the digital process, which universalizes the language (based on bits 0 and 1) for all computers. This process allows the transmitted data to always remain the same after data transport or copy of products. The product presented in an online way presents two fundamental characteristics: Hybridization of the technologies, since the language of the hypermedia allows all the languages to be mixed together and presented in one, and the convergence of the media, in which several media are integrated in a single one (Manovich, 2001; Santaella, 2005, 2007).

The interface is what provides the communication between the computer and the humans, acts as a translator displaying the content to be worked and materializes it as the graphical interface, which is what mediates the humans and the computer. The graphical interface can be considered a new 'reading machine', which allows each reader to be also a content editor and which brings new orientations to paradigms that have set limits to the models and forms of creation of critical discourses (Beiguelman, 2003).

Lev Manovich (2001, p.67) states that the interface is one of the most important elements of the information society and a factor that allows breaking of the old dichotomy between form and content, since the contents and the interface were merged into an entity and can not be separated. As a result, the old media that were incompatible with each other, such as paper photography and sound on magnetic tape, after being digitalized were put together in one virtual site (Santaella, 2004).

The language of hypermedia is characterized as a language that allows simultaneous access to sound, visual and verbal contents, as it is made possible by the digitalization, process that can generate content of any of the three matrices of language and thought, in which access is allowed (e.g. access to icons, texts, etc.), thus representing the possibility of non-linear paths (Santaella, 2005). By offering aligned paths there is the possibility of being offered multiple possibilities of paths to the receiver, which chooses which of them will follow according to what is placed. We thus have an insertion into the content in an interactive way.

Isabel Reis (2012, p.46-47) recalls that the contact of the listener with the AM or FM radio is made through sound, but on the Internet the first contact is visual and sound is what differentiates the contents of the online radios from other kinds of sites. The access to sound can be in two different ways on an online radio. The most common option is the one that provides a link to the access of the audio streaming and that usually presents in this icon the phrases 'click here' or 'live radio'. Another option is to make the audio available when the user accesses the station's page, offering this user an icon to turn off the sound. The first option is more common in webradios that also exist as broadcasters in AM or FM. The second option is more common in broadcasters that only exist on the Internet.

Cebrián Herreros (2008, p. 347) argues that radio renewal is coming through the creation of specific programming by online radios, with the search for authentic interactive communication, content exchanges, participation in the production and application of Internet elements as e-mail, chats, forums, among others, making it an open field for the creativity of professionals.

Meneses (2012, p.175) argues that regardless of the path that the radio follows the focus will be increasingly centered on the listener, which has been raised to the status of user, producer or prosumer, because it seeks more than a receiver-listener, and empowering the listener also means producing other types of content and devising effective ways to distribute them.

Aurora García Gonzalez (2013, p.256) affirms that social networks, as well as radio, help create proximity with the listener and in the current media scenario radio was forced to adapt to avoid losing prominence among other media and, as a result, radio listening has become more individualized and participatory.

When migrating to the Internet the radio obtained new characteristics: Transformation of physical quantity into digital data, which can become sound, image or text (sound, visual and verbal languages); geographical limit breach: Global transmission, provided it is available over the Internet, with the same audio quality; access through the graphical interface; transmission bandwidth equal to the connection bandwidth (the number of listeners interferes in the access); transmission can be maintained by up to one person, it is sufficient to have computers connected to the network and software of execution and transmission of audio; transmission does not need a governmental license (anyone can transmit); and transmission can be produced for many users, but can also be customized.

Online broadcasts are basically bidirectional because every receiver can be an emitter. So we have that any one emits and anyone receives, both downloadable content and streaming content, in a model called by André Lemos (2004) of 'all-all' (all receive and all broadcast).

It is observed in online radio reconfiguration of analogical practices and products, the possibility of the receiver becoming emitter and the conceivability, which allows us to be alone, but together in digital connections.

As a result of the introduction of new possibilities of interaction and use of visual-verbal elements there is a change in the content presented by the broadcasters. In the radio news there is the possibility of simultaneous interaction with several listeners through social network sites and instant messaging applications, the possibility of receiving the contents created by the listeners and put in the air (like accident reported that just happened) and the possibility of using the Internet as a repository (often in the form of podcast) of what was irradiated, breaking the need for immediate access that the radio had before. In music programs, interactions can also occur through social networking sites while songs are listened and songs can be viewed as videoclips on the website and on cable TV. There is also the creation of specific content for the multiplatform environment, which has a common point: the possibility of being understood only by listening, without having to see what is produced. In many cases, the content has spoken and the presenters can be seen, even at different angles, following what is done in television.

Some examples of using new multimedia and interactive languages are from radios such as Radio 538[1] from the Netherlands (which maintains broadcasting focused on orality, channels of communication with users and presentation of content on social networking sites, website with multimedia content that serves as a central point of its digital existence and audiovisual transmissions on its website and on cable TV) and Radio Comercial[2] from Portugal (which maintains broadcasting focused on oral communication, channels of communication with users and presentation of content on the websites of social networks and website with multimedia content that serves as the central point of its digital existence, but that does not yet present audiovisual transmissions in its website or cable TV).

RADIO INTERACTIVITY

Vieira *et al.* (2013b, p.308) argue that radio for many years uses elements for the participation of listeners (such as phone calls, discussion forums, etc.), which are now being rediscovered by the renewed potential for dynamic interaction between producers and consumers possible by digital technologies.

With regard to user participation on the Internet, "it is abundantly clear that the audience wants to contribute to the sphere of public communication. [...] They write, film, record, speak, edit, design, manipulate and publish their material in myriad ways, on myriad digital platforms" (Nyre & Ala-Fosi, 2008, p.43).

On the Internet, listeners participate, not only interacting with the broadcasters, but also among them and even producing materials that are posted online and in some cases used by the broadcaster, such as musical requests, testimonies of some fact or warnings of traffic problems recorded in form of audio. This action makes real the utopia of the radio being a two-way medium, in which we hear but we can also be heard, defended in the 1920s by the german playwright Bertold Brecht (2005, p. 42) in his text *Radio theory*. This is an example of user empowerment in the current radio scenario, which has been made possible by the increased possibilities of interaction.

The contents that are used for the interaction in the radio universe go beyond sound. We must note that text and sound are audiovisual and both are used in the current radio interaction. We can classify radio interactivity as multimedia (including audio, text, video, graphics, images and animations) and multimodal (with audio or image).

Chiumbu and Ligaga (2013, p.247) say that radio programs are ephemeral and that this causes listeners to respond to broadcasters during transmissions, but due to the possibilities of archiving and interacting social networks, listeners were able to engage with the programs even after their broadcasts.

In social networks sites listeners not only respond to the original posting of the broadcaster, but also comment and click on 'like' in their own posts, which enables the emergence of 'community of strangers', where users and broadcasters can communicate, connecting not only radio and public, but users among themselves (Chiumbu & Ligaga, 2013, p.248-249).

Cebrián Herreros (2008, p.347) argues that broadcasters open the way for the creativity of listeners, because with the interactivity exercised by both parties the listener acquires a new status. For the author, everything depends on the interactive model that one wishes to offer, from question / answer to a collaborative model in which the listener participates with drawings, production or co-operation, inciting the creativity of the listeners.

Willems (2013, p.224) cites two possible types of participation, the 'solicited' and the 'unsolicited'. In the first one listeners take the initiative spontaneously to contact the broadcaster to offer their contribution to the production of content; in the second one the stations encourage the audience to participate, whether by phone, SNS or the Internet, such as leaving their opinion about a program displayed in a post on Facebook.

Willems (2013, p.228) also argues that the form of interaction through the SNS offers the producer a greater degree of control in the dialogue with the audience, being less spontaneous than the interaction through the cellular telephones. In the SNS the radio broadcaster can work as moderator, which for Vieira *et al.* (2013, p.322-323) has to foster a close relationship between the radio and its networks, with good oral performance, written dexterity, digital expertise and good editorial ability, working as a gate keeper in the new media.

THE TRANSMEDIA STORYTELLING IN THE RADIO UNIVERSE

With the multiplatform transmission the radio started to work not only with sound elements, but also para-sound, which are understood by Kischinhevsky and Modesto (*apud* Kischinhevsky, 2016, p.32) as photos, videos, icons, infographics, the whole interaction architecture of the broadcaster's website, texts, hyperlinks, broadcaster's or communicator's profiles in the SNS or microblogging services and applications for podcasting and webradio. All these elements come to be present in the production of stories and can be used in the narrative, exploring the potentialities of each medium or platform, enhancing the feedback of the listener and offering multimedia content, which can be produced by the audience and obtained through interaction.

In fact, Kischinhevsky (2016, p.108) argues that social media is seen as a space for the dissemination of content, rather than a space for interaction and participation. What is now is a concern for the construction of stories that uses different media or platforms, each one often tells a piece of history with each collaborating in a specific and valuable way for the whole story, the basic condition of a transmedia narrative, which explores what each media do best, so that history can be expanded for each of them, but can be consumed autonomously, so that it is not necessary to consume one product to understand the other (Jenkins, 2006). For Scolari (2013, p.24) transmedia narratives are a specific type of narrative that expands through systems of meaning and different media. Gosciola (2012, p.12) explains that this narrative has a history divided into parts, which can be linear or not, simultaneous or not, developed in digital support or in multiple platforms, presenting sound, text and image equivalence and connection between the parts of history, with widespread use of social networks, involving either a common audience or an audience that responds to the content displayed.

According to Jenkins, Green and Ford (2013, p.178), the transmedia stories use additional segments to develop their fictional worlds, to build behind-the-scenes stories or to explore alternative viewpoints, all for the purpose of improving the main narrative, the 'mother ship', and for the intensification of public engagement.

Engagement brings models that enable a valuation of the propagation of media texts, since engaged audiences are more likely to recommend, discuss, search, pass on and even generate new material in response (Jenkins, Ford & Green, 2013, p.153). For example, a practice that becomes common in the Facebook pages of radio stations is live video streaming, in which when entering the musical block the interaction between radio and public continues in the video transmission, with images and speech of the announcers and posts of users in an action that is similar to a chatroom.

In radio, the transmedia narrative follows the practice of creating a universe of contents exploring diverse platforms, which creates in the radio a transmedia scenario in which a story, which can be a program, advertising spot or news, is told using multiple media or platforms (Ramos *et al.*, 2012). Content spread across multiple media or platforms often induces the consumption of the story in more detail, which is more detailed on the website of the broadcaster. This is a strategy used to reach visitors to the website and display the numbers of accesses to the advertisers, since each user can theoretically see the ad in the body of the broadcaster's website.

Moreira and Belcavello (2012, p. 347) say that the easy access to the network has made the transmedia narrative known by increasing audiences, with each generation custom establishing itself and reaching expressiveness and coherence.

Some proposals for content production on radio stations are based on posts that serve as a stimulus for audience participation, in which listeners comment and even share the content, putting content in circulation, which allows content to come out of the network of the transmitter and to reach new networks, being able to draw attention of new listeners.

This multiplatform scenario requires new actions by the station's production, which will start to develop content with different types of language, using equipment that was not previously part of the radio universe, such as cameras or softwares for image design work, as well as softwares for the investigation of users' accesses on online platforms. From the point of view of users there is a need for relearning, with each one having to learn how to encode the new types of language presented by the broadcasters.

Van Haandel and Ramos (2015, p.204-205) classify four kinds of elements to develop a transmedia narrative: (1) The radio website, the place where the radio station put all its relevant information; (2) The website interactive zone, the areas (like forums, chatrooms, polls and message areas) where prosumers can interact with the radio station; (3) The social media networks (like accounts and pages in Facebook, Twitter, Instagram, Snapchat, You Tube, Flickr, Tumbrl, Pintrest, VKontatke and Google+) used to develop stories and to let the listeners help to build the contents; and (4) the instant messaging app, developed to cell phones, tablets and iPad, like radio station apps or instant message apps (e.g. WhatsApp, Viber, WeChat and Telegram) to deliver radio content and interact with the prosumers, used as a tool to send their opinions and testemonies about facts that occur in real time.

CONCLUSION

We observed that radio transmissions migrated to digital media and underwent transformations, ecological and with its context, in which technology was the tool, but human adaptation was the agent of transformation, provoking changes in the languages, contents, narratives and interactions of the radio, with reflexes in the production of contents, which becomes multiplatform and with the use the transmedia narrative, and in the reception of the contents, allowing greater participation of the users through the use of spaces of interaction, such as social networks and instant messaging applications, and requiring them a new type of reading, that can understand the interfaces where the contents come to be presented.

From the language point of view, the change to a multiplatform radio, made possible by analogue or digital broadcasting, cable transmission or webcasting through the Internet allowed the radio to present different types of language, such as sonorous-verbal, sonorous-visual-verbal and hypermedia. The first was present on analog radio and the second is present in digital broadcasting and cable transmission, where the image is optional for access to the contents by buttons. The third is present on the Internet, where the image is ubiquitous, because the contact with the contents happens through the graphic interface. It is important to remember that in digital transmission what is transmitted are numerical codes, which can be transformed into any type of language.

With a multiplatform narrative the radio began to present stories, such as programs, commercial spots or news, through the transmedia narrative, in which each platform used tells a piece of the story. From the point of view of the producers, the transmedia narrative demanded new actions from the broadcasters, such as the use of different types of language through the use of multiple platforms, the search for the engagement of its audience, all to strengthen the main narrative of the product and often strengthen the website of the broadcaster, bringing users views that can be displayed to advertisers for new funds. From the point of view of the listener, he was raised to co-producer, being able to help the broadcaster both with its own content (as a report of some fact that it witnessed) as a replicator of content produced by the broadcaster, causing the contents to reach new groups of listeners. In addition, it has the possibility of consuming diverse contents in different platforms, which demands of him a new power of reading. This new reality with different platforms is due to the ease of access to the network and the consolidation of the custom of reading these different spaces.

This research is focused on the transformations that occurred in the universe of radio, but there are several other phenomena that occur simultaneously to this transformation, such as changes in reading content, access to content, access to technologies, among others. As future research, we recommend an investigation to observe the increase in the number of listeners, the age groups of radio consumers, the level of education of radio consumers and the social classes who have access to the new technologies used by radio. Another research suggestion is the investigation of good practices for the production of content following the context detailed in this research.

REFERENCES

Bolaño, C. R. S., & Brittos, V. C. (2007). Rádio. In C. R. S. Bolaño & V. C. Brittos (Eds.), *Televisão brasileira na era digital: exclusão, esfera pública e movimentos estruturalistas* (pp. 255–276). São Paulo: Paulus.

Bonixe, L. (2012). Usos e desusos da rádio informativa nas redes sociais. O caso da visita de Bento XVI. In H. Bastos & F. Zamith (Eds.), Ciberjornalismo. Modelos de negócio e redes sociais (pp. 183-198). Porto: Edições Afrontamento; CETAC.media.

Brecht, B. (2005). Teoria do rádio (1927-1932). Translated from german to portuguese by Regina Carvalho and Valci Zuculoto. In *Teorias do rádio - Textos e contextos* (Vol. 1, pp. 61–98). Florianópolis: Insular.

Cebrián Herreros, M. (2008). A criatividade no contexto do rádio atual. (Translated from spanish by Cláudia Irene de Quadros). In *Teorias do rádio - Textos e contextos* (Vol. 2, pp. 337–348). Florianópolis: Insular.

Chiumbu, S. H., & Ligaga, D. (2013). "Communities of strangerhoods?": Internet, mobile phones and the changing nature of radio cultures in South Africa. *Telematics and Informatics*, *30*(3), 242–251. doi:10.1016/j.tele.2012.02.004

Costa, R. (2003). *A cultura digital* (2nd ed.). São Paulo: Publifolha.

Dubber, A. (2013). Repensando o rádio na era digital. *Significação, 40*(39), 24-43. Retrieved from https://www.revistas.usp.br/significacao/article/view/59949

Fidler, R. (1997). *Mediamorphosis: Understanding new media*. Thousand Oaks, CA: Pine Forge Press.

García González, A. (2013). De la radio interactiva a la radio transmedia: nuevas perspectivas para los profesionales del medio. *Icono14, 11*(2), 251-267. Retrieved from: https://www.icono14.net/ojs/index.php/icono14/article/view/567

Gosciola, V. (2012). Narrativa transmídia: Conceituação e origens. In D. Renó (Ed.), *Narrativas transmedia: Entre teorias y prácticas* (pp. 7–14). Bogotá: Editorial Universidad del Rosario.

Jenkins, H. (2006). *Convergence culture: where old and new media collide*. New York: New York University Press.

Jenkins, H., Ford, S., & Green, J. (2013). *Spreadable media: creating value and meaning in a networked culture*. New York: New York University Press.

Kischinhevsky, M. (2016). *Rádio e mídias sociais: mediações e interações radiofônicas em plataformas digitais de comunicação*. Rio de Janeiro: Mauad X.

Levy, P. (1997). *Collective intelligence: Mankind's emerging world in cyberspace.* Ann Arbor, MI: University of Michigan Press.

Lopez, D. C. (2010). *Radiojornalismo hipermidiático: Tendências e perspectivas do jornalismo de rádio all news brasileiro em um contexto de convergência tecnológica.* Covilhã: LabCom. Retrieved from http://www.livroslabcom.ubi.pt/pdfs/20110415-debora_lopez_radiojornalismo.pdf

Manovich, L. (2015). A ciência da cultura? Computação social, humanidades digitais e analítica cultural. *Matrizes, 9*(2), 67-83.

McLeish, R. (2005). *Radio production* (5th ed.). Burlington: Focal Press.

Medeiros, M. (2007, September). Transmissão sonora digital: Modelos radiofônicos e não radiofônicos na comunicação contemporânea. *Anais do Congresso Brasileiro de Ciências da Comunicação, 30.* Retrieved from: http://www.intercom.org.br/papers/nacionais/2007/resumos/R0773-1.pdf

Meditsch, E. (2010). A informação sonora na webemergência: sobre as possibilidades de um radiojornalismo digital na mídia e pós-mídia. In A. F. Magnoni & J. M. Carvalho (Eds.), *O novo rádio: Cenários da radiodifusão brasileira na era digital.* São Paulo: SENAC.

Meneses, J. P. (2012). R@dio? Cem anos depois, a rádio muda; acaba? In J. P. Meneses (Ed.), *Estudos sobre a rádio. Passado, presente e futuro.* Porto: Mais Leituras.

Moreira, M. C. L., & Belcavello, F. (2012). Transmídia storytelling: fenômeno cultural X engajamento de audiência. In C. Brandão (Ed.), *Televisão, cinema e mídias digitais.* Florianópolis: Insular.

Norbier, D. (2012). Rádio e Internet: Modelos radiofônicos de participação em rede. *Rádio leituras, 3*(2), 45-66. Retrieved from: http://radioleituras.files.wordpress.com/2013/11/ano3num2art2b.pdf

Nyre, L., & Ala-Fossi, M. (2008). The next generation platform: Comparing audience registration and participation in digital sound media. *Journal of Radio & Audio Media, 15*(1), 41–58. doi:10.1080/19376520801978142

Piñeiro-Otero, T., & Ramos, F. (2013). El complejo salto de la radio convencional a la webradio. Usos y percepciones de los universitarios. *Revista de comunicación Vivat Academia, 15*(122), 40-53. Retrieved from: http://www.vivatacademia.net/index.php/vivat/article/view/10

Pitts, M. J., & Harms, R. (2003). Radio websites as a promotional tool. *Journal of Radio Studies*, *10*(2), 270–282. doi:10.120715506843jrs1002_11

Portela, P. (2011). *Rádio na Internet em Portugal: A abertura à participação num meio em mudança*. Ribeirão: Edições Húmus.

Postman, N. (1992). *Technopoly. The surrender of culture to technology*. New York: Knopf.

Prata, N. (2008). *Webrádio: Novos gêneros, novas formas de interação* (PhD thesis). Universidade Federal de Minas Gerais. Retrieved from: http://www.bibliotecadigital. ufmg.br/dspace/bitstream/1843/AIRR7DDJD8/1/nair_prata_tese.pdf

Priestman, C. (2006). Web radio – Radio production for Internet streaming. Oxford, UK: Focal Press. (Originally published 2002)

Ramos, F., Garcia Gonzalez, A., van Haandel, J., & Otero-Pineiro, T. (2012). Radiomorfose em contexto transmídia. In D. Renó (Ed.), *Narrativas transmedia: Entre teorias y prácticas* (pp. 213–227). Bogotá: Editorial Universidad del Rosario.

Rayburn, D. (2007). *Streaming and digital media: understanding the business and technology*. Burlington: Focal Press.

Reis, I. (2012). O áudio nas notícias das ciber-rádios: do hipertexto ao hiper-áudio? In H. Bastos & F. Zamith (Eds.), Ciberjornalismo. Modelos de negócio e redes sociais (pp. 43-54). Porto: Edições Afrontamento.

Ribeiro, N., & Torres, J. (2009). *Tecnologias de compressão multimédia*. Lisboa: FCA - Editora de Informática.

Santaella, L. (2004). *Culturas e artes do pós-humano: da cultura das mídias à cibercultura* (2nd ed.). São Paulo: Paulus.

Santaella, L. (2005). Matrizes da linguagem e pensamento: sonora, visual, verbal: aplicações na hipermídia (3rd ed.). São Paulo: Iluminuras; FAPESP. (Originally released 2001)

Santaella, L. (2007). *Linguagens líquidas na era da modernidade*. São Paulo: Paulus.

Scolari, C. (2013). *Narrativas transmedia: cuando todos los medios cuentan*. Barcelona: Centro Libros PAPF.

Stark, B., & Weichselbaum, P. (2013). What attracts listeners to Web radio? A case study from Germany. *The Radio Journal – International Studies in Broadcast & Audio Media, 11*(2), 185-202. Retrieved from: https://www.intellectbooks.co.uk/ journals/view-Article,id=17152/

Trivinho, E. (2007). *A dromocracia cibercultural. Lógica da vida humana na civilização mediática avançada*. São Paulo: Paulus.

Van Haandel, J. C., & Ramos, F. (2015). The use of transmedia storytelling in the radio universe. In M. Oliveira & F. Ribeiro (Eds.), *Radio, sound and Internet. Proceedings of Net Station International Conference*. Retrived from: http://www. lasics.uminho.pt/ojs/index.php/cecs_ebooks/article/view/2177

Vieira, J., Cardoso, G., & Mendonça, S. (2010). *Os novos caminhos da rádio: Radiomorphosis. Tendências e prospectivas*. Lisboa: OberCom. Retrieved from http://www.obercom.pt/client/?newsId=428&fileName=estudo_tendencias_radio.pdf

Wazlawick, R. S. (2016). *História da computação*. Rio de Janeiro: Elsevier.

Willems, W. (2013). Participation – In what? Radio, convergence and the corporate logic of audience input through new media in Zambia. *Telematics and Informatics*, *30*(3), 223–231. doi:10.1016/j.tele.2012.02.006

KEY TERMS AND DEFINITIONS

Broadcast Radio: Radio that transmits content only through electromagnetic waves, which can be AM (amplitude modulated) or FM (frequency modulated). It also includes digital broadcasts, which use different technologies such as digital audio broadcasting (DAB), DRM (digital radio mondiale), iBOC (in-band on channel), or ISDB-TN (integrated services digital broadcasting – terrestrial narrowcasting).

Multiplatform Radio: Radio that transmits content through different platforms (broadcasting, webcasting, cable, or podcasting).

Podcasting: A type of broadcast in which a warning system is used for audios hosted on a particular channel. Through these warnings the user is informed that a new audio has been published or is presented.

Radio Para-Sound Elements: Term proposed by Kischinhevsky that indicates the elements currently used by the radio, such as photos, videos, icons, infographics, the whole interaction architecture of the broadcaster's website, texts, hyperlinks, broadcaster's or communicator's profiles in the SNS or microblogging services and applications for podcasting and webradio.

Streaming: A technology that allows the transmission of data through packets, which can be continuously sent in small packets (offering live transmission) or can send all the content recorded (which is called streaming on demand and has You Tube as the most famous example).

Transmedia Radio Scenario: The radio's current stage, in which transmissions happen on different platforms and use different services, with their stories migrating from one platform to another.

Webcasting: Process of transmitting content that happens through streaming technology.

ENDNOTES

[1]   Radio 538 can be accessed by the URL: https://www.538.nl
[2]   Radio Comercial can be accessed by the URL: http://radiocomercial.iol.pt

Chapter 9
Immersive Multimedia in Information Revolution

Celia Soares
University Institute of Maia (ISMAI), Portugal & Polytechnic Institute of Maia (IPMAIA), Portugal

Emília Simão
Escola Superior Gallaecia University (ESG), Portugal

ABSTRACT

This chapter describes the immersive multimedia's role in our lives, educational activities, and business, and social media benefits from the growth of this emerging reality. Consequently, this chapter analyses the impact and the use for immersive multimedia in different contexts. In the modern world, technological advancement led to the discovery of the powerful application of multimedia. Education and learning systems have significant contribution to improve this field of research. This chapter is going to help expanded the knowledge and information about multimedia in general and immersive multimedia in particular, and its strong influences on education. How technological innovation can be used by external stakeholders to direct and promote innovation in education, how teaching can benefit from the proximity to technology, and how social networks can seize the advantages of an immersive system are some of the answers the authors try to find in this chapter.

DOI: 10.4018/978-1-5225-5696-1.ch009

INTRODUCTION

The immersive multimedia history began with the concept of virtual reality. In the late 1960s, some of the developer's needs (programmers and artists) were to create experiences digitally made through interactive multimedia. This became known as virtual reality since they produce 'near-to-reality' outputs. Currently, virtual reality can be seen as computer-created environment that users can experience through the senses of sight, hearing and touch. Immersive multimedia is a combination of multimedia elements and Interactivity in virtual reality. On other hand, the Immersion concept and practice is redefining several areas like education, live production industries, arts, and providing new experiences in publics through a combination of creative development and technical innovation.

The companies unites the efforts of directors, artists, programmers, designers, producers and technical specialists, resulting in a deeply collaborative and multidisciplinary approach to making immersive installations, live stage shows, and creative explorations.

Virtual reality and immersive environments are research lines that can be applied to various domains such as scientific or educational. Immersive digital media needs new approaches regarding its interactive and immersive features, which means the new narratives and relationships with users must be rethought. The Immersive term refers to reality simulation computer generated with physical, spatial and visual dimensions. This technology can be interactive and used by different persons with different needs. Architects, engineers, and digital artists are the professionals who take the most advantage from this technology, but industries like entertainment and digital video games are examples of potential creators and users that can create content and projects. Virtual Reality system can simulate everything from aircraft flight simulation to computer games (3D), passing through a simulation from a walkthrough of a building prior to the construction, which means that it is not necessary to invest in the physical objects creation, but it must be done in the virtual environment. As immersive elements becomes more efficient and integrates the technology, it may be available for a wide range of applications. It requires well designed user interfaces and different contents for the new generation like mobile devices, computer games, distributed web systems and desktop application. Immersive and interactive technologies like virtual reality are a new milestone in the form we interact with virtual worlds, and even how we apprehend new methods in our relationship with real world. The Information and Communication Technologies have a high potential for transforming the reality and the way we interact with real things. Virtual reality can be a major tool to potency changes in social reality itself, it is necessary to define and analyze its potential implications and influence on how new media and communication technologies can create new messages and cultural approaches (based on the initial idea of McLuhan "The Medium is the Message") (McLuhan & Fiore, 1967).

In this chapter, we consider virtual reality not only as a technological tool but also a concept related with the power and possibilities of supporting new emerging realities never seen or experienced before. Virtual reality is therefore a technology with many interactive possibilities, especially in an immersive approach related with images and sounds, but also with the possibility of covering other human senses and perceptive channels. The possibilities of creating innovative languages based on the whole range of human perception are almost unlimited, and depend on technological evolution in the first stage. In this chapter, languages are understood as ways of interacting with technology on the expression of cultural reality (Kramsch, 1998) as well as a natural language interface.

Additionally, Information and Communication Technologies evolves through more immersive and interactive circumstances, it being necessary to redesign and consider new forms of representing information and improving users' interaction with immersive worlds. Virtual reality and technologies associated with the *virtuality* such as immersive and digital environments are emerging media. As a medium, this method may help to build concepts and represent ideas, as well as developing new languages. This chapter analyses the cutting-edge expressive, interactive and representative potential of immersive digital technologies and also considers future possibilities regarding the evolution of these immersive technologies, such as virtual reality in coming years, in order to apply them to diverse scientific, artistic or informational and educational domains. Virtual reality consists on technological innovations but is also a concept and a model, proposed to link it with the latest domains such as UX (user experience), interaction design or usability. This all concepts can bring researchers and developers to new paradigms to create and redesign new experiences and imagine new expressive models that can be useful to a wide range of scientific lines of analysis and informative dynamics.

INFORMATION REVOLUTION

Information revolution is a concept that has come to materialize over the last few years. After the Agricultural (Neolithic) Revolution and the Industrial Revolution, we are now living one of the greatest economic revolution of humankind, which is commonly referred as information revolution.

It can be described as the moment when humanity reaches a point when everyone can have access to important and perfect information about everything, everywhere and all the time, this happening on principle guaranteeing equal opportunities for all. It is mainly the result of the growing and mass progress for information and communication technologies, which have advanced over the last fifty years, from data/ information processing, to data production and analysis to a truly massive and sophisticated scale.

The Information Revolution has only begun to reveal a truly relevant role in recent years with the Internet, driven primarily by the digitalization of everything and ubiquitous and permanent access to the web (Makridakis, 1995). The impact in today's world is compounded by the arrival of technologies that can transform information into actual outputs in the physical world. Technologies such as 3D printing, or even cars that do not require a driver, or simple apps to check where people are physically in every moment, carry whole positive charge to the revolution in progress. We argued that technologies change from outside the school and gets inside without the main systems - teachers, be prepared for this scenario (Collins et al., 2018).

The term *Industry 4.0* was introduced in 2011 by Fraunhofer-Gesellschaft Institute and the German Federal Government, as a collective term that draws together various information exchange, automation and manufacturing technologies (Kagermann et al., 2013). That is, the Industry 4.0 is combination of Internet of Things, Cyber-physical Systems and Internet of Services that cooperate with each other and with human within a system (Hermann et al., 2016). Industry 4.0 is primarily based on highly automated smart factories as well as smart products and services. It is based on the establishment of smart factories, smart products and smart services embedded in an internet of things and of services also called industrial internet (Stock & Seliger, 2016).

The question that we should answer is whether it will be possible to compare revolution information with the industrial revolution? The industrial revolution was primarily driven by machines powered by external sources of energy other than humans or animals, such as the steam engine. In general, this revolution can be considered from the industry efficiency point of view, with production level improvement and where the important was to gain competitiveness and more production in less time.

However, the information revolution goes one higher level. It is no longer about the efficiency of individual economic agents but about how they interact with each other. Rather than improving production processes, it makes the real functioning of the market dramatically more efficient.

The lack of information or the imperfect information is one of the main barriers holding back economic activity, as economics studies corroborate. For instance, without perfect information, producers can never identify and sell to all their potential customers or have the components of their products manufactured by the most efficient supplier. As cost have fallen and digitalization has replaced analog technologies, media industries are emerging as a "bit industry", industries capable' s to manipulate voice, image, and computer data, transform technology giants into giants worldwide capable of standing up with the largest financial and economic groups.

Until now, having access to perfect information was as unimaginable as instantly communicating with a person on the other side of the world before the arrival of the telegraph. Nowadays, any company, no matter what they produce and where they are based, can take out information about consumers and the consumers can even contact them throw mobile devices and have perfect information about all the potential suppliers. How? Using global services. Thanks to technologies like additive manufacturing, we can also send the digital file with all the required information and have the component produced by clicking a button on the other side of the world. If we want to travel to a foreign country or town, we can now instantly know all the people who have an empty local accommodation on the dates of travel and would be interested in renting it. In both cases, the result is fewer underutilized assets and a service that much better fits all the needs of all potential users. Even more important, if we are in a major city that we do not know, using services like Google Maps on mobile devices we can now know with perfect precision the best way to get from point A to point B at any given moment and how long it will take. As a result, we may spend time more productively. For example, using advanced artificial intelligence like IBM's Watson, we can in the meantime get access to every article and piece of information that has ever been produced on a given topic and have the results synthesized into a relevant and actionable output.

These are only a few examples of perfect information that we can now access. There has been an increase in interest in the potential social impact of new technologies, such as virtual reality. Researchers and educators argue that virtual reality will lead to a number of important changes in human life and activity, including: (1) Virtual reality will be integrated into daily life and activity, and will be used in various human ways; (2) Another such speculation has been written up on how to reach ultimate happiness via virtual reality; (3) Techniques will be developed to influence human behavior, interpersonal communication, and cognition; (4) As we spend more time in virtual space, there will be a gradual "migration to virtual space", resulting in important changes in economics, worldview, and culture.

Rather than viewing the organizational impacts of multimedia information systems as being inherently positive or negative, we view multimedia information systems as neutral regarding their organizational impacts. The nature of an organization´s use of information technologies and therefore the use of multimedia information systems as well, became an important issue in information revolution. The organizations that make the most will be those that take advantage of new multimedia technologies to integrate the work of people within organizations, to establish new links to other organizations, to build *virtual organizations*, and to allow more efficient use of knowledge, services and 'economies of space.

IMMERSIVE MULTIMEDIA

Multimedia can be seen as media and also content, this designation uses a powerful combination of different content forms, which can sometimes make it ambiguous. The term can be used as a noun or adjective, we use it as a noun describing a medium for multiple contents or as an adjective describing a medium as having multiple content forms. The term is used in contrast to media that only use traditional forms of hand-produced material or printed material. Succinctly, multimedia includes a combination of text, audio, images, animation, video, and interactivity content forms (Thiyagu, 2011). Multimedia is usually recorded and played, displayed or accessed by information content processing devices, such as computerized and electronic devices, but can also be part of a live performance, many times used in artistic productions.

Multimedia, the adjective, also describes electronic media devices used to store and experience multimedia content. Multimedia is distinguished from mixed media in fine art; by including audio, for example, it has a bigger scope (Parthiban & Seenivasan 2017).

Technology can be an important medium and a key tool for transforming learning. It can help and improve the relationships between educators and students, reinvent approaches to learning and collaboration, and adapt learning experiences to meet the needs to all learners (Cibulka, & Cooper, 2017).

Virtual reality is expected to play an important role in education by increasing student engagement and motivation, the technology and even virtual games, brings entertainment closer to education and improves commitment. Nevertheless, little is known about the impact and utility of immersive VR for managing e-learning tools, or the underlying mechanisms that impact learners' emotional processes while learning (Makransky & Lillehol, 2018).

Business analyses and reports calculate that virtual reality could be the biggest computing platform of all time in the future (e.g., Belini et al., 2016; Greenlight & Roadtovr, 2016). Besides that, more than $4 billion has been invested in Virtual Reality startups since 2010 (Benner & Wingfield, 2016) with the expectation that Virtual Reality could transform the entertainment, gaming, and education industries (e.g. Blascovich & Bailenson, 2011; Standen & Brown, 2006).

Companies like Apple, Facebook, Google and Microsoft indicates that virtual reality will be used for many applications including learning, entertainment and gaming. Several projects already exist like Google software Expedition, a virtual reality teaching tool that lets you lead or join immersive virtual trips all over the world — get up close with historical landmarks, dive underwater with sharks, even visit outer space. Built for the classroom and small group use, Google Expeditions allows a teacher acting as a "guide" to lead classroom-sized groups of "explorers" through collections of 360° and 3D images while pointing out interesting sights along the way. NASA's PlayStation VR demo is another example that allows operators to practice using robotic arms. Apollo 11 VR is a new type of interactive virtual reality documentary that not only permits to relive the events of 1969, but also allows to take control and fly the command module, land the lunar lander, explore the Moon's surface and deploy the lunar experiments all before returning to earth in a fiery re-entry. Many more projects are on the way and we have to expect that quality is even better.

Certain on this emerging trend, it is important to gain a better understanding of the utility and impact of virtual reality when it is applied in an educational context. The emotional impact of immersion is one important factor to consider when investigating the utility of virtual reality. This is important because virtual reality promotes a higher level of immersion than standard media, which in turn could facilitate learning through positive emotions such as enjoyment (e.g., Picard et al., 2004), possible thanks to the capability that immersion brings up judgments of control and positive value to the object of learning. However, there is limited empirical evidence of the affective value of immersive virtual reality, and even less research that investigates the psychological process by which added immersion impacts students' interest and motivation, or whether it could facilitate self-regulation and performance in the learning process (Makransky & Lilleholt, 2018).

The 3-D computing is growing quickly, although most current Internet interaction is found when user generates the content and social networks of Web 2.0. Augmented reality enables the enhancement of real-world information through the use and confluence of the Internet and portable/wearable information technology. Virtual Environments, which are beginning to be more efficient and accessible, offer ideal design spaces for social experimentation, rapid-prototyping and customized and distributed production. Every item in the physical world is being mapped, tagged, and data based, as humans build virtual worlds that can be real or unreal moved by a narrative created and manipulated by the user. Second Life, Cyworld and World of Warcraft are examples for virtual worlds innovative and alternative to real world. Social virtual worlds such as Second Life and mapping tools such as Google Earth are overlapping, perhaps predicting the advent of an immersive, 3D world. A 2007 Gartner study estimated that 80% of all active Internet users will have virtual selves by the end of 2011 and the avatars will be increasingly common, although we can see the immersive worlds are not yet massified in part, by the obligation to use appropriate equipment.

VIRTUAL REALITY TYPES AND DEFINITIONS

The very first idea of virtual reality was presented by Ivan Sutherland in 1965 when virtual world in the window look real, sound real, feel real, and respond realistically to the viewer's actions (Sutherland,1965). A lot of research studies has been done since this and currently, several different virtual reality systems exists and cohabit, including computer assisted virtual environment known as CAVE, Head Mounted Displays (HMD), Virtual Reality Glasses, and Desktop Virtual Reality. CAVE is a projection based virtual reality system with display screen faces surrounding the user. As the user moves around within the limits of the CAVE, the correct perspective and stereo projections of the virtual environment are displayed on the screens giving the user a complete sensation of immersion. The user wears 3D glasses inside the CAVE to see 3D structures created by the CAVE, thus allowing for a very life like experience inserting itself into a virtual environment, interacting with objects and becoming an active participant element. Head Mounted Displays usually consist of a pair of head mounted goggles with two LCD screens portraying the virtual environment, by obtaining the users head´s orientation and position from a tracking system the user receives images according (Sousa Santos et al., 2008). The same image may be presented on both eyes – monoscopic or we can see two separate images – stereoscopic – making depth perception a reality. Almost like CAVE, the HMD offers a realistic experience allowing the user to be completely surrounded by the virtual environment.

The virtual reality glasses or goggles are becoming progressively popular in the gaming and entertainment spheres. They are lighter and more comfortable to wear than the standard head mounted display (HMD) and many of them incorporate a range of interactive devices. More advanced versions of these glasses contain head tracking systems. This system is connected to a computer that sends signals to adjust the images seen by the wearer as they move around their environment.

Instead desktop virtual reality enables the user to interact with a virtual environment displayed on a computer monitor using keyboard, mouse, joystick or touch screen (Hounsell et al., 2015).

In order to entirely understand how students process a virtual environment, it is necessary to consider their emotional responses to this environment (Bombari et al., 2015; Kim et al., 2014). This gain special importance when designing educational material, as an understanding of the original instruments that impact students' perceptions and incentives, can guide the optimal development of virtual reality learning simulations which incorporate emotional considerations that can lead to increased use and better cognitive results (Dascalu et al., 2015).

Several categories of virtual reality technologies already exists but is likely others emerge imploded by technology progresses. The various types of virtual reality differ in their levels of immersion and also virtual reality applications and use cases.

The non-immersive simulations are the least immersive implementation of virtual reality technology. In a non-immersive simulation, just a small subset of the user's senses are stimulated, allowing for peripheral awareness of the reality outside the virtual reality simulation. Users enter into these three-dimensional virtual environments through a portal or window using standard monitors.

The semi-immersive simulations provide a more immersive experience where the user is partially but not completely immersed in a virtual environment. Semi-immersive simulations are powered by high performance graphical computing systems, which are often then coupled with large screen projector systems or multiple television projection systems.

Finally fully-immersive simulations provide the most immersive implementation of virtual reality technology. In a fully-immersive simulation, hardware such as head-mounted displays and motion detecting devices are used to stimulate all of a user's senses. Fully immersive simulations are able to provide very realistic user experiences by delivering a wide field of view, high resolutions, increased update rates, and high levels of contrast into a user's head-mounted display (Santos et al., 2009).

VIRTUAL REALITY IMPACT

Several studies have found that virtual reality simulations can have a positive impact on cognitive and non-cognitive results (e.g., Diemer et al., 2015; Kuliga et al., 2015; Makransky et al., 2017). Meta-analysis suggest that students who receive a combination of non-immersive virtual reality and traditional teaching methods and students who either receive traditional teaching, 2-D images or no treatment (Merchant et al., 2014) have different perceptions on learning.

However, early research into the effectiveness of using immersive virtual reality systems in education has been inconclusive. Several studies have found immersive virtual training procedures to produce positive cognitive outcomes in a number of settings including engineering, military research and development and health or even serious games adapted for education (Dinis et al., 2017;Rizzo et al., 2016; Zyda, 2005). Sometimes virtual reality might be compared to traditional teaching with an immersive learning environment presented via a CAVE.

The incomplete and unsettled results suggest that there are a lot of factors that can be playing an important role in how immersive virtual reality leads to educational outputs. Therefore, from a production perspective it is important to understand the process by which students interact with a virtual environment, and how this leads to educational results.

As the potential for an educational revolution begins, it will be necessary for research to be completed in order to determine the best practices and the most meaningful applications of virtual reality for education. Students will need to learn the technical side of virtual reality and how to navigate the relationship of virtual and real life. With the users being thrust into the subject matter, research and exploration into multi-sensory learning will be key factor to improve the relationship. Educators and teachers need to know how the immersive learning environments are impacting students – for good or bad – and be able to adjust how the technology is used based on those answers.

In an effort to harness the potential of virtual reality, institutions will need to think beyond the initial impact factor for learners/students and determine how to take advantage or building knowledge. Standards will also need to be determined in managing how students cross between the physical and virtual world in relationship to project and communication via teachers and fellow students. The applications of virtual reality outside education will progress and inevitably bring up additional considerations for instruction and learning. Like all technology, as it evolves so will the need for regulation and best practices by the educators who implement it.

Virtual reality presents a generous and unused future for education. Learning will transform into something that becomes a full sensory experience available to all students, regardless of background. Students who may not have the means to travel the world may be able to get an up-close look at it anyway with virtual reality technology. Everything that is taught will be linked and embedded into their world. Real and virtual realities will melt together to offer high-impact experiences that immerse students in a way that no other educational resource previously has.

Furthermore, while immediate cognitive results are relevant to control the value of an educational intervention, non-cognitive results such as emotions or stimulus (Makransky & Lilleholt, 2018), enjoyment, and intrinsic value of the learning activity (Hamari et al., 2016) have all been shown to have long-term positive effects on learning and transfer.

Consequently, non-cognitive results may be more relevant for determining the ultimate value of immersive virtual reality based on the expectation that positive emotions and the intrinsic value of the tools will lead to more use and eventually higher long-term cognitive results. Consequently, the method used in this chapter is to explore the process by which the level of immersion through technology impacts non-cognitive and observed learning effects.

While it's more or less evident to say that the technological development of virtual reality is accelerating, we have to understand when, or if, it will really take off, hardware has finally become affordable and that allows most frequent use and headset sales are also rising. When it comes to virtual reality content, many of users or potential users are still thinking about worlds populated by three-dimensional models. When we play video games, we going to see virtual reality as an extension of first-person shooter games like Doom or Halo. Despite that the fact is, outside of gaming, is video that will drive virtual reality implementation. Virtual reality might soon do to video what video did to photography. Photos are still important for engaging people on social media and other digital channels, but it's videos that most take people's attention and prepare customers to invest in a product or experience, it is enough to take into account the advances of tools like Vimeo or Youtube.

Facebook launched its first dedicated virtual reality application - Facebook 360 - serving as a hub for all 360 video and photo content that is posted to the platform. At the time of the release, the social network argues that it was already home to over one million videos and 25 million photos in a 360 format. The figure is likely to increase rapidly going forward, as Facebook's iOS and Android apps can now capture 360-degree photos without the help of a third-party application or an extra device, this allows users to easily take advantage to this functionality.

Use of virtual reality for social is still in its preliminary stage, but one thing is certain: majors advertisers will want to track innovations that make 360 video more immersive and interactive. As social platforms increasingly begin to pursue their own hardware, such as Oculus and Snapchat's Spectacles, we will see the birth of new formats and types of experiences. This will ultimately create more advertising opportunities for brands and more business opportunities.

VIRTUAL REALITY SIMULATIONS IN TRAINING/EDUCATION

Immersive virtual reality could play a predominantly and essential role in virtual simulations used for training or education (Freina & Ott, 2015; Merchant et al., 2014). Most areas of industry need highly expert personnel with major skills and several of these require training through intensive repeated practice, exercise, and active experience, which are frequently expensive and prolonged in time. Virtual learning simulations are useful not only because they are economical and easy to use, and can increase or be an alternative to realistic skills training (Moser, 2017) but also because they promote engagement with learners'. Furthermore, virtual learning simulations provide students and trainees economical and elaborated teaching methods that improve both cognitive and non-cognitive results (Makransky & Cooper, 2017). By learning and training in a virtual environment, students and trainees can practice unusual situations with different scenarios and avoid timewasting in work when the requirement arises, without having to wait for the precise resources.

In comparison, if apprentices had to obtain the same volume of practical experience, that allows to overcome problems with traditional real-world training methods, the cost would far exceed using a virtual learning simulation.

Several meta-analyses and empirical studies have investigated the efficiency and efficacy of simulations in virtual environments have shown that generally, the use of simulations results in at least as good or better cognitive effects or outcomes and approaches concerning learning than do more traditional teaching methods used in general. However, more recent reports conclude that there are still many questions that need to be answered regarding the value of simulations in education (Makransky & Cooper, 2017). In the past, virtual learning simulations were predominantly accessed through desktop virtual reality, the use of computer was the most common method. With the increased use of immersive virtual reality, much by the equipment massification, aided by the costs reduction, it is now possible to obtain a much higher level of immersion in the virtual world, which improves many virtual experiences. However, empirical research is needed to investigate if an immersive virtual reality will enhance the benefits of virtual learning simulations.

As the real world we live in is perceived in three dimensions, studies recommend that this multidimensional demonstration of virtual environments or objects is more appropriate to making us feel part of the digital world, as if it stayed real. This feature is identified in many psychological studies as presence, a cognitive construct believed to be strictly related to immersion and to lead eventually to involvement and interest in learning. In last years, since technology has become accessible to all, recent advances in motivational theory propose with an full understanding of how to create and develop shields on the emotional appeal of e-learning tools is a central issue for learning and instruction, since research shows that initial situational interest can be a first step in promoting learning (Renninger & Hidi, 2016).

Using virtual reality, students can immerse themselves into the topic area to reinforce and highlight the concepts and information they are required to comprehend, and improve their learning experience.

Furthermore, a learner's emotional reaction to instruction can have a great influence on academic accomplishment. There are several educational theories that describe the affective, emotional, and motivational factors that play a role in multimedia learning which are relevant for understanding the role of immersion in virtual reality learning environments. Some theories, such as the cognitive-affective theory of learning with media, and the integrated cognitive affective model of learning with multimedia, include general emotional factors; but they do not describe specific emotional or motivational constructs and their relationships in detail. Accordingly, enjoyment and engagement can be predicted to be the strongest when high intrinsic value is combined with an appraisal that the learning activity is sufficiently controllable (Pekrun, 2016). Establishing both autonomy and intrinsic value instructional designs can reduce the amount of negative emotions, such as anger and frustration, and facilitate enjoyment. As such, intrinsic motivation and enjoyment are important affective factors with regard to the process of learning. Furthermore, cognitive factors such as the appraisal of cognitive benefits and the amount of control or autonomy also play an important role in the learning process.

USABILITY

During the last decade, virtual reality based systems have found positions in new and different industries, powering a wide diversity kind of interactions between humans and machines. As new technologies such as advanced graphics engines, wearable hardware, and innovative interface systems have been created, and the conceptions and applications of virtual reality have transformed along with it, increasing every more varied as different mixtures of the technologies are combined to help designers realize and create their virtually imagined experiences.

Due to this multiplicity and diversity, both in application and in technology, one of the most challenging and inspiring aspects of designing successful virtual reality experiences from a human-centered design perspective has been evaluating the usability of the system throughout the prototyping and implementation phases in order to provide the best guidelines that designers and developers can use to answer the usability concerns and build better interactions possible. While there has been extensive research refining traditional usability evaluation techniques for graphic user interfaces (GUIs) to work for virtual reality, creating new evaluation techniques and classifications of virtual experience, and combining these two methods to account for the variety of Virtual Reality technologies and applications mentioned above, the methodologies have not been synthesized into content that can help designers understand what technique to use, when to use it, and what the costs and benefits are for the methodology (Rogers et al., 2011).

Usability is a dependent research area that is influenced by both the virtual reality features of the virtual environment and an independent variable that influences the affective and cognitive factors in the creation process. Previous research has identified perceived usefulness and perceived ease of use as important components that influence students' interactional experiences when using educational technology (Salzman et al., 1999). Perceived usefulness refers to the consideration to which students believe that using the platforms will enhance their performance. Perceived ease of use was defined as the effort to which students believe that using the platforms is easy or difficult.

One of the major reference on usability studies defines the usability of an interface as being usually associated with five parameters: (1) Easy to learn: a user can get work done fast with the system, (2) efficient to use: once a user has learnt the system, a high level of productivity is possible, (3) easy to remember: a casual user is able to return to using the system after some period without having to learn everything all over again, (4) few errors: users do not make many errors during the use of the system or if they do so they can easily recover them, and (5) pleasant to use: users are subjectively satisfied by using the system; they like it (Nielsen, 1993). In virtual environments and when we use virtual Reality it is sometimes difficult to apply these principles but perhaps two major and important issues regarding the usability of an interface 'transparency' and 'intuitiveness' can be explore on this field (Nielsen, 1993; Preece et al., 1994). Transparency refers to the ability of the interface to fade out in the background, allowing the user to concentrate during his work on what needs to be done and not on how to do it. In this particular case when we try to understand the usability in immersive virtual worlds, this means not interfering with the learning procedure, while intuitiveness refers to its ability to guide the user through it by the use of proper metaphors, adjusted to the situation, and successful mapping to the real world.

Perhaps the biggest difference between virtual environments and traditional user interfaces is the physical environment in which the system is used and which input and output devices are used to interact with it. As outlined above, there are three main types of visual output systems currently in use, and numerous types of input devices from the traditional gamepad to complex computer vision and biometric feedback interfaces. In addition, while most typical user interactions through GUIs don't rely on the position of a user's whole body in space, Virtual Environments may require users to stand or sit, to move around a large space and/or use whole body motions.

The adoption for dedicated virtual reality and augmented reality devices is still low, but public awareness of them has nearly doubled. Thanks to more affordable virtual reality solutions, such as Gear Virtual Reality and Google Cardboard, awareness is increasing all the time. While premier virtual reality experiences might still be behind a paywall of expensive head-mounted displays and hardware to run them, smartphone Virtual Reality offer a decent experience at a much lower cost.

CONCLUSION

Currently, immersive environments and interactive technologies are a research domain with applications in different fields of knowledge, as well as educational approaches and even as a tool for social change. It is necessary to continue building abstract approaches regarding narratives and storytelling for these new media, as well as to go further into research in areas such as interaction design, human-computer interaction, user experience, user interface, and affective computing, between other areas. Thus, virtual reality is an emerging and continuously evolution medium where it is mandatory to explore the possibilities for communication and interaction offered by current technology, and its power to develop immersive experiences regarding the possibilities of integrating human senses into it.

This way, the evolution of virtual reality in short-term approaches will be obviously and necessarily technological, but also, connected to our capacity and ability to conceive and rethink new stories and to make users interact with it, and imagine original and innovative methodologies and applications of a technology with a significant potential to illustrate ideas and concepts as we've never seen formerly. Thus, virtual reality is a technology but also a medium, a communication and narrative research field, and a conceptual idea in some ways and, even, in the future, an immersive different reality which transmits sensations outside visual, audio, haptic or to stimulate the proprioceptive and kinesthetic awareness ones, maybe one step further in the revolution of reality.

Virtual reality content is an emerging technology within various sectors, including education sector. Many examples demonstrate the acceptance in university courses utilizing virtual reality content within their curriculums. Academic should observe this technology and be aware of the development of virtual reality content and resources, as they may be required to provide support to different spaces. Support may include providing classes to develop virtual reality skills, providing Virtual Reality headsets within the collection, and/or providing Virtual Reality content for staff and learners to use.

Many questions emerge related to the virtual reality and immersive environments growth. These questions are the next steps in research in this field, and must be approached by disciplines such as neuroscience, ergonomics, life science or even formal sciences such as systems or decision theories, as well as theoretical aspects of computer science, among others. In this line of expected evolution of the medium and the technology, we need to think about the next phases in the development of simulating alternate sensations as the natural next milestone in virtual reality. Questions such as how can we experience the sensations, or subjective perceptions from other people, or how can we create and feel simulated sensations, not only see, but stay and listen and feel, will be somewhat part of the academic future framework of the virtual reality approach.

REFERENCES

Belini, H., Chen, W., Sugiyama, M., Shin, M., Alam, S., & Takayama, D. (2016). *Virtual & augmented reality: Understanding the race for the next computing platform.* Retrieved from http://www.goldmansachs.com/our-thinking/pages/technology-driving-innovation-folder/virtual-and-augmentedreality/report.pdf

Benner, K., & Wingfield, N. (2016). Apple sets its sights on virtual reality. *New York Times.* Retrieved from http://www.nytimes.com/2016/01/30/technology/apple-sets-its-sights-on-virtual-reality.html

Blascovich, J., & Bailenson, J. (2011). *Infinite reality.* New York, NY: HarperCollins.

Bombari, D., Schmid Mast, M., Canadas, E., & Bachmann, M. (2015). Studying social interactions through immersive virtual environment technology: Virtues, pitfalls, and future challenges. *Frontiers in Psychology*, *6*, 869. doi:10.3389/fpsyg.2015.00869 PMID:26157414

Collins, A., Halverson, R., & Gee, J. P. (2018). *Rethinking Education in the Age of Technology: The Digital Revolution and Schooling in America.* Teachers College Press, Columbia University.

Dascalu, M. I., Bodea, C. N., Moldoveanu, A., Mohora, A., Lytras, M., & de Pablos, P. O. (2015). A recommender agent based on learning styles for better virtual collaborative learning experiences. *Computers in Human Behavior*, *45*, 243–253. doi:10.1016/j.chb.2014.12.027

Diemer, J., Alpers, G. W., Peperkorn, H. M., Shiban, Y., & Mühlberger, A. (2015). The impact of perception and presence on emotional reactions: A review of research in virtual reality. *Frontiers in Psychology*, *6*, 26. doi:10.3389/fpsyg.2015.00026 PMID:25688218

Dinis, F. M., Guimarães, A. S., Carvalho, B. R., & Martins, J. P. P. (2017, April). Virtual and augmented reality game-based applications to civil engineering education. In *Global Engineering Education Conference (EDUCON)* (pp. 1683-1688). IEEE. 10.1109/EDUCON.2017.7943075

Freina, L., & Ott, M. (2015). A literature review on immersive virtual reality in education: state of the art and perspectives. In *The International Scientific Conference eLearning and Software for Education* (*Vol. 1*, p. 133). "Carol I" National Defence University.

Greenlight, V.R., & Roadtovr. (2016). *2016 virtual reality industry report.* Retrieved from http://www. greenlightvr.com/reports/2016-industry-report

Hamari, J., Shernoff, D. J., Rowe, E., Coller, B., Asbell-Clarke, J., & Edwards, T. (2016). Challenging games help students learn: An empirical study on engagement, flow and immersion in game-based learning. *Computers in Human Behavior*, *54*, 170–179. doi:10.1016/j.chb.2015.07.045

Hermann, M., Pentek, T., & Otto, B. (2016). Design Principles for Industrie 4.0 Scenarios. *2016 49th Hawaii International Conference on System Sciences (HICSS)*, 3928-3937. 10.1109/HICSS.2016.488

Hounsell, M. D. S., da Silva, E. L., Filho, M. R., & de Sousa, M. P. (2015). A Model to Distinguish Between Educational and Training 3D Virtual Environments and its Application. *International Journal of Virtual Reality*, *9*(2), 63–72.

Kagermann, H., Wahlster, W., & Helbig, J. (Eds.). (2013). Recommendations for implementing the strategic initiative Industrie 4.0. Final report of the Industrie 4.0 Working Group.

Kim, K., Rosenthal, M. Z., Zielinski, D. J., & Brady, R. (2014). Effects of virtual environment platforms on emotional responses. *Computer Methods and Programs in Biomedicine*, *113*(3), 882–893. doi:10.1016/j.cmpb.2013.12.024 PMID:24440136

Kramsch, C. (1998). *Language and Culture*. Oxford, UK: Oxford University Press.

Kuliga, S. F., Thrash, T., Dalton, R. C., & Hoelscher, C. (2015). Virtual reality as an empirical research tool—Exploring user experience in a real building and a corresponding virtual model. *Computers, Environment and Urban Systems*, *54*, 363–375. doi:10.1016/j.compenvurbsys.2015.09.006

Makransky, G., & Lilleholt, L. (2018). A structural equation modeling investigation of the emotional value of immersive virtual reality in education in Educational Technology. *Research for Development*.

Makransky, J. G., & Cooper, B. S. (2017). *Technology in School Classrooms: How It Can Transform Teaching and Student Learning Today*. Rowman & Littlefield.

Makridakis, S. (1995). *The forthcoming information revolution: Its impact on society and firms*. Elsevier.

McLuhan, M., & Fiore, Q. (1967). *The Medium is the Message* (Vol. 123). New York: Penguin Books.

Merchant, Z., Goetz, E. T., Cifuentes, L., Keeney-Kennicutt, W., & Davis, T. J. (2014). Effectiveness of virtual reality-based instruction on students' learning outcomes in K-12 and higher education: A meta-analysis. *Computers & Education*, *70*, 29–40. doi:10.1016/j.compedu.2013.07.033

Moser, S. (2017). Linking virtual and real-life environments: Scrutinizing ubiquitous learning scenarios. In *Digital Tools for Seamless Learning* (pp. 214–239). IGI Global. doi:10.4018/978-1-5225-1692-7.ch011

Nielsen, J. (1993). *Usability Engineering*. San Diego, CA: Academic Press.

Parthiban, K. T., & Seenivasan, R. (2017). *Forestry technologies- a complete value chain approach*. Scientific Publishers.

Pekrun, R. (2016). Emotions at school. In K. R. Wentzel & D. B. Miele (Eds.), *Handbook of motivation at school* (2nd ed.; pp. 120–144). New York: Routledge.

Picard, R. W., Papert, S., Bender, W., Blumberg, B., Breazeal, C., Cavallo, D., ... Strohecker, C. (2004). Affective learning—a manifesto. *BT Technology Journal*, *22*(4), 253–269. doi:10.1023/B:BTTJ.0000047603.37042.33

Preece, J., Rogers, Y., Sharp, H., Benyon, D., Holland, S., & Carey, T. (1994). *HumanComputer Interaction*. London: Addison-Wesley Publ.

Renninger, K. A., & Hidi, S. E. (2016). *The power of interest for motivation and engagement*. New York: Routledge.

Rizzo, A., Parsons, T. D., Lange, B., Kenny, P., Buckwalter, J. G., Rothbaum, B., & Reger, G. (2011). Virtual reality goes to war: A brief review of the future of military behavioral healthcare. *Journal of Clinical Psychology in Medical Settings*, *18*(2), 176–187. doi:10.100710880-011-9247-2 PMID:21553133

Rogers, Y., Sharp, H., & Preece, J. (2011). *Interaction design: beyond human-computer interaction*. John Wiley & Sons.

Salzman, M. C., Dede, C., Loftin, R. B., & Chen, J. (1999). A model for understanding how virtual reality aids complex conceptual learning. *Presence (Cambridge, Mass.)*, *8*(3), 293–316. doi:10.1162/105474699566242

Santos, B. S., Dias, P., Pimentel, A., Baggerman, J. W., Ferreira, C., Silva, S., & Madeira, J. (2009). Head-mounted display versus desktop for 3D navigation in virtual reality: A user study. *Multimedia Tools and Applications*, *41*(1), 161–181. doi:10.100711042-008-0223-2

Sousa Santos, B., Dias, P., Pimentel, A., Baggerman, J.-W., Ferreira, C., Silva, S., & Madeira, J. (2008). Head-mounted display versus desktop for 3D navigation in virtual reality: A user study. *Multimedia Tools and Applications*, *41*(1), 161–181. doi:10.100711042-008-0223-2

Standen, P. J., & Brown, D. J. (2006). Virtual reality and its role in removing the barriers that turn cognitive impairments into intellectual disability. *Virtual Reality (Waltham Cross)*, *10*(3–4), 241–252. doi:10.100710055-006-0042-6

Stock, T., & Seliger, G. (2016). *Opportunities of Sustainable Manufacturing in Industry 4.0*. Elsevier.

Sutherland, I. E. (1965). The Ultimate Display. *Proceedings of IFIP 65*, *2*, 506–508.

Thiyagu, K. (2011). *Technology and Teaching: Learning Skills*. Kalpaz Publications.

Zyda, M. (2005). From visual simulation to virtual reality to games. *Computer*, *38*(9), 25–32. doi:10.1109/MC.2005.297

Compilation of References

42 Entertainment. (2016). Retrieved July, 30, 2017, from http://www.42entertainment.com/

AA.VV. (2015). *The Right to Have Rights: Citizenship Culture and the Future of Cities, with Antanas Mockus*. Retrieved July 26, 2017, from http://urbandemos.nyu.edu/event/the-right-to-have-rights-citizenship-culture-and-the-future-of-cities-distinguished-faculty-lecture-with-antanas-mockus/

AA.VV. (2017). *Noguchi's Playscapes*. Retrieved July 30, 2017, from https://www.sfmoma.org/exhibition/noguchis-playscapes/

AA.VV. (n.d.). *The Blue Whale Game*. Retrieved July 30, 2017, from https://en.wikipedia.org/wiki/Blue_Whale_(game)

Alexander, B., & Levine, A. (2008). Web 2.0 storytelling emergence of a new genre. *Educause Review*, *43*(6).

Alexander, L. (2015). *Carry the frustration of injustice in this game about racist police violence*. Retrieved July 30, 2017, from http://boingboing.net/2015/08/05/carry-the-frustration-of-injus.html

Alexandrian, S. (1976). *The Surrealism* (Brazilian edition). Sao Paulo: Edusp.

Anceschi, G. (2005). Come si costruisce un'identità istituzionale. In M. Rossi (Ed.), Oltre il logo. Nove progetti di comunicazione visiva per il Palazzo dei Pio a Carpi. Carpi: APM edizioni.

Anholt, S. (2005). *Brand New Justice. How branding places and products can help the developing world* (revised edition). Elsevier.

Anthropy, A. (2011). *Rise of the Videogame Zinesters: How Freaks, Normals, Amateurs, Dreamers, Drop-outs, Queers, Housewifes and People Like You Are Taking Back an Art Form*. Seven Stories Press.

Antinucci, F. (2014). *Comunicare nel museo*. Roma: Laterza.

Appardurai, A. (1996). *Modernity at large: cultural dimensions of globalization*. Minneapolis, MN: University of Minessota Press.

Aretio, L. (2007). *De la educación a distancia a la educación virtual*. Barcelona: *Ariel*. (in Spanish)

Associazione Studi e Ricerche per il Mezzogiorno. (2010). *Mezzogiorno e beni culturali. Caratteristiche, potenzialità e policy per una loro efficace valorizzazione*. Napoli: Cuzzolin.

Augé, M. (2004). *Rovine e macerie. Il senso del tempo*. Torino: Bollati Boringhieri.

Bakhtin, M. (1981). *The dialogic imagination: Four essays*. Austin, TX: University of Texas Press.

Barthes, R. (2002). *A Câmara Clara*. Editora Nova Fronteira.

Bauman, Z. (2006). *Liquid fear*. Cambridge, UK: Polity Press.

Beactive Entertainment. (2017). Retrieved from http://beactivemedia.com/

Beck, U. (2011). Cosmopolitan sociology: outline of a paradigm shift. In M. Rovisco & M. Nowicka (Eds.), *The Ashgate research companion to cosmopolitanism*. Farnham, UK: Ashgate Publishing.

Belini, H., Chen, W., Sugiyama, M., Shin, M., Alam, S., & Takayama, D. (2016). *Virtual & augmented reality: Understanding the race for the next computing platform*. Retrieved from http://www.goldmansachs.com/our-thinking/pages/technology-driving-innovation-folder/virtual-and-augmentedreality/report.pdf

Bell, E., & Owen, T. (2017). The platform press:How silicon valley reengineered journalism. *Columbia Journalism School Tow Center for Digital Journalism*. Retrieved from http://towcenter.org/wpcontent/uploads/2017/04/The_Platform_Press_Tow_Report_2017.pdf

Benner, K., & Wingfield, N. (2016). Apple sets its sights on virtual reality. *New York Times*. Retrieved from http://www.nytimes.com/2016/01/30/technology/apple-sets-its-sights-on-virtual-reality.html

Bennett, A., Taylor, J., & Woodward, I. (Eds.). (2014). *The festivalization of culture*. Surrey, UK: Ashgate.

Bennett, A., & Woodward, I. (2014). Festival spaces, identity, experience and belonging. In A. Bennett, J. Taylor, & I. Woodward (Eds.), *The festivalization of culture* (pp. 11–25). Surrey, UK: Ashgate.

Bernardo, N. (2011). *The Producer's Guide to Transmedia: How to Develop, Fund, Produce and Distribute compelling Stories across multiple platforms.* Lisbon: beActive Books.

Bernardo, N. (2014). *How to build an exciting and convincing transmedia storyworld.* Retrieved July 26, 2017, from https://www.mynewsdesk.com/ie/beactive/blog_posts/nuno-bernardo-how-to-build-an-exciting-and-convincing-transmedia-storyworld-27070

Berthoz, A. (2000). *The Brain's Sense of Movement* (G. Weiss, Trans.). Cambridge, MA: Harvard University Press.

Biocca, F. (1997). *The Cyborg's Dilemma: Progressive Embodiment in Virtual Environments.* International Cognitive Technology Conference. Retrieved February 20, 2017, from https://onlinelibrary.wiley.com/doi/full/10.1111/j.1083-6101.1997.tb00070.x

Blascovich, J., & Bailenson, J. (2011). *Infinite reality.* New York, NY: HarperCollins.

Blashki, K., Lim, L., & Kristensen, M. (2013). The Social Translator: A Game Based learning Simulator to foster cross cultural understanding and adaptation. *IADIS International Journal, 11*(1).

Bock, A. M. (2011). You really, truly, have to be there: Video journalism as a social and material construction. Journalism and Mass Media Quarterly, 88(4), 705-718.

Bogost, I. (2007). *Persuasive Games, The Expressive Power of Videogames.* Cambridge, MA: MIT Press.

Bolaño, C. R. S., & Brittos, V. C. (2007). Rádio. In C. R. S. Bolaño & V. C. Brittos (Eds.), *Televisão brasileira na era digital: exclusão, esfera pública e movimentos estruturalistas* (pp. 255–276). São Paulo: Paulus.

Bolter, J. D. (2001), Writing Space, Computers, Hypertext, and the Remediaton of Print (2nd ed.). London: Lawrence Erlbaum Associates.

Bombari, D., Schmid Mast, M., Canadas, E., & Bachmann, M. (2015). Studying social interactions through immersive virtual environment technology: Virtues, pitfalls, and future challenges. *Frontiers in Psychology, 6,* 869. doi:10.3389/fpsyg.2015.00869 PMID:26157414

Bonixe, L. (2012). Usos e desusos da rádio informativa nas redes sociais. O caso da visita de Bento XVI. In H. Bastos & F. Zamith (Eds.), Ciberjornalismo. Modelos de negócio e redes sociais (pp. 183-198). Porto: Edições Afrontamento; CETAC.media.

Borges, F. (2015). *Tecnoxamanisms, etc.* Avaliable at http://revistageni.org/10/tecnoxamanismos-etc/

Borges, F. (2017). *Ancestrofuturim: free cosmology – do it yourself (DIY) rituals.* Available at https://tecnoxamanismo.files.wordpress.com/2016/05/ancestrofuturismo-cosmogonialivre-rituaisfac3a7avocc3aamesmo.pdf

Bourcier, P. (2001). *Historie de la danse en occident.* Sao Paulo: Martins Fontes.

Bourdieu, P. (1977). Cultural reproduction and social reproduction. In *Power and ideology in education* (pp. 487–511). New York: Oxford University.

Boyd D. & Ellison N. (2007). Social network sites: Definition, history, and scholarship. *Journal of Computer-Mediated Communication, 13*(1).

Brecht, B. (2005). Teoria do rádio (1927-1932). Translated from german to portuguese by Regina Carvalho and Valci Zuculoto. In *Teorias do rádio - Textos e contextos* (Vol. 1, pp. 61–98). Florianópolis: Insular.

Caillois, R. (2001). *Man, Play and Games.* Urbana, Chicago: University of Illinois Press. (Original work published 1958)

Carah, N., & Shaul, M. (2015). Brands and Instagram: Point, tap, swipe, glance. *Mobile Media & Communication, 4*(1), 69–84. doi:10.1177/2050157915598180

Carvalho, M. (2015). *A obra "Faça-Você-Mesmo": Estética da Participação nas Artes Digitais* [The Do-It-Yourself" Work: Aesthetics of Participation in Digital Arts] (Unpublished doctoral dissertation). Faculdade de Ciências Sociais e Humanas, Universidade Nova de Lisboa.

Carvalho, H. (2005). Data fusion implementation in sensor networks applied to health monitoring. In *Departamento de Computação.* Universidade de Minas Gerais.

Castells, M. (2010). The rise of the network society. Wiley & Blackwell Publishing.

Cebrián Herreros, M. (2008). A criatividade no contexto do rádio atual. (Translated from spanish by Cláudia Irene de Quadros). In *Teorias do rádio - Textos e contextos* (Vol. 2, pp. 337–348). Florianópolis: Insular.

Chalcraft, J., & Magaudda, P. (2011). 'Space is the place': The global localities of the Sónar and WOMAD music festivals. In L. Giorgi, M. Sassatelli & G. Delanty (Eds.), *Festivals and the cultural public sphere* (pp. 173-189). Nova Iorque: Routledge.

Chaney, D. (2002). Cosmopolitan art and cultural citizenship. *Theory, Culture & Society, 19*(1–2), 157–174. doi:10.1177/026327640201900108

Chesher, C. (2012). Between image and information: The iPhone camera in the history of photography. In L. Hjorth & ... (Eds.), *Studying Mobile Media: Cultural Technologies, Mobile Communication, and the iPhone* (pp. 98–117). New York: Routledge.

Chiumbu, S. H., & Ligaga, D. (2013). "Communities of strangerhoods?": Internet, mobile phonesand the changing nature of radio cultures in South Africa. *Telematics and Informatics, 30*(3), 242–251. doi:10.1016/j.tele.2012.02.004

Chomsky, N. (2002). *Understanding Power*. New York: The New Press.

Ciotti, F., & Roncaglia, G. (2000). *Il Mondo digitale*. Roma, Bari: Laterza.

Clarke, E., Denora, T., & Vuoskoski, J. (2015). *Music, empathy and cultural understanding*. Swindon: Arts and Humanities Research Council.

Clee, P. (2005). *Before Hollywood, from shadow play to the silver screen*. New York: Clarion Books.

Collins, A., Halverson, R., & Gee, J. P. (2018). *Rethinking Education in the Age of Technology: The Digital Revolution and Schooling in America*. Teachers College Press, Columbia University.

Consani, M. (2015). Moral narratives, Piaget and the flies. In Educommunication and human rights. Sao Paulo. ABPEducom.

Correia, V. (2017). *O Design e a Cultura da Participação na Era dos Média Digitais* [Design and the Culture of Participation in the Era of Digital Media] (Unpublished doctoral dissertation). Faculdade de Ciências Sociais e Humanas, Universidade Nova de Lisboa.

Costa, R. (2003). *A cultura digital* (2nd ed.). São Paulo: Publifolha.

Couchot, E. (1998). *Between trance and algorithm. In Transe: My body, my blood. Exhibition catalogue*. Caxias do Sul: Lorigraf.

Couchot, E. (2002). Real time on artistic devices. In L. Leao (Ed.), *Labyrinths of contemporary though*. São Paulo: Iluminuras.

Crossley, N. (2015). Music worlds and body techniques: On the embodiment of musicking. *Cultural Sociology*, *9*(4), 471–492. doi:10.1177/1749975515576585

Crossley, N., & Emms, R. (2016). Mapping the musical universe: A blockmodel of UK music festivals, 2011–2013. *Methodological Innovations*, *9*, 1–14. doi:10.1177/2059799116630663

Cummings, J., Woodward, I., & Bennett, A. (2011). Festival spaces, green sensibilities and youth culture. In L. Giorgi, M. Sassatelli, & G. Delanty (Eds.), *Festivals and the cultural public sphere* (pp. 142–155). New York: Routledge.

Cunha, M. (2007). Cultural capital Pierre Bourdieu's concept and its ethnographic legacy (Brazilian Edition). Perspectiva, 25(2), 503-524.

Darley, A. (2000). *Visual Digital Culture, Surface Play and Spectacle in New Media Genres*. London: Routledge.

Dascalu, M. I., Bodea, C. N., Moldoveanu, A., Mohora, A., Lytras, M., & de Pablos, P. O. (2015). A recommender agent based on learning styles for better virtual collaborative learning experiences. *Computers in Human Behavior*, *45*, 243–253. doi:10.1016/j.chb.2014.12.027

Davidson, D. (2010). *Cross-media Communications: an Introduction to the Art of Creating Integrated Media Experiences*. Carnegie Mellon University ETC Press.

De Biase, L., & Valentino, P. A. (Eds.). (2016). *Socialmuseums. Social media e cultura, tra post e tweet*. Milano: SilvanaEditoriale.

De Kerckhove, D. (1997). *Connected Intelligence – The Arrival of the web Society*. Toronto: Somerville House Books Limited.

De Rosnay, J. (2000). *L'Homme Symbiotique*. Paris: Éditions du Seuil.

Debord, G. (1992). *La société du spectacle*. Paris: Galimmard.

Deerhunter. (2010). *Desire Lines. On Halcyon Digest* [CD]. London, UK: 4AD.

Deleuze, G. (1987). Qu'est-ce que l'acte de création? Paris: Conference. (in French)

Deleuze, G., & Guattary, F. (1997). Mille plateau (Brazilian edition). São Paulo: Academic Press.

Dennet, D. C. (2000). An Empirical Theory of The Mind: The Evolution of Consciousness-1991. In Cyber_Reader. Critical writings for the digital era. Phaidon.

Denora, T. (2003). Music sociology: Getting the music into the action. *British Journal of Music Education, 20*(2), 165–177. doi:10.1017/S0265051703005369

Deterding, S. (2014). The Ambiguity of Games: Histories and Discourses of a Gameful World. In S. P. Walz & S. Deterding (Eds.), *The Gameful World: Approaches,Issues, Applications* (pp. 23–64). Cambridge, MA: MIT Press.

Dezeuze, A. (2010). *The Do-it-yourself, Artwork, Participation from Fluxus to New Media.* Manchester, NY: Manchester University Press.

Diemer, J., Alpers, G. W., Peperkorn, H. M., Shiban, Y., & Mühlberger, A. (2015). The impact of perception and presence on emotional reactions: A review of research in virtual reality. *Frontiers in Psychology, 6*, 26. doi:10.3389/fpsyg.2015.00026 PMID:25688218

Dinis, F. M., Guimarães, A. S., Carvalho, B. R., & Martins, J. P. P. (2017, April). Virtual and augmented reality game-based applications to civil engineering education. In *Global Engineering Education Conference (EDUCON)* (pp. 1683-1688). IEEE. 10.1109/EDUCON.2017.7943075

Doğan, B.A. (2013). Social sharing sites and participation: a study on academics in İstanbul. *The Journal of İstanbul University Communication Faculty*, (44), 67-84.

Domingues, D. (2003b). *Heartscapes*, Diana Domingues and CNPq collection. The artwork was installed in a cave. *Art + Science Now.*

Domingues, D. (2005). VR AQUARIUM. In *Heartscapes, 2005-2009.*

Domingues, D. (2008). *Research Project: Art and TechnoScience: Expanded Interactions and Cybrid Condition in Software Art.* CNPq Minister of Science and Technology.

Domingues, D. (2012). *Biocybrid ouroborus: ecstasys' geographisms.* The 11th Havana Biennial.

Domingues, D. (2016). Ouroboric perception and the effects of enactive affective systems to the naturalization of technologies. *Media-N, Journal of the New Media Caucus, 12*(1).

Domingues, D., da Rocha, F. A., Hamdon, C., & Miosso, C. J. (2011). Biocybrid Systems and the Reengineering of Life. IS&T/SPIE Electronic Imaging.

Domingues, D., Hamdan, C., & Augosto, L. (2010). Biocybrid Body and Rituals in Urban Mixed Life. In Congreso Internacional Mujer. Arte y Tecnologia en la Nueva Esfera Pública-CIMUAT.

Domingues, D. (1998). The desert of passions and the technological soul. In *Digital Creativity* (Vol. 9). Lisse: Swets & Zeitlinger. doi:10.1080/14626269808567101

Domingues, D. (2003a). *Cyberinstallation exhibited firstly at ISEA 97, at the School of Art Institute in Chicago Isea Montreal, Modern Art Museum, Buenos Aires, 1999, II Bienal do Mercosul, VII Bienal de la Habana, when receiving the 2000 Unesco Prize, Lima 2000, Kibla Multimedia Center, Maribor, Slovenia, 2003 and Exhibition Valfisken Gallery*. Simrishamn.

Domingues, D. (Ed.). (1997). *A Arte no Século XXI: A Humanização das Tecnologias*. São Paulo: Ed. Unesp.

Domingues, D., Lucena, T., Rosa, S., Miosso, C., Torres, R., & Krueger, T. (2016). Walking and health: An enactive affective system. *Digital Creativity, 27*(4), 314–333. doi:10.1080/14626268.2016.1262430

Domingues, D., Miosso, C. J., Rodrigues, S. F., Rocha Aguiar, C. S., ... Raskar, R. (2014). *Embodiments, Visualizations and Immersion with Enactive Affective Systems*. IS&T/SPIE Electronic Imaging. doi:10.1117/12.2042590

Douglas, Y., & Hargadon, A. (2000). *The Pleasure Principle: Immersion, Engagement, Flow*. Retrieved December 15, 2017, from ftp://ftp.cse.buffalo.edu/users/azhang/disc/disc01/cd1/out/papers/hypertext/p153-douglas.pdf

Dowd, T. J., Liddle, K., & Nelson, J. (2004). Music festivals as scenes: examples from serious music, womyn's music and skatepunk. In A. Bennett & R. A. Peterson (Eds.), *Music scenes: Local, translocal and virtual* (pp. 149–167). Nashville, TN: Vanderbilt University Press.

Dubber, A. (2013). Repensando o rádio na era digital. *Significação, 40*(39), 24-43. Retrieved from https://www.revistas.usp.br/significacao/article/view/59949

Duffy, M. (2000). Lines of drift: Festival participation and performing a sense of place. *Popular Music, 19*(1), 51–64. doi:10.1017/S0261143000000027

Dyens, O. (1995). L'émotion du cyberspace. In *Esthétique des Arts Médiatiques*. *Presses de L'Université du Québec*.

Dyens, O. (2016, March 1). The Human/Machine Humanities: A Proposal. *Humanities (Washington), 5*(1). Retrieved from http://www.mdpi.com/20760787/5/1/17

Ermi, L., & Mäyrä, F. (2005). *Fundamental Components of the Gameplay experience: Analysing immersion.* Retrieved May 2018, from http://citeseerx.ist.psu.edu/viewdoc/download?doi=10.1.1.103.6702&rep=rep1&type=pdf

Evans, H., Ginnis, S., & Barlett, J. (2015). #SocialEthics a guide to embedding ethics in social media research. *Wisdom of the Crowd.* Retrieved from https://www.ipsosmori.com/researchpublications/publications/1771/Ipsos-MORI-and-DemosCASMcall-for-better-ethical-standards-in-social-media-research.aspx

Farrel, L. (Ed.). (2004). *Art of contemporary African diaspore.* New York: Museum for African Art.

Fatboy Slim. (1998). *You've Come a Long Way, Baby* [CD]. London: Skint Records.

Fatboy Slim. (1999). *Praise you.* Retrieved from https://www.youtube.com/watch?v=ruAi4VBoBSM

Federculture, F. (2014). *Cultura & turismo. Locomotiva del paese.* Febbraio 2014.

Fidler, R. (1997). *Mediamorphosis: Understanding new media.* Thousand Oaks, CA: Pine Forge Press.

Fischer, S. (2001). Virtual Interface Environments. In *From Wagner to Virtual Reality.* New York: W. W. Norton.

Flanagan, M. (2009). *Critical Play, Radical Game Design.* Cambridge, MA: MIT Press.

Flood, G. (1996). *An Introduction to Hinduism.* Cambridge University Press.

Fonarow, W. (1997). The spatial organization of the indie music gig. In K. Gelder & S. Thornton (Eds.), *The subcultures reader.* London: Routledge.

Foust, J. C. (2011). *Online journalism: Principles and practices of news for the web* (3rd ed.). Routledge Taylor & Francis Group.

Franklin B. (2014). The future of journalism. *Journalism Studies, 15*(5), 481-499. Doi:10.1080/1461670X.2014.930254

Freina, L., & Ott, M. (2015). A literature review on immersive virtual reality in education: state of the art and perspectives. In *The International Scientific Conference eLearning and Software for Education* (*Vol. 1*, p. 133). "Carol I" National Defence University.

Freire, P. (1982). *Cultural activism for freedom.* Rio de Janeiro: Paz e Terra.

Freire, P. (1987). *Pedagogy of the opressed* (17th ed.). Rio de Janeiro: Paz e Terra.

Friedman, S., Savage, M., Hanquinet, L., & Miles, A. (2015). Cultural sociology and new forms of distinction. *Poetics, 53*, 1–8. doi:10.1016/j.poetic.2015.10.002

Frith, S. (1996). *Performing rites. Evaluating popular music.* Oxford, UK: Oxford University Press.

Gallaugher, J.M., Auger, P., & BarNir, A. (2001). Revenue streams and digital content providers: an empirical investigation. *Information & Management, 38*(7), 473-485.

Garbick, J., & Schaefer, S. (2011). In L.A.'s Little Tokyo, a place for your wishes. *Los Angeles Times.* Available at http://articles.latimes.com/2011/aug/14/opinion/la-oe-wishing-tree-20110814

García González, A. (2013). De la radio interactiva a la radio transmedia: nuevas perspectivas para los profesionales del medio. *Icono14, 11*(2), 251-267. Retrieved from: https://www.icono14.net/ojs/index.php/icono14/article/view/567

Garcia, B. (2017). *Technoxamanism: when indigenous and kackers get togethet to save the planet.* Barcelona: Laudano Magazine. Available at http://www.laudanomag.com/tecnochamanismo-indios-hackers/

Garfinkel, H. (1967). *Studies in ethnomethodology.* Prentice-Hall.

Geus, S., Richards, G., & Toepoel, V. (2016). Conceptualisation and operationalisation of event and festival experiences: Creation of an event experience scale. *Scandinavian Journal of Hospitality and Tourism, 16*(3), 274–296. doi:10.1080/15022250.2015.1101933

Giannetti, C. (2006). *Digital Aesthetics.* Belo Horizonte: C/Arte.

Gibson, J. J. (1974). *The perception of the visual world.* Westport, CT: Greenwood Press.

Goodwin, I., Griffin, C., Lyons, A., McCreanor, T., & Barners, M.H. (2016). Precious poplularity: Facebook, drinking photos, attention economy, and the regime of the branded itself. *Journal of Social Media & Society, 1*(13). Doi:10.1177/2056305116628889

Gosciola, V. (2012). Narrativa transmídia: Conceituação e origens. In D. Renó (Ed.), *Narrativas transmedia: Entre teorias y prácticas* (pp. 7–14). Bogotá: Editorial Universidad del Rosario.

Gouveia, P. (2009). Narrative Paradox and the Design of Alternate Reality Games (ARGs) and Blogs. In Proceedings of IEEE Consumer Electronics Society's Games Innovation Conference 2009 *(ICE-GIC 09)* (pp. 231-38.). London Imperial College.

Gouveia, P. (2010b). Playing With Poetry a Portuguese Transmedia Experience and a Serious ARG. In *GIC 2010 Proceedings of 2nd International IEEE Consumer Electronic Society Games Innovation Conference* (pp. 150-56). Hong Kong, China: Academic Press. 10.1109/ICEGIC.2010.5716904

Gouveia, P. (2013). Transmedia experience and the independent game industry: the renascence of old school visual and artistic techniques [Esperiência transmedia e a indústria de jogos independente (indie): o "renascimento" de expressões artísticas e visuais do tipo "old school"]. In Comunicação e Antropologia Social, Seminário Internacional de Rede ICCI Imagens da Cultura Cultura das Imagens (pp. 78-89). ECA, USP.

Gouveia, P. (2015). *Serious gaming: how gamers are solving real world problems*. Academic Press.

Gouveia, P. (2016). Gaming and VR Technologies, Powers and Discontents. In Proceedings of Videojogos'16. Covilhã, Portugal: Academic Press.

Gouveia, P., & Martel, P. (2017). Player Experience, Gaming and VR Technologies (extended version). Journal of Computer Sciences.

Gouveia, P. (2010a). *Artes e Jogos Digitais, Estética e Design da Experiência Lúdica* (11th ed.). Lisbon: Edições Universitárias Lusófonas.

Grau, O. (2003). *Virtual Art: from illusion to immersion*. MIT Press.

Greco, B. (1927). *Storia di Mondragone*. Napoli: Giannini.

Greenlight, V.R., & Roadtovr. (2016). *2016 virtual reality industry report*. Retrieved from http://www. greenlightvr.com/reports/2016-industry-report

Guerra, P. (2010). *A instável leveza do rock: Génese, dinâmica e consolidação do rock alternativo em Portugal* (Doctoral dissertation). Repositório Aberto da Universidade do Porto.

Guerra, P. (2016). Lembranças do último verão. Festivais de música, ritualizações e identidades na contemporaneidade portuguesa. *Portugal ao Espelho*. Retrieved from https://portugalaoespelho.files.wordpress.com/2016/05/ficha_-lembrancas-ultimo-verao.pdf

Guerra, P. (2015). Keep it rocking: The social space of Portuguese alternative rock (1980–2010). *Journal of Sociology (Melbourne, Vic.)*, *52*(4), 615–630. doi:10.1177/1440783315569557

Guerra, P., Moreira, T., & Silva, A. S. (2016). Estigma, experimentação e risco: A questão do álcool e das drogas na cena punk. *Revista Critica de Ciencias Sociais*, *109*(109), 33–62. doi:10.4000/rccs.6206

Gwertzman, B. (2001). *Interviewed by Bill Goldstein on The New York Times*. Retrieved from http://partners.nytimes.com/library/tech/reference/roundtable.html

Hamari, J., Shernoff, D. J., Rowe, E., Coller, B., Asbell-Clarke, J., & Edwards, T. (2016). Challenging games help students learn: An empirical study on engagement, flow and immersion in game-based learning. *Computers in Human Behavior*, *54*, 170–179. doi:10.1016/j.chb.2015.07.045

Hannerz, U. (2006). *Two faces of cosmopolitanism: culture and politics*. Barcelona: Fundació CIDOB.

Hansen, M. (2003). *New philosophy for new media*. London: MIT Press.

Harvey, D. (1989). *The urban experience*. Baltimore, MD: Johns Hopkins University Press.

Hauser, A. (1995). *The story of the Art and the Literature*. M. Fontes.

Hebdige, D. (1990). Fax to the future. *Marxism Today*, *34*(January), 1118–1123.

Hegel, G. W. (n.d.). *Vorlesungen über die ästhetik* (Brazilian edition). Sao Paulo: EDUSP.

Heim, M. (1999). Virtual Realism. In Media and Social Perception. UNESCO/ISSC/EDUCAM.

Heim, M. (1993). *The metaphysics of Virtual Reality*. New York: Oxford Press University.

Hennion, A. (1999). Music industry and music lovers, beyond Benjamin: The return of the amateur. *Soundscapes*, *2*, 1–7.

Henrion, F. H. K., & Parking, A. (1976). *Design coordination and corporate image*. London: Studio Vista.

Hermann, M., Pentek, T., & Otto, B. (2016). Design Principles for Industrie 4.0 Scenarios. *2016 49th Hawaii International Conference on System Sciences (HICSS)*, 3928-3937. 10.1109/HICSS.2016.488

Hertz, G., & Parikka, J. (2012). Zombie Media: Circuit Bending Media Archaeology into an Art Method (pp. 424–430). *Leonardo*, *45*(5), 424–430. doi:10.1162/LEON_a_00438

Hounsell, M. D. S., da Silva, E. L., Filho, M. R., & de Sousa, M. P. (2015). A Model to Distinguish Between Educational and Training 3D Virtual Environments and its Application. *International Journal of Virtual Reality*, *9*(2), 63–72.

Hudson, S., Roth, M. S., Madden, T., & Hudson, R. (2015). The effects of social media on emotions, brand relationship quality, and word of mouth: An empirical study of music festival attendees. *Tourism Management*, *47*, 68–76. doi:10.1016/j.tourman.2014.09.001

Hughes, P. (2001). Making science 'Family fun': The fetish of the interactive exhibit. *Museum Management and Curatorship*, *19*(2), 2001. doi:10.1080/09647770100501902

Huhtamo, E. (2007). Twin-Touch-Test-Redux: Media Archaeological Approach to Art, Interactivity, and Tactility. In O. Grau (Ed.), *MediaArtHistories* (pp. 71–101). Cambridge, MA: MIT Press.

Huizinga, J. (1955). *Homo Ludens*. Boston: The Beacon Press.

ICOM. (2004). *ICOM Code of Professional Ethics, adopted in Buenos Aires in 1986, renamed ICOM Code of Ethics for Museums in Barcelona in 2001, and then revised in Seoul in 2004*. Author.

ICOMOS. (2008). ICOMOS Charter for the interpretation and presentation of cultural heritage sites called Ename Charter. Prepared under the auspices of the Scientific Committee of ICOMOS on Interpretation and Presentation of Heritage Sites (April 10, 2007). Ratified by the 16th General Assembly of ICOMOS, Quebec (Canada), 4 October 2008.

Ihlström, C., & Palmer, J. (2002). Revenues for online newspapers: owner and user perceptions. Electronic Markets, 12(4), 228-236.

Ilan, J. (2012). Street social capital in the liquid city. *Ethnography*, *14*(1), 3–24. doi:10.1177/1466138112440983

Irwin, R. (2009). A/r/tography: A metonymic métissage. In R. L. Irwin & A. de Cosson (Eds.), *A/r/tography: Rendering self through arts-based living inquiry*. Vancouver, Canada: Pacific Educational Press.

Jenkins, H. (2006). *Convergence Culture: Where Old and New Media Collide*. New York University Press.

Jenkins, H. (2006). *Convergence culture: where old and new media collide.* New York: New York University Press.

Jenkins, H. (2006). *Convergence Culture: where old and new media collide.* NYU Press.

Jenkins, H., Ford, S., & Green, J. (2013). *Spreadable media: creating value and meaning in a networked culture.* New York: New York University Press.

Jetto, B. (2010). *Music blogs, music scenes and sub-cultural capital: emerging practices in music blogs.* Paper presented at Cybercultures, 5th Global Conference, Salzburg, Austria.

Jordan, J. (2016). Festivalisation of cultural production: Experimentation, spectacularisation and immersion. *ENCATC: Journal of Cultural Management and Policy, 6*(1), 44–55.

Kagermann, H., Wahlster, W., & Helbig, J. (Eds.). (2013). Recommendations for implementing the strategic initiative Industrie 4.0. Final report of the Industrie 4.0 Working Group.

Kaplan, A.M., & Haenlein, M. (2009). Users of the world,unite the challenges and opportunities of social media. *Business Horizons, 53*, 59-68. doi. doi:10.1016/j.bushor.2009.09.002

Kee, J., Bailey, C., Horton, S., & Kelly, K. (2016). Art at Aché. Collaboration as Creative Assemblage. AAEA Art Education, 69(5).

Kilic, S. O. (2017). *The significant challenges preventing digital newsrooms in Turkey from adapting to new media* (Master thesis). Kadir Has University.

Kim, K., Rosenthal, M. Z., Zielinski, D. J., & Brady, R. (2014). Effects of virtual environment platforms on emotional responses. *Computer Methods and Programs in Biomedicine, 113*(3), 882–893. doi:10.1016/j.cmpb.2013.12.024 PMID:24440136

Kinder, M. (2014). Medium Specificity and productive precursors, an Introduction. In M. Kinder & T. McPherson (Eds.), *Transmedia Frictions, The Digital, the Arts, and the Humanities* (pp. 3–19). University of California Press.

Kischinhevsky, M. (2016). *Rádio e mídias sociais: mediações e interações radiofônicas em plataformas digitais de comunicação.* Rio de Janeiro: Mauad X.

Kitchin, R., & Dodge, M. (2007). Rethinking maps. *Progress in Human Geography, 31*(3), 331–344. doi:10.1177/0309132507077082

Klaxons. (2007). *Myths of the Near Future* [CD]. London: Polydor Records Ltd.

Klaxonsvevo. (2009). *Golden Skans* [Official Video]. Retrieved from https://www.youtube.com/watch?v=q-SJjFcnsGs

Knausgard, K. O. (2015). *A Minha Luta 2: Um Homem Apaixonado*. Lisboa: Relógio D'Água Editores.

Kolb, B. M. (2000). *Marketing cultural organizations: New strategies for attracting audiences to classical music, dance, museums, theatre and opera*. Dublin: Oak Tree Press.

Kramsch, C. (1998). *Language and Culture*. Oxford, UK: Oxford University Press.

Krueger, M. (1991). Artificial Reality Art. Addison-Wesley.

Kuliga, S. F., Thrash, T., Dalton, R. C., & Hoelscher, C. (2015). Virtual reality as an empirical research tool—Exploring user experience in a real building and a corresponding virtual model. *Computers, Environment and Urban Systems*, *54*, 363–375. doi:10.1016/j.compenvurbsys.2015.09.006

Küng, L., Picard, G. P., & Towse, R. (2008). *The internet and the mass media* (1st ed.). Sage Publications.

Kuru, O., Bayer, J., Pasek, J., & Campbell, S. W. (2016). – Understanding and measuring mobile Facebook use: Who, why and how? *Mobile Media & Communication*, *5*(1), 102–120. doi:10.1177/2050157916678269

Kutner, M. (2017). *What is the Blue Whale Game, The Russian 'Challenge' Blamed for Suicides?* Retrieved July 30, 2017, from http://www.newsweek.com/what-blue-whale-game-russia-suicides-637798

Kwastek, K. (2009). Embodiment and Instrumentality. *Proceedings of the Digital Arts and Culture Conference: After Media, embodiment and context*. Retrieved December 21, 2017 from https://escholarship.org/uc/item/0zg3t13v

Larsen, G., & O'Reilly, D. (2005). *Music festivals as sites of consumption: an exploratory study*. Working papers 2005. Braford, The Bradford MBA.

Lee, C., & Shieh, M. (2017) *An action research in photography education for vocational students in the post-true era. 2017 InSEA World Congress. Abstract and power-point presenteation given by the authors*.

Levy, P. (1997). *Collective intelligence: Mankind's emerging world in cyberspace*. Ann Arbor, MI: University of Michigan Press.

Liew, K. K., & Pang, N. (2015). Neoliberal visions, post-capitalist memories: Heritage politics and the counter-mapping of Singapore's cityscape. *Ethnography*, *16*(3), 331–351. doi:10.1177/1466138114552939

Lopez, D. C. (2010). *Radiojornalismo hipermidiático: Tendências e perspectivas do jornalismo de rádio all news brasileiro em um contexto de convergência tecnológica*. Covilhã: LabCom. Retrieved from http://www.livroslabcom.ubi.pt/pdfs/20110415-debora_lopez_radiojornalismo.pdf

Lucena, T. (2013). *Sistemas enativos afetivos em arte e tecnociência: experiências vitais dos deslocamentos na cidade* [Enactive affective systems in art and technoscience: vital experiences of displacement in the city] (PhD diss.). UnB.

Lupton, D. (2012). *Digital Sociology: An Introduction*. Retrieved from https://ses.library.usyd.edu.au/bitstream/2123/8621/2/Digital%20Sociology.pdf

Macdowall, L. J., & Souza, P. (2018). 'I'd Double Tap That!!' Street art, graffiti, and Instagram research. *Media Culture & Society*, *40*(1), 3–22. doi:10.1177/0163443717703793

Machado, A. (2002). Arte e mídias: aproximações e distinções. *Galáxias, 4*, 19-32. Retrieved October 11, 2017, from https://alldocs.net/philosophy-of-money.html?utm_source=ecoacoes-uma-instalacao-de-media-arte

Makransky, G., & Lilleholt, L. (2018). A structural equation modeling investigation of the emotional value of immersive virtual reality in education in Educational Technology. *Research for Development*.

Makransky, J. G., & Cooper, B. S. (2017). *Technology in School Classrooms: How It Can Transform Teaching and Student Learning Today*. Rowman & Littlefield.

Makridakis, S. (1995). *The forthcoming information revolution: Its impact on society and firms*. Elsevier.

Malbon, B. (1999). *Clubbing: Dancing, ecstasy and vitality*. London: Routledge.

Manovich, L. (2001). *Post-media Aesthetics*. Retrieved November 30, 2017, from http://manovich.net/content/04-projects/032-post-media-aesthetics/29_article_2001.pdf

Manovich, L. (2015). A ciência da cultura? Computação social, humanidades digitais e analítica cultural. *Matrizes, 9*(2), 67-83.

Manovich, L. (2016). *Instagram and Contemporary Image*. Retrieved from http://manovich.net/content/04-projects/145-instagram-and-contemporary-image/instagram_book_manovich.pdf

Marcos, A. (2012), Instanciando mecanismos de a/r/tografia no processo de criação em arte digital/computacional. Invisivilidades. Revista ibero-americana de pesquisa em educação, cultura e artes, 3, 138-145.

Marcos, A., Branco, P., & Carvalho, J. (2009). The computer médium in digital art's creative process. In J. Braman & G. Vicenti (Eds.), *Handbook of Research on Computational Arts and Creative Informatics*. IGI Publishing. doi:10.4018/978-1-60566-352-4.ch001

Massumi, B. (2002). Parables for the Virtual: Movement, Affect, Sensation. Durham, NC: Duke University Press.

McGonigal, J. (2011). *Reality is Broken, why games make us better and how they can change the world*. New York: The Penguin Press.

McKay. G. (2000). Glastonbury: A very English fair. London: Victor Gollancz.

McKay, G. (Ed.). (1998). *DIY Culture: Party & protest in nineties Britain*. London: Verso.

McLeish, R. (2005). *Radio production* (5th ed.). Burlington: Focal Press.

McLuhan, M. (2013). Understanding the media the extensions of man (3rd ed.). Gingko Press.

McLuhan, M., & Fiore, Q. (2012). *The Medium is the message an inventory of effects* (J. Agel, Ed.; Haydaroğluİ., Trans.). MediaCat Publishings.

McLuhan, M., & Fiore, Q. (1967). *The Medium is the Message* (Vol. 123). New York: Penguin Books.

McLuhan, M., & Powers, B. (2015). *Global village [global köy]* (2nd ed.; B. Ö. Düzgören, Trans.). Scala Publishings.

Medeiros, M. (2007, September). Transmissão sonora digital: Modelos radiofônicos e não radiofônicos na comunicação contemporânea. *Anais do Congresso Brasileiro de Ciências da Comunicação*, 30. Retrieved from: http://www.intercom.org.br/papers/nacionais/2007/resumos/R0773-1.pdf

Meditsch, E. (2010). A informação sonora na webemergência: sobre as possibilidades de um radiojornalismo digital na mídia e pós-mídia. In A. F. Magnoni & J. M. Carvalho (Eds.), *O novo rádio: Cenários da radiodifusão brasileira na era digital*. São Paulo: SENAC.

Medri, M., & Canonici, T. (2010). L'immagine ricostruttiva nei media: una indagine nei musei archeologici italiani. Virtual Arcaeology Review, 1. doi:10.4995/var.2010.5134

Medyatava. (2017). *Türkiye'nin en çok ziyaret edilen haber siteleri açıklandı!* Retrieved from http://www.medyatava.com/haber/turkiyenin-en-cok-ziyaret-edilen-haber-siteleri-aciklandi_150072

Meneses, J. P. (2012). R@dio? Cem anos depois, a rádio muda; acaba? In J. P. Meneses (Ed.), *Estudos sobre a rádio. Passado, presente e futuro*. Porto: Mais Leituras.

Merchant, Z., Goetz, E. T., Cifuentes, L., Keeney-Kennicutt, W., & Davis, T. J. (2014). Effectiveness of virtual reality-based instruction on students' learning outcomes in K-12 and higher education: A meta-analysis. *Computers & Education, 70*, 29–40. doi:10.1016/j.compedu.2013.07.033

Mesquita, R. (2017). The transition of a traditional newspaper to the internet age: An historical account of Le Monde's case. *The Observatory Journal, 11*, 54–60.

Miller, C. H. (2008). *Digital Storytelling: A Creator's Guide to interactive entertainment* (2nd ed.). Focal Press.

Miller, D. (2015). *Technology and human attainment. Postdigital Artisans. Craftmanship with a new aesthetic in fashion, art, design and architecture*. Amsterdam: Frame Publishers.

Miranda, M. R. (2014). *Desenvolvimento de Bancada para Simulação Veicular Integrando Realidade Virtual e Medição de Dados Fisiológicos*. Tese de Doutorado em Ciências Mecânicas.

Miranda, M. R., Cota, H., Oliveira, L., Bernardes, T., Aguiar, C., & Domingues, D. M. (2015). *Development of simulation interfaces for evaluation task with the use of physiological data and virtual reality applied to a vehicle simulator*. SPIE/IS&T Electronic Imaging; doi:10.1117/12.2083889

Mitchell, B. (2019). *The Immersive Artistic Experience and the Exploitation of Space*. CAT London Conference. Retrieved February 10, 2018 from https://www.bcs.org/upload/pdf/ewic_ca10_s3paper2.pdf

Molz, J. G. (2011). Cosmopolitanism and consumption. In M. Rovisco & M. Nowicka (Eds.), *The Ashgate research companion to cosmopolitanism*. Farnham, UK: Ashgate Publishing.

Montola, M., Stenros, J., & Waern, A. (2009). *Pervasive Games, Experiences on the Boundary Between Life and Play (Theory and Design)*. Burlington, MA: Morgan Kaufmann.

Moreira, M. C. L., & Belcavello, F. (2012). Transmídia storytelling: fenômeno cultural X engajamento de audiência. In C. Brandão (Ed.), *Televisão, cinema e mídias digitais*. Florianópolis: Insular.

Morey, Y., Bengry-Howell, A., Griffin, C., Szmigin, I., & Riley, S. (2014). Festivals 2.0: Consuming, producing and participating in the extended festival experience. In A. Bennett, J. Taylor, & I. Woodward (Eds.), *The festivalization of culture* (pp. 251–269). Surrey, UK: Ashgate.

Moser, S. (2017). Linking virtual and real-life environments: Scrutinizing ubiquitous learning scenarios. In *Digital Tools for Seamless Learning* (pp. 214–239). IGI Global. doi:10.4018/978-1-5225-1692-7.ch011

Murray, J. (2001). *Hamlet on the Holodeck: the future of narrative in cyberspace* (Brazilian edition). Sao Paulo: Itau Cultural.

Museum of Art, Architecture and Technology. (2017). *Post-internet Cities*. Retrieved November, 30, 2017, from https://postinternetcities.weebly.com/

Nachvatal, J. (2011). *Immersion Into Noise*. University of Michigan Library.

Nadais, I. (2010, May 13). A aldeia gaulesa. *Ípsilon*. Retrieved from http://ipsilon. publico.pt/Musica/texto.aspx?id=256596

Neumaier, O. (2004). Space, time, vídeo, Viola. In C. Townsend (Ed.), *The art of Bill Viola*. New York: Times & Hudson.

New Musical Express. (2010). The 50 best festival road-trip songs. *New Musical Express* Retrieved from http://www.nme.com/photos/the-50-best-festival-road-trip-songs/309307

New Musical Express. (2015). 15 Songs you're going to hear everywhere at festivals in summer 2015. *New Musical Express Gallery*. Retrieved from http://www.nme.com/photos/15-songs-you-re-going-to-hear-everywhere-at-festivals-in-summer-2015/377826#/photo/1

New Musical Express. (2016). 30 Years of Festival Anthems: the massive songs which defined every summer, *New Musical Express*. Retrieved from http://www.nme.com/photos/30-years-of-festival-anthems-the-massive-songs-which-defined-every-summer/344628#/photo/14

Newman, N. (2009). *The rise of social media and its impact on mainstream journalism*. University of Oxford.

Nielsen, R. K., & Ganter, S. A. (2017). *Dealing with digital intermediaries: a case study of the relations between publishers and platforms.* Retrieved from http://journals.sagepub.com/doi/pdf/10.1177/1461444817701318

Nielsen, J. (1993). *Usability Engineering.* San Diego, CA: Academic Press.

Nightingale, V., & Dwyer, T. (2007). *New media worlds: Challenges for convergence. front cover.* Oxford University Press.

Noë, A. (2006). *Action in perception.* Cambridge, MA: MIT Press.

Norbier, D. (2012). Rádio e Internet: Modelos radiofônicos de participação em rede. *Rádio leituras, 3*(2), 45-66. Retrieved from: http://radioleituras.files.wordpress.com/2013/11/ano3num2art2b.pdf

Nyre, L., & Ala-Fossi, M. (2008). The next generation platform: Comparing audience registration and participation in digital sound media. *Journal of Radio & Audio Media, 15*(1), 41–58. doi:10.1080/19376520801978142

O'Donnell, D. (2015). *So You Want to be an Artist: when social scientists don the beret.* Retrieved July 30, 2017, from https://medium.com/@darrenodonnell/so-you-want-to-be-an-artist-when-social-scientists-don-the-beret-a9d32f272fb5

O'Donnell, D. (2008). *Social Acupuncture, a guide to suicide, performance and utopia.* Coach House Books.

O'Sullivan, S. (2001). The aesthetics of affect, thinking art beyond representation. *Angelaki, Journal of the theoretical humanities, 6*(3), 125-135. Retrieved May 13, 2018, from https://simonosullivan.net/articles/aesthetics-of-affect.pdf

OECD. (2009). *Education at a glance.* Retrieved from http://www.oecd.org/education/skills-beyond-school/43636332.pdf

Oguibe, O. (2004). *The Culture Game.* Minneapolis, MN: University of Minnesota Press.

Pais, J. M. (1998). As 'cronotopias' das práticas culturais do quotidiano. *OBS, 4,* 7–9.

Pais, J. M. (2010). *Lufa-lufa quotidiana. Ensaios sobre a cidade, cultura e vida urbana.* Lisboa: Imprensa de Ciências Sociais.

Parrish, M., Elliot, N., Riley, N., & Wise, J. (2010). How to create an effective brand presence on Facebook. Forrester Research Online, 2(6).

Parthiban, K. T., & Seenivasan, R. (2017). *Forestry technologies- a complete value chain approach.* Scientific Publishers.

Pastore, A., & Bonetti, E. (2006). Il brand management del territorio. Sinergie, Rapporti di Ricerca, 23.

Pavlik, J. (2010). The impact of technology on Journalism. *Journalism Studies, I,* 229–237.

Pekrun, R. (2016). Emotions at school. In K. R. Wentzel & D. B. Miele (Eds.), *Handbook of motivation at school* (2nd ed.; pp. 120–144). New York: Routledge.

Pennella, G., & Trimarchi, M. (Eds.). (1993). *Stato e mercato nel settore culturale.* Bologna: Il Mulino.

Pereira, B. (2015, June 25). João Carvalho: 'Paredes de Coura tem uma magia que outros festivais não têm'. *Wav Magazine.* Retrieved from http://www.wavmagazine.net/noticias/joao-carvalho-paredes-de-coura-tem-uma-magia-que-outros-festivais-nao-tem/

Perlberg, S., & Seetharaman, D. (2016). Facebook signs deals with media companies, celebrities for Facebook live. *The Wall Street Journal.* Retrieved from https://www.wsj.com/articles/facebook-signs-deals-with-media-%20companies-celebrities-for-facebook-live-1466533472

Phillips, A. (2012). *A Creator's Guide to Transmedia Storytelling: How to Captivate and Engage Audiences Across Multiple Platforms.* McGraw Hill.

Picard, R. W., Papert, S., Bender, W., Blumberg, B., Breazeal, C., Cavallo, D., ... Strohecker, C. (2004). Affective learning—a manifesto. *BT Technology Journal, 22*(4), 253–269. doi:10.1023/B:BTTJ.0000047603.37042.33

Piñeiro-Otero, T., & Ramos, F. (2013). El complejo salto de la radio convencional a la webradio. Usos y percepciones de los universitarios. *Revista de comunicación Vivat Academia, 15*(122), 40-53. Retrieved from: http://www.vivatacademia.net/index.php/vivat/article/view/10

Pink, S. (2001). *Doing visual ethnography.* London: Sage Publications.

Pink, S., Fors, V., & Glöss, M. (2017). Automated futures and the mobile present: In-car video ethnographies. *Ethnography, 0*(00), 1–20.

Pitts, M. J., & Harms, R. (2003). Radio websites as a promotional tool. *Journal of Radio Studies, 10*(2), 270–282. doi:10.120715506843jrs1002_11

Portela, P. (2011). *Rádio na Internet em Portugal: A abertura à participação num meio em mudança.* Ribeirão: Edições Húmus.

Portes, A. (1998). Social capital: Its origins and applications in modern sociology. *Annual Review of Sociology, 24*(1), 1–24. doi:10.1146/annurev.soc.24.1.1

Postman, N. (1992). *Technopoly. The surrender of culture to technology.* New York: Knopf.

Prata, N. (2008). *Webrádio: Novos gêneros, novas formas de interação* (PhD thesis). Universidade Federal de Minas Gerais. Retrieved from: http://www.bibliotecadigital.ufmg.br/dspace/bitstream/1843/AIRR7DDJD8/1/nair_prata_tese.pdf

Preece, J., Rogers, Y., Sharp, H., Benyon, D., Holland, S., & Carey, T. (1994). *HumanComputer Interaction.* London: Addison-Wesley Publ.

Prentice, R. (1994). Perceptual Deterrents to Visiting Museums and Other Heritage Attractions. *Museum Management and Curatorship, 13*(3), 1994. doi:10.1080/09647779409515408

Priestman, C. (2006). Web radio – Radio production for Internet streaming. Oxford, UK: Focal Press. (Originally published 2002)

Purdue, D., Durrschmidt, J., Jowers, P., & O'Doherty, R. (1997). DIY culture and extended milieux: LETS, veggie boxes and festivals. *The Sociological Review, 45*(4), 645–667. doi:10.1111/1467-954X.00081

Putnam, R. D. (1995). Bowling alone: America's declining social capital. *Journal of Democracy, 6*(1), 65–78. doi:10.1353/jod.1995.0002

PwC. (2014). *The digital future of creative Europe.* Retrieved from https://www.strategyand.pwc.com/media/file/The-digital-future-of-creative-Europe-2015.pdf

PwC. (2016). *Leading in changing times making a difference.* Retrieved from https://www.pwc.co.uk/who-we-are/annual-report.html

Quatrèmere de Quincy. (1815). *Considérations morales sur la destination des ouvrages de l'art, ou de l'influence de leur emploi sur le génie et le goût de ceux qui les produisent ou qui les jugent.* Author.

Quéau, P. (1993). Le virtù e le vertigini del virtuale. Bologna: CAPUCCI, Pier Luigi Realtà Del Virtuale. Rappresentazioni Technologique, Communicazione, Arte. Editrice Bologna.

Quesenbery, W., & Brooks, K. (2012). *Storytelling for User Experience: Crafting Stories for Better Design.* New York: Rosenfeld Media.

Rainb. (n.d.). Retrieved November, 30, 2017, from http://rainb.ro/

Ramos, F., Garcia Gonzalez, A., van Haandel, J., & Otero-Pineiro, T. (2012). Radiomorfose em contexto transmídia. In D. Renó (Ed.), *Narrativas transmedia: Entre teorias y prácticas* (pp. 213–227). Bogotá: Editorial Universidad del Rosario.

Rayburn, D. (2007). *Streaming and digital media: understanding the business and technology*. Burlington: Focal Press.

ReflexM. D. (2017). Retrieved from http://mammalian.ca/

Regev, M. (2011). International festivals in a small country: rites of recognition and cosmopolitanism. In L. Giorgi, M. Sassatelli, & G. Delanty (Eds.), *Festivals and the cultural public sphere* (pp. 108–123). New York: Routledge.

Regev, M. (2013). *Pop-rock Music. Aesthetic cosmopolitanism in late modernity*. Cambridge, UK: Polity Press.

Reis, I. (2012). O áudio nas notícias das ciber-rádios: do hipertexto ao hiper-áudio? In H. Bastos & F. Zamith (Eds.), Ciberjornalismo. Modelos de negócio e redes sociais (pp. 43-54). Porto: Edições Afrontamento.

Renninger, K. A., & Hidi, S. E. (2016). *The power of interest for motivation and engagement*. New York: Routledge.

Rettig, J. (2016). *Moby & The Void Pacific Choir – "Are You Lost in the World Like Me?"* [Video]. Retrieved July 27, 2017, from http://www.stereogum.com/1905565/moby-the-void-pacific-choir-are-you-lost-in-the-world-like-me-video/video/

Reuters Institute for the Study of Journalism. (2016). *Digital news report*. Retrieved from http://reutersinstitute.politics.ox.ac.uk/sites/default/files/Digital-News-Report-2016.pdf?utm_source=digitalnewsreport.org&utm_medium=referral

Reuters Institute for the Study of Journalism. (2017). *Digital news report*. Retrieved from https://reutersinstitute.politics.ox.ac.uk/sites/default/files/Digital%20News%20Report%202017%20web_0.pdf

Reynolds, S. (2011). *Retromania: Pop culture's addiction to its own past*. London: Faber and Faber.

Rheingold, H. (2003). *Smart mobs*. Milano: Raffaello Cortina Editore.

Ribaldi, C. (2005). *Il nuovo museo. Origini e percorsi*. Milano: Il Saggiatore.

Ribeiro, N. (2012). Multimédia e tecnologias interactivas (5th ed.). Lisboa: FCA Editora Informática.

Ribeiro, N., & Torres, J. (2009). *Tecnologias de compressão multimédia*. Lisboa: FCA - Editora de Informática.

Ricci, A. (1996). *I mali dell'abbondanza. Considerazioni impolitiche sui beni culturali*. Roma: Lithos.

Rizzo, A., Parsons, T. D., Lange, B., Kenny, P., Buckwalter, J. G., Rothbaum, B., & Reger, G. (2011). Virtual reality goes to war: A brief review of the future of military behavioral healthcare. *Journal of Clinical Psychology in Medical Settings*, *18*(2), 176–187. doi:10.100710880-011-9247-2 PMID:21553133

Rocha, A. F. (2008). As redes de sensores e o monitoramento da saúde humana. In L. Brasil (Ed.), *Informática em Saúde* (pp. 489–510). Brasília: Universa.

Roche, M. (2011). Festivalization, cosmopolitanism and European culture: On the sociocultural significance of mega-events. In L. Giorgi, M. Sassatelli, & G. Delanty (Eds.), *Festivals and the cultural public sphere* (pp. 124–141). New York: Routledge.

Rogers, Y., Sharp, H., & Preece, J. (2011). *Interaction design: beyond human-computer interaction*. John Wiley & Sons.

Ryan, M. (2001). *Narrative as virtual reality: immersion and interactivity in literature and electronic media*. Baltimore, MD: Johns Hopkins University Press.

Salzman, M. C., Dede, C., Loftin, R. B., & Chen, J. (1999). A model for understanding how virtual reality aids complex conceptual learning. *Presence (Cambridge, Mass.)*, *8*(3), 293–316. doi:10.1162/105474699566242

Sandberg, S. (2008). Street capital: Ethnicity and violence on the streets of Oslo. *Theoretical Criminology*, *12*(2), 153–171. doi:10.1177/1362480608089238

Santaella, L. (2003). *Culturas e artes do pós-humano. Da cultura das mídias à cibercultura*. Paulus Editora.

Santaella, L. (2005). Matrizes da linguagem e pensamento: sonora, visual, verbal: aplicações na hipermídia (3rd ed.). São Paulo: Iluminuras; FAPESP. (Originally released 2001)

Santaella, L. (2004). *Culturas e artes do pós-humano: da cultura das mídias à cibercultura* (2nd ed.). São Paulo: Paulus.

Santaella, L. (2007). *Linguagens líquidas na era da modernidade*. São Paulo: Paulus.

Santos, B. S., Dias, P., Pimentel, A., Baggerman, J. W., Ferreira, C., Silva, S., & Madeira, J. (2009). Head-mounted display versus desktop for 3D navigation in virtual reality: A user study. *Multimedia Tools and Applications*, *41*(1), 161–181. doi:10.100711042-008-0223-2

Santos, L. G. (2013). *Transcultural Amazonas: shamanism and technoscience in the opera*. Sao Paulo: N-1 Ed.

Saving the Face. (2015). Retrieved November, 30, 2017, from http://connectingcities. net/project/saving-face-0

Scaltritti, M. (Ed.). (2012). *Comunicare i beni archeologici*. Milano: FrancoAngeli.

Schafer, R. (1977). *The Soundscape: Our Sonic Environment and the Tuning of the World*. Rochester, VT: Destiny Book.

Scolari, C. (2013). *Narrativas transmedia: cuando todos los medios cuentan*. Barcelona: Centro Libros PAPF.

Sennet, R. (2008). *The Craftsman*. London: Penguin Books.

Seo, J. (2015). Aesthetics of Immersion in Interactive Immersive Installation: Phenomenological Case Study. *Proceedings of the 21st International Symposium on Electronic Art*. Retrieved May, 13, 2018 from http://isea2015.org/proceeding/ submissions/ISEA2015_submission_237.pdf

Serota, N. (2009). The Museum of the 21st Century. London School of Economics.

Settis, S. (1981). Introduzione. In N. Himmelmann (Ed.), *Utopia del passato. Archeologia e cultura moderna*. Bari: De Donato.

Sharma, A., Bajpai, P., Singh, S., & Khatter, K. (2018). Virtual Reality: Blessings and Risk Assessment. *Indian Journal of Science and Technology*, *11*(May), 2–20. Retrieved from http://www.indjst.org/index.php/indjst/article/view/112577/87304

Shaw, J. (2017). *Jeffrey Shaw Compendium*. Retrieved January 11, 2017, from http:// www.jeffreyshawcompendium.com/

Shneiderman, B. (1996). *The Eyes Have It: A Task by Data Type Taxonomy for Information Visualizations*. Retrieved December, 22, 2014, from ftp://ftp.cs.umd. edu/pub/hcil/Reports-Abstracts-Bibliography/96-13html/96-13.html

Shobat, E., & Stam, R. (2002). *Unthinking Eurocentrism, multiculturalism and media*. Barcelona: Paidos.

Sicart, M. (2017). *Queering the Controller*. Retrieved August 30, 2017, from http://analoggamestudies.org/2017/07/queering-the-controller/

Silva, H. (2015). *O homem, a obra e o pensamento de Henrique Silva: a intemporalidade ou a temporalidade da obra de arte numa perspectiva polissémica (cosmológica, moral e técnica)* (PhD thesis). Retrieved February 21, 2018, from http://hdl.handle.net/10400.2/5336

Silva, S. A., & Sutko, D. M. (Eds.). (2009). Digital Cityscapes, merging digital and urban playspaces. New York: Peter Lang.

Silva, A. S. (2014). A democracia portuguesa face ao património cultural. *Revista da Faculdade de Letras. Ciências e Técnicas do Património, 13*, 11–32.

Simanowski, R. (2011). *Digital Art and Meaning: Reading Kinetic Poetry, Text Machines, Mapping Art, and Interactive Installations*. University of Minnesota Press. doi:10.5749/minnesota/9780816667376.001.0001

Simão, E., & Guerra, P. (2016). Territórios e mobilidades da (transe) virtualidade. A segunda vida dos freaks. *IS – Working Papers, 3*(11), 1-19.

Simão, E., Silva, A., & Magalhães, S. (2015). Psychedelic Trance on the Web: Exploring digital parties at Second Life. In *Exploring Psychedelic Trance and Electronic Dance Music in Modern Culture*. Hershey, PA: IGI Global. doi:10.4018/978-1-4666-8665-6.ch005

Skeels, M. M., & Grudin, J. (2009). When social networks cross boundaries: a case study of workplace use of facebook and linkedin. *Proceedings of the Group 2009*, 95-104 10.1145/1531674.1531689

Skrbiš, Z., & Woodward, I. (2011). Cosmopolitan openness. In M. Rovisco & M. Nowicka (Eds.), *The Ashgate research companion to cosmopolitanism*. Farnham, UK: Ashgate Publishing.

Soares, I. (2011). Educommunication: Proposals for a high school reform. São Paulo: Ed. Paulinas.

Social Media Research Group. (2016). *Using social media for social research: An introduction. Government Social Research*. Retrieved from https://www.gov.uk/government/uploads/system/uploads/attachment_data/file/524750/GSR_Social_Media_Research_Guidance_-_Using_social_media_for_social_research.pdf

Speridiao, A. (2014). *Connected Drains*. Retrieved November, 30, 2017, from http://www.bueirosconectados.net/

Stack, J. (2010). *Tate Online Strategy 2010–12*. Retrieved from http://www.tate.org.uk/research/publications/tate-papers/13/tate-online-strategy-2010-12

Stack, J. (2013). *Tate Digital Strategy 2013–15: Digital as a Dimension of Everything*. Retrieved from http://www.tate.org.uk/research/publications/tate-papers/19/tate-digital-strategy-2013-15-digital-as-a-dimension-of-everything

Stallabrass, J. (1997). Money, Disembodied Art and the Turing Test for Aesthetics. In J. Stallabrass, S. Buck-Morss, & L. Donskis (Eds.), *Ground Control. Technology and Utopia* (pp. 62–11). Black Dog Publishing.

Standen, P. J., & Brown, D. J. (2006). Virtual reality and its role in removing the barriers that turn cognitive impairments into intellectual disability. *Virtual Reality (Waltham Cross), 10*(3–4), 241–252. doi:10.100710055-006-0042-6

Stark, B., & Weichselbaum, P. (2013). What attracts listeners to Web radio? A case study from Germany. *The Radio Journal – International Studies in Broadcast & Audio Media, 11*(2), 185-202. Retrieved from: https://www.intellectbooks.co.uk/journals/view-Article,id=17152/

Stock, T., & Seliger, G. (2016). *Opportunities of Sustainable Manufacturing in Industry 4.0*. Elsevier.

Sutherland, I. E. (1965). The Ultimate Display. *Proceedings of IFIP 65, 2*, 506–508.

Szope, D. (2003). Peter Weibel. In J. Shaw & P. Weibel (Eds.), *Future cinema: the cinematic imaginary after film*. Cambridge, MA: MIT Press.

Tame Impala. (2015). *Currents* [CD]. Sidney: Modular/Universal Fiction Interscope.

Tame Impala. (2015). *Let it happen* [Official Video]. Retrieved from https://www.youtube.com/watch?v=-ed6UeDp1ek

Teles, P. (2009). *Touchless sensor interfaces: systemic poetics and interactive music* (Unpublished doctoral dissertation). Pontifical University of Sao Paulo, São Paulo, Brazil.

Teles, P. (2015). *The Wishing Forest*. Available at https://www.youtube.com/watch?v=8EmZM_Ybvlw&t=6s recovered at 09/09/2017

Teles, P. (2017). Protagonism, recycling and new sensibilization in technological art international workshop. In *Educomuinicação e suas áreas de intervenção: novos paradigmas para um diálogo intercultural.* São Paulo: ABPEducom.

Teles, P., & Boyle, A. (2015). Psytrance influences on touchless Interactive experiences: new roles for performers and audience within the electronic music scenario. In E. Simão, A. Silva, & S. Magalhães (Eds.), *Exploring psychedelic trance and electronic dance music in modern culture.* Hershey, PA: IGI Global. doi:10.4018/978-1-4666-8665-6.ch007

The New York Times Company. (2014). *Innovation.* Retrieved from http://www.niemanlab.org/2014/05/the-leaked-new-york-times-innovation-report-is- one-of-the-key-documents-of-this-media-age/

The Smiths. (1985). *How Soon Is Now?* [7" single]. London, UK: Rough Trade.

Theory, B. (2018). Retrieved July, 30, 2017, from http://www.blasttheory.co.uk/

Thiyagu, K. (2011). *Technology and Teaching: Learning Skills.* Kalpaz Publications.

Thornton, S. (1996). *Club cultures: Music, media and subcultural capital.* Hannover: Wesleyan University Press.

Tinhorão, J. R. (1984). Short histoty of Brazilian popular music – from "Modinha" to the "Tropicalism". Sao Paulo: Arte Ed.

Tomlinson, J. (2004). Global culture, deterritorialization and the cosmopolitanism of youth culture. In G. Titley (Ed.), *Resituating culture.* Strasbourg: Council of Europe.

Toole, S. J. (2015). *Origin myth of me: reflections of our origins creations of the Lulu.* Lulu Press.

Trivinho, E. (2007). *A dromocracia cibercultural. Lógica da vida humana na civilização mediática avançada.* São Paulo: Paulus.

Turkish Statistics Institute. (2016). Retrieved from http://www.internethaber.com/iste-turkiyede-internet-kullanim-istatistikleri-foto-galerisi-1708499.htm?page=7

Turkle, S. (2011). *Alone Together, why we expect more from technology and less from each other.* New York: Basic Books.

Urry, J. (1995). *Consuming places.* London: Routledge.

Urry, J. (1995). *Lo sguardo del turista.* Roma: Seam.

Van Haandel, J. C., & Ramos, F. (2015). The use of transmedia storytelling in the radio universe. In M. Oliveira & F. Ribeiro (Eds.), *Radio, sound and Internet. Proceedings of Net Station International Conference*. Retrieved from: http://www.lasics.uminho.pt/ojs/index.php/cecs_ebooks/article/view/2177

Vieira, J., Cardoso, G., & Mendonça, S. (2010). *Os novos caminhos da rádio: Radiomorphosis. Tendências e prospectivas*. Lisboa: OberCom. Retrieved from http://www.obercom.pt/client/?newsId=428&fileName=estudo_tendencias_radio.pdf

Vodafoneparedesdecoura. (2017). [Instagram]. Retrieved from https://www.instagram.com/vodafoneparedesdecoura/

Wagner, K. (2016). *Twitter will livestream some Major League Baseball and National Hockey League games starting this fall*. Retrieved from https://www.recode.net/2016/7/25/12260820/twitter-livestream-mlb-nhl-games-mlbam

Wagner, H. R. (Ed.). (1979). *Fenomenologia e relações sociais. Textos Escolhidos de Alfred Schutz*. Rio de Janeiro: Zahar Editores.

Walz, S. P., & Deterding, S. (Eds.). (2014). The Gameful World: Approaches, Issues, Applications. Cambridge, MA: MIT Press.

Wazlawick, R. S. (2016). *História da computação*. Rio de Janeiro: Elsevier.

We Are Social. (2017). *Global digital trends report*. Retrieved from https://wearesocial.com/special-reports/digital-in-2017-global-overview

Weibel, P. (2007). It is Forbidden Not to Touch: Some Remarks on the (Forgotten Parts of the) History of Interactivity and Virtuality. In O. Grau (Ed.), *MediaArtHistories* (pp. 21–41). Cambridge, MA: MIT Press.

Weiser, M. (1991, September). The computer for the twenty first century. *Scientific American*.

Wikipedia. (2018). *Blue Whale Game*. Retrieved July, 30, 2017, from https://en.wikipedia.org/wiki/Blue_Whale_(game)

Willems, W. (2013). Participation – In what? Radio, convergence and the corporate logic of audience input through new media in Zambia. *Telematics and Informatics*, *30*(3), 223–231. doi:10.1016/j.tele.2012.02.006

Willet, F. (2002). *African Arts*. London: Times & Hudson.

Wilson, S. (2010). *Art + Science Now*. London: Thames & Hudson.

Yanatma, S. (2017). Overview of key developments (in Turkey). *Digital News Report 2017*. Retrieved from http://www.digitalnewsreport.org/survey/2017/turkey-2017/

Zyda, M. (2005). From visual simulation to virtual reality to games. *Computer*, *38*(9), 25–32. doi:10.1109/MC.2005.297

Related References

To continue our tradition of advancing information science and technology research, we have compiled a list of recommended IGI Global readings. These references will provide additional information and guidance to further enrich your knowledge and assist you with your own research and future publications.

Adesina, K., Ganiu, O., & R., O. S. (2018). Television as Vehicle for Community Development: A Study of Lotunlotun Programme on (B.C.O.S.) Television, Nigeria. In A. Salawu, & T. Owolabi (Eds.), *Exploring Journalism Practice and Perception in Developing Countries* (pp. 60-84). Hershey, PA: IGI Global. doi:10.4018/978-1-5225-3376-4.ch004

Adigun, G. O., Odunola, O. A., & Sobalaje, A. J. (2016). Role of Social Networking for Information Seeking in a Digital Library Environment. In A. Tella (Ed.), *Information Seeking Behavior and Challenges in Digital Libraries* (pp. 272–290). Hershey, PA: IGI Global. doi:10.4018/978-1-5225-0296-8.ch013

Ahmad, M. B., Pride, C., & Corsy, A. K. (2016). Free Speech, Press Freedom, and Democracy in Ghana: A Conceptual and Historical Overview. In L. Mukhongo & J. Macharia (Eds.), *Political Influence of the Media in Developing Countries* (pp. 59–73). Hershey, PA: IGI Global. doi:10.4018/978-1-4666-9613-6.ch005

Ahmad, R. H., & Pathan, A. K. (2017). A Study on M2M (Machine to Machine) System and Communication: Its Security, Threats, and Intrusion Detection System. In M. Ferrag & A. Ahmim (Eds.), *Security Solutions and Applied Cryptography in Smart Grid Communications* (pp. 179–214). Hershey, PA: IGI Global. doi:10.4018/978-1-5225-1829-7.ch010

Akanni, T. M. (2018). In Search of Women-Supportive Media for Sustainable Development in Nigeria. In A. Salawu & T. Owolabi (Eds.), *Exploring Journalism Practice and Perception in Developing Countries* (pp. 126–149). Hershey, PA: IGI Global. doi:10.4018/978-1-5225-3376-4.ch007

Akçay, D. (2017). The Role of Social Media in Shaping Marketing Strategies in the Airline Industry. In V. Benson, R. Tuninga, & G. Saridakis (Eds.), *Analyzing the Strategic Role of Social Networking in Firm Growth and Productivity* (pp. 214–233). Hershey, PA: IGI Global. doi:10.4018/978-1-5225-0559-4.ch012

Al-Rabayah, W. A. (2017). Social Media as Social Customer Relationship Management Tool: Case of Jordan Medical Directory. In W. Al-Rabayah, R. Khasawneh, R. Abu-shamaa, & I. Alsmadi (Eds.), *Strategic Uses of Social Media for Improved Customer Retention* (pp. 108–123). Hershey, PA: IGI Global. doi:10.4018/978-1-5225-1686-6.ch006

Almjeld, J. (2017). Getting "Girly" Online: The Case for Gendering Online Spaces. In E. Monske & K. Blair (Eds.), *Handbook of Research on Writing and Composing in the Age of MOOCs* (pp. 87–105). Hershey, PA: IGI Global. doi:10.4018/978-1-5225-1718-4.ch006

Altaş, A. (2017). Space as a Character in Narrative Advertising: A Qualitative Research on Country Promotion Works. In R. Yılmaz (Ed.), *Narrative Advertising Models and Conceptualization in the Digital Age* (pp. 303–319). Hershey, PA: IGI Global. doi:10.4018/978-1-5225-2373-4.ch017

Altıparmak, B. (2017). The Structural Transformation of Space in Turkish Television Commercials as a Narrative Component. In R. Yılmaz (Ed.), *Narrative Advertising Models and Conceptualization in the Digital Age* (pp. 153–166). Hershey, PA: IGI Global. doi:10.4018/978-1-5225-2373-4.ch009

An, Y., & Harvey, K. E. (2016). Public Relations and Mobile: Becoming Dialogic. In X. Xu (Ed.), *Handbook of Research on Human Social Interaction in the Age of Mobile Devices* (pp. 284–311). Hershey, PA: IGI Global. doi:10.4018/978-1-5225-0469-6.ch013

Assay, B. E. (2018). Regulatory Compliance, Ethical Behaviour, and Sustainable Growth in Nigeria's Telecommunications Industry. In I. Oncioiu (Ed.), *Ethics and Decision-Making for Sustainable Business Practices* (pp. 90–108). Hershey, PA: IGI Global. doi:10.4018/978-1-5225-3773-1.ch006

Averweg, U. R., & Leaning, M. (2018). The Qualities and Potential of Social Media. In M. Khosrow-Pour, D.B.A. (Ed.), Encyclopedia of Information Science and Technology, Fourth Edition (pp. 7106-7115). Hershey, PA: IGI Global. doi:10.4018/978-1-5225-2255-3.ch617

Azemi, Y., & Ozuem, W. (2016). Online Service Failure and Recovery Strategy: The Mediating Role of Social Media. In W. Ozuem & G. Bowen (Eds.), *Competitive Social Media Marketing Strategies* (pp. 112–135). Hershey, PA: IGI Global. doi:10.4018/978-1-4666-9776-8.ch006

Baarda, R. (2017). Digital Democracy in Authoritarian Russia: Opportunity for Participation, or Site of Kremlin Control? In R. Luppicini & R. Baarda (Eds.), *Digital Media Integration for Participatory Democracy* (pp. 87–100). Hershey, PA: IGI Global. doi:10.4018/978-1-5225-2463-2.ch005

Bacallao-Pino, L. M. (2016). Radical Political Communication and Social Media: The Case of the Mexican #YoSoy132. In T. Deželan & I. Vobič (Eds.), *R)evolutionizing Political Communication through Social Media* (pp. 56–74). Hershey, PA: IGI Global. doi:10.4018/978-1-4666-9879-6.ch004

Baggio, B. G. (2016). Why We Would Rather Text than Talk: Personality, Identity, and Anonymity in Modern Virtual Environments. In B. Baggio (Ed.), *Analyzing Digital Discourse and Human Behavior in Modern Virtual Environments* (pp. 110–125). Hershey, PA: IGI Global. doi:10.4018/978-1-4666-9899-4.ch006

Başal, B. (2017). Actor Effect: A Study on Historical Figures Who Have Shaped the Advertising Narration. In R. Yılmaz (Ed.), *Narrative Advertising Models and Conceptualization in the Digital Age* (pp. 34–60). Hershey, PA: IGI Global. doi:10.4018/978-1-5225-2373-4.ch003

Behjati, M., & Cosmas, J. (2017). Self-Organizing Network Solutions: A Principal Step Towards Real 4G and Beyond. In D. Singh (Ed.), *Routing Protocols and Architectural Solutions for Optimal Wireless Networks and Security* (pp. 241–253). Hershey, PA: IGI Global. doi:10.4018/978-1-5225-2342-0.ch011

Bekafigo, M., & Pingley, A. C. (2017). Do Campaigns "Go Negative" on Twitter? In Y. Ibrahim (Ed.), *Politics, Protest, and Empowerment in Digital Spaces* (pp. 178–191). Hershey, PA: IGI Global. doi:10.4018/978-1-5225-1862-4.ch011

Bender, S., & Dickenson, P. (2016). Utilizing Social Media to Engage Students in Online Learning: Building Relationships Outside of the Learning Management System. In P. Dickenson & J. Jaurez (Eds.), *Increasing Productivity and Efficiency in Online Teaching* (pp. 84–105). Hershey, PA: IGI Global. doi:10.4018/978-1-5225-0347-7.ch005

Bermingham, N., & Prendergast, M. (2016). Bespoke Mobile Application Development: Facilitating Transition of Foundation Students to Higher Education. In L. Briz-Ponce, J. Juanes-Méndez, & F. García-Peñalvo (Eds.), *Handbook of Research on Mobile Devices and Applications in Higher Education Settings* (pp. 222–249). Hershey, PA: IGI Global. doi:10.4018/978-1-5225-0256-2.ch010

Bishop, J. (2017). Developing and Validating the "This Is Why We Can't Have Nice Things Scale": Optimising Political Online Communities for Internet Trolling. In Y. Ibrahim (Ed.), *Politics, Protest, and Empowerment in Digital Spaces* (pp. 153–177). Hershey, PA: IGI Global. doi:10.4018/978-1-5225-1862-4.ch010

Bolat, N. (2017). The Functions of the Narrator in Digital Advertising. In R. Yılmaz (Ed.), *Narrative Advertising Models and Conceptualization in the Digital Age* (pp. 184–201). Hershey, PA: IGI Global. doi:10.4018/978-1-5225-2373-4.ch011

Bowen, G., & Bowen, D. (2016). Social Media: Strategic Decision Making Tool. In W. Ozuem & G. Bowen (Eds.), *Competitive Social Media Marketing Strategies* (pp. 94–111). Hershey, PA: IGI Global. doi:10.4018/978-1-4666-9776-8.ch005

Brown, M. A. Sr. (2017). SNIP: High Touch Approach to Communication. In *Solutions for High-Touch Communications in a High-Tech World* (pp. 71–88). Hershey, PA: IGI Global. doi:10.4018/978-1-5225-1897-6.ch004

Brown, M. A. Sr. (2017). Comparing FTF and Online Communication Knowledge. In *Solutions for High-Touch Communications in a High-Tech World* (pp. 103–113). Hershey, PA: IGI Global. doi:10.4018/978-1-5225-1897-6.ch006

Brown, M. A. Sr. (2017). Where Do We Go from Here? In *Solutions for High-Touch Communications in a High-Tech World* (pp. 137–159). Hershey, PA: IGI Global. doi:10.4018/978-1-5225-1897-6.ch008

Brown, M. A. Sr. (2017). Bridging the Communication Gap. In *Solutions for High-Touch Communications in a High-Tech World* (pp. 1–22). Hershey, PA: IGI Global. doi:10.4018/978-1-5225-1897-6.ch001

Brown, M. A. Sr. (2017). Key Strategies for Communication. In *Solutions for High-Touch Communications in a High-Tech World* (pp. 179–202). Hershey, PA: IGI Global. doi:10.4018/978-1-5225-1897-6.ch010

Bryant, K. N. (2017). WordUp!: Student Responses to Social Media in the Technical Writing Classroom. In K. Bryant (Ed.), *Engaging 21st Century Writers with Social Media* (pp. 231–245). Hershey, PA: IGI Global. doi:10.4018/978-1-5225-0562-4.ch014

Buck, E. H. (2017). Slacktivism, Supervision, and #Selfies: Illuminating Social Media Composition through Reception Theory. In K. Bryant (Ed.), *Engaging 21st Century Writers with Social Media* (pp. 163–178). Hershey, PA: IGI Global. doi:10.4018/978-1-5225-0562-4.ch010

Bucur, B. (2016). Sociological School of Bucharest's Publications and the Romanian Political Propaganda in the Interwar Period. In A. Fox (Ed.), *Global Perspectives on Media Events in Contemporary Society* (pp. 106–120). Hershey, PA: IGI Global. doi:10.4018/978-1-4666-9967-0.ch008

Bull, R., & Pianosi, M. (2017). Social Media, Participation, and Citizenship: New Strategic Directions. In V. Benson, R. Tuninga, & G. Saridakis (Eds.), *Analyzing the Strategic Role of Social Networking in Firm Growth and Productivity* (pp. 76–94). Hershey, PA: IGI Global. doi:10.4018/978-1-5225-0559-4.ch005

Camillo, A. A., & Camillo, I. C. (2016). The Ethics of Strategic Managerial Communication in the Global Context. In A. Normore, L. Long, & M. Javidi (Eds.), *Handbook of Research on Effective Communication, Leadership, and Conflict Resolution* (pp. 566–590). Hershey, PA: IGI Global. doi:10.4018/978-1-4666-9970-0.ch030

Cassard, A., & Sloboda, B. W. (2016). Faculty Perception of Virtual 3-D Learning Environment to Assess Student Learning. In D. Choi, A. Dailey-Hebert, & J. Simmons Estes (Eds.), *Emerging Tools and Applications of Virtual Reality in Education* (pp. 48–74). Hershey, PA: IGI Global. doi:10.4018/978-1-4666-9837-6.ch003

Castellano, S., & Khelladi, I. (2017). Play It Like Beckham!: The Influence of Social Networks on E-Reputation – The Case of Sportspeople and Their Online Fan Base. In A. Mesquita (Ed.), *Research Paradigms and Contemporary Perspectives on Human-Technology Interaction* (pp. 43–61). Hershey, PA: IGI Global. doi:10.4018/978-1-5225-1868-6.ch003

Castellet, A. (2016). What If Devices Take Command: Content Innovation Perspectives for Smart Wearables in the Mobile Ecosystem. *International Journal of Handheld Computing Research*, 7(2), 16–33. doi:10.4018/IJHCR.2016040102

Chugh, R., & Joshi, M. (2017). Challenges of Knowledge Management amidst Rapidly Evolving Tools of Social Media. In R. Chugh (Ed.), *Harnessing Social Media as a Knowledge Management Tool* (pp. 299–314). Hershey, PA: IGI Global. doi:10.4018/978-1-5225-0495-5.ch014

Cockburn, T., & Smith, P. A. (2016). Leadership in the Digital Age: Rhythms and the Beat of Change. In A. Normore, L. Long, & M. Javidi (Eds.), *Handbook of Research on Effective Communication, Leadership, and Conflict Resolution* (pp. 1–20). Hershey, PA: IGI Global. doi:10.4018/978-1-4666-9970-0.ch001

Cole, A. W., & Salek, T. A. (2017). Adopting a Parasocial Connection to Overcome Professional Kakoethos in Online Health Information. In M. Folk & S. Apostel (Eds.), *Establishing and Evaluating Digital Ethos and Online Credibility* (pp. 104–120). Hershey, PA: IGI Global. doi:10.4018/978-1-5225-1072-7.ch006

Cossiavelou, V. (2017). ACTA as Media Gatekeeping Factor: The EU Role as Global Negotiator. *International Journal of Interdisciplinary Telecommunications and Networking*, *9*(1), 26–37. doi:10.4018/IJITN.2017010103

Costanza, F. (2017). Social Media Marketing and Value Co-Creation: A System Dynamics Approach. In S. Rozenes & Y. Cohen (Eds.), *Handbook of Research on Strategic Alliances and Value Co-Creation in the Service Industry* (pp. 205–230). Hershey, PA: IGI Global. doi:10.4018/978-1-5225-2084-9.ch011

Cross, D. E. (2016). Globalization and Media's Impact on Cross Cultural Communication: Managing Organizational Change. In A. Normore, L. Long, & M. Javidi (Eds.), *Handbook of Research on Effective Communication, Leadership, and Conflict Resolution* (pp. 21–41). Hershey, PA: IGI Global. doi:10.4018/978-1-4666-9970-0.ch002

Damásio, M. J., Henriques, S., Teixeira-Botelho, I., & Dias, P. (2016). Mobile Media and Social Interaction: Mobile Services and Content as Drivers of Social Interaction. In J. Aguado, C. Feijóo, & I. Martínez (Eds.), *Emerging Perspectives on the Mobile Content Evolution* (pp. 357–379). Hershey, PA: IGI Global. doi:10.4018/978-1-4666-8838-4.ch018

Davis, A., & Foley, L. (2016). Digital Storytelling. In B. Guzzetti & M. Lesley (Eds.), *Handbook of Research on the Societal Impact of Digital Media* (pp. 317–342). Hershey, PA: IGI Global. doi:10.4018/978-1-4666-8310-5.ch013

Davis, S., Palmer, L., & Etienne, J. (2016). The Geography of Digital Literacy: Mapping Communications Technology Training Programs in Austin, Texas. In B. Passarelli, J. Straubhaar, & A. Cuevas-Cerveró (Eds.), *Handbook of Research on Comparative Approaches to the Digital Age Revolution in Europe and the Americas* (pp. 371–384). Hershey, PA: IGI Global. doi:10.4018/978-1-4666-8740-0.ch022

Delello, J. A., & McWhorter, R. R. (2016). New Visual Literacies and Competencies for Education and the Workplace. In B. Guzzetti & M. Lesley (Eds.), *Handbook of Research on the Societal Impact of Digital Media* (pp. 127–162). Hershey, PA: IGI Global. doi:10.4018/978-1-4666-8310-5.ch006

Di Virgilio, F., & Antonelli, G. (2018). Consumer Behavior, Trust, and Electronic Word-of-Mouth Communication: Developing an Online Purchase Intention Model. In F. Di Virgilio (Ed.), *Social Media for Knowledge Management Applications in Modern Organizations* (pp. 58–80). Hershey, PA: IGI Global. doi:10.4018/978-1-5225-2897-5.ch003

Dixit, S. K. (2016). eWOM Marketing in Hospitality Industry. In A. Singh, & P. Duhan (Eds.), Managing Public Relations and Brand Image through Social Media (pp. 266-280). Hershey, PA: IGI Global. doi:10.4018/978-1-5225-0332-3.ch014

Duhan, P., & Singh, A. (2016). Facebook Experience Is Different: An Empirical Study in Indian Context. In S. Rathore & A. Panwar (Eds.), *Capturing, Analyzing, and Managing Word-of-Mouth in the Digital Marketplace* (pp. 188–212). Hershey, PA: IGI Global. doi:10.4018/978-1-4666-9449-1.ch011

Dunne, D. J. (2016). The Scholar's Ludo-Narrative Game and Multimodal Graphic Novel: A Comparison of Fringe Scholarship. In A. Connor & S. Marks (Eds.), *Creative Technologies for Multidisciplinary Applications* (pp. 182–207). Hershey, PA: IGI Global. doi:10.4018/978-1-5225-0016-2.ch008

DuQuette, J. L. (2017). Lessons from Cypris Chat: Revisiting Virtual Communities as Communities. In G. Panconesi & M. Guida (Eds.), *Handbook of Research on Collaborative Teaching Practice in Virtual Learning Environments* (pp. 299–316). Hershey, PA: IGI Global. doi:10.4018/978-1-5225-2426-7.ch016

Ekhlassi, A., Niknejhad Moghadam, M., & Adibi, A. (2018). The Concept of Social Media: The Functional Building Blocks. In *Building Brand Identity in the Age of Social Media: Emerging Research and Opportunities* (pp. 29–60). Hershey, PA: IGI Global. doi:10.4018/978-1-5225-5143-0.ch002

Ekhlassi, A., Niknejhad Moghadam, M., & Adibi, A. (2018). Social Media Branding Strategy: Social Media Marketing Approach. In *Building Brand Identity in the Age of Social Media: Emerging Research and Opportunities* (pp. 94–117). Hershey, PA: IGI Global. doi:10.4018/978-1-5225-5143-0.ch004

Ekhlassi, A., Niknejhad Moghadam, M., & Adibi, A. (2018). The Impact of Social Media on Brand Loyalty: Achieving "E-Trust" Through Engagement. In *Building Brand Identity in the Age of Social Media: Emerging Research and Opportunities* (pp. 155–168). Hershey, PA: IGI Global. doi:10.4018/978-1-5225-5143-0.ch007

Elegbe, O. (2017). An Assessment of Media Contribution to Behaviour Change and HIV Prevention in Nigeria. In O. Nelson, B. Ojebuyi, & A. Salawu (Eds.), *Impacts of the Media on African Socio-Economic Development* (pp. 261–280). Hershey, PA: IGI Global. doi:10.4018/978-1-5225-1859-4.ch017

Endong, F. P. (2018). Hashtag Activism and the Transnationalization of Nigerian-Born Movements Against Terrorism: A Critical Appraisal of the #BringBackOurGirls Campaign. In F. Endong (Ed.), *Exploring the Role of Social Media in Transnational Advocacy* (pp. 36–54). Hershey, PA: IGI Global. doi:10.4018/978-1-5225-2854-8.ch003

Erragcha, N. (2017). Using Social Media Tools in Marketing: Opportunities and Challenges. In M. Brown Sr., (Ed.), *Social Media Performance Evaluation and Success Measurements* (pp. 106–129). Hershey, PA: IGI Global. doi:10.4018/978-1-5225-1963-8.ch006

Ezeh, N. C. (2018). Media Campaign on Exclusive Breastfeeding: Awareness, Perception, and Acceptability Among Mothers in Anambra State, Nigeria. In A. Salawu & T. Owolabi (Eds.), *Exploring Journalism Practice and Perception in Developing Countries* (pp. 172–193). Hershey, PA: IGI Global. doi:10.4018/978-1-5225-3376-4.ch009

Fawole, O. A., & Osho, O. A. (2017). Influence of Social Media on Dating Relationships of Emerging Adults in Nigerian Universities: Social Media and Dating in Nigeria. In M. Wright (Ed.), *Identity, Sexuality, and Relationships among Emerging Adults in the Digital Age* (pp. 168–177). Hershey, PA: IGI Global. doi:10.4018/978-1-5225-1856-3.ch011

Fayoyin, A. (2017). Electoral Polling and Reporting in Africa: Professional and Policy Implications for Media Practice and Political Communication in a Digital Age. In N. Mhiripiri & T. Chari (Eds.), *Media Law, Ethics, and Policy in the Digital Age* (pp. 164–181). Hershey, PA: IGI Global. doi:10.4018/978-1-5225-2095-5.ch009

Fayoyin, A. (2018). Rethinking Media Engagement Strategies for Social Change in Africa: Context, Approaches, and Implications for Development Communication. In A. Salawu & T. Owolabi (Eds.), *Exploring Journalism Practice and Perception in Developing Countries* (pp. 257–280). Hershey, PA: IGI Global. doi:10.4018/978-1-5225-3376-4.ch013

Fechine, Y., & Rêgo, S. C. (2018). Transmedia Television Journalism in Brazil: Jornal da Record News as Reference. In R. Gambarato & G. Alzamora (Eds.), *Exploring Transmedia Journalism in the Digital Age* (pp. 253–265). Hershey, PA: IGI Global. doi:10.4018/978-1-5225-3781-6.ch015

Feng, J., & Lo, K. (2016). Video Broadcasting Protocol for Streaming Applications with Cooperative Clients. In D. Kanellopoulos (Ed.), *Emerging Research on Networked Multimedia Communication Systems* (pp. 205–229). Hershey, PA: IGI Global. doi:10.4018/978-1-4666-8850-6.ch006

Fiore, C. (2017). The Blogging Method: Improving Traditional Student Writing Practices. In K. Bryant (Ed.), *Engaging 21st Century Writers with Social Media* (pp. 179–198). Hershey, PA: IGI Global. doi:10.4018/978-1-5225-0562-4.ch011

Fleming, J., & Kajimoto, M. (2016). The Freedom of Critical Thinking: Examining Efforts to Teach American News Literacy Principles in Hong Kong, Vietnam, and Malaysia. In M. Yildiz & J. Keengwe (Eds.), *Handbook of Research on Media Literacy in the Digital Age* (pp. 208–235). Hershey, PA: IGI Global. doi:10.4018/978-1-4666-9667-9.ch010

Gambarato, R. R., Alzamora, G. C., & Tárcia, L. P. (2018). 2016 Rio Summer Olympics and the Transmedia Journalism of Planned Events. In R. Gambarato & G. Alzamora (Eds.), *Exploring Transmedia Journalism in the Digital Age* (pp. 126–146). Hershey, PA: IGI Global. doi:10.4018/978-1-5225-3781-6.ch008

Ganguin, S., Gemkow, J., & Haubold, R. (2017). Information Overload as a Challenge and Changing Point for Educational Media Literacies. In R. Marques & J. Batista (Eds.), *Information and Communication Overload in the Digital Age* (pp. 302–328). Hershey, PA: IGI Global. doi:10.4018/978-1-5225-2061-0.ch013

Gao, Y. (2016). Reviewing Gratification Effects in Mobile Gaming. In X. Xu (Ed.), *Handbook of Research on Human Social Interaction in the Age of Mobile Devices* (pp. 406–428). Hershey, PA: IGI Global. doi:10.4018/978-1-5225-0469-6.ch017

Gardner, G. C. (2017). The Lived Experience of Smartphone Use in a Unit of the United States Army. In F. Topor (Ed.), *Handbook of Research on Individualism and Identity in the Globalized Digital Age* (pp. 88–117). Hershey, PA: IGI Global. doi:10.4018/978-1-5225-0522-8.ch005

Giessen, H. W. (2016). The Medium, the Content, and the Performance: An Overview on Media-Based Learning. In B. Khan (Ed.), *Revolutionizing Modern Education through Meaningful E-Learning Implementation* (pp. 42–55). Hershey, PA: IGI Global. doi:10.4018/978-1-5225-0466-5.ch003

Giltenane, J. (2016). Investigating the Intention to Use Social Media Tools Within Virtual Project Teams. In G. Silvius (Ed.), *Strategic Integration of Social Media into Project Management Practice* (pp. 83–105). Hershey, PA: IGI Global. doi:10.4018/978-1-4666-9867-3.ch006

Golightly, D., & Houghton, R. J. (2018). Social Media as a Tool to Understand Behaviour on the Railways. In S. Kohli, A. Kumar, J. Easton, & C. Roberts (Eds.), *Innovative Applications of Big Data in the Railway Industry* (pp. 224–239). Hershey, PA: IGI Global. doi:10.4018/978-1-5225-3176-0.ch010

Goovaerts, M., Nieuwenhuysen, P., & Dhamdhere, S. N. (2016). VLIR-UOS Workshop 'E-Info Discovery and Management for Institutes in the South': Presentations and Conclusions, Antwerp, 8-19 December, 2014. In E. de Smet, & S. Dhamdhere (Eds.), E-Discovery Tools and Applications in Modern Libraries (pp. 1-40). Hershey, PA: IGI Global. doi:10.4018/978-1-5225-0474-0.ch001

Grützmann, A., Carvalho de Castro, C., Meireles, A. A., & Rodrigues, R. C. (2016). Organizational Architecture and Online Social Networks: Insights from Innovative Brazilian Companies. In G. Jamil, J. Poças Rascão, F. Ribeiro, & A. Malheiro da Silva (Eds.), *Handbook of Research on Information Architecture and Management in Modern Organizations* (pp. 508–524). Hershey, PA: IGI Global. doi:10.4018/978-1-4666-8637-3.ch023

Gundogan, M. B. (2017). In Search for a "Good Fit" Between Augmented Reality and Mobile Learning Ecosystem. In G. Kurubacak & H. Altinpulluk (Eds.), *Mobile Technologies and Augmented Reality in Open Education* (pp. 135–153). Hershey, PA: IGI Global. doi:10.4018/978-1-5225-2110-5.ch007

Gupta, H. (2018). Impact of Digital Communication on Consumer Behaviour Processes in Luxury Branding Segment: A Study of Apparel Industry. In S. Dasgupta, S. Biswal, & M. Ramesh (Eds.), *Holistic Approaches to Brand Culture and Communication Across Industries* (pp. 132–157). Hershey, PA: IGI Global. doi:10.4018/978-1-5225-3150-0.ch008

Hai-Jew, S. (2017). Creating "(Social) Network Art" with NodeXL. In S. Hai-Jew (Ed.), *Social Media Data Extraction and Content Analysis* (pp. 342–393). Hershey, PA: IGI Global. doi:10.4018/978-1-5225-0648-5.ch011

Hai-Jew, S. (2017). Employing the Sentiment Analysis Tool in NVivo 11 Plus on Social Media Data: Eight Initial Case Types. In N. Rao (Ed.), *Social Media Listening and Monitoring for Business Applications* (pp. 175–244). Hershey, PA: IGI Global. doi:10.4018/978-1-5225-0846-5.ch010

Hai-Jew, S. (2017). Conducting Sentiment Analysis and Post-Sentiment Data Exploration through Automated Means. In S. Hai-Jew (Ed.), *Social Media Data Extraction and Content Analysis* (pp. 202–240). Hershey, PA: IGI Global. doi:10.4018/978-1-5225-0648-5.ch008

Hai-Jew, S. (2017). Applied Analytical "Distant Reading" using NVivo 11 Plus. In S. Hai-Jew (Ed.), *Social Media Data Extraction and Content Analysis* (pp. 159–201). Hershey, PA: IGI Global. doi:10.4018/978-1-5225-0648-5.ch007

Hai-Jew, S. (2017). Flickering Emotions: Feeling-Based Associations from Related Tags Networks on Flickr. In S. Hai-Jew (Ed.), *Social Media Data Extraction and Content Analysis* (pp. 296–341). Hershey, PA: IGI Global. doi:10.4018/978-1-5225-0648-5.ch010

Hai-Jew, S. (2017). Manually Profiling Egos and Entities across Social Media Platforms: Evaluating Shared Messaging and Contents, User Networks, and Metadata. In V. Benson, R. Tuninga, & G. Saridakis (Eds.), *Analyzing the Strategic Role of Social Networking in Firm Growth and Productivity* (pp. 352–405). Hershey, PA: IGI Global. doi:10.4018/978-1-5225-0559-4.ch019

Hai-Jew, S. (2017). Exploring "User," "Video," and (Pseudo) Multi-Mode Networks on YouTube with NodeXL. In S. Hai-Jew (Ed.), *Social Media Data Extraction and Content Analysis* (pp. 242–295). Hershey, PA: IGI Global. doi:10.4018/978-1-5225-0648-5.ch009

Hai-Jew, S. (2018). Exploring "Mass Surveillance" Through Computational Linguistic Analysis of Five Text Corpora: Academic, Mainstream Journalism, Microblogging Hashtag Conversation, Wikipedia Articles, and Leaked Government Data. In *Techniques for Coding Imagery and Multimedia: Emerging Research and Opportunities* (pp. 212–286). Hershey, PA: IGI Global. doi:10.4018/978-1-5225-2679-7.ch004

Hai-Jew, S. (2018). Exploring Identity-Based Humor in a #Selfies #Humor Image Set From Instagram. In *Techniques for Coding Imagery and Multimedia: Emerging Research and Opportunities* (pp. 1–90). Hershey, PA: IGI Global. doi:10.4018/978-1-5225-2679-7.ch001

Hai-Jew, S. (2018). See Ya!: Exploring American Renunciation of Citizenship Through Targeted and Sparse Social Media Data Sets and a Custom Spatial-Based Linguistic Analysis Dictionary. In *Techniques for Coding Imagery and Multimedia: Emerging Research and Opportunities* (pp. 287–393). Hershey, PA: IGI Global. doi:10.4018/978-1-5225-2679-7.ch005

Han, H. S., Zhang, J., Peikazadi, N., Shi, G., Hung, A., Doan, C. P., & Filippelli, S. (2016). An Entertaining Game-Like Learning Environment in a Virtual World for Education. In S. D'Agustino (Ed.), *Creating Teacher Immediacy in Online Learning Environments* (pp. 290–306). Hershey, PA: IGI Global. doi:10.4018/978-1-4666-9995-3.ch015

Harrin, E. (2016). Barriers to Social Media Adoption on Projects. In G. Silvius (Ed.), *Strategic Integration of Social Media into Project Management Practice* (pp. 106–124). Hershey, PA: IGI Global. doi:10.4018/978-1-4666-9867-3.ch007

Harvey, K. E. (2016). Local News and Mobile: Major Tipping Points. In X. Xu (Ed.), *Handbook of Research on Human Social Interaction in the Age of Mobile Devices* (pp. 171–199). Hershey, PA: IGI Global. doi:10.4018/978-1-5225-0469-6.ch009

Harvey, K. E., & An, Y. (2016). Marketing and Mobile: Increasing Integration. In X. Xu (Ed.), *Handbook of Research on Human Social Interaction in the Age of Mobile Devices* (pp. 220–247). Hershey, PA: IGI Global. doi:10.4018/978-1-5225-0469-6.ch011

Harvey, K. E., Auter, P. J., & Stevens, S. (2016). Educators and Mobile: Challenges and Trends. In X. Xu (Ed.), *Handbook of Research on Human Social Interaction in the Age of Mobile Devices* (pp. 61–95). Hershey, PA: IGI Global. doi:10.4018/978-1-5225-0469-6.ch004

Hasan, H., & Linger, H. (2017). Connected Living for Positive Ageing. In S. Gordon (Ed.), *Online Communities as Agents of Change and Social Movements* (pp. 203–223). Hershey, PA: IGI Global. doi:10.4018/978-1-5225-2495-3.ch008

Hashim, K., Al-Sharqi, L., & Kutbi, I. (2016). Perceptions of Social Media Impact on Social Behavior of Students: A Comparison between Students and Faculty. *International Journal of Virtual Communities and Social Networking*, 8(2), 1–11. doi:10.4018/IJVCSN.2016040101

Henriques, S., & Damasio, M. J. (2016). The Value of Mobile Communication for Social Belonging: Mobile Apps and the Impact on Social Interaction. *International Journal of Handheld Computing Research*, 7(2), 44–58. doi:10.4018/IJHCR.2016040104

Hersey, L. N. (2017). CHOICES: Measuring Return on Investment in a Nonprofit Organization. In M. Brown Sr., (Ed.), *Social Media Performance Evaluation and Success Measurements* (pp. 157–179). Hershey, PA: IGI Global. doi:10.4018/978-1-5225-1963-8.ch008

Heuva, W. E. (2017). Deferring Citizens' "Right to Know" in an Information Age: The Information Deficit in Namibia. In N. Mhiripiri & T. Chari (Eds.), *Media Law, Ethics, and Policy in the Digital Age* (pp. 245–267). Hershey, PA: IGI Global. doi:10.4018/978-1-5225-2095-5.ch014

Hopwood, M., & McLean, H. (2017). Social Media in Crisis Communication: The Lance Armstrong Saga. In V. Benson, R. Tuninga, & G. Saridakis (Eds.), *Analyzing the Strategic Role of Social Networking in Firm Growth and Productivity* (pp. 45–58). Hershey, PA: IGI Global. doi:10.4018/978-1-5225-0559-4.ch003

Hotur, S. K. (2018). Indian Approaches to E-Diplomacy: An Overview. In S. Bute (Ed.), *Media Diplomacy and Its Evolving Role in the Current Geopolitical Climate* (pp. 27–35). Hershey, PA: IGI Global. doi:10.4018/978-1-5225-3859-2.ch002

Ibadildin, N., & Harvey, K. E. (2016). Business and Mobile: Rapid Restructure Required. In X. Xu (Ed.), *Handbook of Research on Human Social Interaction in the Age of Mobile Devices* (pp. 312–350). Hershey, PA: IGI Global. doi:10.4018/978-1-5225-0469-6.ch014

Iwasaki, Y. (2017). Youth Engagement in the Era of New Media. In M. Adria & Y. Mao (Eds.), *Handbook of Research on Citizen Engagement and Public Participation in the Era of New Media* (pp. 90–105). Hershey, PA: IGI Global. doi:10.4018/978-1-5225-1081-9.ch006

Jamieson, H. V. (2017). We have a Situation!: Cyberformance and Civic Engagement in Post-Democracy. In R. Shin (Ed.), *Convergence of Contemporary Art, Visual Culture, and Global Civic Engagement* (pp. 297–317). Hershey, PA: IGI Global. doi:10.4018/978-1-5225-1665-1.ch017

Jimoh, J., & Kayode, J. (2018). Imperative of Peace and Conflict-Sensitive Journalism in Development. In A. Salawu & T. Owolabi (Eds.), *Exploring Journalism Practice and Perception in Developing Countries* (pp. 150–171). Hershey, PA: IGI Global. doi:10.4018/978-1-5225-3376-4.ch008

Johns, R. (2016). Increasing Value of a Tangible Product through Intangible Attributes: Value Co-Creation and Brand Building within Online Communities – Virtual Communities and Value. In R. English & R. Johns (Eds.), *Gender Considerations in Online Consumption Behavior and Internet Use* (pp. 112–124). Hershey, PA: IGI Global. doi:10.4018/978-1-5225-0010-0.ch008

Kanellopoulos, D. N. (2018). Group Synchronization for Multimedia Systems. In M. Khosrow-Pour, D.B.A. (Ed.), Encyclopedia of Information Science and Technology, Fourth Edition (pp. 6435-6446). Hershey, PA: IGI Global. doi:10.4018/978-1-5225-2255-3.ch559

Kapepo, M. I., & Mayisela, T. (2017). Integrating Digital Literacies Into an Undergraduate Course: Inclusiveness Through Use of ICTs. In C. Ayo & V. Mbarika (Eds.), *Sustainable ICT Adoption and Integration for Socio-Economic Development* (pp. 152–173). Hershey, PA: IGI Global. doi:10.4018/978-1-5225-2565-3.ch007

Karahoca, A., & Yengin, İ. (2018). Understanding the Potentials of Social Media in Collaborative Learning. In M. Khosrow-Pour, D.B.A. (Ed.), Encyclopedia of Information Science and Technology, Fourth Edition (pp. 7168-7180). Hershey, PA: IGI Global. doi:10.4018/978-1-5225-2255-3.ch623

Karataş, S., Ceran, O., Ülker, Ü., Gün, E. T., Köse, N. Ö., Kılıç, M., ... Tok, Z. A. (2016). A Trend Analysis of Mobile Learning. In D. Parsons (Ed.), *Mobile and Blended Learning Innovations for Improved Learning Outcomes* (pp. 248–276). Hershey, PA: IGI Global. doi:10.4018/978-1-5225-0359-0.ch013

Kasemsap, K. (2016). Role of Social Media in Brand Promotion: An International Marketing Perspective. In A. Singh & P. Duhan (Eds.), *Managing Public Relations and Brand Image through Social Media* (pp. 62–88). Hershey, PA: IGI Global. doi:10.4018/978-1-5225-0332-3.ch005

Kasemsap, K. (2016). The Roles of Social Media Marketing and Brand Management in Global Marketing. In W. Ozuem & G. Bowen (Eds.), *Competitive Social Media Marketing Strategies* (pp. 173–200). Hershey, PA: IGI Global. doi:10.4018/978-1-4666-9776-8.ch009

Kasemsap, K. (2017). Professional and Business Applications of Social Media Platforms. In V. Benson, R. Tuninga, & G. Saridakis (Eds.), *Analyzing the Strategic Role of Social Networking in Firm Growth and Productivity* (pp. 427–450). Hershey, PA: IGI Global. doi:10.4018/978-1-5225-0559-4.ch021

Kasemsap, K. (2017). Mastering Social Media in the Modern Business World. In N. Rao (Ed.), *Social Media Listening and Monitoring for Business Applications* (pp. 18–44). Hershey, PA: IGI Global. doi:10.4018/978-1-5225-0846-5.ch002

Kato, Y., & Kato, S. (2016). Mobile Phone Use during Class at a Japanese Women's College. In M. Yildiz & J. Keengwe (Eds.), *Handbook of Research on Media Literacy in the Digital Age* (pp. 436–455). Hershey, PA: IGI Global. doi:10.4018/978-1-4666-9667-9.ch021

Kaufmann, H. R., & Manarioti, A. (2017). Consumer Engagement in Social Media Platforms. In *Encouraging Participative Consumerism Through Evolutionary Digital Marketing: Emerging Research and Opportunities* (pp. 95–123). Hershey, PA: IGI Global. doi:10.4018/978-1-68318-012-8.ch004

Related References

Kavoura, A., & Kefallonitis, E. (2018). The Effect of Social Media Networking in the Travel Industry. In M. Khosrow-Pour, D.B.A. (Ed.), Encyclopedia of Information Science and Technology, Fourth Edition (pp. 4052-4063). Hershey, PA: IGI Global. doi:10.4018/978-1-5225-2255-3.ch351

Kawamura, Y. (2018). Practice and Modeling of Advertising Communication Strategy: Sender-Driven and Receiver-Driven. In T. Ogata & S. Asakawa (Eds.), *Content Generation Through Narrative Communication and Simulation* (pp. 358–379). Hershey, PA: IGI Global. doi:10.4018/978-1-5225-4775-4.ch013

Kell, C., & Czerniewicz, L. (2017). Visibility of Scholarly Research and Changing Research Communication Practices: A Case Study from Namibia. In A. Esposito (Ed.), *Research 2.0 and the Impact of Digital Technologies on Scholarly Inquiry* (pp. 97–116). Hershey, PA: IGI Global. doi:10.4018/978-1-5225-0830-4.ch006

Khalil, G. E. (2016). Change through Experience: How Experiential Play and Emotional Engagement Drive Health Game Success. In D. Novák, B. Tulu, & H. Brendryen (Eds.), *Handbook of Research on Holistic Perspectives in Gamification for Clinical Practice* (pp. 10–34). Hershey, PA: IGI Global. doi:10.4018/978-1-4666-9522-1.ch002

Kılınç, U. (2017). Create It! Extend It!: Evolution of Comics Through Narrative Advertising. In R. Yılmaz (Ed.), *Narrative Advertising Models and Conceptualization in the Digital Age* (pp. 117–132). Hershey, PA: IGI Global. doi:10.4018/978-1-5225-2373-4.ch007

Kim, J. H. (2016). Pedagogical Approaches to Media Literacy Education in the United States. In M. Yildiz & J. Keengwe (Eds.), *Handbook of Research on Media Literacy in the Digital Age* (pp. 53–74). Hershey, PA: IGI Global. doi:10.4018/978-1-4666-9667-9.ch003

Kirigha, J. M., Mukhongo, L. L., & Masinde, R. (2016). Beyond Web 2.0. Social Media and Urban Educated Youths Participation in Kenyan Politics. In L. Mukhongo & J. Macharia (Eds.), *Political Influence of the Media in Developing Countries* (pp. 156–174). Hershey, PA: IGI Global. doi:10.4018/978-1-4666-9613-6.ch010

Krochmal, M. M. (2016). Training for Mobile Journalism. In D. Mentor (Ed.), *Handbook of Research on Mobile Learning in Contemporary Classrooms* (pp. 336–362). Hershey, PA: IGI Global. doi:10.4018/978-1-5225-0251-7.ch017

Kumar, P., & Sinha, A. (2018). Business-Oriented Analytics With Social Network of Things. In H. Bansal, G. Shrivastava, G. Nguyen, & L. Stanciu (Eds.), *Social Network Analytics for Contemporary Business Organizations* (pp. 166–187). Hershey, PA: IGI Global. doi:10.4018/978-1-5225-5097-6.ch009

Kunock, A. I. (2017). Boko Haram Insurgency in Cameroon: Role of Mass Media in Conflict Management. In N. Mhiripiri & T. Chari (Eds.), *Media Law, Ethics, and Policy in the Digital Age* (pp. 226–244). Hershey, PA: IGI Global. doi:10.4018/978-1-5225-2095-5.ch013

Labadie, J. A. (2018). Digitally Mediated Art Inspired by Technology Integration: A Personal Journey. In A. Ursyn (Ed.), *Visual Approaches to Cognitive Education With Technology Integration* (pp. 121–162). Hershey, PA: IGI Global. doi:10.4018/978-1-5225-5332-8.ch008

Lefkowith, S. (2017). Credibility and Crisis in Pseudonymous Communities. In M. Folk & S. Apostel (Eds.), *Establishing and Evaluating Digital Ethos and Online Credibility* (pp. 190–236). Hershey, PA: IGI Global. doi:10.4018/978-1-5225-1072-7.ch010

Lemoine, P. A., Hackett, P. T., & Richardson, M. D. (2016). The Impact of Social Media on Instruction in Higher Education. In L. Briz-Ponce, J. Juanes-Méndez, & F. García-Peñalvo (Eds.), *Handbook of Research on Mobile Devices and Applications in Higher Education Settings* (pp. 373–401). Hershey, PA: IGI Global. doi:10.4018/978-1-5225-0256-2.ch016

Liampotis, N., Papadopoulou, E., Kalatzis, N., Roussaki, I. G., Kosmides, P., Sykas, E. D., ... Taylor, N. K. (2016). Tailoring Privacy-Aware Trustworthy Cooperating Smart Spaces for University Environments. In A. Panagopoulos (Ed.), *Handbook of Research on Next Generation Mobile Communication Systems* (pp. 410–439). Hershey, PA: IGI Global. doi:10.4018/978-1-4666-8732-5.ch016

Luppicini, R. (2017). Technoethics and Digital Democracy for Future Citizens. In R. Luppicini & R. Baarda (Eds.), *Digital Media Integration for Participatory Democracy* (pp. 1–21). Hershey, PA: IGI Global. doi:10.4018/978-1-5225-2463-2.ch001

Mahajan, I. M., Rather, M., Shafiq, H., & Qadri, U. (2016). Media Literacy Organizations. In M. Yildiz & J. Keengwe (Eds.), *Handbook of Research on Media Literacy in the Digital Age* (pp. 236–248). Hershey, PA: IGI Global. doi:10.4018/978-1-4666-9667-9.ch011

Maher, D. (2018). Supporting Pre-Service Teachers' Understanding and Use of Mobile Devices. In J. Keengwe (Ed.), *Handbook of Research on Mobile Technology, Constructivism, and Meaningful Learning* (pp. 160–177). Hershey, PA: IGI Global. doi:10.4018/978-1-5225-3949-0.ch009

Makhwanya, A. (2018). Barriers to Social Media Advocacy: Lessons Learnt From the Project "Tell Them We Are From Here". In F. Endong (Ed.), *Exploring the Role of Social Media in Transnational Advocacy* (pp. 55–72). Hershey, PA: IGI Global. doi:10.4018/978-1-5225-2854-8.ch004

Manli, G., & Rezaei, S. (2017). Value and Risk: Dual Pillars of Apps Usefulness. In S. Rezaei (Ed.), *Apps Management and E-Commerce Transactions in Real-Time* (pp. 274–292). Hershey, PA: IGI Global. doi:10.4018/978-1-5225-2449-6.ch013

Manrique, C. G., & Manrique, G. G. (2017). Social Media's Role in Alleviating Political Corruption and Scandals: The Philippines during and after the Marcos Regime. In K. Demirhan & D. Çakır-Demirhan (Eds.), *Political Scandal, Corruption, and Legitimacy in the Age of Social Media* (pp. 205–222). Hershey, PA: IGI Global. doi:10.4018/978-1-5225-2019-1.ch009

Manzoor, A. (2016). Cultural Barriers to Organizational Social Media Adoption. In A. Goel & P. Singhal (Eds.), *Product Innovation through Knowledge Management and Social Media Strategies* (pp. 31–45). Hershey, PA: IGI Global. doi:10.4018/978-1-4666-9607-5.ch002

Manzoor, A. (2016). Social Media for Project Management. In G. Silvius (Ed.), *Strategic Integration of Social Media into Project Management Practice* (pp. 51–65). Hershey, PA: IGI Global. doi:10.4018/978-1-4666-9867-3.ch004

Marovitz, M. (2017). Social Networking Engagement and Crisis Communication Considerations. In M. Brown Sr., (Ed.), *Social Media Performance Evaluation and Success Measurements* (pp. 130–155). Hershey, PA: IGI Global. doi:10.4018/978-1-5225-1963-8.ch007

Mathur, D., & Mathur, D. (2016). Word of Mouth on Social Media: A Potent Tool for Brand Building. In S. Rathore & A. Panwar (Eds.), *Capturing, Analyzing, and Managing Word-of-Mouth in the Digital Marketplace* (pp. 45–60). Hershey, PA: IGI Global. doi:10.4018/978-1-4666-9449-1.ch003

Maulana, I. (2018). Spontaneous Taking and Posting Selfie: Reclaiming the Lost Trust. In S. Hai-Jew (Ed.), *Selfies as a Mode of Social Media and Work Space Research* (pp. 28–50). Hershey, PA: IGI Global. doi:10.4018/978-1-5225-3373-3.ch002

Mayo, S. (2018). A Collective Consciousness Model in a Post-Media Society. In M. Khosrow-Pour (Ed.), *Enhancing Art, Culture, and Design With Technological Integration* (pp. 25–49). Hershey, PA: IGI Global. doi:10.4018/978-1-5225-5023-5.ch002

Mazur, E., Signorella, M. L., & Hough, M. (2018). The Internet Behavior of Older Adults. In M. Khosrow-Pour, D.B.A. (Ed.), Encyclopedia of Information Science and Technology, Fourth Edition (pp. 7026-7035). Hershey, PA: IGI Global. doi:10.4018/978-1-5225-2255-3.ch609

McGuire, M. (2017). Reblogging as Writing: The Role of Tumblr in the Writing Classroom. In K. Bryant (Ed.), *Engaging 21st Century Writers with Social Media* (pp. 116–131). Hershey, PA: IGI Global. doi:10.4018/978-1-5225-0562-4.ch007

McKee, J. (2018). Architecture as a Tool to Solve Business Planning Problems. In M. Khosrow-Pour, D.B.A. (Ed.), Encyclopedia of Information Science and Technology, Fourth Edition (pp. 573-586). Hershey, PA: IGI Global. doi:10.4018/978-1-5225-2255-3.ch050

McMahon, D. (2017). With a Little Help from My Friends: The Irish Radio Industry's Strategic Appropriation of Facebook for Commercial Growth. In V. Benson, R. Tuninga, & G. Saridakis (Eds.), *Analyzing the Strategic Role of Social Networking in Firm Growth and Productivity* (pp. 157–171). Hershey, PA: IGI Global. doi:10.4018/978-1-5225-0559-4.ch009

McPherson, M. J., & Lemon, N. (2017). The Hook, Woo, and Spin: Academics Creating Relations on Social Media. In A. Esposito (Ed.), *Research 2.0 and the Impact of Digital Technologies on Scholarly Inquiry* (pp. 167–187). Hershey, PA: IGI Global. doi:10.4018/978-1-5225-0830-4.ch009

Melro, A., & Oliveira, L. (2018). Screen Culture. In M. Khosrow-Pour, D.B.A. (Ed.), Encyclopedia of Information Science and Technology, Fourth Edition (pp. 4255-4266). Hershey, PA: IGI Global. doi:10.4018/978-1-5225-2255-3.ch369

Merwin, G. A. Jr, McDonald, J. S., Bennett, J. R. Jr, & Merwin, K. A. (2016). Social Media Applications Promote Constituent Involvement in Government Management. In G. Silvius (Ed.), *Strategic Integration of Social Media into Project Management Practice* (pp. 272–291). Hershey, PA: IGI Global. doi:10.4018/978-1-4666-9867-3.ch016

Mhiripiri, N. A., & Chikakano, J. (2017). Criminal Defamation, the Criminalisation of Expression, Media and Information Dissemination in the Digital Age: A Legal and Ethical Perspective. In N. Mhiripiri & T. Chari (Eds.), *Media Law, Ethics, and Policy in the Digital Age* (pp. 1–24). Hershey, PA: IGI Global. doi:10.4018/978-1-5225-2095-5.ch001

Miliopoulou, G., & Cossiavelou, V. (2016). Brands and Media Gatekeeping in the Social Media: Current Trends and Practices – An Exploratory Research. *International Journal of Interdisciplinary Telecommunications and Networking*, 8(4), 51–64. doi:10.4018/IJITN.2016100105

Miron, E., Palmor, A., Ravid, G., Sharon, A., Tikotsky, A., & Zirkel, Y. (2017). Principles and Good Practices for Using Wikis within Organizations. In R. Chugh (Ed.), *Harnessing Social Media as a Knowledge Management Tool* (pp. 143–176). Hershey, PA: IGI Global. doi:10.4018/978-1-5225-0495-5.ch008

Mishra, K. E., Mishra, A. K., & Walker, K. (2016). Leadership Communication, Internal Marketing, and Employee Engagement: A Recipe to Create Brand Ambassadors. In A. Normore, L. Long, & M. Javidi (Eds.), *Handbook of Research on Effective Communication, Leadership, and Conflict Resolution* (pp. 311–329). Hershey, PA: IGI Global. doi:10.4018/978-1-4666-9970-0.ch017

Moeller, C. L. (2018). Sharing Your Personal Medical Experience Online: Is It an Irresponsible Act or Patient Empowerment? In S. Sekalala & B. Niezgoda (Eds.), *Global Perspectives on Health Communication in the Age of Social Media* (pp. 185–209). Hershey, PA: IGI Global. doi:10.4018/978-1-5225-3716-8.ch007

Mosanako, S. (2017). Broadcasting Policy in Botswana: The Case of Botswana Television. In O. Nelson, B. Ojebuyi, & A. Salawu (Eds.), *Impacts of the Media on African Socio-Economic Development* (pp. 217–230). Hershey, PA: IGI Global. doi:10.4018/978-1-5225-1859-4.ch014

Nazari, A. (2016). Developing a Social Media Communication Plan. In G. Silvius (Ed.), *Strategic Integration of Social Media into Project Management Practice* (pp. 194–217). Hershey, PA: IGI Global. doi:10.4018/978-1-4666-9867-3.ch012

Neto, B. M. (2016). From Information Society to Community Service: The Birth of E-Citizenship. In B. Passarelli, J. Straubhaar, & A. Cuevas-Cerveró (Eds.), *Handbook of Research on Comparative Approaches to the Digital Age Revolution in Europe and the Americas* (pp. 101–123). Hershey, PA: IGI Global. doi:10.4018/978-1-4666-8740-0.ch007

Noguti, V., Singh, S., & Waller, D. S. (2016). Gender Differences in Motivations to Use Social Networking Sites. In R. English & R. Johns (Eds.), *Gender Considerations in Online Consumption Behavior and Internet Use* (pp. 32–49). Hershey, PA: IGI Global. doi:10.4018/978-1-5225-0010-0.ch003

Noor, R. (2017). Citizen Journalism: News Gathering by Amateurs. In M. Adria & Y. Mao (Eds.), *Handbook of Research on Citizen Engagement and Public Participation in the Era of New Media* (pp. 194–229). Hershey, PA: IGI Global. doi:10.4018/978-1-5225-1081-9.ch012

Nwagbara, U., Oruh, E. S., & Brown, C. (2016). State Fragility and Stakeholder Engagement: New Media and Stakeholders' Voice Amplification in the Nigerian Petroleum Industry. In W. Ozuem & G. Bowen (Eds.), *Competitive Social Media Marketing Strategies* (pp. 136–154). Hershey, PA: IGI Global. doi:10.4018/978-1-4666-9776-8.ch007

Obermayer, N., Csepregi, A., & Kővári, E. (2017). Knowledge Sharing Relation to Competence, Emotional Intelligence, and Social Media Regarding Generations. In A. Bencsik (Ed.), *Knowledge Management Initiatives and Strategies in Small and Medium Enterprises* (pp. 269–290). Hershey, PA: IGI Global. doi:10.4018/978-1-5225-1642-2.ch013

Obermayer, N., Gaál, Z., Szabó, L., & Csepregi, A. (2017). Leveraging Knowledge Sharing over Social Media Tools. In R. Chugh (Ed.), *Harnessing Social Media as a Knowledge Management Tool* (pp. 1–24). Hershey, PA: IGI Global. doi:10.4018/978-1-5225-0495-5.ch001

Ogwezzy-Ndisika, A. O., & Faustino, B. A. (2016). Gender Responsive Election Coverage in Nigeria: A Score Card of 2011 General Elections. In L. Mukhongo & J. Macharia (Eds.), *Political Influence of the Media in Developing Countries* (pp. 234–249). Hershey, PA: IGI Global. doi:10.4018/978-1-4666-9613-6.ch015

Okoroafor, O. E. (2018). New Media Technology and Development Journalism in Nigeria. In A. Salawu & T. Owolabi (Eds.), *Exploring Journalism Practice and Perception in Developing Countries* (pp. 105–125). Hershey, PA: IGI Global. doi:10.4018/978-1-5225-3376-4.ch006

Olaleye, S. A., Sanusi, I. T., & Ukpabi, D. C. (2018). Assessment of Mobile Money Enablers in Nigeria. In F. Mtenzi, G. Oreku, D. Lupiana, & J. Yonazi (Eds.), *Mobile Technologies and Socio-Economic Development in Emerging Nations* (pp. 129–155). Hershey, PA: IGI Global. doi:10.4018/978-1-5225-4029-8.ch007

Ozuem, W., Pinho, C. A., & Azemi, Y. (2016). User-Generated Content and Perceived Customer Value. In W. Ozuem & G. Bowen (Eds.), *Competitive Social Media Marketing Strategies* (pp. 50–63). Hershey, PA: IGI Global. doi:10.4018/978-1-4666-9776-8.ch003

Pacchiega, C. (2017). An Informal Methodology for Teaching Through Virtual Worlds: Using Internet Tools and Virtual Worlds in a Coordinated Pattern to Teach Various Subjects. In G. Panconesi & M. Guida (Eds.), *Handbook of Research on Collaborative Teaching Practice in Virtual Learning Environments* (pp. 163–180). Hershey, PA: IGI Global. doi:10.4018/978-1-5225-2426-7.ch009

Pase, A. F., Goss, B. M., & Tietzmann, R. (2018). A Matter of Time: Transmedia Journalism Challenges. In R. Gambarato & G. Alzamora (Eds.), *Exploring Transmedia Journalism in the Digital Age* (pp. 49–66). Hershey, PA: IGI Global. doi:10.4018/978-1-5225-3781-6.ch004

Passarelli, B., & Paletta, F. C. (2016). Living inside the NET: The Primacy of Interactions and Processes. In B. Passarelli, J. Straubhaar, & A. Cuevas-Cerveró (Eds.), *Handbook of Research on Comparative Approaches to the Digital Age Revolution in Europe and the Americas* (pp. 1–15). Hershey, PA: IGI Global. doi:10.4018/978-1-4666-8740-0.ch001

Patkin, T. T. (2017). Social Media and Knowledge Management in a Crisis Context: Barriers and Opportunities. In R. Chugh (Ed.), *Harnessing Social Media as a Knowledge Management Tool* (pp. 125–142). Hershey, PA: IGI Global. doi:10.4018/978-1-5225-0495-5.ch007

Pavlíček, A. (2017). Social Media and Creativity: How to Engage Users and Tourists. In A. Kiráľová (Ed.), *Driving Tourism through Creative Destinations and Activities* (pp. 181–202). Hershey, PA: IGI Global. doi:10.4018/978-1-5225-2016-0.ch009

Pillay, K., & Maharaj, M. (2017). The Business of Advocacy: A Case Study of Greenpeace. In V. Benson, R. Tuninga, & G. Saridakis (Eds.), *Analyzing the Strategic Role of Social Networking in Firm Growth and Productivity* (pp. 59–75). Hershey, PA: IGI Global. doi:10.4018/978-1-5225-0559-4.ch004

Piven, I. P., & Breazeale, M. (2017). Desperately Seeking Customer Engagement: The Five-Sources Model of Brand Value on Social Media. In V. Benson, R. Tuninga, & G. Saridakis (Eds.), *Analyzing the Strategic Role of Social Networking in Firm Growth and Productivity* (pp. 283–313). Hershey, PA: IGI Global. doi:10.4018/978-1-5225-0559-4.ch016

Pokharel, R. (2017). New Media and Technology: How Do They Change the Notions of the Rhetorical Situations? In B. Gurung & M. Limbu (Eds.), *Integration of Cloud Technologies in Digitally Networked Classrooms and Learning Communities* (pp. 120–148). Hershey, PA: IGI Global. doi:10.4018/978-1-5225-1650-7.ch008

Popoola, I. S. (2016). The Press and the Emergent Political Class in Nigeria: Media, Elections, and Democracy. In L. Mukhongo & J. Macharia (Eds.), *Political Influence of the Media in Developing Countries* (pp. 45–58). Hershey, PA: IGI Global. doi:10.4018/978-1-4666-9613-6.ch004

Porlezza, C., Benecchi, E., & Colapinto, C. (2018). The Transmedia Revitalization of Investigative Journalism: Opportunities and Challenges of the Serial Podcast. In R. Gambarato & G. Alzamora (Eds.), *Exploring Transmedia Journalism in the Digital Age* (pp. 183–201). Hershey, PA: IGI Global. doi:10.4018/978-1-5225-3781-6.ch011

Ramluckan, T., Ally, S. E., & van Niekerk, B. (2017). Twitter Use in Student Protests: The Case of South Africa's #FeesMustFall Campaign. In M. Korstanje (Ed.), *Threat Mitigation and Detection of Cyber Warfare and Terrorism Activities* (pp. 220–253). Hershey, PA: IGI Global. doi:10.4018/978-1-5225-1938-6.ch010

Rao, N. R. (2017). Social Media: An Enabler for Governance. In N. Rao (Ed.), *Social Media Listening and Monitoring for Business Applications* (pp. 151–164). Hershey, PA: IGI Global. doi:10.4018/978-1-5225-0846-5.ch008

Rathore, A. K., Tuli, N., & Ilavarasan, P. V. (2016). Pro-Business or Common Citizen?: An Analysis of an Indian Woman CEO's Tweets. *International Journal of Virtual Communities and Social Networking*, 8(1), 19–29. doi:10.4018/IJVCSN.2016010102

Redi, F. (2017). Enhancing Coopetition Among Small Tourism Destinations by Creativity. In A. Kiráľová (Ed.), *Driving Tourism through Creative Destinations and Activities* (pp. 223–244). Hershey, PA: IGI Global. doi:10.4018/978-1-5225-2016-0.ch011

Reeves, M. (2016). Social Media: It Can Play a Positive Role in Education. In R. English & R. Johns (Eds.), *Gender Considerations in Online Consumption Behavior and Internet Use* (pp. 82–95). Hershey, PA: IGI Global. doi:10.4018/978-1-5225-0010-0.ch006

Reis, Z. A. (2016). Bring the Media Literacy of Turkish Pre-Service Teachers to the Table. In M. Yildiz & J. Keengwe (Eds.), *Handbook of Research on Media Literacy in the Digital Age* (pp. 405–422). Hershey, PA: IGI Global. doi:10.4018/978-1-4666-9667-9.ch019

Resuloğlu, F., & Yılmaz, R. (2017). A Model for Interactive Advertising Narration. In R. Yılmaz (Ed.), *Narrative Advertising Models and Conceptualization in the Digital Age* (pp. 1–20). Hershey, PA: IGI Global. doi:10.4018/978-1-5225-2373-4.ch001

Ritzhaupt, A. D., Poling, N., Frey, C., Kang, Y., & Johnson, M. (2016). A Phenomenological Study of Games, Simulations, and Virtual Environments Courses: What Are We Teaching and How? *International Journal of Gaming and Computer-Mediated Simulations*, *8*(3), 59–73. doi:10.4018/IJGCMS.2016070104

Ross, D. B., Eleno-Orama, M., & Salah, E. V. (2018). The Aging and Technological Society: Learning Our Way Through the Decades. In V. Bryan, A. Musgrove, & J. Powers (Eds.), *Handbook of Research on Human Development in the Digital Age* (pp. 205–234). Hershey, PA: IGI Global. doi:10.4018/978-1-5225-2838-8.ch010

Rusko, R., & Merenheimo, P. (2017). Co-Creating the Christmas Story: Digitalizing as a Shared Resource for a Shared Brand. In I. Oncioiu (Ed.), *Driving Innovation and Business Success in the Digital Economy* (pp. 137–157). Hershey, PA: IGI Global. doi:10.4018/978-1-5225-1779-5.ch010

Sabao, C., & Chikara, T. O. (2018). Social Media as Alternative Public Sphere for Citizen Participation and Protest in National Politics in Zimbabwe: The Case of #thisflag. In F. Endong (Ed.), *Exploring the Role of Social Media in Transnational Advocacy* (pp. 17–35). Hershey, PA: IGI Global. doi:10.4018/978-1-5225-2854-8.ch002

Samarthya-Howard, A., & Rogers, D. (2018). Scaling Mobile Technologies to Maximize Reach and Impact: Partnering With Mobile Network Operators and Governments. In S. Takavarasha Jr & C. Adams (Eds.), *Affordability Issues Surrounding the Use of ICT for Development and Poverty Reduction* (pp. 193–211). Hershey, PA: IGI Global. doi:10.4018/978-1-5225-3179-1.ch009

Sandoval-Almazan, R. (2017). Political Messaging in Digital Spaces: The Case of Twitter in Mexico's Presidential Campaign. In Y. Ibrahim (Ed.), *Politics, Protest, and Empowerment in Digital Spaces* (pp. 72–90). Hershey, PA: IGI Global. doi:10.4018/978-1-5225-1862-4.ch005

Schultz, C. D., & Dellnitz, A. (2018). Attribution Modeling in Online Advertising. In K. Yang (Ed.), *Multi-Platform Advertising Strategies in the Global Marketplace* (pp. 226–249). Hershey, PA: IGI Global. doi:10.4018/978-1-5225-3114-2.ch009

Schultz, C. D., & Holsing, C. (2018). Differences Across Device Usage in Search Engine Advertising. In K. Yang (Ed.), *Multi-Platform Advertising Strategies in the Global Marketplace* (pp. 250–279). Hershey, PA: IGI Global. doi:10.4018/978-1-5225-3114-2.ch010

Senadheera, V., Warren, M., Leitch, S., & Pye, G. (2017). Facebook Content Analysis: A Study into Australian Banks' Social Media Community Engagement. In S. Hai-Jew (Ed.), *Social Media Data Extraction and Content Analysis* (pp. 412–432). Hershey, PA: IGI Global. doi:10.4018/978-1-5225-0648-5.ch013

Sharma, A. R. (2018). Promoting Global Competencies in India: Media and Information Literacy as Stepping Stone. In M. Yildiz, S. Funk, & B. De Abreu (Eds.), *Promoting Global Competencies Through Media Literacy* (pp. 160–174). Hershey, PA: IGI Global. doi:10.4018/978-1-5225-3082-4.ch010

Sillah, A. (2017). Nonprofit Organizations and Social Media Use: An Analysis of Nonprofit Organizations' Effective Use of Social Media Tools. In M. Brown Sr., (Ed.), *Social Media Performance Evaluation and Success Measurements* (pp. 180–195). Hershey, PA: IGI Global. doi:10.4018/978-1-5225-1963-8.ch009

Škorić, M. (2017). Adaptation of Winlink 2000 Emergency Amateur Radio Email Network to a VHF Packet Radio Infrastructure. In A. El Oualkadi & J. Zbitou (Eds.), *Handbook of Research on Advanced Trends in Microwave and Communication Engineering* (pp. 498–528). Hershey, PA: IGI Global. doi:10.4018/978-1-5225-0773-4.ch016

Skubida, D. (2016). Can Some Computer Games Be a Sport?: Issues with Legitimization of eSport as a Sporting Activity. *International Journal of Gaming and Computer-Mediated Simulations*, 8(4), 38–52. doi:10.4018/IJGCMS.2016100103

Sonnenberg, C. (2016). Mobile Content Adaptation: An Analysis of Techniques and Frameworks. In J. Aguado, C. Feijóo, & I. Martínez (Eds.), *Emerging Perspectives on the Mobile Content Evolution* (pp. 177–199). Hershey, PA: IGI Global. doi:10.4018/978-1-4666-8838-4.ch010

Sonnevend, J. (2016). More Hope!: Ceremonial Media Events Are Still Powerful in the Twenty-First Century. In A. Fox (Ed.), *Global Perspectives on Media Events in Contemporary Society* (pp. 132–140). Hershey, PA: IGI Global. doi:10.4018/978-1-4666-9967-0.ch010

Sood, T. (2017). Services Marketing: A Sector of the Current Millennium. In T. Sood (Ed.), *Strategic Marketing Management and Tactics in the Service Industry* (pp. 15–42). Hershey, PA: IGI Global. doi:10.4018/978-1-5225-2475-5.ch002

Stairs, G. A. (2016). The Amplification of the Sunni-Shia Divide through Contemporary Communications Technology: Fear and Loathing in the Modern Middle East. In S. Gibson & A. Lando (Eds.), *Impact of Communication and the Media on Ethnic Conflict* (pp. 214–231). Hershey, PA: IGI Global. doi:10.4018/978-1-4666-9728-7.ch013

Stokinger, E., & Ozuem, W. (2016). The Intersection of Social Media and Customer Retention in the Luxury Beauty Industry. In W. Ozuem & G. Bowen (Eds.), *Competitive Social Media Marketing Strategies* (pp. 235–258). Hershey, PA: IGI Global. doi:10.4018/978-1-4666-9776-8.ch012

Sudarsanam, S. K. (2017). Social Media Metrics. In N. Rao (Ed.), *Social Media Listening and Monitoring for Business Applications* (pp. 131–149). Hershey, PA: IGI Global. doi:10.4018/978-1-5225-0846-5.ch007

Swiatek, L. (2017). Accessing the Finest Minds: Insights into Creativity from Esteemed Media Professionals. In N. Silton (Ed.), *Exploring the Benefits of Creativity in Education, Media, and the Arts* (pp. 240–263). Hershey, PA: IGI Global. doi:10.4018/978-1-5225-0504-4.ch012

Switzer, J. S., & Switzer, R. V. (2016). Virtual Teams: Profiles of Successful Leaders. In B. Baggio (Ed.), *Analyzing Digital Discourse and Human Behavior in Modern Virtual Environments* (pp. 1–24). Hershey, PA: IGI Global. doi:10.4018/978-1-4666-9899-4.ch001

Tabbane, R. S., & Debabi, M. (2016). Electronic Word of Mouth: Definitions and Concepts. In S. Rathore & A. Panwar (Eds.), *Capturing, Analyzing, and Managing Word-of-Mouth in the Digital Marketplace* (pp. 1–27). Hershey, PA: IGI Global. doi:10.4018/978-1-4666-9449-1.ch001

Tellería, A. S. (2016). The Role of the Profile and the Digital Identity on the Mobile Content. In J. Aguado, C. Feijóo, & I. Martínez (Eds.), *Emerging Perspectives on the Mobile Content Evolution* (pp. 263–282). Hershey, PA: IGI Global. doi:10.4018/978-1-4666-8838-4.ch014

Teurlings, J. (2017). What Critical Media Studies Should Not Take from Actor-Network Theory. In M. Spöhrer & B. Ochsner (Eds.), *Applying the Actor-Network Theory in Media Studies* (pp. 66–78). Hershey, PA: IGI Global. doi:10.4018/978-1-5225-0616-4.ch005

Tomé, V. (2018). Assessing Media Literacy in Teacher Education. In M. Yildiz, S. Funk, & B. De Abreu (Eds.), *Promoting Global Competencies Through Media Literacy* (pp. 1–19). Hershey, PA: IGI Global. doi:10.4018/978-1-5225-3082-4.ch001

Toscano, J. P. (2017). Social Media and Public Participation: Opportunities, Barriers, and a New Framework. In M. Adria & Y. Mao (Eds.), *Handbook of Research on Citizen Engagement and Public Participation in the Era of New Media* (pp. 73–89). Hershey, PA: IGI Global. doi:10.4018/978-1-5225-1081-9.ch005

Trauth, E. (2017). Creating Meaning for Millennials: Bakhtin, Rosenblatt, and the Use of Social Media in the Composition Classroom. In K. Bryant (Ed.), *Engaging 21st Century Writers with Social Media* (pp. 151–162). Hershey, PA: IGI Global. doi:10.4018/978-1-5225-0562-4.ch009

Ugangu, W. (2016). Kenya's Difficult Political Transitions Ethnicity and the Role of Media. In L. Mukhongo & J. Macharia (Eds.), *Political Influence of the Media in Developing Countries* (pp. 12–24). Hershey, PA: IGI Global. doi:10.4018/978-1-4666-9613-6.ch002

Uprety, S. (2018). Print Media's Role in Securitization: National Security and Diplomacy Discourses in Nepal. In S. Bute (Ed.), *Media Diplomacy and Its Evolving Role in the Current Geopolitical Climate* (pp. 56–82). Hershey, PA: IGI Global. doi:10.4018/978-1-5225-3859-2.ch004

Van der Merwe, L. (2016). Social Media Use within Project Teams: Practical Application of Social Media on Projects. In G. Silvius (Ed.), *Strategic Integration of Social Media into Project Management Practice* (pp. 139–159). Hershey, PA: IGI Global. doi:10.4018/978-1-4666-9867-3.ch009

van der Vyver, A. G. (2018). A Model for Economic Development With Telecentres and the Social Media: Overcoming Affordability Constraints. In S. Takavarasha Jr & C. Adams (Eds.), *Affordability Issues Surrounding the Use of ICT for Development and Poverty Reduction* (pp. 112–140). Hershey, PA: IGI Global. doi:10.4018/978-1-5225-3179-1.ch006

van Dokkum, E., & Ravesteijn, P. (2016). Managing Project Communication: Using Social Media for Communication in Projects. In G. Silvius (Ed.), *Strategic Integration of Social Media into Project Management Practice* (pp. 35–50). Hershey, PA: IGI Global. doi:10.4018/978-1-4666-9867-3.ch003

van Niekerk, B. (2018). Social Media Activism From an Information Warfare and Security Perspective. In F. Endong (Ed.), *Exploring the Role of Social Media in Transnational Advocacy* (pp. 1–16). Hershey, PA: IGI Global. doi:10.4018/978-1-5225-2854-8.ch001

Varnali, K., & Gorgulu, V. (2017). Determinants of Brand Recall in Social Networking Sites. In W. Al-Rabayah, R. Khasawneh, R. Abu-shamaa, & I. Alsmadi (Eds.), *Strategic Uses of Social Media for Improved Customer Retention* (pp. 124–153). Hershey, PA: IGI Global. doi:10.4018/978-1-5225-1686-6.ch007

Related References

Varty, C. T., O'Neill, T. A., & Hambley, L. A. (2017). Leading Anywhere Workers: A Scientific and Practical Framework. In Y. Blount & M. Gloet (Eds.), *Anywhere Working and the New Era of Telecommuting* (pp. 47–88). Hershey, PA: IGI Global. doi:10.4018/978-1-5225-2328-4.ch003

Vatikiotis, P. (2016). Social Media Activism: A Contested Field. In T. Deželan & I. Vobič (Eds.), *R)evolutionizing Political Communication through Social Media* (pp. 40–54). Hershey, PA: IGI Global. doi:10.4018/978-1-4666-9879-6.ch003

Velikovsky, J. T. (2018). The Holon/Parton Structure of the Meme, or The Unit of Culture. In M. Khosrow-Pour, D.B.A. (Ed.), Encyclopedia of Information Science and Technology, Fourth Edition (pp. 4666-4678). Hershey, PA: IGI Global. doi:10.4018/978-1-5225-2255-3.ch405

Venkatesh, R., & Jayasingh, S. (2017). Transformation of Business through Social Media. In N. Rao (Ed.), *Social Media Listening and Monitoring for Business Applications* (pp. 1–17). Hershey, PA: IGI Global. doi:10.4018/978-1-5225-0846-5.ch001

Vesnic-Alujevic, L. (2016). European Elections and Facebook: Political Advertising and Deliberation? In T. Deželan & I. Vobič (Eds.), *R)evolutionizing Political Communication through Social Media* (pp. 191–209). Hershey, PA: IGI Global. doi:10.4018/978-1-4666-9879-6.ch010

Virkar, S. (2017). Trolls Just Want to Have Fun: Electronic Aggression within the Context of E-Participation and Other Online Political Behaviour in the United Kingdom. In M. Korstanje (Ed.), *Threat Mitigation and Detection of Cyber Warfare and Terrorism Activities* (pp. 111–162). Hershey, PA: IGI Global. doi:10.4018/978-1-5225-1938-6.ch006

Wakabi, W. (2017). When Citizens in Authoritarian States Use Facebook for Social Ties but Not Political Participation. In Y. Ibrahim (Ed.), *Politics, Protest, and Empowerment in Digital Spaces* (pp. 192–214). Hershey, PA: IGI Global. doi:10.4018/978-1-5225-1862-4.ch012

Weisberg, D. J. (2016). Methods and Strategies in Using Digital Literacy in Media and the Arts. In M. Yildiz & J. Keengwe (Eds.), *Handbook of Research on Media Literacy in the Digital Age* (pp. 456–471). Hershey, PA: IGI Global. doi:10.4018/978-1-4666-9667-9.ch022

Weisgerber, C., & Butler, S. H. (2016). Debranding Digital Identity: Personal Branding and Identity Work in a Networked Age. *International Journal of Interactive Communication Systems and Technologies*, 6(1), 17–34. doi:10.4018/IJICST.2016010102

Wijngaard, P., Wensveen, I., Basten, A., & de Vries, T. (2016). Projects without Email, Is that Possible? In G. Silvius (Ed.), *Strategic Integration of Social Media into Project Management Practice* (pp. 218–235). Hershey, PA: IGI Global. doi:10.4018/978-1-4666-9867-3.ch013

Wright, K. (2018). "Show Me What You Are Saying": Visual Literacy in the Composition Classroom. In A. August (Ed.), *Visual Imagery, Metadata, and Multimodal Literacies Across the Curriculum* (pp. 24–49). Hershey, PA: IGI Global. doi:10.4018/978-1-5225-2808-1.ch002

Yang, K. C. (2018). Understanding How Mexican and U.S. Consumers Decide to Use Mobile Social Media: A Cross-National Qualitative Study. In K. Yang (Ed.), *Multi-Platform Advertising Strategies in the Global Marketplace* (pp. 168–198). Hershey, PA: IGI Global. doi:10.4018/978-1-5225-3114-2.ch007

Yang, K. C., & Kang, Y. (2016). Exploring Female Hispanic Consumers' Adoption of Mobile Social Media in the U.S. In R. English & R. Johns (Eds.), *Gender Considerations in Online Consumption Behavior and Internet Use* (pp. 185–207). Hershey, PA: IGI Global. doi:10.4018/978-1-5225-0010-0.ch012

Yao, Q., & Wu, M. (2016). Examining the Role of WeChat in Advertising. In X. Xu (Ed.), *Handbook of Research on Human Social Interaction in the Age of Mobile Devices* (pp. 386–405). Hershey, PA: IGI Global. doi:10.4018/978-1-5225-0469-6.ch016

Yarchi, M., Wolfsfeld, G., Samuel-Azran, T., & Segev, E. (2017). Invest, Engage, and Win: Online Campaigns and Their Outcomes in an Israeli Election. In M. Brown Sr., (Ed.), *Social Media Performance Evaluation and Success Measurements* (pp. 225–248). Hershey, PA: IGI Global. doi:10.4018/978-1-5225-1963-8.ch011

Yeboah-Banin, A. A., & Amoakohene, M. I. (2018). The Dark Side of Multi-Platform Advertising in an Emerging Economy Context. In K. Yang (Ed.), *Multi-Platform Advertising Strategies in the Global Marketplace* (pp. 30–53). Hershey, PA: IGI Global. doi:10.4018/978-1-5225-3114-2.ch002

Yılmaz, R., Çakır, A., & Resuloğlu, F. (2017). Historical Transformation of the Advertising Narration in Turkey: From Stereotype to Digital Media. In R. Yılmaz (Ed.), *Narrative Advertising Models and Conceptualization in the Digital Age* (pp. 133–152). Hershey, PA: IGI Global. doi:10.4018/978-1-5225-2373-4.ch008

Related References

Yusuf, S., Hassan, M. S., & Ibrahim, A. M. (2018). Cyberbullying Among Malaysian Children Based on Research Evidence. In M. Khosrow-Pour, D.B.A. (Ed.), Encyclopedia of Information Science and Technology, Fourth Edition (pp. 1704-1722). Hershey, PA: IGI Global. doi:10.4018/978-1-5225-2255-3.ch149

Zervas, P., & Alexandraki, C. (2016). Facilitating Open Source Software and Standards to Assembly a Platform for Networked Music Performance. In D. Kanellopoulos (Ed.), *Emerging Research on Networked Multimedia Communication Systems* (pp. 334–365). Hershey, PA: IGI Global. doi:10.4018/978-1-4666-8850-6.ch011

About the Contributors

Emília Simão is a university professor and researcher, PhD in Information and Communication in Digital Platforms, Master in Multimedia, Master in Arts and Degree in Communication. The main research themes are immersive environments, digital culture, media and digital arts, art and technology, human-computer interaction, electronic dance music cultures, retrofuturism and neotribalism vs post-modern aesthetics. Professor in several areas such as new media aesthetics, semiotics, emerging arts practices, virtual languages, human-computer interaction and multimedia, at Escola Superior Gallaecia University (ESG); Polytechnic Institute Cavado e Ave (IPCA) and Catholic Portuguese University (UCP), Portugal. Coordinates ObEmMa - Scientific Observatory of Electronic Music and Media Art - UP (Porto University) and member of CiESG-Arts and Multimedia Research Center (ESG) / CITCEM-Digital Culture Research Department (UP). Published the book "Exploring Psychedelic Trance and Electronic Dance Music in Modern Culture".

Celia Soares is a university professor and researcher. Is Invited Professor at Higher School of Technology and Management, Polytechnic Institute of Maia (IP-MAIA), Portugal and invited Professor at the Communication Sciences and Information Technologies Department, University Institute of Maia (ISMAI), Portugal. She focuses and develops her research in the "Information and Communication in Digital Platforms" area - "Information Systems and Usability" context. She is involved in practice-based research on projects such as "teaching foreign language for children with dyslexia using immersive technologies and Virtual reality" and she also develops research focused on digital art preservation in ObEmMa - Scientific Observatory of Electronic Music and Media Art - UP (Porto University). She is member of CITCEM-Digital Culture Research Department (UP), Portugal, CITEI - Research Center for Technologies and Intermedia Studies (ISMAI), Portugal and Ni2- Research Center (IPMAIA), Portugal.

* * *

Johan Cavalcanti van Haandel is Brazilian and Dutch. He has a degree in Art and media from the Federal University of Campina Grande (UFCG), a master's degree in Communication and semiotics from the Pontifical Catholic University of São Paulo (PUC-SP) and a PhD in Information and Communication in Digital Platforms from the University of Aveiro and the University of Porto. He was executive producer of 98 FM in Campina Grande and today is a professor at the FIAM-FAAM University Center.

Diana Maria Gallicchio Domingues is the founder and director of LART (Art and TechnoScience Research Laboratory). She is a CNPq (National Research Board, Ministry of Science Technology and Innovation) researcher, and senior artist/researcher of the National Program of Visiting Professors (PVNS) of the Ministry of Education, Capes (20102014), Brazil. She has traced the plan of 'New Leonardos' at the University of Brasilia, based on the creative minds of artists and scientists to redefine the boundaries of art and contemporary science, building innovative practices that contribute to contemporary forms of art and technoscience. She is a senior professor at the PostGraduate Program in Biomedical Engineering at UnB Gama and at the PostGraduate Program in Science and Technologies in Health at UnB in Ceilândia and a Research Collaborator at the Computig Institut – UNICAMP. She is involved in projects with international collaborations such as MIT – Camera Cultura/CNPq, advisory board of the Program MediaAC, Department for Image Science (Danube University Krems), and OCADU in Toronto. Results of her researches have been published in high impact communities such as IEEE, ISEA, Leonardo, SPIE. She holds a postdoctoral degree from ATI – Art & Technologies de l'Image, Université Paris VIII, and a PhD in Communications and Semiotics from PUC São Paulo. She has published and organized around 10 books such as EDUNESP: Arte, ciência e tecnologia: passado, presente e desafios (2009); Arte e vida no século XXI: tecnologia, ciência e criatividade (2003); A arte no século XXI: a humanização das tecnologias (1997); Criação e interatividade na ciberarte, Experimento (2002). She has written approximately 100 chapters in books, articles in journals from Harmattan, Presses UQAM, LAVAL, and other publishers in Mexico, Spain, Italy, France, the UK, China, Japan, and the US, including Leonardo and Digital Creativity. She is an artist with over 50 individual exhibits, and over 130 collective exhibitions in São Paulo Biennials, Bienal de la Habana, Bienal do Mercosul, HKW (Berlin), MN Belas Artes (Rio de Janeiro), MAM and MAC (São Paulo), and in galleries and museums in France, Italy, Sweden, the US, Greece, China, Mexico, Peru, Argentina and Colombia. She has curated international events such as Ciberarte Zonas de Interação (II Bienal do Mercosul), engaging with over 300 scientists and artists. Awards include The 2000 UNESCO PRIZE – 7th Biennial la Habana; The First

LEONARDO Global Crossing Prize; 2004 Rockefeller Foundation; Personalidade do século XX (Caxias do Sul, Brazil); and Prêmio Sergio Motta 2011. Her work is published in reference books such as Art + Science Now, by Stephen Wilson, Thames and Hudson, 2009; Information Arts, MIT Press 2002; Bruce Wands; Digital Art, 2004; Latin American Art in the 20th Century, by Edward Lucie Smith, Thames and Hudson, 2003.

Zeynep Genel completed her undergraduate degree at İstanbul University in 1998 on Public Relations She took her first MA degree in 2004 at Marmara University on Public Relations and Advertising, and second MA degree in 2008 at Marmara University on Journalism. Dr. Genel took her doctoral degree in 2015 at Yeditepe University, on Media Studies. She has lectured at Okan University's Public Relations and Advertising department since 2016. Her research and publications focus corporate reputation, marketing communications, city branding, participation management, community management, social media and sustainability.

Patrícia Gouveia is Associate Professor and New Media Art Department Director at the Fine Arts Faculty at Lisbon University [Faculdade de Belas-Artes da Universidade de Lisboa]. Works in Multimedia Arts and Design since the nineties. Her research focus on playable media, interactive fiction and digital arts as a place of convergence between cinema, music, games, arts and design. Previously she was Associate Professor at the Interactive Media (Games and Animation) department at Noroff University College (2014-16) in Kristiansand, Norway, Invited Assistant Professor at FCSH/UNL (2007-14) and Assistant Professor at ULHT (2008-13) both in Lisbon. From 2006 to 2014 Patrícia edited the blog Mouseland. In 2010 she published the *book Digital Arts and Games, Aesthetic and Design of Ludic Experience [Artes e Jogos Digitais, Estética e Design da Experiência Lúdica]* (ed. Universitárias Lusófonas), a synthesis of her doctoral thesis and some articles she published.

Paula Guerra is professor of sociology at the University of Porto. Researcher at the Institute of Sociology of the University of Porto (IS-UP) and Centre of Studies on Geography and Spatial Planning (CEGOT), and Adjunct Associate Professor of the Griffith Centre for Social and Cultural Research (GSCR). She is the main coordinator of the KISMIF project — Keep it simple, make it fast!, and the founder and coordinator of the KISMIF Conference and the network Todas as Artes [All the Arts]. Over the years, she has researched and published widely on themes related to youth cultures, sociology of the arts and culture, indie rock, underground music scenes, DIY and punk.

Sukru Kilic graduated from Istanbul University in 2012 with a bachelors degree in Economics. He completed his MA in New Media program at Kadir Has University in 2017 with the thesis on the current state of digital journalism in Turkey. He has started working in the field of journalism as an intern correspondent in Turkish language daily newspaper Radikal in 2011 and currently working for Al Jazeera English as a senior producer. His research and articles mainly focus on digital journalism, social media, newly emerging platforms, technologies, tools and storytelling techniques.

Mateus Miranda received his Postdoctoral in Transportation Design and Product Ergonomics at University of Quebec in Montreal - UQÀM (2015). - PhD in Mechanical Sciences at University of Brasilia (2014). - Masters in Aeronautical and Mechanical Engineering at Technological Institute of Aeronautics / ITA (2004). - Degree in Mechanical Engineering at University of Brasilia (2000) Adjunct Professor at the University of Brasilia - UNB (Campus Gama) on Automotive Engineering and Aerospace Engineering, teaching courses and conducting research in the areas of Automotive Design, Product Ergonomics and Aerospace Systems. Professional experience in the fields of Mechanical Engineering, Aeronautical Engineering, Product Design and Ergonomics, including work done at the EMBRAER (2004-2009), where he worked as Product Development Engineer. Also acted professionally in areas such as automation and vehicle inspection. Member of the Art Lab and Technoscience - LART, conducting research in the areas of Product Design, Design, Ergonomics, Simulation and Virtual Reality. Also a member of LAICA (Laboratory of Innovation in Aerospace Sciences) where he develops research and academic production in the areas of Aeronautical Design and Aerospace Systems.

Manuela Piscitelli is Associate Professor at the Department of Architecture and Industrial Design, Università degli Studi della Campania Luigi Vanvitelli, Italy. She has been Researcher and Assistant Professor at the same Department from 2008 to 2017. PhD in Drawing and survey of the building heritage at the University of Rome La Sapienza (Italy) in 2001. Member of the teaching staff of the PhD School in Architectural Disciplines, she currently teaches courses in architectural drawing and survey and in graphic communication. Her main research area includes the architecture drawing, the survey and documentation of architectural heritage and landscape, the representation and communication of cultural heritage. She has lectured on those subjects in several international conferences. She is author of 6 books and more than 50 scientific articles.

Henrique Silva is born in 1933, in Portugal, is a plastic artist with more than 50 individual and 200 collective exhibitions in Portugal, Spain, France, Belgium, USA and other countries. PhD in Digital Media Art by Universidade Aberta (PT) and Universidade do Algarve (PT) and bachelor of Fine Arts by Universitée de Paris VIII (FR). He is currently the director of Fine Arts and Multimedia degree at Escola Superior Gallecia University (PT) and the co-founder of Fundação Bienal Internacional de Arte de Cerveira - Cerveira Art Biennial. Henrique Silva was executive director of the artistic cooperative Árvore from1978 to 1995, pedagogical director in Escola Profissional de Economia Social (PT) from 1989 to 1991 and 1998 to 2000, and director of the Museum of Contemporary Art of Cerveira Art Biennial since 2003.

Paulo Cesar Teles is a Brazilian new media artist, researcher and Professor Doctor of Media Studies and Visual Art at The Art Institute of University of Campinas, Brazil. PhD in Communication and Semiotics by Pontifical Catholic University, Master Degree in Multimedia, by University of Campinas and Graduated in Social Communication - Radio & TV by Paulista State University. He has been working on technological art and new media for the past 13 years and, nowadays, is current focused on transcultural literacies and multi-platform art expressions.

Index

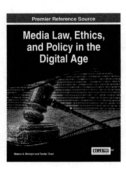

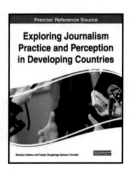

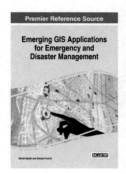